ROMANTIC TALES FROM THE PANJAB WITH INDIAN NIGHTS' ENTERTAINMENT

ROMANTIC TALES FROM THE PANJAB WITH INDIAN NIGHTS' ENTERTAINMENT

BY

CHARLES SWYNNERTON, F.S.A.

(SENIOR CHAPLAIN, INDIAN GOVERNMENT, RETD.)

NEW EDITION IN ONE VOLUME

GYAN

Published by

Gyan Publishing House
5, Ansari Road
Daryaganj, New Delhi-110002
Phone: 011-47034999, 9811692060
E-mail: books@gyanbooks.com

Distribution Network
gyanbooks.com
India, USA, Canada, UK, Australia, France

ISBN : 978-81-212-3969-1 (PB)
First Published, 1908

2nd Impression 2020

Printed at: Gyan Press, Delhi.

Romantic Tales from the Panjab with Indian Nights' Entertainment
Author: Charles Swynnertona

ROMANTIC TALES FROM THE PANJÂB WITH INDIAN NIGHTS' ENTERTAINMENT

BY

CHARLES SWYNNERTON, F.S.A.

(SENIOR CHAPLAIN, INDIAN GOVERNMENT, RETD.)

NEW EDITION IN ONE VOLUME

LONDON

ARCHIBALD CONSTABLE & CO. LTD.

1908

The Original Dedication of ROMANTIC TALES, here reproduced by the King's gracious Privilege, ran as follows—

TO HER MOST GRACIOUS MAJESTY,

QUEEN VICTORIA, EMPRESS OF INDIA,

WHOM THE PEOPLE OF INDIA CALL BY

THE ENDEARING NAME OF "MOTHER," THIS

SERIES OF INDIAN STORIES IS (BY HER

MAJESTY'S KIND PERMISSION)

RESPECTFULLY DEDICATED

PREFACE

In this volume are comprised all the stories which I had previously issued in two separate works, entitled respectively, *Indian Nights' Entertainment* and *Romantic Tales from the Panjâb*.

In now re-publishing the full tale of these stories, in a complete edition intended for popular use, it is not needful to write much by way of introduction, and much which I write I have written before. As translations from the Panjâbi of the Upper Indus, they are as literal as idiom and faithful freedom of expression would permit. Their collection and compilation from purely original sources were the work of years, bringing solace in trouble and respite from the weariness of the long glowing days of summer in that hottest of all hot places, the Peshawur Valley. As popular legends and tales they claim of course the highest possible antiquity, being older than the Jâtâkâs, older than the Mâhâbhârâta, older than history itself. From age to age, and from generation to generation, they have been faithfully handed down by people rude and unlearned, who have preserved them through all the vicissitudes of devastating wars, changes of rule and faith, and centuries of oppression. They are essentially the tales of the people. They are truly representative of the quaint legends and stories which form the delight of the village *hûjrâ* or guest-house on winter-nights, when icy winds are blowing over mountain and plain; when the young men of the village community gather round the blazing logs to be charmed by the voice of some wandering minstrel, to listen agape to his incredible descriptions of the miseries and the joys of hapless love, or to revel in the fantastic tales of giants, goblins and fairies; or when the weary wayfarer, if not too spent to sit up, alternates the recital of fictitious wonders by news from the outer world, or commands the attention of auditors, as simple as himself, by circumstantial accounts of disastrous chances of his own by flood and fell. It was at the little village of Ghâzî, on the river Indus, thirty miles above Attock, and upwards of a thousand miles due north of Bombay, that many of these tales were written down from the mouths of the simple narrators themselves. There, at the solitary house of my old friend, Thomas Lambert Barlow, a master of every variety of local dialect, whose assistance and encouragement were of the greatest possible value to me, they were, many of them at least, gathered together. There, within sight and hearing of the majestic river of history and romance, quite close to the ancient ferry over which Alexander the Great threw his bridge of boats, in a district exclusively pastoral, which comprises within its area the fabled mountain of Gandghar, the stronghold of the last of the giants, in the midst of many a ruined temple and fallen fortress pertaining to a nobler race and a former faith, we used to sit late into the night, round the leaping log fire in winter, under the dewless sky in summer, and enjoy hearing, as much as the villagers enjoyed telling, the tales which had charmed their forefathers for scores of generations.

A few miles north of Ghâzî, at the point where the Sirin, a river abounding in noble fish, falls into the Indus, stands a collection of hamlets known as Torbêla, the people of which, like the savages of the Orinoco, are addicted to a curious habit of eating a certain saponaceous clay. Opposite Torbêla, on the other side of the Indus, stands the warlike independent Pathân village of Kabbal. It is here, between these two rival villages, that the "Father of Rivers" breaks through the gorge of the opposing systems on either side, the last bulwarks of the Himalayas, which form the territory, in part independent, in part under British control, called by the inhabitants Yâkistân. Wonderfully beautiful is the view miles and miles up the river, where the descending lines of the precipitous mountains, one behind the other, recede ever more and more into the blue haze until crowned by distant snows. As we sit in the warm winter sun among the river-boulders at Ghâzî, where several gold-washers are busy rocking the sand in their rude cradles, and as the eye is directed northwards into the dim distance past the bare tawny peaks of Banêr to the west and the dark pine-clad heights of the Black Mountain to the east, we remember that all this land was once in the hands of a dynasty of Greeks, of helmed Menander, or lightning-wielding Antialkides, whose coins attest the excellency of the arts in these remote places when under their accomplished sway, but of whose influence every living trace seems to have disappeared, unless in the classical designs of village basket-work or in the graceful devices in red and green on the country rugs of felt, may be detected a remnant, however slight, of Grecian taste and Western refinement. Or again, listening to the murmuring of the river, always low and rapid during the bright months of winter, we think of the enlightened rule of the great Buddhist convert, Azoka, several of whose rock-cut edicts which are the delight of Oriental epigraphists are close at hand, one of them across the stream in Yusufzai, and three others within a ride of fifty miles to the north at Mansêrah. And not only Azoka; for here reigned also the representatives of other famous dynasties as well: the brilliant Scythian chief, Kanishka; the Hindu Kings of Kabul—of whom Râja Rasâlu of the legends was possibly one; the revived line of the Sassanians; the pitiless Muhammadan Mâhmûd, the Image-breaker of Ghazni; and lastly, the Mogul Emperors of Delhi. No wonder this region abounds in footsteps of the speechless past, and that every separate village contains within itself an unwritten library of old-world legends, stories, and proverbs, of which the present volume offers comparatively but a few examples.

For further information concerning the legends of this volume, their origin, their history, the places where and the circumstances under which they were gathered together, I must refer the reader to my long introduction and to the appendix in *Romantic Tales from the Panjâb* (Constable, 1903). All the stories, the five score and seven, presented here are issued in this cheap edition in the hope that they may form a treasure-house of amusement, and for that reason I have ventured on no scientific arrangement of them nor classified them in any way. Some little arrangement there is, inasmuch as the longer stories have been divided one from the other by fables and anecdotes, thrown in for the sake of variety in reading, but on the whole they may be compared to lots shaken up in a bag, falling into their places by the rule of haphazard, to be a moment's delight, then to be laid aside, and anon to be resumed. For men and women doomed from week to week to live laborious days, for busy merchant and leisureless professional man, for readers of ease and culture whether in the East or in the West, for old folks sitting snug and warm in the chimney corner, and, above all, for the young, for boys and girls freed from the term's weary round, this collected volume of old stories is now published anew. And if in ever so slight a degree they tend to lighten the burden of life, which seems to grow heavier as the years roll on, if for five minutes now and then they serve to mask a sorrow or force a smile, reward so great, as I have already said elsewhere, will far exceed my desert.

In conclusion, I have to acknowledge an error of fact which appeared in my introduction to *Romantic Tales* in 1903, and which was pointed out by a writer in the *Athenæum*. I was not the first, as I supposed, to present a version of the beautiful tale of *Hîr and Rânjha* to English readers. That honour belongs to Sir Richard Temple, whose monumental work should be consulted by all students interested in the stories of the Panjâb. At the same time it should be stated that my version differs so completely from his, coming as it does from a different quarter, as to constitute a new story in itself, while at the same time it differs considerably also from a much earlier version published in French by Garcin de Tassy in 1857.[1] That is a translation, highly embellished, from the Hindustâni, a version to charm the fine ladies of an Eastern court, but not to win the sympathies of the simple auditors in a village *hûjrâ*.

C. S.

[1] *Revue de l'Orient*, VI, 113. I am indebted to the Librarian at the India Office for the reference.

CONTENTS

Note.—A few hints as to pronunciation of the proper names :—

â (circumflex) like *a* in *father*—*Rânjhâ*.
a (unmarked) like *u* in *but*—*Chand* = Chund.
e like *a* in *fate*—*bêlâ*.
î (circumflex) like *ee* in *feet*—*Dhîdo* = Dheedo.
ô like *o* in *home*—*Hôm Bâdshâh*.
û like *oo* in *room*—*Gûl Bâdshâh*.

ROMANTIC TALES FROM THE PANJÂB

WITH

INDIAN NIGHTS' ENTERTAINMENT

I

THE LOVE STORY OF HÎR AND RÂNJHA[1]

MANY years ago, in quite the olden time, there lived three brothers, Nûr Khân, Chûnd Khân, and Rânjha. Of these three the two elder were married, but Rânjha, whose pet name was Dhîdo, was only a stripling.

One day Nûr Khân and Chûnd Khân came to Rânjha and said, "Dhîdo, our father is now dead, and as for us we have families to feed. But you, Brother, do nothing at all on the farm. All you do is to ramble uselessly after the buffaloes and goats, playing old tunes. So we two have decided to divide the inheritance into three parts, and we now tell you plainly that from this time forth you will have to manage your own land yourself :—

" Up, Brother, up—thy piping days forego—
See where the blacksmith sweats beneath the shade!
These useless bars, with many a lusty blow,
Quickly he'll change to ploughshare and to spade;
Then haste we home again to fix the line
That shall divide our heritage from thine."

In vain Rânjha, and in vain his sisters, the wives of his brothers, urged that he was still but young and untrained. The iron was wrought up, the land was divided, and the

[1] The verses in this tale are translations of verses in the original Panjâbi.

lad was left to do the best he could. To make matters worse, the portion assigned to him was wild uncleared jungle. He merely got barren land which had never been broken at all, and of which the soil was poor, bearing stones, and scrub, and coarse grass. It was land far too savage for him to reduce to order at all. Nevertheless, taking with him his yoke and his plough, and driving his oxen before him, the boy set out early in the morning to clear it and till it. Hard was the task and stiff the ground, and soon his arms began to tire, and his bullocks to flag, and when at last his ploughshare snapped in twain in the stony furrows, he sat himself down, and bitterly weeping complained—"I was the son of my father's old age, and nothing of this kind have I ever seen before. Cruel unnatural brothers are mine to give me barren land!" Saying these words he loosed his oxen from the yoke to wander at will, and lay down to sleep under the shade of a tree.

By-and-by, when the sun was high in the heavens, out stepped his two sisters from the house, bearing in their hands some *chûri*,[1] and calling the boy by his name. As they came along the fields they passed their husbands busy at the plough, and they stopped a moment and said, "Do you know where Dhîdo is?" And their husbands looked up and told them where to seek him. But when the women reached the spot they found him lying asleep, his work unfinished and his oxen loose. So they slapped his cheeks with the tips of their fingers and woke him up, and began to reproach him, saying, "O Dhîdo, for shame!—

"You love to tend the lazy herd,
To sleep beneath the shady tree;
You love to startle beast and bird,
Playing your flute's soft minstrelsy.
But now thy sisters stand and weep,
They cry, 'O thou whom others keep,
When wilt thou learn
Bread of thine own to earn?'"

Saying these words they took him, and the broken plough, and the oxen, and coming to their husbands they complained about him. "O Dhîdo," said the brothers, "it is not lawful food you eat, and, unless you work and

[1] *Chûri*, sweet cake.

earn for yourself, no longer can you remain with us. See to it, therefore, for we mean what we say!"

Rânjha felt grieved as he listened to these words which vexed his very soul, and all the night long he lay awake, turning them over and over. He could not sleep, and at last he determined that when the morning came he would leave the village and never return again. In vain his sisters strove with him, coaxing him to stay. He left them as the day broke, and with only his scarf and his staff started off on his travels. All day long he walked, never stopping for a moment to rest, and in the evening it so happened that he approached a certain village named Khârlân-dî-Mâri, and, because he was worn with hunger and fatigue, he entered it, and made his way to the mosque, intending to spend the night there.

Now it was then close on the hour for prayers, and soon the people began to assemble, and one of them saw him and said, "Son, you look like a wayfarer; have you had anything to eat?"

"No," answered he, "I have eaten nothing at all. Early in the morning I left my house in Takht-Hazâra, and I have only just arrived." Then went a lad to his home and brought him some food, and he ate and drank and revived. But it was winter time, and he, lying on the floor in the open mosque, became sick with the pangs of fever, and his fever and sickness troubled him sore. And when the people came together again to say their morning prayers, they looked at him, and, seeing how ill he had been, they said to him, "And how have you passed the night?" Then said Rânjha, "I came from Takht-Hazâra—

"At dawn of day I broke away,
Nor lingered once to rest,
Till in your village mosque I lay,
By want and grief oppressed;
A little boy went round, by pity led,
And begged me alms—some butter-milk and bread.—

"I tell you I am the son of a good man," said he, "and one well-to-do, and never before have I seen such troubles. I have become sick from the cold, and I pray you therefore to let me warm myself somewhere at a fire."

One of the villagers at once took him to the village smithy, and he sat down and began to warm himself over the glowing charcoal. Meanwhile the smith snatched out a bar of hot iron, and holding it on the anvil he told his two lads to beat it with their hammers. Then, looking at Rânjha and observing that he seemed a fine stout young fellow, he bade him also take a hammer, and smite while the others rested. Rânjha felt ashamed to refuse the man so small a service, so he sprang into the pit, and seizing a sledge, he struck the red-hot iron three or four times, but, as he struck, the blood started from the veins of his arms. And when he laid the hammer down he said—

> "Cold was the night, a homeless wanderer I,
> Vainly for fire I searched from door to door,
> And when I raised the ponderous sledge on high,
> My very blood came trickling to the floor."

But the blacksmith was astonished. "Ah, what delicate limbs!" cried he. "Are you a King's son, or born of some fairy race? In my house you would never earn even your keep, and therefore, boy, go, seek your fortune elsewhere, in the name of God!"

So Rânjha left that place, and his heart was sad, but as he went along he chanced, to his great joy, to see a certain woman putting some fire into an oven, for she was a bread-seller, and he determined to go near to her, and to sit down and warm himself. As soon as he entered the door of the court, however, he was arrested by the cries of three or four young girls. "O youth," cried they, "whoever you are, is it among a parcel of girls you wish to sit? Surely a house full of women is no place for you!" But the mistress of the house, whose name was Mîrabân, observing how handsomely he carried himself, called him in and made him sit down by the side of the stove, and the boy did as he was bidden and came into the courtyard and sat down, and the heat of the stove warmed his blood, and his eyes began to shine. By-and-by the woman glanced at him again, and perceiving that he had something hidden away under his arm, she asked him what it was. "Whenever I am sad," said he, "I take my flute and play upon it, for it amuses me, and I carry it wherever I go." Then all the girls, and the woman herself as well, would have him play them a tune to pass the time, and at first he refused to play at all, saying it was better not, but, when they came clustering round him, crying,

"Play us something, play us something!" he put the flute to his lips and began to play. But the effect of that music was such that the girls and even the woman of the house herself became possessed, being rendered utterly distraught by the sound which filled their ears, and they began to dance like mad things, all over the court, keeping time with feet and hands. Yea, the very cakes in the stove danced till they turned as black as coal. Seeing her cakes burnt to ashes, Mîrabân was filled with grief and sorrow of heart, and, waxing wrath, she snatched up her *kûndi*[1] and gave Rânjha two or three strokes on the back with it, saying, "O you sorcerer, you have made us all silly! Out of my house at once—you are not worth a pin!" Thus the boy would have had to wander forth again, but, looking at the woman, he said, "O you lady-compounder of loaves, listen to the words of your spiritual guide! Go to Madam Oven, lift up the cover from her mouth, and look within!" Then she took off the top of the oven and looked down and saw that the cakes were no longer burnt as before, but all done to a turn; and when she considered the thing, she guessed that Rânjha had mystic power in him, and she approached him humbly, and besought him to stay with her for a time, seeing also indeed that her own good man was but a poor creature, and that Rânjha, on the contrary, was young and stout.

Soon after, her husband, who had gone to the forest for fuel, came back with a load of logs on his head, and as he threw them to the ground he observed the youth seated, like a prince, on a couch, with the best carpet in the house spread under him, and so he said to his wife, "Who is your visitor?"

"You do not know him," answered she. "But I know him, for he is my family *pîr*,[2] come from my father's village."

So Rânjha remained in the house of Mîrabân for three or four days, but at the end of that time he began to get tired of his dull life and longed to go away. In the middle of the night, therefore, when husband and wife were both asleep, he arose softly and stole away; but as he stepped over the threshold the woman heard him and

[1] *Kûndi*, the hooked stick with which the cakes or loaves are taken out of the oven.

[2] Spiritual guide.

awoke, and when she found that he had gone she also went after him. Pursuing him along the stony footpath she soon drew nigh him, but Rânjha turned and threw stones at her, telling her to be gone. So she stopped and cried, "O you cursed of God, why would you hide yourself? Mîrabân is calling you. Have you eaten poison, or wholesome food, in my house?" Then came also her husband, and he, overhearing all that was said, bade her return. "Come here, Mîrabân," said he. "Was this man your lover, that you speak him fair and foul in the same breath?"

"And do you not know?" answered she. "You were sleeping, I think. But understand he is a thief. He took up all our precious things and was going off. We were ruined indeed if I had not wakened in time."

Then as she caught Rânjha by one arm, her husband seized him by the other, and as a captured thief he was dragged back to the house and put in the stocks, and there in the chamber alone he was left to pass the night.

Now in the morning, when her husband had gone forth as usual for a load of wood, Mîrabân came privately to the lad, bringing him *chûri*, and she opened her heart to him, saying, "My dear love, do you not see that I love you? I love you, and how then can I bear to part with you!" This speech Rânjha heard, but keeping silence he uttered not a word, but remained still, and by-and-by she gave him some *chûri* and left him alone.

This woman used to parch quantities of corn and to leave much of it lying on the oven. One day a blind man groped his way in and coming to the stove began to pick up the grains and put them in his mouth. Presently Rânjha caught sight of him and cried, "O blind man, what are you doing?"

"I am eating the parched grain," answered he.

"Come to me," said Rânjha. "If you come to me, I will put some healing medicine on your eyes, and then you will be able to see."

So the blind man rose up, and coming to Rânjha he began to feel his body, and, as he did so, he touched the stocks, and by feeling soon found out what they were. Then Rânjha took up a handful of *chûri* and crammed it into his mouth, and when the blind man found out how delicious it was, he stretched out his leg and tried to put it into one of the holes of the stocks. "What are you doing now?" said Rânjha.

"I think," answered the blind man, "you get *chûri* here, and if I sit in the stocks with you, of course I shall get *chûri* too."

"Blind man," said Rânjha, "do not waste your time to no purpose. You cannot put your foot into the stocks unless you first take out the peg."

Then the blind man felt for the peg, and when he had found it he seized it, and, applying his full force to it, drew it out at once. Then Rânjha lifted up the plank and put the blind man in the stocks instead of himself, after which he took up the wooden peg and drove it home with a stone. "O blind man," said he, "take this plate of *chûri* and eat it up! If you want more, call aloud—'O God, send me *chûri*, O God, send me *chûri!*' and *chûri* will come to you." So Rânjha left the blind man in the stocks, and escaped from the house.

Now the blind man was not long before he had finished the whole of his *chûri*, and as he still felt unsatisfied he began to cry out, "God, God, send me *chûri*, send me *chûri!* O God, send me a mouthful!" And he made such a din in the darkness of the night that he roused Mîrabân, who rose in wrath, crying, "Who are you? and what in the world are you saying?"

"I am a blind man," roared he of the stocks, "and I am doing nothing whatever but asking God to send me *chûri*."

Then thought the woman to herself, "Rânjha perhaps has gone mad!" So she got up, and came into the chamber to see him and to find out what had gone wrong with him. Great was her surprise to discover that it was not Rânjha at all, but the old blind beggar who passed her door every day. Her anger was beyond everything, and dragging him out of the stocks she threw him down, and seizing her *kûndi* she applied it well to the old fellow's shoulders, who struggled in vain and howled horribly. Louder and louder grew the noise of the fray, until at last it ended by rousing the husband, who came rushing into the room, and who laid hold of his wife by the throat. "O shameless hussy," cried he, "you have come out here to carry on your tricks with Rânjha, have you?" So saying, he punished her well.

Meanwhile, as they were thus contending, all three one with another, Rânjha came back, and standing beside the door, peeped in to watch the fun, and when he saw his chance he cried aloud, "O woman, so tall and so slender, whose name is Mîrabân, get up, you sleep too long; Rânjha is leaving you!" These words said he, and then he ran away. But Mîrabân and her husband Sowâri ran after him, and while one cried "Thief!" the other cried "Rogue!" until Rânjha lifted some stones and stoned them, saying, "Neither my father's sister nor my mother's sister are you, Mîrabân, that I should not put a knife to your throat. Love indeed! What can you know of love, you sorry jade?"

Now when Sowâri heard this speech, he left following Rânjha, and again turned on his wife in a fury. "Ah, faithless female dog!" cried he. "You told me the lad was your village *pîr*, and behold now he speaks to you of love! Verily you have harboured him for tricks of your own and nought else!" And with these words he belaboured her front and rear with her own *kûndi* until she cried "Peccavi!"

Meanwhile Rânjha laughed. "Ha, ha!" quoth he, "How now, sly puss?—

"Sowâri suspects
Some things have been missed, Mîrabân—
Is it true?
Sowâri believes
A thief has been kissed, Mîrabân—
Was it you?
Sowâri declares
He will give you his fist, Mîrabân—
So, vixen, adieu!"

Leaving the contending couple to settle the difference between them, Rânjha went on his way, and coming to the river Chenâb which flows into the Râvi, he plunged in, and swam with the current many a mile, until at last he saw on the bank a beautiful garden. So he made for it, and, landing, entered it. The beauty of the place captivated him, because being only a simple countryman he had never seen the like of it before. It was dawn, and the worshippers of God were making preparations for their accustomed prayers. While sitting alone under a shady tree his mind went back to his native village, and he thought of his brothers and sisters and the fields and the cattle, and the nooks and corners of his father's house, and then he thought of his present miserable condition. All at once he raised his eyes, and perceived five venerable men standing before him. To see them there he was astonished and amazed, but they all spoke very kindly to him, saying, "O good young sir, give us some milk!" All five of them, standing together, joined in prayer to Rânjha, saying—

> "Who beg and implore, dost thou ken?
> O we the Five *Pîrs*[1] beg of thee!
> What name shalt thou bear among men?
> Mîyân Rânjha for aye shalt thou be!
> So buffalo's milk do thou bring us, for, lo,
> We have given thee Hîra for weal or for woe!"

But on Rânjha fell sorrow that he had no milk to offer them, which when the Pîrs perceived, they said, "Why are you troubled?"

"Alas, sirs," answered he, "my buffaloes are far away in Takht-Hazâra. Here I have no animal at all. Where then can I find milk for you?"

"O son," said they, "have you ever given anything away in the name of God?"

"No, never," replied the lad. "I am a mere boy; but of course my brothers have."

"Recollect well," said they again. "Perhaps you may have given something at least!"

Then Rânjha considered, and after a while he again spoke and said, "Sirs, I remember that once, when a calf of mine was ill and about to die, I gave it to a beggar."

"How old was your calf then?" inquired the Pîrs.

"She was but two months," answered he.

"By this time she has grown up," said they, "and you can call her, and when you call her we hope that she will come to you. What was her name—do you remember?"

"Yes," said he, "I used to call her Brownie!"

"Then call her," said the Pîrs. "Call her by the same name."

So Rânjha called out, "Brownie! Brownie!" and in a

[1] Pîr—a saint, a spiritual director. When a man is in sickness or peril, he supplicates God and his Pîr.

little time his buffalo came running towards him with her tail cocked up over her back. Now as she approached, he saw plainly enough that she had no milk at all in her. "Now what shall I do?" thought he. "How am I going to milk a dry buffalo?" The Pîrs perceiving the drift of his mind then said to him, "What is the matter now?"

"The buffalo has no milk," answered he.

"Never mind that, my son," said they. "Pat her and sit down to milk."

So he did as he was told, and sat down, but again he considered that he had no vessel for the milk, and he looked towards the Pîrs, who, understanding at once the whole matter, brought him a little wooden begging-bowl which they gave him for the milk, and he began to milk the creature, thinking all the time if she let down any milk at all, how soon that small vessel would be filled. But, to his great surprise, when the milk began to flow, neither did the milk stop nor did the vessel fill. At last he got very tired, and looked once more towards the Five Pîrs, who came near, and one said, "Do not be distressed, my son. Get up now, ,you have milk enough."

Then Rânjha rose, and presented the bowl to the Pîrs who drank of the milk turn by turn, and who gave the remainder to Rânjha himself. When all this was done, the Five Pîrs ordered the boy to close his eyes, and he did so. "Shut your eyes," said they—

"Now close thine eyes, O duteous son,
For, lo, she's thine, by virtue won,
Mâhr Chûkak's daughter Hîr!
O close thine eyes, she's freely thine,
We cede her in the name divine,
The lovely and the dear!"

So Rânjha closed his eyes and waited for a long long time for orders to open them again, but, as no one ordered him to do so, at last he opened them himself, when to his great astonishment he no more saw Pîrs or buffalo or garden, all had vanished away, but he found himself in another garden far more beautiful than the other, and he saw close at hand some couches decorated with all manner of handsome trappings, but no one to sit or to lie on them. At the same time he remembered that he had some cakes with him, so he took them out of his turban and sat down and began to eat. All at once he noticed some lovely damsels, well dressed and adorned with rich jewels, coming towards him, and some of them were singing and dancing, and others walking sedately. Being so young he felt afraid, and ran away towards the bank of the river, intending to cross over to the other side. Now Hîr was chief among them all, and when she saw him she sent her damsels to persuade him not to enter the river, and they followed, but could prevail nothing. So Hîr herself went forward then, and gently reproved him, saying—

"O tall of form, and fair of face,
O youth whose turban's close embrace
Enfolds thy shapely brow—
Who but a fool, in haste to die,
A river's fordless depths would try,
As thou art trying now?"

Then, as he was struggling on, the girl plunged in after him, and seizing him by the hand, she said, "Brother, do not kill yourself, the river here is too deep to be crossed." Her words and her action gave him confidence, and he returned with her to the garden, where she put some questions to him, as to who he was, why he had left his home, and whether or not he could do anything. While she was thus speaking to him, it came into her heart that this youth was the servant of God and endued with grace divine. And in answer to her questions he told her that he had come from Takht-Hazâra, that injustice had driven him away, and that as for employment all he could do was to graze buffaloes. "Ah, then you are in luck," said she, "for I can get you work to do. I will ask my father to-day."

So they wandered about the garden together, spending the whole day there, she and he and her company of maidens, and in the evening she parted from him and returned home. Then when her father came in from the fields, she went to him, and sat down by his side, and spoke to him, thus—

"O father, I have engaged a servant for you. He grazes buffaloes and understands them. Well content will he be with a *pakka*[1] of four yards and a *bhûra*[2] of eight yards, nor during twelve years will he ever ask for more.

[1] *Pakka* is a sheet of cotton cloth.
[2] *Bhûra* is a coarse country blanket.

No buffalo touched by his rod will ever bring you a bull-calf. He sits on a rock or he stands on a mound, and when he plays on his flute all the herd will follow him home."

"Very well, daughter mine," said her father. "All this is very good. What more need we ask from God? He is a good man, you say. No buffalo touched by him but brings a she-calf, and, besides all this, you say that when he likes he plays on a flute, and that when he plays all the whole herd comes trooping home to the sound of his music. This is very good, my dear, and we will take him and keep him, so bring the lad hither to me."

The next day, therefore, Hîr brought Rânjha home to her father's house and he was at once engaged. At first he had charge of the horses, but the work was irksome to him, and after a time he complained to Hîr and said, "You never promised to make me a horse-keeper, Hîr, and the work does not suit me at all. Ask your father therefore to give me charge of his herds of buffaloes, for that was the bargain." And when she had spoken to her father, saying, "O father, Rânjha is weary of keeping the horses, and he was promised only the buffaloes," her father at once answered, "Hîr, my daughter, it was a mistake of the steward, and you can send him to our island of Bela[1] to take care of the buffaloes there."

So to Bela Rânjha went, and there he became the sole master of a herd of three hundred buffaloes. Before his arrival at the place it took eight or nine herdsmen to manage so many, but Rânjha managed them all himself. The simple creatures loved him from the first. He would sit all day in the shade with his flute, and towards sunset he would mount a hillock or climb a tree, and there he would play a certain lively tune, and gradually the whole herd would respond to the call, and then follow him whithersoever he went. And so passed the jocund hours away.

One night Hîr dreamed that a man clothed in white garments came to her bedside and spoke to her. "Listen, O daughter," said the voice. "The Five Pîrs have met together and have married you with solemn rites to Rânjha." Hearing these words, Hîr trembled and awoke. As she was in the habit of honouring the prophet Christ

[1] *Bela* is the term for any islet formed by a river.

every Sunday, and as it was then Sunday eve, she took the phantom which had appeared to her to be a vision of Christ himself, and she received his word with joy, believing that already she was the wife of Rânjha. So the next morning she went up to her father and said, "Father, you know the buffaloes never come to the village. They are kept at Bela, and our messengers being very dishonest do not bring us all the milk nor yet the butter which comes from them. Will you then permit me, father, to go for a few days, and look after these things myself?" And her father was glad, and said, "Go, my child, you have my full consent to do so."

So away went Hîr, and when she came to the island she found Rânjha there, but Rânjha was displeased. "Dearest one," said he, "I never enslaved myself to your father for a morsel of bread and a cup of butter-milk. One motive I had, and that was that I might see you day by day. Perhaps you are not aware that even now you are my wife, and that upon me the Five Pîrs have bestowed your hand. But tell me, dear one, do you for your part accept me as your husband?"

Hearing these words she at once called to mind her dream, and she answered, and said, "I have dreamed a dream—this night I dreamt it—

"I slept, and, lo, a dream I had—
Some heavenly One, in glory clad,
Came nigh me in the night!
'Rânjha,' cried he, 'hath wedded Hîr,
They, the great Five, each one a Pir,
Performed the sacred rite!'"

So then, joyfully and peacefully, they began to live together one with the other on that little island in the midst of the river Chenâb. Rânjha had no work to do but to sit by the side of Hîr all day long playing his flute, and in the evening he had only to strike up his sunset-tune for all the buffaloes to come running home to the fold. Soon, however, prying people began to whisper about them, and by-and-by some of them went to her father's house and told tales about them. Then there came a certain beggar-man who reported that whenever he went across to Bela to beg an alms he always found the herdsman sitting on a couch with a plate of *chûri* before him.[1]

[1] Chûri is a food much eaten by the newly married.

Now when this was said, Mâhr Chûkak called his sons together, and, finding them very angry at the misfortune which had befallen the family, he strove to appease them, saying, "My sons, you know well that people are in the habit of spreading lies of this description. For my part I think the scandal is false, but let us sift the matter well and then take steps to stop people's tongues. And for this purpose I tell you there is a man—my brother—whose name is Kaido, who is lame of a leg, and who lives in a hut outside the village like a beggar, and keeps dogs and fowls and a goat or two. Call that man to me. I think he will be the proper person to ascertain if these things are true or false."

Kaido therefore was summoned, and Mâhr Chûkak asked him whether he would go over to Bela and bring back word what was right and what was wrong there. And Kaido said "Yes," and having so determined he prepared for his visit, for he got a bag made of a leopard's skin, and a staff and a begging-bowl, and a brass *lotah* for water, and he put on him a turban of twisted ropes of goat's hair, and being so disguised as a poor wandering fakîr he went across to the island. Now Hîr was then absent, having gone to gather *bêr*[1] berries, but before going she had laid before Rânjha some freshly-made *chûri*. And when Kaido arrived at the door of the hut in which they lived he cried in a feigned voice, "Give me some alms! O you resident in this noble mansion, give me some alms in the name of God!" Rânjha then began to consider what there was which he could offer the man, and after thinking awhile he said, "O beggar, come in! Take this platter of fresh *chûri* and begone, for it is all I have." So Kaido took the *chûri*, and right glad he was to get it, because in the *chûri* he had the proof of all the stories told by the town's folk. Therefore, putting the *chûri* in his bag of leopard-skin, he limped away with it as fast as he could.

He had scarcely left the house when Hîr, returning, missed the *chûri*, and addressing Rânjha, she said, "What has become of all the *chûri?*"

"I have eaten it all myself," answered he.

"No, dear," said she, "I do not think you have. You always kept some of it till the evening, and you could not

[1] A little wild plum.

have eaten the whole of it. You say that to-day you have eaten it all? Tell me the truth, please."

Then said he, "It is true that I have not eaten the *chûri*, for I gave it to a poor fakîr."

Hîr felt alarmed when she heard him speak thus, and said, "What kind of man was he?"

"He was an old fellow," answered Rânjha, "and lame of a leg."

Then she understood the whole matter, and became exceedingly sorrowful, saying, "You have done very wrong, my dear. No beggar was that at all, but my uncle Kaido. He will now take the *chûri* to my father, and you, as well as I, will be brought into shame and disgrace." And then, without losing another moment, she took up a heavy stick and ran after the pretended fakîr. Going out of the door she espied him running away at a great distance, and he also, looking behind him, saw his niece in full pursuit, but as he was lame of a leg and she a fine active girl, he was soon overtaken. And when she reached him she gave him four or five good cracks over his head with her stick and knocked him down. Then she tore off his turban of goat's hair, and snatched away his begging-bowl, and seized his leopard-skin bag which she at once opened, and emptied of the *chûri*, while the old rascal lay flat on the ground crying and lamenting and saying, "O daughter, would you lift your hand against your uncle?"

"Yes, a thousand times yes," cried she, "because like a villain you are going to put me to shame."

So with a parting thrust she left him and betook herself back to Rânjha.

But Kaido, gathering himself up, collected all the crumbs of *chûri* he could find, and so went weeping and wailing to his brother, who was just then sitting in his courtyard in the midst of some of his neighbours. To him he presented himself, and, throwing down the scraps of *chûri* before the whole company, he said, "Listen to me, O ye Siyâls—

"O hear me speak, for sage advice I give,
No woman-child henceforth permit to live,
Soon as your teeming wives are brought to bed,
Be yours to strike their female children dead!
For know, my kinsmen, Hîr is Rânjha's slave,
His she is now, and his will be beyond the grave!"

Then Mâhr Chûkak rose up in wrath, and ordered his sons to go to the island, to put Rânjha to death, and to bring their sister home. So to Rânjha they went, and sitting down by his side began to seek for some excuse to slay him. "O Rânjha," said they, "the smell of musk comes from you. Whence got you the smell of musk?"

"There is a certain wood," said he, "and the name of that wood is sandal wood. Sandal wood came floating down the river, and the buffaloes drank of the water thereof, and they carry the smell of musk with them wherever they go. But as for me I have not robbed a caravan, still less have I embraced your sister Hîr."

"You utter a lie!" cried they. "You go with our sister Hîr, and out of her bosom comes the smell of the musk that comes from yourself."

Then the two men drew their swords, and they were in the act to cut the lad down, when he spoke again. "Brothers, look here," said he. "Go to the herd and smell the buffaloes' mouths—yea, the odour is in their very dung. You will find that the smell of the musk comes, not from me, but from them. I do not tell you a lie."

The brothers then lowered their weapons and went out, and when they found some buffaloes' dung they smelled it, and, lo, the smell was as the smell of musk. But it availed not Rânjha, for their father's command was to kill and not to spare him. Going back to his hut, therefore, they again raised their swords to smite him, but in the very act their arms stiffened and remained uplifted, nor could any effort of theirs cause them to descend again. They tried to bring them down, working their bodies now this side, now that, but they tried in vain. Then they began to suspect that Rânjha was different from other men, and believing him to be a prophet of God, they all four fell down at his feet. "Pardon us," said they, "and we will return to our father, and commend you to him that he may give you our sister Hîr to wife. But do you pray for us that our arms may be restored, and for this favour we promise never to move foot or hand against you again." So Rânjha prayed, and the use of their arms came back to them as before.

Now, as they were conferring together, Hîr also came in, and began to taunt and upbraid her brothers for what they had done. "Dear sister," protested they, "we were only acting a part, nor had we any idea of killing Rânjha at all. But we have come to summon you home, for your father wishes to see you for a couple of days, while your mother also is far from well. Get leave, therefore, from Rânjha and go with us back." So she turned to Rânjha and said, "My dear, give me leave now to return with my brothers, and in two days we shall meet again."

On the way to the village she thought much of the treachery of her uncle Kaido in coming to Bela disguised as a poor fakîr, and she saw plainly that he alone could have betrayed her, and that all her troubles had their origin in him. So she said, "Brothers, take me round by the way of our uncle's hut, as I have business with him of great importance." And they turned aside out of their way, and it was so that when they were passing the hut, and when the two men had gone a little before her, Hîr took some fire and put it to the thatch, and the fire at once burst into a blaze and consumed the whole place, while the lame beggar began to dance and yell with rage. "Ah, Hîr," cried he, "you have done me a wrong in burning my hut! I jumped and danced and O you have burnt up my heart! You have burnt up Khairi, my little Beauty, which had twelve chickens, you have burnt Lohi, my little red bitch that barked at every door, my vessels are burnt, all my household stuffs are burnt, and the bag in which I stored my *bhang*. Countless were the things I had in my house. You have burnt them all—yea, in a word, I may say you have burnt up a very apothecary's shop!" Thus he complained, and then he said, "But I go to your father's house to denounce you."

"Go," said she. "You have burnt fire on my head, and I have burnt fire on yours."

With these words she hastened away and entered her mother's chamber, leaving her wretched uncle without, wringing his hands and bemoaning his hard fate.

That night Mâhr Chûkak and his wife talked only of their daughter Hîr, and the end of it was that her mother said, "Husband, to kill a human being would be the greatest sin, and how much more so when the victim would be your own daughter! No, we must send for the Kâzi and get him to persuade and correct her."

Early in the morning, therefore, a man was despatched to the mosque for the Kâzi, and he was asked to take her in hand, to admonish her with wise counsel, and to bring her to reason. And the Kâzi called her in, and when she came to him he said to her, "O Hîr, you are a good child, your mother is a good woman, and a good man is your father. Listen then to good advice, for I have taught you from your childhood up, and I am your master. My dear daughter, do you think it is right or proper to bring trouble and disgrace on your father and mother? You know that long ago they betrothed you to the chief of the Khera tribe, and well you know that every child should obey its father."

"My Pîr is a spirit," answered she, "and he has married me to Rânjha. I have accepted Rânjha, and his shall I be as long as I live."

These words filled the Kâzi's soul with rage, and he said, "O Hîr, artful girl that thou art, listen to me and attend to the words of God! You will be expelled from Paradise to find your portion in Hell!"

"Kâzi," said she, "from my earliest years you have been my instructor, but never from you, O Kâzi, should I have looked for language like this! Rânjha is mine and I am his."

Then the priest opened his book, and showed Hîr some lines written therein, saying to her, "O child of disobedience, do you not see this? Do you dare to bandy words with your Kâzi? I tell you that you are on the straight road to Hell."

"O you consumer of bribes!" cried Hîr. "They have bribed you with five rupees and a betel leaf! A precious *Mûlwâna*[1] are you! What are you doing, you cunning Kâzi, you deceiver of the people? Why make white the black letters of the Alkorân? May your children perish at home and your oxen abroad! What connection, tell me, is there between love and the doctrines of the Muhammadan Law?"

Then thought the Kâzi within himself, "This girl is too infatuated to listen to a word spoken against Rânjha, since she puts even me to disgrace." As he was thus considering, one of the people of the Kheras came to the door and made signs as though he had somewhat to tell him.

[1] A priest.

But the priest dismissed him with a look, and turning again to Hîr, he said, "I have no power to write, I have not even ink for my pen to describe, the sin you are about to commit. A place will be found for you in the lowest pit of Hell if you do not submit yourself to the Law. O Hîr, you will render yourself infamous, and an outcast from your parents, from me, and from all your kin, if you do not obey my order, and give Rânjha up. O believe what I tell you! If you will not accept the Khera as your husband, your father has fully determined to hand you over, body and soul, to the lowest scavenger in all the village."

But Hîr, like the foundations of the earth, remained unmoved. "Hear me, O Kâzi," said she. "To me you are a father, and you, too, have daughters at home in your house. I have begged you, I have prayed you, I have besought you with tears, and ever I call you Miyân.[1] For Rânjha I am going distracted—

"He is my soldier lad, yea more,
My chosen knight is he!
Him madly, madly I adore,
His life is life of me!

If Rânjha seek the battle-field
To fight against the foe,
O I will be his sheltering shield,
On me shall fall the blow!

Could I in Mecca's sacred place
E'er hope to bow my head,
If I from Rânjha turned my face,
Or Khera loved instead?"

"O blasphemy!" cried the priest. "Listen to me and attend, O Hîr, thou crafty one! Fearlessly you utter words without sense, but may speedy death put an end to him, may that Rânjha of whom you are so proud be numbered with the lost!"

"Can prayer be made in vain?" said she.—

"When the sun breaks the power of night
I rub my nose-ring clean and bright;
When the sun halts in mid career,
A gem I choose to deck my ear;
When he marks half the western sky,
My burnished necklace then I try;

[1] *Miyân*, master.

Soon as he sinks adown the west,
I don the robe that suits me best;
When bed-time comes my beads I take,
And all my faith's confessions make."[1]

"O Kâzi," continued she, "neither you nor my father can be judge between Rânjha and me. Let us go to the King and let him be my judge."

The Kâzi then ordered one of his pupils to call in her mother, and when the mother entered the room she looked at her daughter and said, "Hear me, my daughter! Doubtless the Kâzi has explained to you everything. Know then that you have been given in marriage to Sattar, the chief of the Kheras. Why do you bring so much trouble upon us?"

"Mother," answered she, "if you have a single particle of the true Faith in you, do not vex me. Otherwise I will thrust a dagger into my heart, and die here at your feet!"

Her mother then made signs to her younger daughter, who went out and brought in her father, and all four sat down together. "O my daughter," said her father, "you must simply be ruled by us, and obey the orders we give you. Why will you not accept the Khera? God will give you the true Faith."

"O father," said she, "hear me!—

"One day I ran, urged by some secret power,
And to the ferry came, just as a boat
Came floating in. Within her lay a youth,
And from his face I lifted up the veil,
But when he raised his eyes to look at mine,
Straightway I, swooning, fell. The Khwâjâ Pîr[2]
Betrothed me to him; angels whispering low
Performed the ceremony of *Mâyân;*[3]
To deck me out came jewels down from Heaven,
Pearls for my neck and bracelets for my arms,
And, O, to Rânjha, father, was I wed!
The angel Jibrâil was there to speak
The solemn words, and Isrâfil stood by
As witness to the rite, while in the train,
The wedding-train, walked the Five Holy Pîrs,
And God, yea, God Himself, was good to me!
All turned to Rânjha, and they gave him Hîr,
In this world now, and in the world to come."

[1] In other words she observes the five fixed times of prayer in vogue among Muhammadans.

[2] *Khwâjâ Pîr*—the deity of the river.

[3] *Mâyân*, the betrothal ceremony.

Meanwhile the Kâzi was muttering to himself, "There are sixteen rubies and seventeen diamonds with five pearls. Five of the rubies are of excellent lustre—what a garland they would make! Who can read me the parable? The men, forsooth, are asses and the women she-asses!" He then addressed himself to Mâhr Chûkak, and said, "Very rich is the Khera. When he was betrothed to Hîr he sent her rubies, diamonds, and pearls of price. And yet notwithstanding all this and much besides, in spite of my precepts and her father's injunctions, she is going to marry a homeless beggarly wanderer, so that your only remedy now is to do away with her altogether."

But here her mother interposed and said, "God forbid —to kill the child must in any case be a sin! The whole world would point the finger of scorn and say we had killed her because she was worthless and bad, and our good name would be for ever lost. No, no, let us rather marry her off to the Khera at once!"

Her advice was approved, and the father Mâhr Chûkak at once proceeded to act upon it. He summoned his family bard as well as a barber and a Brahmin, and despatched them all three to Sattar, the chief of the Kheras, to give him notice that his wedding ceremony would be celebrated in eight days. So the tribe of the Kheras assembled together and held a council, and it was announced to them that Mâhr Chûkak had sent his messengers, saying, "Make your preparations of marriage!" And the news was very welcome to them, and they all began to get ready.

And now Hîr, considering within herself that her fate was inevitable, unless God himself could help her, decided to see Rânjha once more. So, taking with her a bevy of maidens, she set off for the island, and when she arrived there she found Rânjha sitting under a tree engaged in prayer. "Dear Rânjha," said she, "what about the buffaloes? Are they quite well?"

"What do I know about the buffaloes?" answered he.

She, supposing him to be angry, sat down by his side, and said, "It is not on the buffaloes' account I have come—let them go! I have come to tell you something." Then in a little while she spoke to him thus—

"My father's buffaloes are mine—whole herds
He now has given me. Fairies are some,
And some are lovelier than birds
Of Paradise, that go and come,
Or houris soft and fair.

Look at their dazzling teeth! No jasmine flower,
No dainty bud, can boast so pure a white!
And, O, their curving horns! What power,
And what rare symmetry unite
Magnificently there!

When they go forth, is there a pasture sweet
But puts on warmer smiles for them?
When they troop home, our tiny street
Wears beauty like a diadem,
Though mean enough before.

Perdition seize them! Yea, may they devour
Their owners, Rânjha!—But, for me
And you, O snatch this fleeting hour,
And in my arms content yourself to be—
Perchance you may embrace me nevermore!"

Moreover, she told him of her approaching marriage with the Khera, and said, "I will send for you the day before the wedding, and then shall I see whether or not the power of God is upon you."

"My dear heart," said Rânjha. "I have no such power at all. I am a simple man and cannot pretend to favour or grace more than another. But let us trust in God, who only can make darkness light."

When Hîr returned to her house, she found that the *mâhdi*[1] had been prepared for her, and as she entered her apartment a certain woman whose duty it was called her and said, "Dear child, come, stretch out your hand!" But, instead of giving her hand, she slàpped the woman's face, saying, "O mother, you have distilled the *mâhdi*, but whose hands would you redden therewith? I am betrothed to Rânjha, and would you give me to the Khera?"

At last the marriage procession arrived, and after the performance of all the preliminary rites, the ceremony itself began to be solemnized. For the girl's mother had sent for the Kâzi and her father and several other persons. First of all came her father and the Kâzi, who addressed her

[1] *Mâhdi*, a red vegetable stain, similar to henna, for staining the nails, the palms of the hands, and soles of the feet.

and said, "Dear child, we hope you will consider us, and not put us to disgrace in the presence of so many people."

"O let me be," said she, "for well you know that I have already been married to Rânjha!"

Then was Sattar Khera made to sit down, and the Kâzi began the ceremony, but Hîr sprang up from her place, and seizing a rod, smote the priest upon the head. "Ah," cried he, "the bridegroom sat down ready to begin, but she, the insolent and perverse, has plucked out my beard!"

"O Kâzi," said she, "listen to me—

"The month of July has descended in flood,
And the barrier-sands have been carried away;
Deep, deep, and as fierce in my heart and my blood
Rolls the river of love—
Can you turn it with threats, or with menaces stay?"

Also she said, "But for you, O stony priest, may God consign you to lamentable shame and disgrace without end, and may like disgrace befall your daughters as well!"

Then she went out of the house, her mind fixed wholly on Rânjha. But her mother, who was not willing that further forbearance should be shown her, now ordered that she should be taken by force and made over at once to the Khera. So the servants seized her, and with violence thrust her into the pâlki which was waiting ready to receive her.

That same morning Rânjha was lying asleep among the trees of Bela when the Five Pîrs appeared to him and said, "Sir, are you asleep? Know you not that your wife is going away with the Khera?" All five of them stood at his head, saying, "Rise up, O wretched one,—the Kheras are about to bear her away!"

Then Rânjha sprang to his feet, and, by the power of the Pîrs, he at once found himself standing close to the pâlki in which Hîr had been seated. Now no one was able to lift that pâlki. The very strongest of the Kheras tried to raise it, but he tried in vain. In spite of all their struggles the pâlki remained immovable. And all the time Rânjha stood by, while the Five Pîrs stood behind him. And when the people, notwithstanding every endeavour, found themselves unable to lift the pâlki, then they called the Kâzi, and the Kâzi, coming to Hîr, spoke and said, "O daughter, you shall have all the wealth you desire. We will give you apparel and ornaments, rubies and diamonds; but for God's sake dismiss Rânjha from your mind, forget him for one moment, so that the pâlki may be raised and the honour of your family preserved." But Hîr answered him not, only she looked towards the Five Pîrs and towards Rânjha, and she said, "Let the Five Pîrs speak. If they do, another pâlki will descend from Heaven, and in one pâlki shall sit Hîr and in the other Rânjha!"

So the Five Pîrs prayed before God, and immediately, to the surprise of all men, another pâlki descended from Heaven. But the Kheras, bewildered and astonished, turned towards Mâhr Chûkak and his wife, who, answering, said, "We were her parents, and truly we brought her into the world, but that Hîr was married to Rânjha is news indeed—we never understood it before."

And now Rânjha stepped forth and took his place, and the Five Pîrs ordered angels of God to come down and bear the pâlkis away. And there appeared two angels, beautiful and strong, who, lifting the pâlkis in their hands, bore them upwards, and carried them swiftly to Mecca. And there, having paid their devotions, the two lovers lived happily together for many years, and if, as we believe, they never died, they are living still in one of the islands of Arabia.

Told by the bard, Sher, at Abbottâbâd, October 1889.

II

A STORY OF GÛL BÂDSHÂH

The true King is God; I tell of Kings who vanish away.

HEAR a story of Gûl Bâdshâh, the name of whose queen was Manavûr.[1] He was just and good, very jealous of his name, and all the world spoke well of him. One day his vizier came to him and said—

"O King, the Queen goes and comes just as she pleases. Let her go out, but only at stated times. It is not good for queens to go out so much."

"But the Queen," answered the King, "gets tired of the house, and she goes out and comes back refreshed. So best,—let the Queen be, vizier!"

Again, after some days, the vizier came to the King and mentioned the name of the Queen to him in such a way that he set the King a-thinking, and by-and-by the King began to suspect something.

Now Queen Manavûr had a sister whose name was Senâh, and the two lived in the palace together. One day when these two went out walking as usual, the King took his bow and his quiver, and, with his dog at his heels, he followed them. On they went until they came to a garden of trees, and the King having tracked them, stole up and saw both ladies sitting with two huge men called dhehs, that is to say, two demons or ogres. At that moment the Queen glanced back, and spied the King coming, and said to her dheh, "The King, the King, he is coming and will strike!" Then she shrank away as if in fear of the dheh, and so crouching, awaited events.

Now when the King came quite close up, the second dheh rose, and snatching up the Princess Senâh, flew off with her after the manner of dhehs; but the Queen's dheh rushed at the King and would have slain him, had not the King's dog seized him by the leg and held him fast until the King, fitting an arrow to his bow, took aim and laid the monster low. Thus, the dheh being dead, the Queen Manavûr ran away home for her life, and went trembling

[1] From *Manauhâr*, "heart-ravishing."

to her rooms. But the King entered moody and sullen, and sat down in his hall of audience and awaited the coming of his vizier, who, when he saw him, said, "O King, you are upset, your mind is disturbed!"

At that time, however, the King did not answer, but remained silent, and soon he went in; and as he sat by himself he began to consider and to meditate, saying, "Surely nothing in the world is so faithful as a dog. O excellent hound, O faithful friend, but for you, your master would be lying cold and stiff in the garden of cypresses!" So the King sent for his vizier and told him the whole story,—how the Queen was false, how the Princess had vanished, and how one of the dhehs lay dead in the garden. "But I do not wish to kill her," said he, "for if I killed my Queen, the people would not understand, they would believe even worse things of her, and on me and on my house would fall trouble and disgrace, and everywhere in my kingdom men would give me a bad name. To save my honour, therefore, contrive something; invent what scheme you please, but whatever you do, let it be settled that the Queen shall eat day by day of the leavings of my dog, since, when she was false, my dog was true!"

So it came to pass that a house was built covered all over with bristling spear-heads so that the Queen could not possibly escape, or in any way be reached; and every day when the faithful dog had finished his daily meal the vizier carried his leavings to that dismal place and gave them to the Queen with his own hands. So passed many days. But the King was not satisfied, and sometimes he sent forth his vizier disguised into the city to listen to the speech of the people and to report their sayings. And when the vizier returned and the King inquired, "What are the people saying?" the vizier would answer, "No one suspects, for no one knows that the Queen is not in the palace." These reports, however, the King never believed, and for greater secrecy he ordered all his servants to live without the walls. "Let no one spend the night within the palace grounds," said he. But even that precaution did not ease the mind of the King, who, growing more and more suspicious, at last retired to the top of a certain mountain, where he had a strong castle, in which he took up his abode and in which the Queen languished miserably, feeding like a beast on the leavings of the old dog. And no guard or attendant or servant, once engaged, was allowed to leave the premises, under pain of sword or gibbet. Nor could any one approach from without, for on one side were steep places, and on the other, at the foot of that mountain, flowed a river twelve miles broad, on which no boat was suffered to ply.

Now it had so happened, that it was in the very country which lay on the opposite side of the river that the second dheh had settled when he had flown away with the Princess Senâh. But he had died, leaving the Princess alone. And in the place where the dheh had died and the Princess was living, there were heard every Thursday night the most dismal wailings and moanings, nor could any one find out what they were. And when the Kings of that part came to see the Princess Senâh and to ask her to marry them she always imposed conditions, saying to them, "First I will only marry the man who will stop the wailing, and, secondly, I will only marry the man who will bring me tidings of Gûl Bâdshâh." Many were the Princes who essayed the tasks imposed on them, but none of them succeeded. No one was able to stop the wailings, and no one could bring her news of Gûl Bâdshâh, for the Queen was too straitly confined; and as for the wailings, all the old men declared they had gone on for years time out of mind, so that the Kings had all to return to their homes as they came.

It chanced, however, that in those parts there was one King named Chand Bâdshâh, who had seven sons by one Queen, and one son only by another Queen. All the seven elder brothers were married, but not so the half-brother. This young Prince, whose name was Ahmed, sometimes visited his brothers' wives, who never failed to taunt him, saying, "If you were worth anything at all, you would go and stop the wailing and marry the Princess." Stung by these reproaches, he at last answered them, "Now I go! If I stop the wailing, all's well; if not, I will return no more." So he left his home, and after wandering from place to place, he at last arrived at the palace of the Princess and asked her hand in marriage. But she answered him, "Stop the wailing noise and marry me, and bring me news of Gûl Bâdshâh and marry me, but never shall man marry me until both my behests are fulfilled." Having received his answer, he repaired to the place of the wailings to observe, climbing the hills and going down to the valleys, sometimes by night, sometimes by day, and all to no purpose, But, when he inquired of the neighbours, he heard that in such a place lived a very old man who by trade was a goldsmith. To him he went, and when he spoke to him the old man answered, "Why have you come to me, and for what purpose do you ask such things? For this is a most difficult enterprise, and you are merely a lad. Better go home again!"

"Nay," answered the Prince, "only tell me the story, for learn the secret I must!"

"Heed then my words," said the old man. "In former times that was a place where evil men were wont to rob and murder the innocent. In those days there once came a wedding party who implored the inhabitants to escort them through the dark defiles where the robbers used to lurk and where the murders took place, but, out of all the people, only ten men would venture to go. As soon as they got down to a certain place, as they were travelling along, out rushed the robbers and massacred every soul of the party. And, because those ten men had gone freely to their death, therefore the people reckon them as martyrs. Yet, out of the ten, nine only were good men. The tenth was a usurer. And every Thursday night, week by week, for the souls of the nine good men, rice comes down from heaven, but for the soul of the usurer come only stones, and ever as he gnaws his stones he keeps wailing and wailing. Hence the dismal noise which is heard in all the country-side."

Having heard this story, the Prince set out for the mountain defile, and on Thursday night he sat down near the spot at which those men had fallen under the sword. And as he sat, the souls of those ten men gathered, and came to the place, and also sat down. And the nine good men said among themselves, "To-night we have a guest, let us spare a little for him from every mess." So they all gave, each of them dropping a little of his rice into a dish, which they then presented to the Prince. And when the tenth saw that, he said, "As you have given of yours, I too must give of mine," and he gave the Prince a stone, and having so done, he went away and sat down by himself. Then said the Prince, "Food you have brought me, but wherefore this stone?" All that mystery they explained to him fully, and they also said, "In a little while you will hear the sound of the wailing."

"But what is the meaning of it?" asked the Prince.

Then the nine answered, "In life he was worth lacs and lacs of rupees, yet never gave a pice in charity. All his treasure he buried in the ground, while the poor starved, and that is why he is now so punished."

"But may I not speak to him," said the Prince, "if only to say to him 'God bless you!'?"

So the nine good martyrs took him to their fellow-martyr, and when the Prince saw him he had pity on him, and begged him to tell him the reason of his misery.

"When I was in life," said the usurer, "and when my debtors came to me with their supplications, I used to say to them, 'First pay your interest and then take your principal, first pay your interest and then take your principal!' But, O sir, if you could only find my money, which is a vast sum, and distribute it all in charity, then God perhaps would release me! It lies buried in the village of the old goldsmith."

When morning came all the ghosts disappeared, and the Prince returned to the village. But he had forgotten to ask the bad man his name, so he went to the old goldsmith and said to him, "What were the names of the ten martyrs?" And the old man answered so and so. "But what was the name of the rich usurer?" asked Ahmed.

"That man," said he, "was named Dîn."

"Can you tell me anything about him?" said the Prince.

"I can tell you everything," said the goldsmith.

"Then has he any relations left still in this place?"

"None of his own descendants," answered the man, "but some of his daughter's descendants are here."

But when the Prince went to inquire, he found only one great-grand-daughter left, and she in the greatest poverty. At that very moment she was so poor that she was patching up her wretched hovel herself, with mud. So he addressed her and said, "Was not your great-grandfather named Dîn?"

"Yes," answered she. "Dîn was my grandfather's name."

"Alas," said he, "that ancestor of yours is now a cursed

being. For the sake of his name, then, give something away in charity."

At this the woman got angry, and throwing some of her mud to one side, "Here—take this!" cried she. "This I will give, if you like,—it is all he ever left me."

"But had he never a house of his own, your great-grandfather Dîn?" asked the Prince.

"O yes, he had," said she, "but poverty compelled us to sell it to a grain-seller."

"Come, show me the place," said he.

So they both went together, and having reached the house, the Prince said to the bunniah, "Did you buy Dîn's property from this woman?"

"Yes," answered the man.

"But," said the Prince, "did you buy the house only, or did you buy the land as well?"

"I bought the house only," said he.

On hearing this, the Prince began digging. After some time he came upon three large jars full of money, which he lifted out, and then said to the woman, "All this money was your great-grandfather's."

"I have nothing to do with it," said she. "Give me but enough to live upon, and the rest take yourself."

Then said he to the bunniah, "If for twenty rupees you bought this house, take now thirty and quit."

"You speak so handsomely," said the bunniah, "and have behaved so well, why should I ask more than I paid?"

The Prince then took the money and divided it into three parts. One part with the house he gave to the woman, but with the other two parts he bought horses and goods and raiment and food, and began to distribute them day by day in charity, but always in the name of Dîn. Each Thursday the wailing sounded less and less dreadful, and it ceased completely to be heard as soon as the whole of the money had been given to the poor. Then went the Prince back to the Princess and said, "One of my tasks is done."

"I know it," said she, "but the other still remains. Bring me now news of Gûl Bâdshâh, and my hand shall be yours."

So the Prince set out again, and coming to the old goldsmith, he stated the case to him and said, "What shall I do now?"

"Alas," said he, "this is a most difficult business, and you such a stripling! First of all you must pass through jungles full of tigers and monkeys and huge birds of prey."

"If I die," said the Prince, "go I must."

"Come," said the old man. "I will advise you, and if you will follow my counsels you will succeed."

"What do you advise?" asked the Prince.

"First of all," said the old man, "when you come to the country of the tigers, be not afraid, but go forward, and say unto them, 'In the name of God!' Then they will allow you to pass, and none will molest you. Again, when you get to the country of the great birds, say in like manner, 'In the name of God!' and they too will let you pass. But the monkeys will not obey that charm. Therefore be careful to take with you some grain, as much as you can carry, and when they begin to swarm about you, scatter it on the ground, for monkeys are greedy folk, and they will stop to fill their mouths, and meanwhile you can pass safely through."

So the Prince took with him a bag full of grain and started on the adventure. When he came to the tigers he cried, "In the name of God!" and so passed on. And when he came to the monkeys he threw at them handfuls of the grain which monkeys love. Grain by grain, the monkeys stopped to pick it up, while the Prince passed on in safety. Then he came to the huge birds, numbers of which came flying round him and spoke to him, and thanked God for his grace in sending them a human being for their dinner that day. And their words were so alarming that the Prince had need of all his courage.

"You speak of eating me," said he. "But see my bow and my arrows—I can shoot you down two at a time."

Then said the king of the birds to him, "Who then are you?"

"I am a king," answered he.

"You a king?" cried the bird. "And do you understand shooting?"

"Yes, I do," answered the Prince.

"Be it so," said the bird. "I will hold up my claw, and if you can hit my claw with one of your arrows, pass in peace in the name of God!"

So the bird held up a claw, but the Prince, suspecting a

trick, determined to aim at the leg, "for," said he, "I think that bird will lower his claw, and if he do, then I shall hit him fair."

As a matter of fact the bird did lower his claw, and the arrow hit it and pierced it through. And the Chief of the birds was so astonished at this exploit that at once he ordered an escort of birds to see the Prince safely out of his territory. Nevertheless the wounded bird remained behind, but it was not to waylay the Prince, though the Prince thought it might have been so; and when they arrived at the boundary of the kingdom of the birds, their leader begged a token from the Prince, who gave him a ring as a pledge that his engagement had been faithfully kept, and then the escort returned, while the Prince continued his journey alone.

At last he came to the banks of the river, but neither boat nor boatman, nor any person whatsoever, was to be seen anywhere, and how to cross no one could tell him. Now there grew there an enormous *sîsam* tree, and as he was very tired he sought the shade of it, and lying down commended himself to God and went to sleep. In his sleep he dreamed that he heard the loud cries of birds, and started up, but could see no one. But there the cries were just the same, and they seemed to come from a great nest high up in the tree. And as he looked he saw a huge snake crawling up from branch to branch, and the higher he went, the more loudly shrieked the young birds, and the more they fluttered. When the Prince understood the affair, he drew his bow and the snake fell dead, pierced by a sharp arrow, while he himself, weary with travel, lay down and went to sleep once more.

After a time the two old birds returned, bringing food for their young ones, and seeing a strange man lying there, they began to say to each other,—"For six years past, this fellow has been coming here stealing our young ones. Now, before feeding them, let us kill him!"

But the youngsters, overhearing this speech, cried, "The man has saved our lives in such sort that to the end of our days we can never be thankful enough."

"Nay," said the old birds. "The rogue is an enemy, and an enemy he has been for six years past."

"O no," said the young ones, "not he at all, but that monstrous snake. See where he lies!"

And when the old birds saw the snake, they were convinced, and straightway wetting their wings in the river, they spread them over the sleeping Prince to shade and refresh him. When, however, he at last awoke, he looked up, and began to think he was to be devoured, but the birds said, "Don't be afraid!"

"I am distressed," said the Prince, "because it would seem that God has only given me trouble on trouble."

But the birds reassured him by telling him their story, and by thanking him for his kindness, after which they said to him, "Can we do anything for you? Other people can work with their hands, but we will work with our eyes for you!"

"I wish to cross the river," said he, "to get news of Gûl Bâdshâh and his *begam*."

Then said the male bird, "You rest awhile here, and I will cross and bring you all the news possible."

"O no," said the Prince, "my promise was that I should go myself and see with my own eyes."

"In any case it is now too late," said the bird. "Remain therefore with us and rest. We can give you food, we can catch you a deer. Shall we bring it alive or dead?"

"Bring it to me alive," said the Prince.

So it was said, and so it was done. The deer was brought in alive, and the Prince killed it, and, having made a fire, he roasted the flesh of it, and ate, and slept. And when the morning came the male bird descended from the tree and bade the Prince mount on his back and close his eyes. And swiftly he rose, and swiftly flying over the river set the Prince down close to the castle. "Now I am going," said he, "but, as you have done us a service so great that we can never repay it, take from me this feather, and if ever you are in danger or in need of help, burn the end of it in a flame, and one or both of us will come to your aid."

Having so said, the bird took wing once more, and instantly disappeared. But the Prince entered first a neighbouring town, and the people took note of him, and when they asked him why he was there, he answered, "I have come to enter the service of the King." And they said, "Are you mad to think of such a thing? For neither will you have leave to go, nor will you even save your life if you attempt it."

"What does it matter," said the Prince, "since I have made up my mind to face the risk?"

At the castle gate, the sentry warned him too, and an old domestic said to him, "Ah fool, to come to a place like this," but still he persisted, until some one went and told the King, who came and said to him, "Whence come you?" And while the Prince answered something, the King said, "Why have you come?"

"I am merely one of the King's servants," said the Prince. "Let me be one of your bodyguard."

"My servants come, but they never go," said the King. "Neither absence nor leave is theirs, and death is the penalty of desertion. So come or else go at once."

"Try me," said the Prince; "these conditions I accept."

So Prince Ahmed entered the service of Gûl Bâdshâh, who furnished him with arms and sent him to guard the Queen. She was confined in a tower by herself, and her cell was dark and narrow. There she languished from day to day, fed upon the leavings of a dog, though still she looked like a human being. All these things the Prince soon discovered, and when he had seen and learnt everything he determined to get away. So he went to the King and said, "I have made a great mistake, and as this service does not suit me I wish to go, or at least to take leave."

"One thing you may do," answered the King, "and one only. You can remain living or dead."

"Nay," answered the Prince. "I will not stay here either living or dead, but I will go."

So the King called for a sword, but Prince Ahmed said, "First let me have respite merely so much as to allow me to take my farewell of the world from the house-top."

The King consenting, the Prince took with him a little fire, and running up the steps to the top of the tower, he took out his feather and held it for a moment over the ember, and, when it flamed, at once both the birds appeared ready to do him service. Meanwhile the King had sent up some of his guards, saying, "If he refuse to descend, kill him on the spot." Hearing their approach, the birds advised despatch, saying, "Make your salaams and mount at once, lest you be overtaken by an arrow." So the Prince turned towards the palace, and with a respectful salaam he thanked the King for his hospitality, and exclaiming, "Now, I am off!" mounted the male bird, and in a moment was carried far away to the other side of the river. Thus when the slaves reached the top of the tower they found no one there, and at once returned to report the circumstance to the King, who, falling into a rage, seized a sword and ran up himself, but when he saw the place deserted, he cried, "Ah, the fellow was some traitor from another land! He has escaped me, and now my dishonour will be published to the world."

But the Prince had landed in safety under the great tree on which sat the young ones, now well able to fly. And he said to the male bird, "Carry me, I pray you, over the jungles." And the male bird said, "Take one of my young ones also to remain with you always and to be your attendant." At first the Prince refused this gift, but afterwards he consented. Then he mounted once more, and away they flew over hills and plains of forest and jungle, where lived the monkeys and the tigers and the birds that devoured travellers, and at last they alighted not many marches from the house of the Princess Senâh. There the old bird made his salaams to him, and committed to him the young one, who promised to be faithful and bring news when trouble threatened, and after that he took his leave of them both, and returned to his mate. But the Prince continued his journey on foot, until he reached the village of the old goldsmith, who, when he had heard of all his adventures, said, "Now go boldly to the Princess and claim her." This the Prince did not fail to do, and when he saw her he said, "I have obeyed your orders. I have fulfilled both the conditions; do you believe it, or not?"

"Tell me," said she, "the whole story from first to last, and then I will tell you whether I believe it or not."

So she sat and listened, while the Prince related his adventures in wild places, in the countries of the tigers and the monkeys and the savage birds, and told her of the enormous snake, and how God had shown him kindness at the river, and brought him two great fowls to carry him over and to carry him back. "And your sister the Queen," said he, "is still alive; she lives in a barred chamber, and eats the leavings of the King's dogs, and yet, in spite of it all, she has still something of the look of a woman."

"All this is true," cried the Princess when he had ended.

"I knew beforehand that this would happen, and so now I accept you."

But by this time she had become very poor, and for that reason she would have put him off, he being a Prince, and she a Princess. "But see," said she, "I have left a ruby chain of great price—pledge it, and procure me suitable conveyance, and I will go with you to your country."

So after the wedding was over, a handsome doolie was brought, into which the Princess got in her loveliest robes, and they both started for the court of Chand Bâdshâh, the Prince's father. When within two marches of the capital, a herald was sent forward to announce their coming, and the news spread far and wide. His mother was overjoyed, and his father saddled his horse and rode out with a brilliant retinue to welcome his long-lost son, and, having met him on the road, he embraced him, and escorted them both with great ceremony into the town. But Princess Senâh delayed to visit her seven sisters, the wives of the other seven Princes, until she had new apparel provided to visit them in state. "I must put off my call," said she, "until my things are ready."

"Nay," answered her mother-in-law, "you shall not need to wait. You shall have all you require immediately. See, I have brought with me gold, apparel and jewellery in abundance, trinkets and bangles, a mirror of pearls for your finger, pendants for your head, a ring for your nose, and slaves withal to attend you. What need you more?"

So then she began to adorn herself handsomely, and her ornaments jingled like bells the moment she moved. And when she was ready, her husband, Prince Ahmed, escorted her forth, and her doolie bore her to the palace of her new sisters, who already possessed her likeness, but who were forced to admit that the reality far surpassed the picture.

Now the seven Princes were of old envious of their youngest brother because he was the son of another woman, and they began to conspire. "We had got this fellow," said they, "out of the way, but here he is back again in greater glory than ever." Their hatred against him increased when Prince Ahmed demanded territory to maintain his dignity, and especially after he had said to them, "You are seven sons of one mother, I am the only son of another mother. By custom and law, therefore, half the kingdom should be yours, and the other half should be mine."

"No," said the brothers, "make eight parts of it and take one, and do not expect any more."

While these disputes were raging among his children, the old King Chand Bâdshâh died and was buried. And when he was dead the wife of the eldest brother spoke and said to her husband, "Give him half the kingdom, and then fight him and take all his land from him, since you are seven to one." But the seven brothers scorned this advice as being the advice of a woman, and with Ahmed they agreed to call in a neighbouring king as umpire, who, when he had come and feasted for seven days, said to the seven, "Give your youngest brother one half of the kingdom, since it is his by right." This then accordingly they did, but when the land was divided, they soon picked a quarrel against him and began to make war upon him, and to take from him his towns and his castles. In his extremity Prince Ahmed summoned his favourite heron, but it was not to be found in its house or elsewhere, and search was made for it in vain. But the people heard say that the brothers had poisoned it with oil, because a wise man had informed them that it could fly one hundred miles in a single breath to bring news to its master and to fetch him assistance. Then in his trouble Prince Ahmed turned to his friend the umpire King, who promised speedy relief, which when the seven heard, they sent ambassadors to their brother desiring peace. "Let us agree to lay down our arms," said they, "and let us quarrel no more."

"I am the youngest," answered Ahmed, "and you are my elders. For that reason, if for no other, I desire to be on neighbourly terms with you."

Now at that time there was living with the seven Princesses an old woman whose name was Badnâmi. She, coming to the wicked Princes, as they sat together, said, "Give me the order, and I will contrive the death of Prince Ahmed at once." So they gave her leave.

There was then peace between the brothers, and they were all together at the capital of the seven, for Prince Ahmed and his wife had come on a visit to them. And Badnâmi went to the Princess Senâh and said, "Alas, Lady, your husband has accused you to me only this very day of freedoms with one of his brothers, but O do not repeat what I say, lest I fall into trouble." Then she went to the Prince and whispered to him privately under a similar promise of secrecy, "Alas, how men are always suspected! Only this very day your wife accused you to me of freedoms with one of her slave-girls."

Thus this wicked old woman sowed the seeds of jealousy between the husband and the wife, and one day when the Prince was away in the garden, she ran to him and said, "At this very moment one of your brothers is walking off with your wife."

Then she ran to the Princess and cried, "O haste, Lady, haste, your husband at this very moment is running off with your beautiful slave-girl!" Hearing these words, the young Queen rushed out into the garden, and Prince Ahmed seeing her as he approached the house, and believing as he did that she was hastening to meet her lover, shot her dead, without a moment's delay, with the bow which he bore in his hand. But when he came up to her and looked at her quivering body, it smote him to the heart that he had never questioned her. The seven brothers of course rejoiced, and, as they sat together in the evening, they said among themselves, "Half the work is already done, half only now is left!" But as for Prince Ahmed, he wandered forth, and sat him down in a lonely spot by himself. There his minister found him, and when he came to him he said, "What answer will you give before God in the next world for the murder of that poor Princess?" And as he thought of all the perils he had gone through in order to win her, his heart broke, and, falling backwards, he died.

Then was the whole realm seized by the seven brothers, and they enjoyed it; but their pride was not for long, for Prince Ahmed's mother went to the umpire King and to various other kings, and having brought an army, declared war against those unnatural brothers, two of whom were slain, and the rest banished, while the old Queen, ascending the throne herself, had the obsequies of Prince Ahmed and Princess Senâh performed with suitable splendour, and their memories preserved in sumptuous tombs set in the midst of gardens of fountains and flowers.

Told at Hâji Shâh, near Attock, by Gholâm, a Muhammadan villager, 1880.

III

OF THE WEAVER WHO MISSED THE MARE HE WAS RIDING

It happened one dark night, that a certain wise man, on a journey, was riding his mare through a gloomy forest, in which highwaymen and thieves sometimes lay in wait. Suddenly he cried out with a loud voice, "*Nafr, Nafr*,[1] where on earth is my mare?"

"Your mare?" answered his man. "You are riding your mare, are you not?"

"Am I?" said his master. "Well, so I am. But all the same we should be very careful going through a place like this."

Told by the bard, Sher, at Abbottâbâd, November 1889

IV

OF THE BLIND FAKÎR AND THE GOLD MOHARS

Once upon a time there was a blind fakîr who used to sit day by day begging at the gate of a city. As he was accounted a saint, his simple neighbours called him Hâfiz.[2] It was the custom of Hâfiz to cry out at intervals in a loud voice, "Who is the beloved of God, who will let me feel, only feel, one hundred gold mohurs?"

It happened one day that a certain soldier, returning from the wars, passed by the spot where Hâfiz was sitting and heard his doleful cry. Said the soldier to himself, "I vow before God that if ever I have a hundred gold

[1] A servant.

[2] *Hâfiz*, a title of honour bestowed upon any one who can say the Korân by heart.

mohurs, I will carry them to this good old man and let him feel them!"

He had not gone far on his way, when, as if in answer to his prayer, he picked up a bag of money which had been dropt in his path, and which contained a hundred gold mohurs, neither more nor less. So the good man retraced his steps, and going up to Hâfiz, he said, "Sir, by the kindness of God and yourself I have found a hundred gold mohurs. Be good enough to feel them, O good old man!"

Blind Hâfiz took the soldier's bag, untied the string, picked out the coins one by one, counting them carefully as he passed them from hand to hand, then restored them, tied up the precious treasure again, and gave the soldier hundreds of benedictions.

"But," said the soldier, "I also want my money, good Hâfiz!" At once the blind beggar set up a dismal cry, "Friends, neighbours, help! Thieves! All my wretched life I have been scraping together a little money, here a pice, there a cowrie, and now this son of a thief would rob me of all!" The people who came rushing together with great tumult instantly seized the unfortunate soldier, tore his clothes to rags, beat him to a jelly, and finally hustled him out of the town.

But the soldier, determined to have his revenge, still waited about. A cat watches a mouse, and so in like sort the soldier watched the blind fakîr. By-and-by Hâfiz takes up his *hamzah*,[1] and begins to feel his way home, passing down into the street of the blind beggars. His house was the last in the row near to the open country, and having undone the clasp, he entered and sat down on the floor, thanking God for all his mercies. But he was not aware that the soldier had dogged his steps, and that, at that very moment, he was standing behind him with drawn sword ready to cut off his head.

"Four hundred gold pieces before," muttered old Hâfiz, "and one hundred now. Four hundred and one hundred make five hundred!" And Hâfiz laughed long and merrily.

The blind man now rose up and groped his way to a corner where he turned up the earth, revealing a flat stone. which he lifted, and, lo, beneath it a brass pot! Divesting himself of his broad belt, which was heavy with treasure,

[1] *Hamzah*—here, a stick with a crescent top.

he deposited that, and the gold he had just acquired, in the brass pot aforesaid, and restoring everything to its proper place, returned to his cot.

Now came the turn of the soldier. Stooping down, he slyly uncovered the brass pot, which he lifted out with the utmost care; but, as ill luck would have it, in the act of rising, he knocked his head against a shelf. Instantly the old man bounded from his seat, and, seizing his stick, began to career madly round the centre of the room, revolving like a wheel, and uttering the most frightful cries. Round and round he danced like a madman, striking out right and left with his stick, breaking his waterpots to shivers and flooding his room with water. His cries were so frantic as to be heard by another blind man who lived hard by, and who now came running over to see what was the matter. But scarcely had he entered the room when Hâfiz closed with him, believing him to be the robber, and over the two blind men went on to the floor, fast locked in each other's arms, rolling here and rolling there in the mud, and with cries and yells tearing each other to pieces.

Taking advantage of the noise, and bursting with laughter, the soldier now slipped out of the house with all his booty, and got away as fast as his legs would carry him.

Told at Ghâzi on the Indus, by Sher Khân, a blind man, September 1879.

V

OF THE CRAFTY FAKÎR AND THE FOOLISH KING

ONCE upon a time some sturdy fakîr came to a certain town in which every commodity was sold at precisely the same rate. Gold was as cheap as iron, and wheaten bread could be bought for the same price as barley cakes.

"This must be a fine place to live in," said one of the fakîrs. "Let us rest a bit here!" But the chief of the band answered, "No, no, for if everything is sold at the same rate, justice is probably sold too. We are too poor. So I, for one, shall move on." The first speaker, however, who was a great lazy fellow, caring only for his ease, determined to remain, in order to eat and drink and live his life. His comrades therefore left him behind.

As ill-luck would have it, that night there was a great robbery with murder, and the people set upon the strange fakîr and charged him with the crime. In vain he protested innocence, and the upshot of the matter was that the King condemned him to be hanged. So he found himself in a fix, but somehow he managed to send word to his chief, who arrived on the scene just as the gallows had been set up, and the people were only waiting for the King to come and give the word of command.

"Save me, O my *Pîr*, save me!" was the petition of the doomed fakîr.

"Listen," said his master. "I shall speak to the King and beg to be hanged in your place, but do you keep saying all the time, 'No, no, I want to be hanged myself!' and then we shall see what we shall see!"

When the King arrived the old fakîr approached him and said, "O King, this unfortunate one is strong and young, with an old mother to maintain, whereas I am old and useless. Be pleased, therefore, to hang me instead of him!"

"Nay, nay," cried the other fakîr, "I want to be hanged myself, I want to be hanged myself!"

This farce was repeated several times over, which so astonished the King that he called the old fakîr aside and said to him, "What's the meaning of this, that you two gentlemen are both so eager to be hanged?"

"Sir," answered that deceitful one, "the sacred books and in short all the writings of the fakîrs pronounce this day to be the most fortunate day for death in the whole history of Islâm. He who dies to-day is in luck, for he will go on angels' wings straight away to Paradise!"

"Ah, then," cried the King, "that being so, hang me, O good people, hang me!"

So the King was hanged instead of the fakîr, who, rejoicing in his luck, went off with his master, and both instantly cleared away.

Told at Attock on the Indus, December 10, 1879, *by Karan Khân, a villager.*

VI

OF THE PATHÂN WHO WANTED HIS ASS TO BE MADE A MAN

Once upon a time a priest was teaching the village children at a mosque, when a Pathân came by. Hearing the babbling, he halted outside the wall and looked over. There he saw the priest flogging one of the boys and exclaiming, as he flogged him, "From an ass I have made a man of you, yea, made a man of you out of a jackass, and yet you will not understand!"

Hearing these extraordinary words, the Pathân pricked up his ears and said to himself, "What power this priest must possess to turn asses into men!" So, taking fifty rupees out of his waist-cloth, he stepped into the court and laid them down before the priest. "I am going," said he, "to bring you my old donkey and I give you in advance these fifty rupees on condition that you make a man of him."

"Well," said the priest, "I shall want the money if only for the feed of the ass; but do you call again some other day!"

The priest, therefore, took the man's money and put it by, and when the donkey came he handed it over to his wife, who used it day by day to fetch and carry.

At the end of six months, the Pathân came back and said to the priest, "Now, if you have finished the job, hand me over my man!"

"You have come too late," answered the priest. "The truth is I spiced your ass so highly that it was not long before he turned into the nawâb of the next village. Go to the nawâb of the next village, and tell him so!"

For the next village, therefore, the Pathân set off, and going to the house of the nawâb, he explained the matter, saying, "My fifty rupees I gave to the priest, and now come along—you are my man!"

Thereupon the nawâb waxed wrath and turned him out, and the Pathân had to return empty-handed to the priest, to whom he made his complaint. "I went to the nawâb," said he, "but he got angry and refused to give himself up!" Then said the priest, "That nawâb was once a pupil of mine, and you must therefore go to him again, and remind him that he was taught by me from a child; tell him I put too much spice in him, and that, nawâb or no nawâb, he is most certainly your old donkey!"

So the Pathân did as he was told, and when the nawâb had heard his story again, he began to think within himself, "It would appear that my old teacher must have said something to this stupid ass, which he has not understood. So I had better go with him to the priest myself."

Coming to the mosque, the nawâb, inasmuch as the priest was his old master, paid him great respect, and begged to be enlightened as to the capers of the blockhead of a Pathân. "He is certainly a blockhead, but not more so than other Pathâns," said the priest. "The fact is he was passing when I was administering the rod to a dunce, and hearing me using my accustomed phrase, 'From an ass I have made a man of you,' he gave me fifty rupees to make a man out of his own ass. Then I sent him on to you, but even now, as you see, he does not understand."

"I have an idea," said the nawâb. "Do you tell him that his ass has now become the village fakîr, and send him there, and I'll warrant that, by the exercise of some miracle or other, that holy man will be able somehow to knock sense into his head."

No sooner was it said than it was done, and presently the Pathân was seen standing by the lowly shed of the village fakîr, to whom he told his message, saying, "The priest informs me that you are my old donkey, and I want you to come home with me at once." On hearing these words, the fakîr thought to himself, "This man is daft!" Then he said, "Yes, it is all right! I was once your old donkey true enough, my master. But first I want you to do something for me, and then you must come back for me. I have a friend, another fakîr, who lives across the river. Take him these cakes, and having given them to him, with my salaams, fail not to return." Taking the cakes, the Pathân went to the river, but he had forgotten to ask for a boat in which to cross over, so he had fain to retrace his steps. "Return to the river," said the fakîr, "make respectful salaams to it, and say I have sent you, and then you will be able to cross." So he went again, and made obeisance, and received an answer, and then he was permitted to cross over the water to the other side. There he saw the second fakîr, to whom he handed the cakes, saying, "Such and such a fakîr has sent you this bread." By this time the Pathân had begun to experience some faint glimmerings of reason, and he now considered within himself, "How am I to get back? I will ask the fakîr!" This therefore he did, saying, "How am I to cross the river again?"

"Go to the bank," answered the holy man, "and say to the river, 'He who needs not food sends you a salaam, and begs you to suffer this Pathân to cross.'"

The Pathân obeyed him, and coming to the river he spoke as directed, and, as before, the same voice said "Cross!" and he crossed over in safety. And all the time he was puzzling his brains as to what things meant, seeing that the fakîr had eaten up all the cakes. So he said he would go back to the first fakîr and ask him to explain.

To him therefore he went again, and, reporting to him all that had hapt, he begged for some explanation. And the fakîr, seeing he was ripe, took him in hand. "Ah!" said he to him, "you are a Pathân, and therefore I suppose a foolish fellow, void of understanding. If you had had any wit at all, you would have seen for yourself. That man, being a fakîr, does not need food, but as I sent it, and as you took it, he ate it out of civility!" Furthermore he said to him, "O son, we are fakîrs. If any one could turn donkeys into men, it would be ourselves, of course, but that schoolmaster merely meant to say that he had turned a stupid lad into a wise one, a fool into a reasonable being."

So, having been enlightened, and understanding at last what a fool he was, the Pathân went back to the mosque, and, stooping low, he touched the feet of the priest and said, "An ass I came and an ass I went. Take me, I pray you, in hand yourself, and make a man of me!"

Hearing these words, the priest commended him, and, restoring his money and his ass, bade him enter his school, which he did, and there in time he acquired some knowledge and even some sense, saving the fact that he was still a Pathân.

Told at Ghâzi, February 14, 1883, by Nazâm Dîn, a villager of Ghargûshti.

VII

A JUNGLE TALE

ONCE upon a time there was a donkey, and also a bullock, and neither the one nor the other had any regular master, but any one who wished used to catch them, and load them with stones or with timber, and work them to death. So one day the bullock said to the donkey, "Look here, we have no master and both our backs are sore. Every one puts upon us. Let us then go to the hills together and shift for ourselves!"

"All right," said the donkey, "let us!" and they started off. After living freely in the jungle for some time, they got into good condition, and the donkey said to the bullock, "O bullock, bullock, I feel to-day as if I should like to bray!"

"Hold!" said the bullock, "and don't be an ass! Have you forgotten the time when your back was so sore, and now do you want to bray, merely because you have been living at your ease for a day or two? Here we are in the jungle, and, if you bray, a tiger will assuredly come, and kill either you or me! What then, O donkey?"

"Let him come," said the donkey; "let as many tigers

come as like. I feel I should like to bray, and therefore bray I must."

So the donkey began braying terribly, until the earth seemed to shake, and the bullock said to him, "So, you are braying, are you? Well, now I must shift for myself."

So the two friends separated. But the bullock had gone only a few steps, when a famished tiger began to wag his head and say, "I am hungry, very hungry, and God has brought into these jungles a donkey for me!"

The bullock also, as he moved away, was saying to himself, "Now something unpleasant is sure to happen, or I am not the true son of a bullock."

And the tiger was also saying, "I will set on the bullock first, and then settle with the donkey."

And the donkey, seeing how things were going, was saying, "The tiger has made for the bullock, and then I suppose he will come and devour me!"

Presently the tiger sprang on the bullock, so the donkey flew to the rescue, kicking and biting savagely. At last he fixed his teeth in the tiger's flesh, right between the shoulders, which forced him to let go, and the bullock, set free, ran away to a place of safety.

At this moment a ploughman came strolling by, and he said, "What a thing—a donkey has laid hold of a tiger!" The tiger seeing him called out, "O you ploughman, come to my aid, save me from this wretched donkey!"

"Nay," answered he, "I save you not, you deserve all you will get!"

"For the sake of God, and in the name of the Prophet," cried the tiger, "I beseech you, take me out of the jaws of this wretched donkey!"

Thus adjured, the ploughman went up, and smote the donkey with his staff. But this only made the donkey rear and kick and struggle all the more, until the tiger said, "O he bites me harder than ever, his very teeth meet in me! For mercy's sake don't hit him any more, or I am a dead tiger this day! O ploughman, take your plough-rope, and passing it round the villain's teeth, saw his very jaws off!"

Thus assailed, the donkey was fain to let go his hold, and seeing that he had now two foes to fight instead of one, he scampered off, and joined his friend the bullock in a place of safety, leaving the miserable tiger lying exhausted on the ground. Then thought the tiger to himself, "Far better to have died at once than to have suffered such dishonour from a donkey! This ploughman, too, will talk of it everywhere, and all the tigers will come to hear of it. I had therefore better kill him out of the way." So he glared at the ploughman, and said, "O ploughman, I am going to kill you!"

"But why kill *me?*" said the ploughman.

"I am going to kill you," answered the beast, "because you will go and tell everybody about this infamy, and then all the whole tribe of tigers will be disgraced for ever. But dead men tell no tales, and once I kill you, my story is safe!"

"O you ungrateful beast!" said the ploughman. "I released you from death, and is this all the thanks I get? Not a word will I speak, nor mention a thing about it." And he solemnly promised to hold his tongue.

After this the ploughman went his way home, followed by the dejected tiger. And the man said to his wife, "I have seen a wonderful thing this day, but I won't tell you what it was."

Now, in this family, the grey mare was the better horse, so she said to her husband, "If you don't tell me, I'll thrash you!"

"Well," said her husband, "I *will* tell you, but remember, if I do, I shall be killed."

"Don't be a fool," said she, "but tell me at once!"

So he told his wife the whole story which he had promised to keep secret, and the tiger, listening outside, heard every word, and he cried out, "You wait till I catch you!" And the man said to his wife, "Now, you see!"

Next day the ploughman would have kept to the house, being afraid to go out to till the land, but his wife hustled him, saying, "Off with you! Snakes and tigers never come to the same place twice! Get along!" and she took up a stick and gave him a drubbing. Then thought the man to himself, "Better for me to be killed by a tiger than struck by a woman!" So out he went, but presently came across the tiger, who began to upbraid him for his perfidy, and would have eaten him, if the wife, hearing the noise, had not issued forth, armed with her bludgeon. The tiger, seeing her fury, took fright and ran away, leaving the man to his plough. And so the wife returned triumphant to the cottage. Who then will say that a woman is not as good as a donkey, seeing that if a donkey routed a tiger, a woman was more than a match for man and tiger too?

Told by Nûr Khân, a farmer, at Torbêla, Upper Indus. November 21, 1880.

VIII

A STORY OF A RUBY

"Of a really deserving man no one knows the value"

Once upon a time there was a potter, who owned thirty or forty donkeys. Having loaded them up with pots one day, he was going his rounds, when he found a precious stone, which he tied round his largest donkey's neck. After a time he came to a ferry, and as he was crossing over, the ferryman saw the stone and admired it. "What a pretty stone," said he. "Give it to me, and your donkey may go over free!"

"All right," said the potter, and he handed over the stone to the ferryman, who tied it to his stern oar.

After a time, a traveller wanted to cross. He was by trade a lapidary, and seeing the stone he said to himself, "That stone is simply a priceless ruby!" So he said to the boatman, "Will you take five rupees for your stone?"

"You can have it for ten," answered the boatman, having no idea of its value; and so the lapidary became the possessor of the ruby.

Having paid the money, and received the stone, he wrapped it most carefully in several soft napkins, and then laid it within several jewel cases, which he placed under lock and key in the safest place in his shop.

Some time after, the King, wanting a ruby, sent his

minister to look for one. Without delay they went straight to the lapidary, who at first denied having any such stone as the King would care to possess. "If I had," said he, "you would seize it, and give me but a small sum for it."

"Never fear," said the minister. "As you have such a ruby, show it to us! But first, how much do you ask for it?"

"Not less than twenty thousand rupees," answered the lapidary.

"Well, bring it, and show it!" said the minister.

So he brought out his boxes, which he proceeded to open. But, alas, he found his precious ruby shivered to atoms! "Ah, my kismet, my kismet, my ruby, my ruby!" cried he.

So the minister went away. And the lapidary, looking at the shattered ruby, began to upbraid it. But the ruby murmured, "Can you wonder that I am broken? First I was found by a potter and tied round the neck of a donkey, but he, poor man, was a simple villager. Then I was owned by a boatman who bound me to an oar, but he too was ignorant, and knew no better. But you!—you offered five rupees for me, and gave ten! And even now, when you had the chance of proclaiming my true value, what did you do? You asked a wretched twenty thousand rupees for me! These slights were too much—my heart broke, and now I am worthless!"

So with people really worthy of honour. They are never appreciated by their fellow-men, until, with broken hearts, they lie in their graves!

Told by Sher Khân, the blind Khân of Hazro.
December 27, 1881.

IX

THE RASÂLU LEGENDS

I. RASÂLU'S EARLY LIFE[1]

"On a Tuesday he entered his narrow domain,
A Saturday smiled when he left it again;
O then was brought forth that monarch of might,
And Rasâl on the day of his birth was he hight."

RÂJA SÛLWÂHÂN (SALIAVAHAN) OF SIÂLKÔT, a descendant of the great king famous in story, whose name was Vîkrâmâjît, of the empire of Ujâin, had two Queens, the elder of whom was Ichrân, and the younger Lûna, a tanner's daughter. By the former whom he had married first, he had a son Pûran, who by the advice of the astrologers was secluded from the sight of his father in a lonely palace from the moment of his birth until he was twelve years old. On his release from duress, he was permitted to appear at court, and his father on one occasion sent him to pay his respects to his newly-married wife, Râni Lûna, who was about the same age as the young prince and exceedingly fair. Pûran also was remarkable for his great beauty, and Râni Lûna, when she saw him, fell deeply in love with him. But because he absolutely refused to listen to her, she procured his disgrace, and his deluded and incensed father condemned him to exile and death. The executioners to whom he was committed carried him far away into the wilds, where they cut off his hands and feet and cast him into a ruined well, there to languish and die. In that dismal place he lingered for many a year until he was rescued by the great saint Gûrû Gorakhnâth, who restored his limbs to him sound and whole as before, and showed him kindness and protection.

Prince Pûran now determined to turn fakîr, and concealing his identity, he temporarily took up his abode, by his director's advice, in a certain abandoned garden close to the palace of his father in Siâlkôt. The fame of his sanctity spread far and wide, until it was reported to the King Sûlwâhân that the very trees of the garden, which

[1] This and the following chapter are compiled from scattered fragments and traditions. The verses represent verses in the original story.

had withered up to the roots and died, were miraculously beginning to bud and to put forth leaves. So the King and his younger Queen, desiring the same favour, went to visit him. As they approached the spot, Pûran said to himself —"Here comes my father, and not only he, but my step-mother as well; if she should chance to recognize me, she will again plot to work me ill."

But being a good man he considered once more,— "Never mind, I trust in God. Whatever she does she must account for hereafter; and so, whether she remember me or not, still out of respect I will rise and do obeisance to them."

When the King and his consort arrived at the place, Pûran stood up and bowed himself humbly, with his eyes fixed on the ground.

"Ah!" cried the King, "you have acted amiss; you are a fakîr, and it is I who should have humbled myself to you."

"O King," answered he, "I had a master once, but he is dead, and, as I do remember, his face and form were not unlike those of your Highness: that is the reason I rose and salaamed at your approach."

Then the Queen addressed him and said, "I also have come to see you, for I have no children."

"You shall certainly have a son," replied the fakîr, "but your son's mother will always be crying, even as the mother of your step-son was always crying. And just as by reason of the fraud contrived by you the son of Râni Ichrân fell upon evil days, so, though, as a mighty hero vowed to solitude, your son shall conquer his foes, yet he shall at last perish through the guile of a woman."

With these words Pûran handed to his father a single grain of rice, bidding him administer the same to Râni Lûna, in order that the promised son should come into the world.

In due time the event as foretold came to pass, and the King named the child Rasâl or Rasâlu. Sorrow and heaviness attended his birth, for the conjunction of his stars presaged a life of storm and strife, and the astrologers prophesied evil to the King on account of him. Scarcely had he opened his eyes on the world, therefore, when he was banished to a solitary place, and, like his half-brother Pûran before him, he was not permitted to see his father for twelve weary years. As he advanced in growth, however, he enjoyed a foretaste of his future glory in the stories of kings and heroes, which were recited or sung to him day by day by bards and minstrels, until the very name of war and the sound of arms tingled in his ears like music. All that was suitable to his position and agreeable to his destiny he practised and learnt; but most of all he excelled in magic, in archery, in riding, and in the use of the sword and lance, while the pleasures of chess-playing and deer-hunting filled up his lighter hours.

Thus passed the early boyhood of Prince Rasâlu, until he was free to approach the capital and to set foot over his father's threshold. He was remarkably strong and agile for his years, more like a man than a boy; and he was skilled in every generous accomplishment, and in every warlike exercise. Yet there was then one pastime which, beyond all others, he was fond of indulging in, and that pastime was shooting marbles from the pellet-bow. He used to watch for the women of the city as they returned from the river, bearing on their heads full chatties or pitchers of water, and shooting his hard pellets with an unerring aim from the walls of the palace, he would break the pitchers into atoms, and laugh gaily when he saw the released water pouring down in floods over their shoulders.

At last his victims made complaint to the wazîr, and the wazîr complained to the King, and as the Prince had been warned again and again, he proposed his banishment for a season. But the King answered, "One son of mine I dismissed to exile and death before, for which I shall ever mourn. See, here is my treasury, take money sufficient for the purpose, and let the women of the city be provided with vessels of brass." Moreover, he laid his commands on his son that he should cease to molest them.

But if the women imagined that their pitchers of brass would make the slightest difference, they were soon undeceived, for Rasâlu fashioned a bow of steel, and cast him pellets of iron; and so great was his strength of arm that, with faultless aim, he drove his bullets right through the brazen pitchers even when full charged with water. In dismay the people turned their steps again to the palace, and in answer to their prayers the wazîr once more proposed the banishment of the Prince.

"Nay," answered the King, "this is my only son; he must not be sent away. I therefore order that in every enclosure in the city a well shall be sunk, so that the women of each household may draw their abundance of water undisturbed."

So, in accordance with the King's directions, numerous wells were built throughout the city, and the people fondly reckoned on supplying their needs in freedom and quiet. But again they were disappointed, for the irrepressible Prince ascended to the top of a high tower which commanded every homestead and walled enclosure within the gates, and from that vantage-ground he continued to discharge his artillery at the brazen pitchers, to the despair of the unfortunate owners.

Then was the King petitioned for the last time either to banish or to put to death his rebellious son; and his patience being at length exhausted, he answered,—"Would to God Rasâlu had never been born, or that even now he were taken away! Let him leave my country, let him go wheresoever he pleases, but let me not look upon his face again." And to his mother Lûna he said,—"Tell that son of thine to quit my kingdom and never to trouble me more!"

Full of distress, the Queen sent for Rasâlu and said to him,—"Henceforth, my son, we shall be as strangers, for the King has pronounced your doom. You must leave your mother, your home, and your country, and go into exile."

"But why," asked the Prince, "am I to leave you, mother, and why must I quit the country? What crime have I committed? Speak to the King, my father, and let him declare for what fault I am deserving of exile."

That night the Queen entreated the King for her son with repeated solicitations and tears, but he answered her harshly, steadily refusing to listen to her prayers, saying, "Rasâlu's crime admits of no excuse, he has plunged the good people into distress in the matter of water, and his exile is the only remedy."

When the Prince heard that his fate was irrevocable, he sought his father's presence and said to him, "I will obey you in all things if on your side you will accept my two conditions. The first is, that you make me a Mussulman; and the next is that you become a Mussulman yourself."

Hearing these words, the King lost control of himself, and in a fury he ordered his son to instantly quit the palace. At the same time he sent for his ministers and said to them, "Set up a figure fashioned like a man with his hand behind his back, and let the face of the figure be blackened. By this symbol my son will understand that he is doomed to banishment."

One day, as Rasâlu was returning from the chase, he caught sight of the figure standing without his mother's palace, and, turning to his followers, he said: "This figure is a sign that I must quit the kingdom. Lo, the goodness of the King my father! We are the descendants of the great King Vikrâmâjît, who sold himself away in charity three hundred times; and for a mere trifle my father decrees my banishment. Nevertheless, I will obey."

So he gathered together a chosen band of valiant men, the flower of the youth of Siâlkôt, and armed them with bows, lances, and swords. He also provided himself with fleet horses and ample treasure, and when all was ready, he mounted his famous mare Folâdi,[1] which was born on the same day as himself, and passing under the windows of his mother's palace he bade her a long farewell, and set out from the city at the head of his followers, all eagerly bent on foray and spoil.

But the Râni Lûna, weeping and beating her breast, loosed her ringlets and looked out from her lattice and watched the retreating figure of her son as he rode away into the wilds. There she remained straining her eyes, until a distant cloud of dust alone showed her the route which he had taken, and as she watched and wept she stretched out her hands and cried through her falling tears—

"O little, little can I see of you,
My son Rasâlu!
Your crest the rolling dust obscures from view,
My own Rasâlu!
With knives of hardened steel my heart is riven,
It burns like flames within the furnace driven.
O hear, Rasâlu!
Whose son goes forth to exile, storm, and strife,
How doubly, trebly vain that mother's life!"

1 *Folâdi* means *made of steel* (Persian). Sometimes Rasâlu's horse, like Rustem's, is named *Baurâki, the Grey Mare.*

RÂJA RASÂLU

2. HE GOES TO GÛJERÂT

HAVING turned his back upon his native land, Râja Rasâlu rode towards the kingdom of Gûjerât. Wherever he halted on his route the whole country was made aware that he was bound on an expedition of adventure, and that he would enrol all good men and true who would join his standard. Thus, by the time he arrived at the capital of Gûjerât he found himself in command of a strong force of hardy warriors, all eager to do battle for their youthful leader.

The King of Gûjerât was a Gûjar, the head of a race of Râjpûts in alliance with the house of Siâlkôt, and friendly to Râja Sûlwâhân. Hearing that a foreign force had encamped within sight of his walls, he went forth to hold a parley with them, and, when he met Rasâlu, he addressed him courteously, saying,—" Who are you?

" What Râja's son are you,
 And say what name you bear;
Where lies your fatherland,
 What city owns you there?"

And to him Rasâlu made answer—

" Râja Sûlwâhân's son am I,
 Rasâlu is my name;
Siâlkôt is my fatherland,
 My city is the same."[1]

Then was Rasâlu received and welcomed with befitting honour, and festivities were held to celebrate his arrival at Gûjerât.

" But," said the Gûjar King, " you are heir to a kingdom; why then do I see you at the head of an army so far away from your own dominions?"

" Near Jhîlam," answered Rasâlu, " there is a territory

[1] The reader will scarcely need to be reminded of the similar doggerel put into the mouth of Captain Cuttle—

Captain Cuttle is my name,
 England is my nation,
London is my dwelling-place,
 And blessèd be creation!—

a variant of a rhyme as old as Rasâlu!

containing numbers of giants who have been turned into stone, but it is held by usurpers. Of that country my father claims a fourth share, as being near of kin to the former râjas; and, as his rights are denied, I am now on my way to maintain them, and to recover my patrimony."

Then the Gûjar King offered help to Rasâlu, saying, "Take with you a contingent of my troops, chosen marksmen, with arms and munitions of war, and go, and prosper against your enemies." And to his own men he said, "Go, fight for Râja Rasâlu, and do not return until you are dismissed."

When the Prince arrived at the land of the Petrified Ones he at once began his warlike operations, besieging forts, throwing up earthworks, and cutting off supplies. Rasâlu's strength was the strength of a giant; his bow, made out of steel, could be drawn by no one but himself, and he had three arrows, each of them weighing a hundred pounds, which never failed to hit, and which he never failed to recover.

After a short blockade the principal fortress was carried, and the city fell into the hands of Rasâlu. Much spoil was taken, gold and silver and precious stones, and splendid raiment, and many a fair damsel, all of which was divided among his captains and men of war.

Then, while the petty princes fled away, or else submitted, and consented to acknowledge Rasâlu as lord and master, the kingdom was reduced to order, laws were enforced, and under chosen governors prosperity once more smiled on the land.

It was during his halt at Jhîlam that Râja Rasâlu heard of a certain famous fakîr, or saint, whose abode was at the village of Tillâh, and as this man's reputation for miracles and signs was in everybody's mouth, he determined to pay him a visit. The hermit's power was so great that he knew of the King's approach long before he came to the foot of the hill on which he lived, and addressing his disciples, he said, "Râja Rasâlu is at hand with purpose to put my knowledge to the test. But as he is the son of a Hindu, he ought to have known his duty better. However, I will forestall him, and test him first, and we shall see whether his own power is so great as rumour declares."

His pupils answered him, "True, O master; they say

his arrow is so strong and swift that it will pierce a stone. Therefore devise something."

The hermit then turned himself into an immense hungry tiger, and when the King's followers saw the wild beast prowling round about the jungle, they were alarmed, and said, "See, so great is the power of this hermit that even the tigers acknowledge his sway. Come, let us return!"

But Râja Rasâlu answered, "He is a wise man who will finish an enterprise; foolish are they who falter!"

Then the King challenged the tiger, and said, "You are indeed a mighty full-grown tiger, but I am a Râjpût. Come, let us do battle together!"

In reply, the tiger uttered a terrific growl like the roar of a coming earthquake, and crouching down, he prepared to spring. But Rasâlu fitted two of his tremendous arrows to his bow of steel, when immediately the tiger was confounded with fright and vanished away.

The King now went forward to the house of this famous hermit, whom he found sitting in the midst of his disciples, and who at once arose and made a salutation to the man who was more powerful than himself.

"Pretty hermit this," cried the King, "to stand up to me or to any one else!"

The saint, feeling ashamed, said, "O King, this hill is only the abode of mendicants. It is not Gandgarh, which is the home of giants. If single-handed you engaged the giants of Gandgarh, and if you slew them, you would win glory and renown; but there can be no renown and no glory in lording it over poor fakîrs."

"O sir," answered the King, "you taunt me! Now, as I am a descendant of the great king Vikrâmâjît, I vow never to abide in my home in peace, until I have conquered the giants of Gandgarh."

"As for me," said the old prophet, "I can only pray for you. Yet I know full well that you will prosper, and overcome them all—yea, every one—if you will but remember and do what I bid you:—First, draw not your sword against the poor, and next, lift not your hand to smite fakîrs."

Then Râja Rasâlu, dismissing his retinue, left that place, and continued his journey alone.

3. RASÂLU'S REVOLT

AND now, having ended his labours in the borders of Jhîlam, Râjâ Rasâlu, whose term of exile was drawing to a close, set out for other parts, regardless of home and kindred. And wherever he went he took with him Shâdi, his parrot, and Folâdi, his grey mare. Thus he went on his way, and when his mother heard of it she sent forth a messenger, but the messenger returned, saying, "Rasâlu has gone off, and will not return." And when his father heard of it, he sent forth a messenger, but his messenger returned with the same story. And when his foster-mother heard of it, she also sent forth a messenger, and the messenger came, and Rasâlu inclined his ear, and went back to Siâlkôt. And when his foster-mother saw him in the courtyard, the milk simmered in her breasts, and she cried to him—

"Hast come, my son, from lands afar?
Hast come, my son, from wounds and war?
Hast played a manly part?
I am thy mother, who but I?
And thou art the babe I travailed by,
The offspring of my heart!"

But Rasâlu did not regard her. Only as he passed he looked up and answered her thus—

"In my hand I carry a mendicant's stick,
And my head is bound up with a clout,
Your son may be whole and your son may be sick,
I'm a beggar-man out and out!"

Thus came Rasâlu back to Siâlkôt. And his mother was glad and his father too.

Now Rasâlu had not been long at home before he yielded to counsel and began to incline his mind to marriage. So he sent his groom to his mother with this message,—"If I did not tell you so before, it was only shame that held me back. But now choose me a wife, for I am willing to be guided."

Hearing these tidings, his mother became highly pleased, for she had often spoken to him on the same subject, but every time Rasâlu had turned away and put it off. Now, however, he himself had made the first advances, and she told the King, his father, who, delighted equally with herself, told the groom to hasten back to his son and say, "I will summon the great ones, I will order our family Brâhmin to open his tables, Motî Râm also shall be called, and the wedding ceremonies shall be put in train without delay."

Then the King, Râja Sûlwâhân, called together his council, especially his wazîr, Motî Râm, who was the father of the chosen bride, and he fixed the wedding for the fifth day of the month Assa.

The day after, early in the morning, at the time of the drawing of water, Rasâlu went down to the river to bathe. On his way back he passed along the street in which stood the house of Motî Râm. There, loitering about the well, he saw a parcel of girls with their pitchers. They were laughing and talking together as women do. Foremost among them was the maiden who had been betrothed to him and whom he was shortly to marry. Being a girl of free spirit, always ready with a jibe or a jest, she called out in that public place to the man she was to wed—

"Ho, rider of the dark grey mare,
Did you forget to bind your hair?
Like some young girl's, all loosely tied,
It bobs about from side to side.
Take care, O Râja, I implore,
Lest, as you pass some lady's door,
Her watchman flout you,
And jest about you!"

Rasâlu was vexed to be put to shame, and he answered her—

"Hear me, my wife not now but soon to be!—
For all your words of shame addressed to me
I swear, as I am Râni Lûna's son,
Your insults I'll repay you every one!"

And, retorting, the girl cried—

"You son of Lûna, do not be so proud,
Nor vent your anger thus before a crowd,
For men as good as you,
Not one, but quite a crew,
Lead forth by miry ways
My father's calves to graze!"

Then said Rasâlu to her—

"O bride betrothed, O wife to be,
Mark thou the words I speak to thee!
By the mother who bore me,
By the pangs she had o'er me,
My wife thou shalt be, but I swear to thy face,
I'll marry and leave thee to shame and disgrace."

So he passed on his way. And when the marriage preparations were sufficiently advanced, his father and himself and all the guests, being a great company, went to the house of Motî Râm, and there the wedding feast was spread and the people all sat down. But Motî Râm, the bride's father, sat not down with the rest, but, girding up his loins, he went in and out among the guests, saying, "O friends, ye who have come in with the procession, welcome you are! And I pray you not to feel displeased or offended, for I am one of your slaves!" And when the meal was over and the men had retired to smoke and to recline, troops of girls came in and played *bero-ghôri*.[1] With singing and dancing came they in, all the maidens of the place in full tale, and they jested with the King and the Prince, and made free with everything, and Rasâlu gave them largess, throwing among them fifty rupees, and one gold piece thrown in too. Then they took his hands, and brought him to the chamber in which he was to be married, all fun and laughter, and he went with them in company with his father and a great following of friends. But as he passed through the court, he made secret signs to his groom not to fail to have Folâdi, his grey mare, saddled and bridled and ready at hand.

Then entered the Brâhmin priests, who called in also the parents, and the two, the man and the woman, were made to sit down in the middle of that room, while the Brâhmins read to them words out of a book. And to the principal one said Rasâlu, "O Sûndar Dâs, I, the Râja, speak to you! To cut the matter short, I pray you not to marry me at all!"

"O Râja Rasâlu," answered he. "Hear me! You come of a noble stock. I pray you do not disgrace your name by conduct unworthy of your birth!"

This counsel Rasâlu disdained, keeping silence all the time. And when the reading was over these men tied together the ends of the skirts of the bride and the bride-

[1] Scrambling for money or sweetmeats.

groom, and made them pass round and round the burning fire. And as Rasâlu passed round, he glanced up, and, lo, in the court without, his horse stood ready. So all at once he drew his sword and severed the skirts at the knot, the one from the other, and he leapt forth, while his wife reproached him, saying,—" O Rasâlu, you have done me a wrong to cut off marriage-knot of mine, and in the day of judgment I will call you to account for it!—

> " Ah me! How foul a trick to play
> Your wedded wife!
> Before great God what will you say
> To save your life?"

But he taunted her, and said, " Remember your words, O Râni, the words that you spoke that day at the well! Since you call me a beast, go marry some one else!"

In vain all the four parents, afflicted by so great a disgrace, besought him to return, standing with heads bare and imploring him. "I brought you up from a child," said the King, " only to be a grief to me, and now you have degraded your father before all this assembly!"

Rasâlu did not note the words spoken by his father, and on his way forth he bethought him that he should have answered him too, so he returned, and, while his whole body trembled, he said thus,—" Hear me, my father! Me have you ever embittered. But I go hence to Mecca, and when I come again, it will be with a Muhammadan army at my back to pull down Siâlkôt."

Then he went off, riding day and night, until he came to a noble city having walls and towers all round, and, going to the gates, he inquired, " Who is the chief of this place?"

" This is the city of Mecca," said a watchman, " and the lord of Mecca is the Hazrat Imâm Ali Lâk."

So Rasâlu entered, and he went to the Imâm Ali, and addressed him, saying, " Receive me, I pray you!"

The Imâm, seeing that he was a Hindu, said to him, " Whence come you?"—

> " What Râja's son are you?
> What is the name you bear?
> Where lies your fatherland?
> What city owns you there?"

And Rasâlu made answer, "I am a Râjpût"—

"Râja Sûlwâhân's son am I,
Rasâlu is my name,
My city is Siâlkôt,
My fatherland the same."

Then the Imâm Ali ordered the two prophets, the Pîr Panjâbi and Sûrkru Sobâh, to embrace him, and they all three took him and all embraced him, and their embraces so purified his heart that the locks of infidelity were broken asunder. Also they taught him the prayers, and so Rasâlu ceased to be a Hindu and became a Muhammadan.

One day he said to the chief priest, "My father is a great infidel and a follower after evil customs. Give me help to enable me to return and overcome him."

"What evil customs do you speak of?" asked the priest.

"First," answered Rasâlu, "he takes to himself a new guest every night, but early in the morning he takes his life, or sends him forth to perish in the jungles. Next, the robe he wears by day he burns at night, and that which he wears at night he burns in the morning. And lastly, he will not drink two days together from the same well. Every morning, therefore, a new well must be dug for him, and lives are sacrificed in vain."

When they heard these things, the priests became convinced that Rajâ Sûlwâhân was a very great infidel indeed, but they answered, saying, "It would not be right for you, his son, to lead an army against your own father. Such behaviour would ill become you, for a son should respect his father!" Still, however, he continued to urge his petition, and so the Imâm told the rest of the priests not to refuse his request absolutely, but to put him off with promises, which when Rasâlu perceived he became more eager than ever to have his request complied with.

Meanwhile Râja Sûlwâhân had set to work to repair the walls of Siâlkôt, for the armies of Muhammad were overrunning all the world. One of the great towers, however, repeatedly fell down at the moment of completion. Three times the builders laid stone upon stone and three times the work crumbled to the dust. Then the King consulted his astrologers, who said, "Never will the wall stand, until the head of a young Muhammadan, who must be also an only son, has been buried under the foundations!" So the King sent officers, and they came to the house of the old woman Zabêro, and, seizing her son, they hauled him forth, saying, "Are you not a Muhammadan?" And boldly the lad answered, loving the truth, "I am a Muhammadan; I do not deny it, for in any case I must die at last and pass into the presence of God."

And the men who had him took him off to the King, before whom he came, and on his arm he wore a wedding-bracelet and on his neck a garland of flowers. And when the King saw him he said, "For whose feast art thou thus decked out, O son?"

"For my own feast am I thus decked out," answered he, "for to-day is the day of my marriage."

"It matters not," said the King. "Ho, fellows, off with this youngster's head, and down with it into the earth!"

So the lad was at once beheaded, even there, in the presence of his widowed mother, who wept at that sight, and who, snatching a dagger from a soldier, cried out, "I, too, am ready to die. O wicked Râja, may the lightnings of God fall upon you!"

Now as she spoke these words, meditating death, the head and the body of her lifeless son began moving towards her on the ground, which when she perceived, she dropped her weapon, and taking up those bloody tokens one by one, she pressed them to her bosom. Then addressing the King, she cried, "Now will I go to Mecca and bring back with me those that will avenge my cause!"

Rising at once, the old woman started on her journey, but, seeing that she was aged and feeble, she could not cover more than half-a-mile a day. With limbs fatigued and feet swollen, she prayed in her distress to God and said, "I am an old woman and cannot walk. May Pîr Panjâbi come to my succour!" Then she lay down in the desert, and that same night, as she slept, she had a dream. In her dream she saw an old man with a white beard, who came to her and said to her, "Shut your eyes!" and she shut them and at once found herself in Mecca. That was her dream. Early in the morning when she woke, she looked about her, and her dream had come true, for she saw that she was standing on the steps of the Great Mosque, and she saw also the priests of that mosque, and she addressed them, saying, "Behold in me a helpless old woman, having no protector. A Hindu Râja, the biggest infidel in Hindustân, has cruelly killed my son to build him a wall. If you are indeed followers of the Prophet, come and avenge me!"

"Mother, do not weep," answered they. "Our heads shall answer for your son's."

"I could wish not to weep," said she, "but my heart weeps, and I cannot restrain myself. I must weep and weep until you come and plough up the city."

"The son of our chief priest," answered they, "is to be married in three days. After that we shall set out for Siâlkôt."

"O priest," replied she, "you are quite right! You are going to marry your son, and at home sits my daughter robbed of her husband, and in short I cannot wait any longer!"

Then they set out for the kingdom of Siâlkôt. But as they marched along, she looked and saw that they were only five horsemen all told, so she said to Rasâlu, "You are but a few. What will you do against all the hosts of Siâlkôt?" And the Hazrat took up the answer and said, "Mother, put your trust in us!"

"Of course," said she, "I put my trust in you. But I see also that you are only five in number."

"Close your eyes!" said the priest. So she closed her eyes forthwith, and when in a moment more she opened them again, she saw a large army, the numbers whereof were so vast, that the pommel of one horseman jostled against the pommel of the next, and the sound of their riding went up. So she was satisfied, and she counselled them to bring their army on in the same invisible manner.

At last they arrived at the city of Siâlkôt and invested it, being encamped round about the walls. And early in the morning when the people came out they saw the whole place surrounded, and they went in and told Râja Sûlwâhân. And when the King looked out, he said, "It is only my son, Rasâlu, no one else, who has brought this evil upon me. He went to Mecca and now he has come back with a Muhammadan army to destroy me!"

Then began the great fight between Sûlwâhân on the one side and his son Rasâlu on the other. Long held out Siâlkôt, but it was taken at last, and when the enemy swarmed through the gates and over the walls, so great was the slaughter that the horses walked the streets fetlock deep in blood. But first, before that happened, the people of that city looked down and saw a horseman fighting sword in hand, but without his head, which he had hurled at the gates. That man was the Hazrat himself. And the people marvelled at it, expressing their astonishment each to the other. But passing strange it was to see how the body stopped fighting on hearing their remarks, and how falling down from its horse, it lay quite still among the slain.

Meanwhile Sûndar Dâs, thé Brâhmin priest, never ceased praying to God for peace. But he prayed in vain, for the Muhammadans fought on until they had gained the citadel and the palace of the king. And when they had entered therein, they saw the Râja Sûlwâhân sitting on his stool, smoking his hookah. Then the priests said to Rasâlu, "Go forward to your father and bid him become a Muhammadan!" So Râsâlu went in and bade his father either turn Muhammadan or die.

"My son," answered the king, "you whom I have brought up to manhood, spare your father's life!"

But Rasâlu seized him by his long hair, which he twisted, and throwing him on the ground, he put his foot on his breast and would have cut off his head. Then said his father unto him, "Neither your mother nor I have ever been unfaithful the one to the other. You are therefore my own undoubted son, and at the bar of Heaven, I, your father, will lay my hands upon you!" And when Rasâlu would have smitten, the priests held back his hand, forbidding the deed. Then came he away, and going forth, he buried the bodies of the Muhammadans who had fallen in the assault.

After a time it came to pass that father and son became reconciled, and that Motî Râm offered his second daughter, in lieu of his first, as a wife for Rasâlu. But the priests returned to Mecca, and by-and-by Rasâlu also left the city, and once more, mounted on Folâdi, went roaming over the world.

4. THE HUNTER KING

When he had established a new government in Siâlkôt it was that Râja Rasâlu set out alone for the Deccan because he wished to meet and to see Mîrshikâri, the renowned hunter.

As he was riding along, his horse suddenly heard the strains of distant music proceeding from the depths of the forest. "Sir," said she to her master, "what is that sweet sound which I hear, and whence is it coming?"

"I have been told," answered Rasâlu, "that there is a certain king of the greenwood, named Mîrshikâri, who sits in the forest playing on a lute which was given to him by the Water-King, the immortal Khwâjah Khizar.[1] All the animals when they hear the melodious music come and gather around him to listen. Then when he finds a chance, he shoots at them with his bow, and kills whatever game he favours."

Saying this, Râja Rasâlu with his horse and with Shâdi his parrot, followed the direction of the sound, and approached the glade in which Mîrshikâri was sitting.

Now Mîrshikâri had been informed by astrologers that in the course of time one Rasâlu would come, who should be his master in magic and fighting and in woodcraft. So he was always expecting him; and now, when he saw a mounted stranger approaching, he inquired of him, "Who are you?"

"What Râja's son are you?
And say what name you bear;
Where lies your fatherland?
What city owns you there?"

And Rasâlu answered him—

"Râja Sûlwâhân's son am I,
Rasâlu is my name;
Siâlkôt is my fatherland,
My city is the same."

Then asked Mîrshikâri, "Are you the Rasâlu that should come?"

[1] *Khwâjah Khizar;* the tutelary deity of the Indus.

"Yes," answered the King.

"As I have heard about you," said Mîrshikâri, "so now have I seen you."

"What have you heard about me?" inquired Rasâlu.

"The real Rasâlu," answered Mîrshikâri, "carries an arrow weighing one hundred pounds. By this token I know you are the real Rasâlu, and to-day, by the grace of God, I have met you in the forest, where I had scarcely hope of seeing you at all."

Then said Rasâlu, "What are you doing? Why are you playing on a lute?"

"It is my usual custom," answered Mîrshikâri. "Every day of my life I play on my lute in order to entice the animals, because, when my lute is playing, all the animals of the forest gather round me to listen to it, and then, watching my chance, I choose my sport and shoot at them and kill them, since I cannot live without flesh-meat every day. But, O my master, as you have come to the green-wood at last, I pray that you will make me your disciple."

"So let it be," said Rasâlu, "but first, if you will be a follower of mine, there are three conditions which you will have to observe."

"Whatever shall be told me," said Mîrshikâri, "that shall I observe to do implicitly."

Then said Rasâlu, "The first condition is this: Let no one know of my coming here, and tell no one that you have seen me. The second is this: You may go and shoot over three sides of the forest, the north, east and the west, but on the fourth side you shall not shoot. And the third condition is this: On the forbidden side of the forest there live two deer, a buck and a doe. On no account must you kill them."

"How shall I know," then asked Mîrshikâri, "which of all the deer of the forest the two reserved ones are?"

To him Rasâlu returned answer, "On the south side of the forest those two deer live, and to that side alone they resort. You will never meet them and you will never see them unless you go there. But if you do go there, and if you shoot them, O remember, you will lose your own life!"

All these terms were accepted by Mîrshikâri, and Rasâlu having shown him his mode of using weapons of war and of the chase, went away from that place, and tarried in another part of the forest.

So Mîshikâri, after playing on his lute and killing some deer, returned to the city, and when he had eaten his food he went to his chamber, and there he began to address sweet words to his wife. In the midst of their colloquy he broke the first condition imposed upon him by Râja Rasâlu, for he said to her, "To-day I have seen Rasâlu in the forest."

The woman turned round and said, "You are speaking a jest. What, is Rasâlu a madman to be wandering about in the woods? What a wise man are you!"

Feeling ashamed and abashed on account of his wife's words, he took an oath to God before her, and said, "I have verily seen Râja Rasâlu to-day with my own eyes."

But his wife believed not his words, and she said to him, "Hold your tongue and do not vex me so, seeing you cannot beguile me."

After a short time Mîrshikâri ordered his wife to prepare his breakfast over-night, "because," said he, "to-morrow I must be in the forest long before dawn."

Hearing this speech, his wife thought to herself, "It is useless to take so much trouble at so late an hour of the night. Everything can be got ready for him before he starts in the morning."

At the fixed time on the morrow, while it was yet dusk, she awoke, and having bathed, she went to the cook-room to prepare some food for Mîrshikâri, but she was astonished at finding that there was no meat of any description in the house. Then said she, "Mîrshikâri will not eat anything but meat. I must go into the street, to the stalls of the butchers, and bring home two pounds of goat's flesh."

So she went to a butcher and said to him, "Give me two pounds of goat's flesh, and to-morrow I will give you four pounds of venison instead of it."

"At this time of night," answered the butcher, "I cannot possibly open my door. I hear your voice, but what you are God knows; some witch, perhaps, or a giantess, or it may be an evil spirit."

"I am the wife of Râja Mîrshikâri," replied the woman.

Then said the butcher, "If you are the wife of Mîrshikâri, bring me the money, and I will give you the two pounds of meat."

In the meantime, while his wife was arguing with the butcher, Mîrshikâri woke up, and he called and looked, but in the palace his wife was nowhere to be found. For some time he waited, but he waited in vain, for she did not return. Then, as it was growing late and as he was tired of waiting, he took up his lute, his quiver, and his bow, and without any breakfast he went out to his shooting. When he arrived at the ground he broke the second condition, for he chose for his sport the side of the forest which had been forbidden to him by his master Rasâlu.

Having fixed on a place, he sat himself down, tuned the strings of his lute, and began to play. The beautiful strains floated on the morning air, and penetrated into the depths of the forest, so that, as Râja Rasâlu was wandering about, his mare again heard the sweet woodland notes, and said to the King, "Sir, it is the sound of the lute we heard in the woods yesterday."

"You are right," answered Rasâlu, "but my man has not fulfilled my behest, nor has he regarded my word, and now we shall witness the turning of his fate."

Meanwhile, as Mîrshikâri was playing his lute, the two deer, a buck and a doe, came out of the forest into the open glade, and there stood still to listen. As they felt themselves drawn towards the spot where the lute was playing, the doe said to the buck, "Let us wait here and see. Perhaps it is Râja Mîrshikâri playing on his lute. I am afraid lest, seeing us, he will kill us dead, because by means of his treacherous lute he has already done much to empty the woods."

On hearing these unexpected words, Mîrshikâri stopped his music, and glancing all round him, he saw a *chachra* tree covered with large green leaves. Then moving softly to it, he plucked some of the foliage, and having fastened it all over his body, he made himself leafy and green like the tree, and taking up his lute, he began to play on it once more, and as he played he slowly advanced towards the buck and the doe.

When the two deer saw him approaching, the buck said to the doe, "See, he is coming towards us for something, let us go and meet him."

But the doe said, "Do not move a step further," to which the buck made answer—

> "In the forest I was bred,
> In the forest I was fed,
> And the forest is my home;
> Some little leafy tree,
> To discover you and me,
> In perplexity doth roam."

Then said the doe to her simple husband—

> "In the forest I was bred,
> In the forest I was fed,
> And the forest is my home;
> Such a thing could never be
> For a little leafy tree
> On two little feet to roam."

But the buck, being resolved to go forward, said—

> "In the forest I was bred,
> In the forest I was fed,
> In the forest I abide;
> And if hunger be his plea,
> Or if forced by fate he be,
> We may venture to his side."

"No, no," cried the doe; "be well advised—

> "In the forest I was bred,
> In the forest I was fed,
> In the forest I abide;
> By his acting I can see
> He would capture you and me,
> And our flesh he would divide."

"O my husband," continued she, "you should not go nearer."

Saying this, she stopped; but the wilful buck went nearer and nearer, listening to the dulcet music, and when Mîrshikâri saw him well within flight of his arrow, he took his lute between his teeth and, drawing his bow, he shot at him, and the foolish deer, being pierced by the sharp weapon in the shoulder, fell to the ground. Then ran Mîrshikâri swiftly forward, and drawing his knife, he prepared to cut the throat of his quarry according to custom.

But all the time Râja Rasâlu was watching his proceedings, saying to his horse, "He has disregarded my counsel; look and you will see the trouble which shall shortly fall upon him."

Mîrshikâri now lifted his knife to despatch his victim, when the deer addressed him in reproachful words, and said—

> "Thou tyrant-thrower of the pointed dart,
> Thine edgeless knife, O lay it by;
> But take the lute, the lute that pierced my heart,
> And strike some chords before I die;
> O tyrant, sweep the trembling strings again,
> I fain would hear one fleeting dying strain!"

Then said Mîrshikâri, "His death has been caused by my lute, and I must therefore play for him something more. Yet I am in fear lest, as I play, he may suddenly turn his head and gore me with his horns."

So he sat upon him astride, pressing him down with the weight of his body, and thus seated he began to play upon his lute once more, while the dying buck, as his life ebbed away, listened to the ravishing sounds.

When he had finished playing, Mîrshikâri laid aside his lute again, and lifting his knife, he passed it over the throat of the buck, and let out his life-blood.

After this he looked about him for some water, "For," said he, "if the knife be not washed, my game will not be fit for eating." But no water was to be seen, excepting the heavy dew which lay all round about upon the earth. So he wiped his bloodstained knife in the grass, and when it was cleansed he held it between his teeth in order that he might also wipe the blood from his hands in the same manner. But it so happened that no sooner had he put his hands into the wet grass than he was stung by a viper. Uttering a loud cry, he dropped his knife from his mouth, which, falling upon the serpent, cut it into two pieces so that it died, and presently Mîrshikâri himself, as the poison pervaded his system, gave up the ghost and expired as well.

Seeing this, Râja Rasâlu, who was watching all these fatal consequences, said to his mare, "Now see what will come to pass next."

After a little while the doe stole out from the jungle to look for her husband, and she found him dead. She also saw Mîrshikâri lying still upon the ground. Then thought she to herself, "The hunter-king has been shooting for a long time, and now, being tired, he is taking his rest." But, venturing nearer, she espied the dead snake cut into two pieces, and the knife resting close by. Then understood she that her husband had been killed by Mîrshikâri, that Mîrshikâri had been killed by the snake, and that the snake had been killed by the knife.

Having looked upon this dismal spectacle, she said to herself:—"Now for me to live longer in the world is useless, for God knows who may not kill me, or what suffering it may not be my lot to endure." And she began to wonder how she should destroy herself. After thinking and considering, she said, "O my husband's horns, they are sharp as spears! I shall put straight his head and jump upon them, and their points will pierce through my body and kill me."

So saying, she set the buck's head upright, and going to a little distance she leaped upon his sharp, tapering horns, which, penetrating her body, ripped her open and killed her. In her dying struggles she gave birth to two little kids, a male and a female; but they, after breathing the air for a few short moments, expired likewise by the side of their dam.

And all the time Râja Rasâlu was gazing at the scene, watching every hapless circumstance, and he now said to his mare, "Let us see what will come to pass next."

In a few minutes a jackal came out of the forest, and finding so many dead bodies lying prone upon the ground, he began to trim his moustachios, and to leap and frisk for joy, saying to himself, "God has given me lots of good things to-day! I shall eat my fill, and sleep, and eat again. But Mîrshikâri is a strong man and a famous hunter, and if he wakes up he will certainly kill me. So my best plan will be to steal his bowstring and throw it away, because then, if he awake, he will never without it be able to harm me, and meanwhile I shall have time to escape."

Saying this, the jackal came silently towards Mîrshikâri, and, taking away his bow and skipping into the jungle, he endeavoured to break it. But the string was made of twisted wire which proved too tough for his teeth. At last, putting the side of the bow on his hind legs and one end of it under his chin, he succeeded in slipping the wire, but the rebound of the weapon was so sharp and so sudden that it tore him in two, and the upper part of his body went flying towards the sky.

When Râja Rasâlu saw the jackal's fate he laughed and said, "Let us go and look at them now." Coming to the spot, he said to his mare, "What shall we do? What arrangements shall we make for conveying the body of Mîrshikâri?"

"Lay it on his own horse," answered she, "and she will carry it straight to his house."

Then Rasâlu lifted the body and was going to lay it on Mîrshikâri's horse, but the animal refused, saying, "As he failed to obey your orders, I will never carry him more."

"At least," said Rasâlu, "guide me to your master's palace," and taking from the fatal spot Mîrshikâri's turban, his quiver, his bow, and his lute, he followed the dead hunter's horse, which led them on through the grassy glades and the leafy alleys of the forest.

As they entered the city, Râja Rasâlu caught sight of a woman standing at the stall of a butcher who was weighing out some meat, and he overheard her saying, "Do not longer delay. My husband Mîrshikâri is waiting."

Then Rasâlu stopped and said to her, "O woman! what are you doing there?—

"You weigh the flesh within the scale,
But say for whom the flesh you weigh;
The flesh you weigh will ne'er avail,
The man who looked his last to-day."

Hearing these words, the woman hastily turned and said, "Who are you thus cursing my husband?"

"I am Rasâlu," answered he. But the woman did not believe him.

"A wise Rasâlu too," replied she, "to curse another man needlessly. It is no good thing which you do."

"But," said Rasâlu, "would you recognize your husband's things if they were shown to you?"

"Yes," answered she, "wherefore not?"

Then he laid down before her Mîrshikâri's turban, his lute, and his weapons, and said, "Examine and see if these things are your husband's."

As soon as she looked upon them, the woman swooned and fell senseless to the ground.

When she came to herself she arose and ran to the palace of the King who was lord of all that country, weeping and beating her breast, and Rasâlu followed her. There she cried aloud, "Sir, this man has killed my husband Mîrshikâri!"

The King, hearing her distressful cries, ordered a trial, and at the hour appointed one hundred men were despatched to bring Râja Rasâlu into the court. But Rasâlu, collecting them all in one place, covered them under the broad expanse of his shield, and then sent a message to the King, saying, "Come if you can, and take your men from under my shield."

When the King understood what a wonderful master of magic he was, and how great was his might to cover one hundred men with his shield, he sent other messengers, saying to them, "Do not use force with him. Bring him by solicitations and prayers." And they, as soon as they arrived, humbly requested Rasâlu to come before their lord, beseeching him with courteous words.

"I come," answered he, and so, lance in hand, and with the king's messengers behind him, rode to the city and so to the palace. When he entered the King's presence he said, "Wherefore have you sent for me?"

"Why have you slain Mîrshikâri?" inquired the King.

"I will also ask you a riddle," replied Rasâlu, "and if you can answer it, you will know of the death of Mîrshikâri—

"One was killed and two died;
Two were killed and four died;
Four were killed and six died;
Four were males and two were females."

But the King was unable to guess the answer. Therefore said he to his ministers, "Go with this stranger, whoever he is, and see if he tells the truth, and let us beware lest he be the real Rasâlu."

So Rasâlu conducted them to the forest, where they came and saw all the six bodies lying lifeless together on the ground. Taking up the corpse of Mîrshikâri, they took it into the presence of the king, who, having heard their tale, looked upon it and said of Rasâlu, "This man has indeed spoken the word of truth."

Then Râja Rasâlu carried the body of his disciple, Mîrshikâri, back into the forest, and there he laid it down, and he dug a grave for it, both long and deep, with his own hands, and buried it under the shade of the trees. And over the spot he erected an enduring tomb, and proclaimed to the whole city and to all the country around, "Whosoever would go hunting, let him first go visit the tomb, and do homage at the grave, of Mîrshikâri!"

Having performed this last act of piety to the remains of the hunter-king, he engraved on his tomb the following epitaph, and then went his way—

> "King Dhartli, peerless he for deeds of might,
> Abandoned all his pomp to die:
> And this fair world shall sink in endless night,
> As fades a star-bespangled sky."

RÂJA RASÂLU

5. RASÂLU AND THE SWANS

RASÂLU, in his wanderings, once came to a certain city, on the gate of which he read an inscription setting forth that Rasâlu of Siâlkôt, the son of Sûlwâhân, would one day appear, and that he would shoot an arrow of iron one hundred feet into the air, and that his reward should be a turban one hundred feet in length.

There Rasâlu determined to tarry; and one day in the presence of the inhabitants, when feats of strength were being exhibited, he took one of his arrows and shot it towards the sky. All the people stood still to gaze, waiting for the return of the arrow, but as it never came back, they said, "This must be the real Rasâlu!"

Then they wove for him a turban one hundred feet in length and proclaimed him as the real Rasâlu throughout the city, and for his great strength he was held in honour of all men.

The next day he entered on his travels again, and as he was walking by a river-side he saw a crow and his mate sitting fondly together, and he heard the female bird saying, "Please take me up to the sky."

"No one can go up to the sky," answered the male bird.

But she insisted and said, "Take me up as high into the air, then, as you can."

Saying this, she mounted up and the male bird followed her, and both went flying skywards until they were out of sight, and Rasâlu, wondering what would come of this adventure, continued his wanderings.

Now the two birds flew up so high that at last they came to a region of rain, hail, and snow, which kept falling continually, and the female bird, drenched and terrified, cried, "For God's sake, save my life and take me to some place of shelter."

"What can be done now?" said her companion. "It is your own fault, why did you not listen to good advice?"

With these words they began to descend, and, worn out with fatigue, they at last fell on to a certain island away in the sea. Then said the female crow, "Let us go and look for some place of shelter."

Searching here and there, at last they saw a swan with his mate, sitting in a nest in the midst of a tree. So the crow approached, and offered his salaams. "What do you want, O crow?" said the swan to his unwelcome guest.

"For the sake of God," answered the crow, "be good enough to give us a corner to shelter in to save our lives."

"Although between you and me," said the swan, "there is no relationship, come in and take your rest."

On hearing this, the female swan protested vehemently. "I cannot allow the creature to come into any house of mine," cried she. "He is a mean fellow, and our kins-people will reproach us, not to speak of our good name."

"He is asking for shelter in the name of God," said her husband, "and I am therefore bound to allow him to enter and rest."

The crow and his mate then crawled into the nest, and the swan gave them pearls to eat, and whatsoever else his house afforded.[1]

The next morning, the rain being over, the crows stepped forth, and the male bird said to the swan, "Dear friend, against the wicked you should always be on your guard."

[1] Swans are said to feed on pearls.

"He who will do evil shall suffer evil," answered the swan.

"True," said the crow, "but whether a man do evil or not, he should always keep the base and the unworthy at a distance."

"What do you mean by saying that?" inquired the swan.

"Do you not know," said the crow, "that in a single night you have robbed me of my swan-wife whom I have tenderly reared for twelve years? You had better give her back to me."

"Is this your return for all my kindness?" asked the swan.

"I do not know the meaning of kindness," replied the insolent crow; "give me back my wife! Otherwise, you must either fight with me, or go to the King's court for judgment."

"I have no desire to fight with you," answered the swan meekly. "Come, let us go to the court of the King!"

All the birds at once set out and came to the palace of Rajâ Bhôj. When they entered the court the King inquired, "Why have those four birds come here to-day? Bring them before me first!"

Then were they marshalled by officers before the judgment seat, and they said, "Sire, we have come to you for a decision; condescend to listen!"

"What is it that you want?" asked the king.

"Inquire from the crow," said the swan.

"Nay," replied the crow, "I do not wish to say anything whatever—please ask the swan."

Then the swan stated his case—

"Struck down by storm, and rain, and driving snow,
With cries for shelter came this crafty crow;
In God's great name he proffered his request,
We gave him all we had—our place of rest;
But lo! when morning dawned, good turned to ill,
He sat and mocked us, and he mocks us still."

Then the crow stood forward, and stated his own side of the question thus—

"One day upon the river-side
I chanced to take a stroll,
And there I found some creature's egg
Within a sandy hole.

This egg I carried in my bill,
  And cherished it with care,
I hatched it underneath my breast,
  Till all my breast was bare.

At last, the young one burst the shell,
  No useless cock was he,
Or else he might have wandered forth,
  And roamed the jungle free.

It was a female, and I said,
  'I will preserve her life,
When twelve years old she'll doubtless prove
  A most deserving wife.'

Then came this swan, struck down by rain,
  By storm and driving snow,
And begged me for the love of God
  Some pity to bestow.

I took him in without a word,
  But lo! when morning came,
On score of caste he took my wife,,
  And vilified my name."

Râja Bhôj, having heard both stories, said to the swan, "This crow appears to me to be in the right, so hand him over his wife!"

The poor swan made no reply, but gave up his wife at once to the crow, and then he went crying and sobbing to a distant place, where he lived in a certain solitary garden.

The triumphant crow, leading out his prize, thought to himself, "As my new wife is so handsome, no doubt, if I go to my own house, my kinsfolk will come and snatch her away from me. It is better therefore to take her away to some distance."

It chanced, however, that the spot which he chose was the very garden in which the male swan was already living, and so it came to pass that all the four birds once more found themselves together.

One day it happened to Râja Rasâlu that, in the course of his travels, he rode by that way, and that, as he went, he was saying to his mare, "To pass the time let us look for some friend and get him to talk."

Just then he saw a jackal, and making for him he ran him down and caught him.

"Sir, why have you caught me?" said the jackal.

"Merely to make you talk," answered Rasâlu, "and to pass the time."

Then the jackal, seated on Rasâlu's saddle-bow, began to tickle them both with hundreds of lying stories which amused them excessively. While thus employed they approached the city of Râja Bhôj, when Rasâlu told the jackal to be off.

"But," answered the jackal, "it would be cruel to leave me here, since all the dogs of the town would set on me and kill me. You had better take me with you."

Rasâlu consenting entered the city, and the people seeing him, paid him salutations and said, "Who are you?"

"I am Rasâlu, the son of Sûlwâhân," answered he.

Hearing his name, all the inhabitants came and surrounded him, saying, "This day God has fulfilled our desires."

Thence Rasâlu went to the court of Râja Bhôj, for whom he conceived a strong feeling of friendship, and dismounting from his horse, he entered and sat down. Then Râja Bhôj called for chess and invited his visitor to play. Rasâlu, who had taken a fancy for his amusing little friend the jackal, caused him to sit close to him whilst he began the game. First Râja Bhôj, on his side, laid a bet of one thousand rupees and threw the dice, but, his cast being spoilt by the jackal falling violently against his arm, Rasâlu won. Râja Bhôj became angry with the jackal, but the latter said, "Pray, sir, pardon my offence! I have been awake the whole night, and being sleepy, I touched your side quite by an accident."

Once more Râja Bhôj laid and began to play, but his cast of the dice was again spoilt by the jackal falling as before against his side. Then cried Râja Bhôj, "Is there any one there? Ho! some one cut this jackal to pieces!"

"I have been awake the whole night," said the jackal, excusing himself again; "forgive me, as I have not committed this fault wilfully."

"What is this talk about your being awake the whole night?" inquired Rasâlu. "What do you mean by that?"

"I will tell the secret," said the jackal, "to Râja Bhôj only."

"Tell me then, O jackal," said Râja Bhôj, "what it was you were doing all the night through?"

"Sir," replied the jackal, "tormented with hunger I went to the river-side to look for food. But finding none I grew desperate, and taking up a stone I threw it against another stone, and from the two stones came out fire."

Having said so much, the jackal came to a stop, and Râja Bhôj said, "Well, what else did you do?"

"Sir," said the jackal, "I caught the fire in some dry fuel, out of which a small cinder flew and fell into the river, when at once the whole river was in a blaze. Then I, being afraid of my life on account of you, endeavoured to quench the fire with dry grass, but though I tried my best I am sorry to say two-thirds of the river were burnt up and one-third only remained."

Listening to this tale every one began to laugh, and to say, "What a fib! Can water catch fire, and, even if it could, can dry grass quench it?"

"Sirs," said the jackal, "if water cannot quench fire, how can a crow possibly claim a female swan as his wife?"

Hearing this mysterious answer, Râja Rasâlu said, "Jackal, what in the world are you talking about?"

"Sir," answered the jackal, "Râja Bhôj pronounced a judgment in this court yesterday between a crow and a swan, and without due consideration he snatched away the swan's wife, and made her over to the crow. This judgment I listened to myself. And now the wretched swan is crying all round the jungle, while the crow is enjoying his triumph without let or fear."

"Can this be true?" asked Rasâlu, to which Bhôj replied, "Yes, this fellow tells the truth. I was undoubtedly wrong."

Then Râja Rasâlu sent for those four birds, and when they came he ordered them to sit in a row on the branch of a tree and to close their eyes. The birds did so, and Rasâlu, taking a bow and pellets, shot at the crow and killed him dead on the spot, saying, "This is a just reward for fraud and treachery."

At the same time he restored the female swan to her proper mate, who, delighted with the judgment, extolled his wisdom thus—

"All other kings are geese, but you
 The falcon wise and strong;
A judgment just you gave, and true—
 O may your life be long!"

RÂJA RASÂLU

6. RASÂLU AND RÂJA BHÔJ

WHEN Rasâlu had spent a brief season of rest at the court of Râja Bhôj, he requested that king's permission to take his leave. But his host, unwilling to part with him, said, "As you have blest my palace with your presence, so you will confer on me a still greater favour, if you will abide here a little longer, and make me your disciple."

"In the same spot," answered Rasâlu, "my destiny forbids me to tarry long. Nevertheless I will accept your invitation and impart to you whatever I know myself."

So he remained in that city some time longer, dwelling in the house of his friend, and teaching him the art of fighting and wrestling.

At last Rasâlu set out once more on his travels, and many of the inhabitants, out of love and admiration for him, saw him out of their borders; but Râja Bhôj and his wazîr, together with some few attendants, accompanied him several days' marches.

As they journeyed pleasantly along, Râja Bhôj said to Rasâlu, "Pray tell me, what in your opinion are the five most cursed things in the world."

Then Rasâlu answered him—

"A thriftless wife who ruins house and home;
A daughter grown whose head is bare and bald;
A daughter-in-law of sour forbidding face;
A crooked axle to the garden-well;
A field that lies athwart the village path;
A man may search the world where'er he please,
And never find more cursèd things than these."[1]

Hearing this answer, Râja Bhôj was pleased exceedingly, and praised Rasâlu's wisdom. And so the two kings, engaged in pleasant converse, continued their way.

At last they arrived one morning at a delightful garden which belonged to the Râni Sobhôn,[2] and entering therein, the whole company dismounted, and laying aside their arms, they reclined along the margin of a fountain of cool, delicious water.

[1] A string of favourite Panjâbî proverbs.
[2] *Sobhâ*—Beauty, charm.

Scarcely had they taken their places, when they saw approaching them from the midst of the shrubs and trees one hundred beautiful damsels, all armed with drawn swords. Rasâlu, with a smile, then said to Bhôj, "These fair ladies appear to be very formidable. Let us amuse ourselves a little at their expense."

Having thus spoken, he looked at the girls and said, "O ladies, why have you come out against us with drawn swords in your hands?"

"Whosoever," answered they, "trespasses within the bounds of this garden or comes hither to take water out of the fountain forfeits his ears and his hands, and is then expelled with ignominy."

"Alas," said Rasâlu, "what dire mishap has brought us here!"

Putting on sterner looks, the girls then said, "Have any of you touched the water of the fountain?—If you have, confess it, in order that we may cut off your hands and your ears, for such is the order we have received from the Queen, our mistress, who has bidden us cut off the hands and ears of all who dare to drink from her fountain."

"O fair ones," replied Rasâlu, "we have not yet presumed to drink. But, as we are merely poor wayfarers, do not hinder us. Suffer us to drink, and then let us depart in peace."

"Who are you?" inquired the damsels.

"As for me," said the King, "men call me Rasâlu."

Hearing his name, all the girls fluttered together, and began to whisper among themselves, "If he be the real Rasâlu," said they, "he will catch us and kill us. We had better let him go, and seize only the others."

But Rasâlu divined their thoughts, and so he said—

"If you let me go, O beauteous ones, will you not also release the others, seeing we are all wayfarers together?"

Then said one of the maidens—

"Wayfarers number three, they say,—
The brook, the moon, the shining day;
Of all these three,
Pray tell to me,
Who is your father, and who is your mother?"[1]

[1] Common children's rhyme.

"It is true we are wayfarers," replied Rasâlu, "but we are not so much wayfarers as world-travellers."

"Indeed," said the same lady, "but—

> "Travellers o' the world are also three,
> A sheep, a woman, a bullock they be;
> With quibbling words no longer play,
> But tell me your name without delay."[1]

"It is evident," said Rasâlu, "that we poor fellows, whether wayfarers or world-travellers, shall have fain to implore your clemency."

"We have power, of course," observed the ladies, relenting, "to let you off. But what answer shall we make to our mistress?"

"Go to your hard-hearted mistress," answered Rasâlu, "and tell her this—

> "Beside your spring three men reclined,
> Your father's family priests were they;
> They saw our swords, and, vexed in mind,
> They rose at once and walked away;
> God knows their route—we greatly fear
> They've gone to Kâbul or Kashmír."

Accordingly these simple damsels left Rasâlu and his friends, and going to the palace, they reported to the Râni Sobhân all that had been told them. "Alas," said the Queen, beginning to grieve, "it is twelve long years since our family priests were here before! And now, when they had journeyed so great a distance to visit me, my foolishness has driven them away. Who knows whether they will ever return again to me or not?"

So speaking the Queen began to sob, and rising from her seat, she prepared to descend into the garden with her train of belted maidens.

Meanwhile, however, Rasâlu and his companions, having rested sufficiently, had left the fountain and gone on their way. Towards evening they halted at a pleasant spot in the open wilderness, where there were some beautiful well-laden mango-trees, and a fair babbling brook. Here they determined to tarry for the night, and having dismounted, they sat down under the cool, shady boughs.

Just then a deer appeared in the distance, and Rasâlu, drawing his bow, brought it down, after which, a fire

[1] Common children's rhyme.

having been kindled, the game was dressed and served, and every one with glad, contented mind partook of the feast.

Now it happened that about the same time Râja Hôm of Delhi had been routed in a great battle by another Râja. Great was the slaughter, and Râja Hôm, abandoning his capital, fled away with only a few of his attendants. Coming to the mango-trees under which Rasâlu and his friends were sleeping, the fugitives there pitched their camp, and having eaten a frugal supper, they all retired to rest. The night was very lovely, and Râja Hôm's Queen was lying asleep in her litter next to her husband's tent, while the Râja sat by her side. As he was unwilling or unable to sleep himself, he began to gaze with a certain tender melancholy, now at the slumbering lady, and now at the shining moon. When some time had thus elapsed, he called up his wazîr and said to him, " I have just made some verses."

" Pray, sir, tell them to me," said the wazîr.

Then Râja Hôm repeated the following lines—

> " No water's like the Ganges, river dear;
> No light is like the moon, serenely clear;
> No sleep is like the sleep that fondly lies,
> So calm and still, upon a woman's eyes;
> Of every fruit that hangs upon the tree,
> The luscious mango is the fruit for me."[1]

" Bravo!" cried the wazîr, applauding vehemently. " Excellently good, sir, and right nobly expressed!"

Suddenly the silence was broken by the voice of Râja Rasâlu, who, with his friend Bhôj, had not been as soundly asleep but that he had heard every word of this pretty interlude, and who now interrupted the conversation with these words—

> " In lonely woods I walk, Râja,
> I walk, a poor recluse;
> However wise your talk, Râja,
> Your friend's a learnèd goose."

" Who is that?" cried Râja Hôm with sudden anger. " What means this intrusion on our privacy? Ho! catch the fellow, and bring him here!"

[1] These lines consist of common sayings of the people.

One of the attendants approached Rasâlu, and said with some insolence, "Get up, sir; how dare you interfere with our Râja's talk?"

"If you value your life," answered Rasâlu, "return to your master at once."

"Why?" said the man. "Who are you and whence come you?"

"I am Rasâlu the son of Sûlwâhân," replied he, "and my home is the blessed Siâlkôt. If you are not a stranger to courtesy and to the customs of kings, and if you will request me civilly to visit your Râja, I may go to him. But never yield I to force."

The servant was astonished, and returning to his master he reported to him all his adventure.

"Go to him again," said Râja Hôm, "and entreat him courteously to come to me. I wish to speak with him."

Then went the attendant back to Rasâlu, and delivered his message, saying, "Sir, Râja Hôm of Delhi sends you his compliments and would speak to you."

So Rasâlu arose, and approaching the tent he saluted the King of Delhi with grave politeness.

"Are you really Rasâlu?" inquired the latter. "Why did not my verses commend themselves to you?"

"However well expressed," answered Rasâlu, "the sentiment was scarcely true. So I ventured to interrupt you."

"I may of course be wrong," said Râja Hôm; "but if so, you will doubtless correct me."

"Willingly," replied Rasâlu; "the idea, in my judgment, should be this—

"No water like the limpid stream
  That ripples idly by;[1]
No light so glorious as the beam
  That sparkles from the eye;
Of all the sleep that mortals know,
  The sleep of health's the best;
Of all the fruit the gods bestow,
  A son exceeds the rest."

"How is that?" said Râja Hôm. "Let me hear your explanation."

"When you were born into the world," answered

[1] Literally, "No water like the water at your arm-pit"—a proverb referring to the flask always borne under the arm by travellers and shepherds in the East.

Rasâlu, "who gave you Ganges water then? And when a thirsty fugitive you fled away before your foes, what good was Ganges water to you then? If you had not eyes you might look for the moonlight in vain; if health forsook you, sleep would forsake you too; and if you were to die fruitless, you would die a barren stock, with never a son to succeed or to perpetuate you."

Having heard this answer, Râja Hôm, admiring Rasâlu's wisdom, praised him greatly, and said to him, "Sir, you are undoubtedly right, and I was wrong."

The next morning Râja Rasâlu embraced his friend Râja Bhôj and bade him adieu, after which he continued his journey alone, ever seeking for fresh adventures.

RÂJA RASÂLU

7. RASÂLU AND THE GIANTS OF GANDGARH

ONCE Râja Rasâlu was out hunting in the forest when, overcome with fatigue, he lay down under a tree and went to sleep. In his sleep he had a vision in which he saw approaching him the Five Holy Men, who addressed him, saying, "Get up, Râja, and root out the race of the giants!"[1] Disturbed in mind, he arose and instantly set off on the expedition, having determined without delay to achieve the exploit. Many a league rode the hardy King on his renowned war-horse Folâdi, now over hills, now over moors, and now through gloomy forests, intent on his arduous quest. One day in the depths of a lonely wood he reached a large city which was as silent as the grave. He entered the streets, but they were deserted; he gazed in at the open shops, but they were all tenantless. Amazed at the solitude, he stood in an open space and surveyed the scene. Just then he caught sight of some smoke issuing from a distant corner, and making his way to it he saw there a miserable old woman kneading and baking quantities of bread and preparing abundance of sweetmeats, but all the time she was either weeping or laughing. Surprised at a spectacle so extraordinary, Rasâlu halted and said, "Mother, in this solitary place who is to eat all that food, and why are you both weeping and laughing?"

[1] "Five Holy Men"—The five chosen Apostles of Muhammad—The Five *Pîrs*.

"My son, where have you come from?" answered the woman, "from the skies or out of the earth? Do you know this country belongs to giants and man-eaters? You are a stranger; it is better for you to pursue your way and not to question me."

"Nay," said Rasâlu, "I cannot bear to see you in such trouble, and I would fain know the cause of it."

"The king of this place," said the woman, "is Kashu-dêo,[1] and he has ordered that a human being, a buffalo and four hundred pounds of bread, shall be sent daily to a certain place for the giants. Once I had seven sons, of whom six have been devoured, and to-day it is the turn of the seventh, and to-morrow it will be the turn of myself. This is my trouble, and it makes me cry. But I am laughing because also to-day my seventh son was to have been married, and because his bride—ha! ha!—will have now to do without him."

With these words the woman fell to laughing and crying more bitterly than ever.

"Weep not," said Râja Rasâlu.—

"Good wife, your tears no longer shed,
If God will keep the youngster's head,
I swear my own shall fall instead."

But the old woman had not so learnt her lessons of life, and replying through her tears, "Alas! what man was ever known to give his head for another?" she went on with her dismal task. But Rasâlu said, "I have come here for no other reason than to extirpate the kingdom of the giants."

"Who are you then?" inquired the woman. "What is your father's name and where is your birthplace?"

"The blessed Siâlkôt is my birthplace," replied he. "I am the son of Sûlwâhân, and my name is Rasâlu."

Then the woman began considering, and she thought to herself, "Whether he be the real Rasâlu, I know not; yet he may be, because it is written, 'One Rasâlu shall be born, and he will destroy the kingdom of the giants.'"

Then Rasâlu, gazing round, inquired, "Why is there no one in the city?

[1] Kashu-Dêo, a Hindu deity held in high honour in Kashmir.

"Here temple domes and palace towers,
Bazaars and lowly shops abound,
But silent as the passing hours,
Idly they lift themselves around;
What luckless hap hath chanced the world, that all
Deserted are the doors of house and mart and hall?"

"Let not this surprise you," answered the old woman, "the people have all been eaten up by the giants."

Rasâlu now dismounted from his horse, and having tied him under shelter, he stretched himself on a small low bedstead and at once fell into a deep slumber. Meanwhile the young lad arrived with the buffalo which was laden with the bread and the sweetmeats, and when all was ready he drove it before him through the empty streets and went out into the forest. After a time the old woman came close to the sleeping king and began to cry piteously, so that the King started up from his sleep and inquired the reason of her distress. She answered him—

"Thou rider of the dark-grey mare,
Rasâlu, bearded, turbaned stranger,
O for some saviour to repair,
A champion, to the field of danger!
I weep because those tyrants come to-day,
To lead my one surviving son away."

Then Rasâlu arose, and with a word of comfort to the mother, he mounted and rode off in pursuit of her son. Having overtaken him he said, "How shall we know boy, when the giants are coming?"

"First," answered the boy, "there will be a strong wind with rain, and when that is over the giants will come."

Continuing their journey, they arrived at the banks of a river, where the boy halted, while Rasâlu rambled about hunting. In his absence one of the giants named Thirya[1] came down to fetch some water. So huge of body and mighty of limb was he, that his water-skin was composed of the hides of twenty-seven buffaloes all sewn together so as to form one vast receptacle, and he carried a bucket made up of the hides of seven buffaloes. When he filled his water-skin the river absolutely groaned, so that Rasâlu, hearing, gazed at it in wonder.

[1] *Thirya*—Unprincipled one.

Thirya, seeing the lad and the buffalo, and the full load of bread, grinned with greedy delight, saying, "Glad am I to see all these good things."

Then seizing some of the loaves, he shuffled away into a thicket and began to munch. But by-and-by Rasâlu returned, and then the boy said to him, "One of the giants has already come and has taken away his toll of the loaves, and others will soon come and eat me together with the buffalo. What is the use of your advancing further?"

"Who is he that has taken away the loaves?" asked Rasâlu.

"He is the water-carrier," answered the lad. "His name is Thirya, and he generally comes first and takes his bread beforehand as a tax which is allowed him."

"Where is he?" asked Rasâlu.

"There he is," said the boy, "in the thicket, eating the loaves."

Rasâlu, sword in hand, rode into the thicket, and going up to the giant he smote him with his iron whip and cut off his right hand, and recovered the loaves.

Then, with a howl which was so loud and dreadful that it roused his companions the other giants from their sleep or from their labours and brought them out from their dens in the mountain, the giant cried, as he gazed at the hero's enormous quiver and his threatening aspect, "What man, what demon, are you?"

"I am Rasâlu," answered the King.

And when he heard the name, the disabled monster, crying and weeping, ran back to his brothers, traversing the distance in two or three strides. His brothers were surprised, and said, "What has come over you? You look quite perplexed. Where is the skin and where the pitcher?" And Thirya answered, "The leathern pitcher I left with the buffalo, the skin I hung on the pommel of the horse. Run, brothers, run!—

> "Here comes Rasâlu, the champion brave,
> Let us haste and hide in the mountain cave;
> Whether prophet of God or Beelzebub,
> Upon his shoulders he carries a club!"

Saying these words, Thirya cried out and ran in terror.

But the eldest of the crew, whose name was Kabîr,[1] and who was bald-pated, offered to go and see what was the matter and who the person was who had cut off Thirya's arm. Now this Kabîr was very bold. He advanced confidently, running along to the side by which Rasâlu was coming. Scarcely had he gone far, when he saw a buffalo, a boy, and a horseman moving up towards him. So at once he understood the whole matter, and he said to himself, "Here will I stay, for the things to be divided are the buffalo, the boy, and the loaves. But the horse and his rider are things over and above all that, and these shall be mine. I will have them at once, and tell my brothers I have devoured them in vengeance for my brother's arm. So they won't be angry with me!"

While he was planning all this out, Râja Rasâlu saw him, but he was so tall in stature and so awful in aspect, that the Râja could not take him for a man at all, but, as the head was moving, he asked the boy; "O boy, boy," said he, "let me know what that mountain is in front of me with the moving top! Are the hills of this country moving?"

"No, sir," answered the boy. "That is not a hill. It is a sturdy giant. His name is Kabîr. He is waiting for us. He will undoubtedly devour us all!"

"All right!" said Rasâlu. "Let us go forward!"

Meanwhile the Râja took his bow, and placing an arrow in it, he drew and shot it with such force, that it went straight into the upper part of Kabîr's skull. So the giant cried out with a bitter cry and went running in terror to his brothers, who were more astonished than ever. And they asked him, saying, "What is the matter with you? Why are you running so wildly? Perhaps you have eaten something!" He was just going to answer them, when his brains came oozing out from his wound, and he fell prone upon the earth right in front of his brothers, saying, as he fell—

"Hear me, brothers, though we live long enough, still we must die! But be advised by me, and beware of the horseman coming up the hill!"

Then fell rage on them all for the loss of their two brothers, and they all began to boast, and to utter foul words. "Who is the man," said they, "who has treated

[1] A certain Hindu philosopher.

our brothers thus?" Tûndia and Mûndia declared they would go at once, and devour him there where he stood. But Akâldêo[1] told them to calm themselves, and not be too hasty. "Let him come, brothers," said he, "and we will see how we can avenge ourselves for our loss!" So they began to make preparations.

Meanwhile Rasâlu, the boy, and the buffalo, came within sight of them, and the Râja said, "Hail, giants, hail!" And Akâldêo returned answer, saying—

"Hail to you, and hail to your father and mother! But stop there, whoever you are, and let me first know your name. Are you Râja Rasâlu? Our fathers told us we should be killed by one Râja Rasâlu, but it does not matter whether you are he or not, as we are quite prepared to have a fight with you. So what is your name anyhow?"

At first Rasâlu hesitated to say, but the giant insisted, and when he saw that he was growing angry he spoke and said, "Siâlkôt is my country and Siâlkôt is my town. My father's name is Sâribân (Sûlwâhân) and my mother was Râni Lûna." Now his mother's name he gave them because she was of the race of the fairies; and when the younger brothers heard it they would have fled at once. But Tûndia and Mûndia said, "Flee who will, we will stand by Akâldêo!"

And Akâldêo counselled them, saying, "Brothers, do not run! My parents taught me a charm, and we shall soon see if this horseman stands or runs. If he stands, then no doubt he is Râja Rasâlu." Then turning to the Râja, he said, "One snort of mine will sweep you away!"

At once the monster laid his forefinger on his right nostril and blew with his left. Instantly there passed over the land a sudden and thick darkness, the atmosphere was filled with lurid dust, and by means of magic and enchantment the winds and the clouds rushed up from afar. Then beat the rain for forty days and forty nights, and the hailstones smote, the thunders roared, and the lightnings flashed, and the very earth was shaken.

"Now keep your feet, good steed," cried Râja Rasâlu; and to the lad he said, "Here, boy, grip well my stirrup and fear them not!"

And while the wind swept by with the force of a hurricane so that the trees were uprooted, the King sat firm

[1] Akâldêo—Immortal God.

and undaunted in the midst of the tempest and never flinched or cowered a jot. Nay, so firm was his seat, that his horse sank up to his knees in the earth.

When the storm had driven by and the darkness had sped, Akâldêo boastfully cried, "Now see if Rasâlu is there!"

And as the light dawned they saw him in the same spot. Then Akâldêo, bursting with rage, snorted with both his nostrils, and it continued raining and hailing with two-fold violence, and the storm raged furiously for eighty days and eighty nights, so that no stone, or tree, or animal, or bird, was left within a radius of a hundred miles. And when this was over, Akâldêo cried once more, "Now see if Rasâlu is there!" And they looked and still they saw him standing in the same position, calm and unmoved as the Angel of Death. Then fear and consternation filled their hearts, and they were in a mind to flee, when one of them said, "But if you are indeed Rasâlu, you will pierce with your arrow seven iron griddles, for so it is written in our sacred books."

"Bring them forth!" said Rasâlu.

And the giants brought out the seven griddles, each of which weighed thirty-five tons, and setting them up in a row one behind another, they challenged Rasâlu to pierce them. Drawing his bow, Rasâlu launched one of his shafts of iron, weighing a hundred pounds, and drove it at the seven griddles, so that it pierced them through and through and fixed itself immovably in the earth beyond.

"You have missed!" cried all the giants in a breath.

"I never missed in my life," returned Rasâlu. "Go, look at the griddles and see!"

They went to the spot, and saw the griddles really pierced, and the arrow stuck in the ground beyond.

Then said Rasâlu, "Pull out the arrow!"

They all pulled and tugged, but not one of them could stir it, so, at that, Rasâlu drew it forth himself.

"Of a truth this man is a giant," said one. "Let us try him with some iron gram. If he will eat it, we shall know that he comes of the blood of the demons."

Then the giants brought ten pounds of iron gram and gave it into his hands; but Rasâlu, deftly changing it for the gram which he had in his horse's nose-bag, began to eat before them, and when he had so done, he cried, "Now look out for yourselves!"

Then they all got really alarmed. "No doubt," thought they, "it is the real Râja Rasâlu: no doubt our destruction is certain." But Akâldeô chanted a charm and turned himself into a stone. Two others, Thirya and Wazîr, fled for their lives; but Tûndia and Mûndia, feeling ill, stayed where they were. Then said Rasâlu to Folâdi, his horse, "Now what shall we do?"

"Their chief has turned himself into a stone," answered the horse, "by virtue of his magic. You cannot therefore do anything with him. Much better that you should fight the two who are remaining behind."

So Rasâlu advanced to them and bade them strike the first blow.

"No strength is left to us at all!" answered they.

"Râja," said the parrot, "kill them at once!"

"O Rasâlu," said they, "evil is the deed you have done us this day! O tyrant, two of our brothers you have killed! What poison have you served out to us? In the name of God, take our lives soon!"

Then Rasâlu, drawing his bow, struck first at Tûndia, and the arrow sent him flying to Maksûdabâgh. Then with another arrow he smote Mûndia, who, with the arrow, went flying away to Alikhân. Down they fell, both of them, Tûndia and Mûndia. They fell like mountains, and their blood gushed out like rivers of water in the hills.

After that he advanced to Akâldêo, and smote him two or three times, but, finding his efforts useless, he asked his parrot and his horse to advise him. "Râja," said the parrot, "it is useless to break your arm over this stone. Three of them have been killed, and of the two who have fled one has lost his arm. You can't do any harm to this figure of stone. Let us then go to the place where the smoke is rising; perhaps some of their women are there. Make them tell you what to do with this figure, and then despatch them as well!"

Then went Rasâlu forward to that place from which the smoke was issuing, and there he found a large building with a wild garden round it. At the same time he spied a woman coming out, whose features were most repulsive, who was covered with hair to her ankles, and whose teeth were just like the iron points of ploughshares. She was coming forward as if to meet her husband, and she bore in her hand an iron bar, from one end of which was hanging a whole roasted camel. The sight of her scared even Rasâlu, for he had never seen anything so hideous in his life, and he cried out to his parrot, "O Shâdi, woe to you, and woe to me, and woe to us all! Our lives were preserved from those monsters, but now you have led your master to a most awful thing. No doubt we shall here be eaten alive!"

"Be careful, Râja!" answered the parrot. "Don't lose your presence of mind! It is a woman, and it cannot be so courageous as the men. Frighten her, and you will see that she will give way!"

Then Rasâlu, drawing his sword, spoke, "O Bhagalbatt, in a towering rage I draw my sword! Tell the secret at once, and show me your husband's magic art!"

At the same time he flashed his sword in front of her as if to cut her in pieces. The woman stood aghast, and, folding her hands, she said, "I will obey all your orders."

"Tell me the secret, then, at once!" said Rasâlu, "Your husband is a stone. Can you make him alive again?"

"Yes, I can," answered she, "and I will go with you to the place."

And so she did. But no sooner had she approached the figure of her husband than she ran back again, and would have escaped, if Rasâlu had not caught her, refusing to let her go. Then said she, "I will not bring my husband back to life unless you promise to marry me after you have put him to death. Oh, I do not want to become a widow! If you kill me it does not matter, because in that case my husband will save himself and remain alive. But give me your promise, and I will call him back to life, and then you can kill him, and marry me!"

At this speech Rasâlu laughed. But Shâdi said, "Râja, why hesitate? Give her your promise. You will never have such a chance again! You will certainly have to buy up all the cotton in the country to dress her, but then see what a beauty she is! She is indeed most lovely, and well worthy of your Highness!"

Rasâlu, however, was much perplexed, not wishing to make a false promise, and besides he did not want her as a wife. Yet, after all, he promised; and when he had done so, the giantess said—

"O Râja, make haste, make no delay! The whole body of the giant has become rigid as stone, but not so his heart. Up, Râja, and strike him through the heart!"

Then Rasâlu went up at a bound, his horse leaping a leap of one hundred yards, and passing round the figure, he saw that the heart was indeed beating very heavily. So he stabbed him there, right through the heart, and his sword came out on the other side of the body. And as the sword drove in, that one-eyed monster began to tremble like a quaking mountain, and in a short time he grew cold.

Then said his horse to Rasâlu, "Râja, now is the time for you to marry this woman, that is, to strike her dead, lest she play us a trick!"

"No, horse," answered Rasâlu, "she cannot do harm, and besides she is only a woman, so let her live till we come back. First and foremost we must think of the giants who have run away, and who are far more dangerous than she. One of them is without an arm, so I don't care for him; but the other is sound and stout, and we must settle him at once!"

So Rasâlu set off in pursuit of Thirya and Wazîr. These both ran together for a little while, but afterwards Thirya, who was wounded and bleeding, said to Wazîr, "Brother, my blood is flowing apace, and will, I think, get us into trouble, because Rasâlu can follow us upon the track of the blood. But you, being in sound health, had better get away to some safe place and leave me alone." Wazîr, thinking Thirya meant him to return to Akâldêo, went back, because he hoped to escape to Mount Sarbân, but on the way he saw Rasâlu galloping his horse. Puzzled and perplexed what to do, he tore up thick bushes and large trees and made a pile of them and hid himself under them. Thirya, happening to look back, was quite astonished at his sudden disappearance, and he said—

"He left me only just now, and what's become of him I do not know!" And, being quite confounded by grief and sorrow, he spoke and said, "The fire of pain burns in my breast, on our family has fallen calamity. O Brother, escape while yet you can, run anywhere, to this side or to that side, if only you are still alive!"

Then Rasâlu again conferred with his horse and his parrot, and ordered them to advise him, whether first to go in pursuit of Thirya, or to kill the giant concealed under the trees. Both of them advised him to kill Wazîr first. So the King came to the pile of trees and brushwood, and they saw that underneath lay a large flat slab of heavy stone, which was moving up and down as the giant breathed beneath. Now the Râja had learnt some magic from his mother Lûna, so he chanted some words, by virtue of which the stone rolled away, and the giant beneath became visible. Then the Râja began to pull away the trees and the bushes, but the horse and the parrot stopped him, saying, "O Râja, what a foolish thing to do! If you are going to tear away those trees one by one, it will take ages, and, besides, the giant will suddenly jump up all at once and catch you in his arms, and you will not be able to kill him, but get killed by him yourself instead. You have killed four of them, and now we think the fifth will kill you. You had better cut him through with your sword, together with the trees." And right glad was Rasâlu that he did so. He drew his sword, making it flash like lightning, and, taking God's name on his lips, he struck with his sword, which was so sharp, that it passed through the trees and the bushes, and cut the giant in two. Then, setting a light to it, he made a bonfire of the whole mass.

When all this was being done, Thirya again looked back, and saw that his brother Wazîr was dead. He also saw Rasâlu preparing to pursue him with all his strength, and he cried, "You have cut off my arm and killed my brothers. Why still pursue me? I feel an arrow piercing my heart!" Then he hurried on up the mountain, moaning, "O God, you alone are my saviour! He won't let me alone!" And when he got to the cliff, all at once the rock before him began to split open, and taking advantage of it, he climbed up and ran into the cleft. So Rasâlu lost him, to his great surprise, and he spoke to his parrot and his horse, saying—

"I am astonished! You see the state of affairs. No sooner had I begun to overtake him, than he disappeared. What's to be done now?"

"Sâhîb," answered Shâdi, "you did not see what I did. I was higher than you, and I think that the rock must have opened for the giant to go in. Let me go and see where he is!" So the parrot flew to the hill and found him hidden in the Cave of Gandghar. Then, flying back to his master, he said, "The giant is hidden in the cave of the mountain."

Going to the place, Rasâlu saw Thirya crouching in the gloom of Gandgharri-ki-ghâr,[1] and he cried, "Are you inside, Thirya?"

"Yes," answered he.

"Why are you here?" asked Rasâlu.

"Because, sir," said Thirya, "you cut off my hand, and I was afraid of you, and I have come in hither to hide."

Then, as he heard the approaching tramp of Folâdi, he ran further in, and lifting up his voice in a lament, cried aloud and said—

"Strange is Thy nature always, God most dread,
To Thee the poor and needy cry for bread;
Thou givest life where life lived not before,
And those who live Thou biddest live no more.
My bark is drifting o'er the stormy deep,
While all her crew are wrapt in deadly sleep;
Asrâil himself grips fast the guiding oar,
And, through the waves that hoarsely round her roar,
His shuddering freight he hurries to the shore.
O how can I foreknow what words of doom
Against my soul proclaim beyond the shadowy tomb!"

As he spoke thus, Rasâlu alighted, and tying his horse to a stone, he took his shield and his sword and went into the cave. Then said the parrot, "Râja, Râja, what are you doing? We advise you not to go alone into that cave, lest in the darkness the giant catch you in his arms and eat you up!" But the Râja insisted, and went in, but as he found no limit to the length of that cave, and as Thirya continued to evade him, and as it was getting darker and darker at every step, he cried out, "Thirya, it is unmanly to flee away to such a place! Come out if you are brave, and you shall have the first blow!"

"No, no, no," roared the giant, "I won't come out, and I will never come out till the Day of Judgment!" And as he rushed further and further in, the echoes of his voice reverberating through the vast chambers resounded far and wide. But the darkness then became so black and so confusing that Rasâlu searched for him in vain. Therefore at last he gave up the hopeless task and came out.

[1] That is, *The Cave of Gandghar*.

But having engraved a likeness of his stern face on the surface of the rock just within the cave, he rolled a great stone to the mouth of it, and fixed thereto his bow and arrow. At full stretch, with the arrow fitted to the string, hangs the bow, and from the arrow hangs a tuft of Rasâlu's hair. Then having closed up the entrance, he cried out to the imprisoned giant, "Thirya, remember if you dare to stir forth you will be killed on the spot!"

Thus he shut the monster in, and there he remains to this day. Sometimes, even now, he endeavours to escape, but when in the sombre twilight he catches sight of the awful look of King Rasâlu's pictured face, and sees the threatening arrow, and the nodding tuft of hair, he rushes back dismayed and baffled, and his bellowing fills the villages round with dread.[1]

Then said the son of the old woman to Rasâlu, "Râja, let us now go back!" And the Râja, listening to the words of the boy, turned to go home again. When they got near the castle of the giants, the boy again spoke. "Râja," said he, "let the giantess remain where she is. Go not nigh her gate, but let us go straight home!"

"No, child," said Rasâlu, "this plan will not work at all. The giantess will prove as great a plague to the world as the giants were. So we must kill her too!"

They went to the castle, and there saw the giantess sitting and waiting. She had dressed herself up in most splendid clothing, in the hope of becoming the wife of Rasâlu. She now stood up and began to catch the Râja by his skirt, but he ordered her to keep off and not to touch him.

"Râja," said she, "I am to be your wife, and do you order me not to touch you? What is the meaning of that?"

"When you are my wife, you can touch me," said the Râja, "of course!"

"Then make haste, Râja," cried she. "Be quick and marry me!"

"We must do the thing properly," said Rasâlu. "Hear me, you Bhagalbatt! Let us put the cauldron on the fire, and fill it full, and let us march round it seven times. Thus shall the wedding rite be accomplished!"

[1] Subterranean noises are often heard in the neighbourhood of Gandghar.

Then brought she out a huge iron cauldron, and the Râja bade her to fill it with oil, and set it in the midst, and light a large fire under it. All this she did, as she was told, saying to Rasâlu, "Is it a way of marrying, Râja!"

"Yes, my wife," answered he.

Now Rasâlu had determined to throw her into the burning oil, but she suspected him, and she had also made up her mind to throw him in, if she got the chance. Meanwhile he told her to compass the fire with him seven times, according to the custom of Hindus at their marriages, and she began to trip round and round. And as Rasâlu eyed her, he was thinking how best he could lift her up, and he decided that the best plan would be to catch her by the neck with one hand, and by the lower part of her body with the other. So, in accordance with this plan, all of a sudden he thus caught her, as she was prancing round the fire, and, using the utmost force, he heaved her up, and cast her into the boiling cauldron, where she was burnt up. And when her skull split with the heat of the fire, so great was the shock thereof, that it brought on an earthquake which lasted for three hours. And Rasâlu said—

"Forever cursèd be the wife,
The wretch, who sells her husband's life,—
Burn, burn, O leaping flame!
I've killed her dead, that famous slut,
The cauldron reeks of Bhagalbatt,[1]
All open lies her shame!"

Then Rasâlu took the boy back to Uda-nâgiri, where the house of the old woman was, and there they saw her waiting for them outside the door. And when they drew near, alive and safe, joyfully she spoke and said—

"I saw you coming on your way,
As I stood beside the door,
O sit and rest while now you may,
And let me be, I humbly pray,
Your slave for evermore!"

Thus the old woman entreated him to stop with her, but he was not willing to do so, for in three days he mounted his mare and rode away to other parts.

[1] When the *a* is not accented it is pronounced like *u* in English *butt*. The giantess's name therefore pronounce *Bhuggulbutt*.

8. TILYAR NAG THE SNAKE AND SUNDAR KAG THE RAVEN[1]

THEN after many days, Rasâlu came by the way of Nûrpûr Jehân to Mejât, and so to Avellia, and then to Maksûdàbâgh in Hazâra. At that time there was a large dragon or serpent in that country which was very destructive to every living thing. The country was all uninhabited, and waste, on account of the serpent. And it rained and continued raining for seven days and nights. And when the rain was over, and the weather clear, Rasâlu happened to see a hedgehog.

The hedgehog, trying to leap a stream, fell into it, and became entangled in weeds, and got into trouble, and he addressed Râja Rasâlu, saying thus—

"O rider of the dark-grey mare,
Rasâlu, bearded, turbaned stranger,
A drowning hedgehog craves your care,
For God's sake save his life from danger!"

When Rasâlu heard these words he was surprised, and began to look about him. And he said to his parrot, "You are flying above me. Did you hear a voice? Who calls to me?" Instantly the parrot looked about, and seeing the black hedgehog, he said to Rasâlu, "It is the hedgehog. He begs you, in the name of God, to rescue him. So pray help him!"

Then Rasâlu looked at the hedgehog, and said, "You are a hedgehog, and I am a man. What connection there is between you and me I know not. But as you have challenged me with the name of God, I will help you!" He then dismounted, and stretched out his hand to help the hedgehog out. But the hedgehog struggled, and some of his spines ran into the Râja's hand. To get rid of the little beast, the Râja threw him back into the water, and he fell into the very same place whence he had been taken. And Rasâlu said to him, "Your body is very small and very insignificant, but you seem to have many

[1] *Tilyâr Nâg, i.e.* Tilyâr the Snake (Cobra). *Sundar Kâg, i.e.* Sundar the Raven or Crow.

arms. I do not touch you again, seeing that your sharp quills have pierced my hand!"

So the Râja left him where he found him, and went on his way. And when the hedgehog saw that, he put his hands together, and besought him, saying, "Neither touch me with your hand, nor keep me in your lap. Take me out of the stream and put me in your horse's feeding bag!" But Rasâlu was in doubt, so he said to the parrot, "Shâdi, the hedgehog wants me to put him in the nose-bag. What is your opinion about that?" And the parrot as well as the horse begged him to rescue the hedgehog from his miserable plight. So the Râja lowered the end of his bow, and so took him out of the water, and he set him on the ground and left him there a little while to dry. And when he was dry he put him in Folâdi's nose-bag, which hung from the saddle-bow.

It was then mid-day, and Rasâlu made up his mind to go to Maksûdabâgh, and there take rest from the heat of the sun. So he set out. And as they journeyed the hedgehog began to think to himself, "I have been exposed to storm and rain for seven days, and to-day there is a good sun shining. I wonder if I am any the worse. Better see!" So he swelled himself out, and stretched his spines. And the spines on the horse-side pierced through the nose-bag, and pricked Folâdi most terribly, so that she shuddered again. And Rasâlu was astonished and said to his horse, "O you horse! you have been in many a battle, you have fought with giants and savages without number, and you never trembled. I think it must be either your last day or mine. Let me know the cause of this trembling!"

"My trembling," answered the horse, "has been all caused by that wretched animal you took out of the water!"

Then Rasâlu dismounted to see, and found his horse's body pierced by the spines. So he said to the hedgehog, "I took you out of that horrible mess, and carried you with me. Why, pray, did you pierce my Folâdi with your thorns?"

"It was a joke," answered the hedgehog, "my first joke! It was not malice, it was not a bad heart! Indeed I may have to play some other jokes with Mr. Horse!"

So they all laughed and joked together, one with the other.

By-and-by they began to draw nigh to Maksûdabâgh.

Now as they were riding along, Rasâlu observed a spacious castle, beautifully built, and surrounded on all sides with gardens, but it was entirely deserted. There Rasâlu dismounted and sat down under a *baherâ*[1] tree, close to a running fountain of pellucid water. At that moment the parrot began to say something, when the hedgehog exclaimed from the nose-bag, "Take me out, take me out!"

The King lifted him out, and then addressing his parrot, he said, "Tell me, O Shâdi, what you were going to say."

"Sir," answered the parrot, "it seems to me that this house is enchanted. It must belong to some demons or giants, because I can see the carcases of dead men lying all about close to the walls. It is better that we should leave this place and go pass the night elsewhere."

"I have no wish to do that," answered Rasâlu, "and in brief I intend to remain. But tell me, what monster is that which has killed all these men?"

"Sir," replied the parrot, "what do I know about them? Ask the hedgehog, since he has the look of one who belongs to these parts."

Then said the King to the hedgehog, "O Friend, what monster is it which has destroyed all these animals and all these men?"

"Sir," answered the hedgehog, folding his hands, "in this place live Tilyâr, the great flying serpent, and his friend Sundar Kâg, the sea-raven. They are villains in grain, and having come here they trouble and molest wretched wayfarers, and whosoever ventures this way, whether he be hunter or prince or king, they never permit him to quit the place alive."

"What do they do?" enquired Rasâlu.

Kneeling down before the King as if at his prayers, the hedgehog meekly replied, "Sir, travellers who come to this fountain, being overcome with fatigue, lie down here and rest. Then this Tilyâr the serpent, in the middle of the night, steals out upon them and sucks away their breath as they lie asleep, after which he goes away and informs the sea-raven, who comes in his turn and pecks out their eyes from their sockets."

"Is it true?" said Rasâlu.

[1] A tree yielding a medicinal fruit.

"Yes, it is quite true," answered the hedgehog.

Then said the King, "I cannot now mount again, because I have already said that here I will certainly remain. But you shall all act as I bid you."

"We await your orders," said the hedgehog.

"God is master over all," said Rasâlu. "He has power to kill and He has power to save. But one thing, in good sooth, you people should not omit to do. Altogether we number four persons. Let us therefore wake and sleep by turns, and thus let us pass the four watches of the night in safety."

Having so ordained, Rasâlu again spoke, and said, "The first watch of the night shall be taken by me, the second by Folâdi my horse, the third by Shâdi my parrot, and the fourth by the hedgehog."

But, alas! all Rasâlu's plans availed him not, for before night-fall that fiery serpent came. And thus it befell.

As it was still early in the day, he ordered the horse to go and graze in the meadows, and the parrot to go and pick fruits in the woods, and the hedgehog to have a ramble, and so they were scattered.

Now Tilyâr, the serpent, had made a vow twelve years before that he would suck away Rasâlu's breath. And Tilyâr's friend, the raven, whose name was Sundar Kâg, knew it. It so happened that Rasâlu, feeling weary with the heat, had fallen asleep, and Sundar Kâg, hopping round, saw him, and at once went to Tilyâr's hole, and woke him up with a loud croak. The serpent, feeling angry at being disturbed, said, "What business have you coming here at this hour?"

"Come out!" said the raven. "The man you have vowed to kill is to-day in this very garden, and I have come to tell you so."

The serpent at once came out of his den, and crawled softly to the spot where Râja Rasâlu was sleeping. Taking the Râja at advantage he mounted on his breast, and putting his mouth to Rasâlu's mouth, drew up all his breath, so that the Râja became lifeless. Just after this, Shâdi returned from the jungle, and, seeing the Râja lying asleep, he sat on the tree, waiting for him to wake and have a talk.

Meanwhile the serpent went back, and reported the whole adventure to his friend the raven, and ordered him to go and make a feast on the Râja's body. But the raven had a wife whose name was Shârak,[1] and she said to her husband, "O Sundar Kâg, bring me the Râja's eyes and tongue, and eat the rest yourself!" So the raven set off, and the first thing he did was to sit on the Râja's instep, which he began to peck, in order to find out if he was really dead or not. Finding that he did not stir, he hopped on to one of his knees, and the parrot, who was watching the whole thing, was quite surprised the Râja did not move, because he knew well that his master's aim never failed of its mark. After this, the raven hopped up and sat on the Râja's breast. Then the parrot concluded that Rasâlu was dead. So he pounced down on to the raven and broke his back, and when the raven saw that his back was broken, he flew away. But he was so amazed and bewildered, that he could not find his own house, but went blundering along elsewhere through streams and bushes.

The parrot now began to weep for his master. And he thought of the hedgehog, and longed for his friend the horse; but neither of them came. Indeed, the poor hedgehog had himself got into trouble. For, when rambling in the jungle, he began to pursue a little grasshopper, and he was so eager in the pursuit that he never saw a pool of water right in his way, and fell flop into it. And very sorry he was when he found, as he quickly did, that he could not get out again. But what was his horror when he overheard Tilyâr, the serpent, saying to his friend Sundar Kâg, "I have taken his breath, go along and feast away!"

"O God," said he, "what has happened? All this trouble has been caused by me!" He was just thinking about all this, when a rat, having got scent of him, began to throw mud at him, because rats and serpents naturally are the enemies of hedgehogs. The poor hedgehog begged him to leave off, and help him out. But the rat refused, saying, "Shall I help one that is my enemy? No, never!" and, to show his malice, he got on the hedgehog's back, and kept pushing him down into the water. Then the hedgehog prayed him again. "In the name of God," said he, "take me out, and I promise never to do anything

[1] The *Graculus religiosa*.

to injure you. O rat, it is a time of trial; if you will do me this little kindness, you shall be repaid!"

At last the rat relented. But he said, "O hedgehog, please hide your snout, I am afraid of your snout! And oh, please hide your teeth, as I am also afraid of your teeth! Consent to this, and I will help you!" So the hedgehog did so, and the rat laid hold of one of his spines, and, snatching him out of the water, landed him safely on dry ground. Then ran the hedgehog back with all speed, and was surprised to find the Râja sleeping, and the parrot weeping copiously. "O parrot," said he, "what is the cause of your trouble?" Then answered the parrot as he sobbed—

"Of the fruits of the garden we feasted at will,
By the waters we wandered and drank to our fill,
But, ah, for the weeping,
Our Râja is sleeping,
Our Râja is sleeping forever in death,
For Tilyâr the serpent has drawn up his breath!"

"O Shâdi, parrot Shâdi," answered the hedgehog, "the Râja is not dead, though his breath has been drawn up by the snake. Within twenty-one days he can be restored to life. Please get some milk and two *chûpâtties* and some rice cooked in the milk. Get them soon!" And the hedgehog continued, "I am a very weak little body, and cannot speak to any one. I cannot persuade any one to bring them. The horse also is a thing to be coveted, and, if he goes, people will catch him and tie him up. Neither he nor I can help. Only you, who are a bird and who can fly far away in a little time, can bring those things!"

So Shâdi went, and going he said, "I, Shâdi, leave this place trusting in God, and saying that I will come back in eight days. O hedgehog, carefully watch the Râja's eyes, that they be not destroyed!"

Then flew the parrot away to the village of Kabbal and perched on the roof of the house of a widow, who was a Hindu. And the parrot cried, "O God most merciful, O most bounteous God!" The woman was going down to the Indus with a little vessel in her hand, but hearing the voice of the bird she stopped, and said—

"O parrot, where is your home,
And where is the place of your dwelling?
What Râja sent you to roam?
O speak to me, truthfully telling!"

And the parrot made answer—

"Siâlkôt is my Râja's court,
His mother comes from Indra Fort;
In beauty, theme of endless praise,
He shames the moon of fifteen days;
But Tilyâr Nâg has sucked his breath,
And now my Râja lies in death!
For love of God, behold this tear,
And make for me a little *khîr!*"

Now the woman made up her mind to catch the parrot, because, as it was a Râja's, his master would come and pay high ransom for it. So she prepared the *khîr*—the milk, the rice, and the sugar—and invited the parrot to come and eat. But the parrot was too clever to be taken in, and refused. "I belong to a great Râja," said he. "I am not accustomed to eat of one dish, but of two. Make me also some *chûpâtties!*" And this he said then, because he wanted to engage both her hands, so that he might not be caught. So she baked the cakes which she held in one hand, while she held the *khîr* on the other, and she invited Shâdi to the feast. Then the parrot flew down straight on to her head, with his face over her face, and glad beyond measure she was when she noticed that every feather in his body was set in gold. "No doubt," thought she, "he belongs to some great Râja!" And now the parrot, in order to engage her attention, began to peck up *khîr*, grain by grain, but afterwards, getting a chance, he flew away with two *chûpâtties*, and, wrapped in the *chûpâtties*, a little *khîr*. Seeing this, the woman stood surprised, and cried—

"Around my lattice, gaily nested,
Bulbuls trill by night and day;
Upon my house-top, golden crested,
Peacocks sing melodious lay;
O parrot, you alone have rested,
Only rested to betray!"

By-and-by the parrot came to the hedgehog, and saluted him, and he took note that the hedgehog was sitting close by the ear of the Râja. And the hedgehog said, "I have been watching the Râja all this time; so much I have done. Have you also done something?" And the hedgehog, taking from the parrot one of the *chûpâtties*, wrapped it well round his own body, and keeping a little *khîr* in front of his mouth, he again sat close to the ear of the Râja.

But how about the raven? When the raven flew away from the garden, having his backbone broken, he stayed away for several days, but when his back got well, he returned to his own house, thinking that by that time his friends would have forgotten the story. But his wife Shârak received him with anger, and spoke roughly to him. "What have you done?" cried she to him. "Where have you been? Have you brought the Râja's eyes and tongue for me? If not, you are no good!" The raven, at these reproaches, felt sad, saying to himself, "Wives are always nagging their husbands!" To satisfy her, he spoke, saying, "Keep quiet! I am again going to the place, and will fetch you the things as soon as possible!"

"Then go at once," said she, "and bring them!"

So early in the morning the raven flew to the garden once more, and there he saw some white *khîr* close to Râja Rasâlu's ear. At first he stood at some distance, fearful that the parrot might pounce on him again, and break his backbone. But soon he drew nearer, and at last came right up to the *khîr*, and began to peck at it, because it was delicious and he was not accustomed to nice things. When he had eaten up all the *khîr*, the greedy raven then began to dig his beak into the *chûpâtty*, minded to devour that as well, but at once the hedgehog seized his head with his jaws. Alarmed at this, the raven spread his wings and flew away, carrying the hedgehog with him. But the hedgehog was very clever. He at once sent his teeth well into the raven's back, and bit him hard, and so the fight went on, until the raven, helpless and exhausted, came fluttering down to the ground in the maw of his enemy. Then thought the raven to himself, "I will converse with the hedgehog, and induce him to open his mouth!" So he spoke, saying, "Well, hedgehog, did you take hold of me knowingly, or unknowingly? Did you want to catch me, or somebody else?" But the hedgehog, being very cunning, spoke not a word. Then began the raven to cry out with a great outcry, and his friend the serpent, hearing his voice, was surprised, wondering what had happened to his old chum, the raven. To find out, he thrust his head out of his hole, and said, "Who is there? Let my friend go!"

Then said the hedgehog, "First go and restore *my* friend, and then I will leave yours!"

"Leave my friend first," said the serpent. "I have done yours no harm—only drawn up his breath. And promise me peace as well. I will then go and pour his breath back into him, and take out all the poison."

So the hedgehog vowed him peace, and the snake went to Rasâlu and took out the poison, and poured life into his body again. But Shâdi, who was watching, said, "Take care, Bâshâ[1] Nâg! My Râja was as powerful as twenty-two champions. Do not keep back even a little of that power!" Then the snake moved aside, and Shâdi said, "What is the reason my Râja does not rise? He is lying as senseless as before!"

"Shâdi," answered the serpent, "take two or three leaves of the *shere*[2] tree, and put them into Rasâlu's mouth with a few drops of water, and you will see his power will come back, and he will rise!"

This therefore the parrot proceeded to do.

Now when the snake was thus engaged, the hedgehog, getting a chance, took the lifeless raven in his mouth to the snake's den, where, releasing him, he laid his head under one of his wings, and set him up at the entrance. When the snake returned, he found the smell of hedgehog coming from the hole of his den, and he said, "You hedgehog, you! Why have you gone into my den?"

"I have set your friend sitting at the entrance," said the hedgehog, "and that is the only reason I entered your den!"

"Make haste, then," said the serpent. "Get out that I may go in! It is hot weather, and some ant will be coming and creeping on my body!"

"I have made your friend sit here," said the hedgehog. "Look at him: here he is, right before your eyes. He does not speak because he is so angry with you for delaying."

But the hedgehog was watching his chance, being afraid of being devoured by the serpent, and all of a sudden he

1 Artful one.

2 A small fruit-bearing shrub, the *Coriaria Nepalensis.*

made a leap and, springing on to the serpent's head, began to thrust all his thorns into the serpent's brain, and there was a great fight between them.

"O unworthy one," then cried his victim, "do not break your vow!"

"I am a hedgehog," answered he. "What have I to do with vows? My business is to kill my enemy!"

Then said the serpent—

> "In former ages, write the sages,
> Snakes and hedgehogs were akin;
> Then cease your strife and spare my life,
> And you shall God's approval win!"

But the hedgehog answered him—

> "In former ages, write still wiser sages,
> We tore each other more than tongue can tell;
> O fool and daft, where was your wonted craft?
> On your own foot the axe uplifted fell!"[1]

Meanwhile Râja Rasâlu rose up, and found the parrot sitting close by, but he was very angry to have been wakened from such a sweet sleep, and had a mind to take hold of the parrot and punish him for it. But the parrot said, "My Liege, let us go to the serpent's den that I may show you the wonderful kindness done you by the hedgehog. You indeed had done a little service to that creature, but now I will inform you of the great service he has done to you!"

So the Râja went, and there he saw the hedgehog fastened to the head of the serpent, and the serpent struggling, and trying to get rid of him. So the Râja drew his sword and cut the snake to pieces, and from his fragments he made great heaps. Then understood he all the greatness of the service which had been done for him, and he was glad, and said to the hedgehog, "O hedgehog, this favour which you have done me is past recompense since you have saved my life, but you will be rewarded of God!" At the same time the hedgehog advanced to the Râja's feet and spoke thus—

[1] "Kohârâ mâriâ tudh âpon âpen pair"—"The axe you have struck on your own foot." A proverb very common in a country where every one cuts his own fire-wood. So, in English, "the biter bit," "Hoist on his own petard," etc.

"A dish was filled with pearls and in it was poured size. Having now done you a service, I am your son and you are my father!"

Then Rasâlu took off his turban, and threw it at the hedgehog's feet, and the hedgehog said, "The dish is filled with pearls and the pearls had black lines upon them. If you talk sweetly, I am only as the dust of your feet." Then the hedgehog folded his hands, and begged the Râja to take up his turban and put it on his head, saying, "I am as one of your sons, and you are my father. As a son should serve a father, so will I serve you!"

"I will keep you always with me," said the Râja, "yea, I will set you in gold and make a locket of you."

"Let me remain here," answered the hedgehog. "I do not wish to go with you for the great trouble I should be to you. I want to remain in the hole of the snake so that no other serpent may venture to come and trouble this place again."

The parrot and the horse also commended him highly, saying, "O friend, you have saved our master's life. May God preserve you in happiness!"

"Sir Horse and Sir Parrot," said the hedgehog, "I have merely returned the favour which the Râja did to me."

Very unwillingly Râja Rasâlu consented to part with him, but at last leaving him at that spot, he mounted and rode off. Hardly had he turned his back when the hedgehog looked after him and said, "Where are you going to now, O King?"

"I am going," answered the King, "to see Râja Sirikap."

"O sir," said the hedgehog, "be warned by me! Go not to Râja Sirikap, for he is a magician, and he will surely bring you into trouble."

"Nevertheless to Râja Sirikap I shall go," replied Rasâlu.

"If you are really fixed to go," said the hedgehog, "take advice and act as I beg you. Lying on the road halfway to Sirikap's capital you will find the body of Râja Sirisûk his brother. Go to him, speak to him, and mark well his words."

Then the king left that place, and rode away to look for the body of Sirisûk, the brother of Sirikap the Beheader, while the hedgehog remained still in that garden.

RÂJA RASÂLU

9. RASÂLU AND RÂJA SIRIKAP

THAT very day, having departed from thence, Râja Rasâlu journeyed on towards Sirîkot, the "Fort of Skulls."[1]

At the close of the day he halted, and having pitched his tent and eaten his supper, he walked forth to look for the body of Sirisûk, the brother of Râja Sirikap, who, as his name implies, was surnamed "The Beheader." He found the corpse lying stiff and cold on the ground, and turning to his parrot, he said, "This man is dead. Who now will advise us about Râja Sirikap?"

"Offer up your prayers to God," answered the parrot, "and I think the body will sit up, because it is not really dead, but it lies here under the spell of Sirikap's magic."

Then Rasâlu, when he had first washed his face, his hands and his feet, stood and prayed in these words—

> "God, within the forest lonely
> Night hath fallen o'er the dead;
> Grant him life a moment only,
> Light within his eyelids shed;
> Then this corpse that lieth pronely,
> Four words to speak will lift his head."

The King's prayer was heard and God granted Sirisûk his life, for at once the dead man trembled, and, raising himself, he began to speak. "Who has disturbed me?" said he.

"Here you have been lying asleep for twelve years," answered Rasâlu. "What kind of sleep is this?"

"Who are you?" asked Sirisûk.

"I am Rasâlu," answered the King.

"Are you the real Rasâlu or another?" said Sirisûk. "Where are you going?"

"I journey towards the castle of your elder brother Sirikap in order to wage battle with him," said Rasâlu.

Then began Sirisûk to laugh a dead man's laugh.

"What are you laughing at?" inquired Rasâlu.

"I was his own brother," replied Sirisûk, "and yet he killed me without pity. We often played *chaupat* together,

[1] The popular notion. Really *The Head Fort*.

and I was always the winner excepting once. Once only my brother won, and then he claimed my head; and when in joke—not thinking that, as he was my brother, he meant what he said—I bent my head, he took it off at a single blow, and then, fastening a rope to my feet, threw me out of the city. Do you think then he will spare you? Besides, you have not even an army, while his army is numerous. How do you intend to cope with him?"

"Assisted by your advice," answered Rasâlu, "I trust I shall be fully able to fight and to subdue him."

Then said Sirisûk, "When you begin to draw near the city he will raise his magical storm and blow you away to some other country. And if you evade that, he will bury you under a storm of magical snow. And if you escape that, then when you strike the gong which hangs before the castle-gate, and when the noise of the gong shall sound in your ears, you will lose your senses, and becoming crazed you will be driven out of the place. And if peradventure you avoid that peril, then when you pass under the swing of his daughter Chandei who swings in the porch of the palace, which is fifty yards high, you will begin to rage with frenzy and you will become the sport of the inmates, because the effect of that swing is that whosoever passes beneath it goes raving mad. And if by good fortune and the favour of God you overcome that danger, Râja Sirikap will then play *chaupat*[1] with you, and his wife and daughters will sit before you to divert your eyes, and in the meantime you will lose the game and Sirikap will win it, after which he will cut off your head. But if he cannot prevail over you in that way, he will call forth his rats, Harbans and Harbansi,[2] who are kept for that very purpose, and who will come and take away the wick out of the lamp, and there will be confusion, and Sirikap will make you the loser and himself the winner, after which he will take your head from off your shoulders. It is better for you to turn back and not go to Râja Sirikap."

"I will certainly go to him," answered Rasâlu.

"If you insist upon going," said Sirisûk, "you must endeavour to avoid all the perils of which I have warned

[1] *Chaupat.* A game somewhat like draughts.

[2] *Harbans.* A person of many resources, a Jack of all trades.

you. Therefore do you now take out of me two of my ribs. On your way you will meet a cat which you must carry with you and which you must feed from time to time with my ribs. Then when you are playing *chaupat* and when the Râja cries out 'Harbans!' let loose your cat, so the cat will kill the rat, and the game will be yours." Saying these words, Sirisûk drew out of his side two of his ribs and gave them to Râja Rasâlu, who took them and kept them carefully by him as he journeyed along.

Having started afresh, he came to a village where a cat was busy assisting an old weaver in his work. "O weaver," said Rasâlu, "have you no son, nor any servant, that this wretched cat is helping you?"

"I am a poor man," answered the weaver, "and no other creature in the house have I excepting my cat."

Rasâlu, offering the man twenty rupees, bought the cat, and took her with him, and as they went along she sucked at the ribs of Sirisûk.

Rasâlu came next to a certain place where he saw two boys playing together. One of them made a small pool of water and called it the river "Râvi", and the other made a similar pool and called it the river "Chenâ." Just then up came a third boy, who stooped down and drank up the water out of both the pools.

Resuming his journey, Rasâlu next saw an old soldier washing clothes on the bank of a river. He was a discharged pensioner who had done good service, and who had received as his reward the grant of a horse and sixty villages. His vouchers or pension-papers were tied up in his turban, which was lying at some distance from him upon the ground. When his back was turned a stray goat came by and ate up both his turban and his vouchers, and on discovering his loss the poor soldier, who was on his way to claim his recompense, began to lament most bitterly.

Having observed these things, Rasâlu continued his march, and at last approaching the city of Sirîkot, the capital of Râja Sirikap, he pitched within a mile of the fortress, and there he tarried.

When the king of that place heard of the arrival of this redoubtable champion, he raised his magic storms, in which many trees and houses were swept away. The next morning he inquired of his wife Ichardei,[1] saying, "See if that man is still there!"

The Queen looked out of the window and said, "He and his horse are there still."

Then Sirikap proclaimed in the city, "To-night there will be a heavy fall of snow. Take care of yourselves!"

As the evening approached the snow began to come down, and it continued falling all night until every place in the city was buried many a yard deep. When morning broke the King again addressed his wife, saying, "See if the man is still there!"

"Sir," answered she, looking out, "he is standing there still, and the snow has not touched him."

When the storm was over, Râja Rasâlu entered the city, and going to the castle-gate, he took up the mallet and smote the gong such a terrific blow that mallet and gong were both smashed into pieces. Then said he to his horse, "If I venture to pass beneath the lady's swing my senses will leave me."

"Sit firmly in your seat," answered the horse; "I will reach her at a single bound, and the moment I reach her do you sever the swing with your sword."

With these words the horse leaped into the air and carried her rider to the lofty archway under which the Princess Chandei, with her two sisters, was then swinging in their cradle-swing, when Rasâlu with one stroke cut through the silken cords, and down fell the three to the ground. Alarmed and indignant, they went running to their father, and Chandei spoke, crying out and saying—

> "Some one has come to-day, O King,
> Who kills and kills throughout the town;
> He smote my ropes, and spoilt my swing,
> And I, Chandei, came tumbling down;
> The mallet flew in fragments eight,
> Down fell the gong in fragments nine;
> O flee, my sire, evade thy fate,
> The doom of all thy kingly line!"

"Daughter," said Râja Sirikap, "do not distress yourself and do not fear. Soon I shall kill him, and you shall

[1] *Ichardei*, i.e. *A woman of God*. It was also the name of the mother of Pûran Bhaghat, the prince-saint, the immaculate "Joseph" of the Panjâb. See his story.

see his head upon the bloody walls which I have built of the heads of others despatched before him."

Then, inflamed with anger, he placed guards in the different corridors of the palace with orders not to allow Rasâlu to pass them, but to lead him in by the gateway which was built of men's skulls. This then the guards did. Rasâlu was led in by the Gate of Skulls, where he saw piles of heads, grim and ghastly, which first laughed and then wept at him as he passed them by, and Rasâlu addressed them and said, "O heads, pray that I may have luck—

> "Since I must try my fortunes too,
> O Heads dissevered, pray
> That God will grant me victory,
> When I sit down to play,
> For then one yard of cloth I'll bring
> For every head in turn,
> And on a pyre of sandal-wood
> Each one of you shall burn!"

So Rasâlu entered the palace, and Sirikap rose, and salaamed him. Then he said to him, "O stripling, wherefore have you come? You have come to the city of Gangû to burn coals of fire on your head. But come on, Rasâlu! Tell me, if you can, how many glories there are in the world?"

Now Rasâlu was always helped in secret by the Five *Pîrs*, and they now came to his aid, and he at once answered, "O fool, void of understanding not to know yourself! The glory of the house is the house-wife, the glory of the body is dress, the glory of the land is the falling rain, and the glory of the battle-field is verily a goodly son!"

Then Sirikap offered him a couch covered with a green embroidered cloth, on which were cabalistic symbols, the work of women versed in magic and spells, and upon that he invited his visitor to sit and rest.

But Rasâlu waved him aside, rejecting his advances. "Give me not coloured couches," said he; "give me a carpet all woven in white."

"White shall it be," answered Sirikap, "but first you must answer another question and read me the riddle I shall set you, for that is the custom; and if you guess it aright, the white-woven couch shall be yours."

"Say on!" said Rasâlu.
Then spoke Sirikap to him thus—

> "Who of four-fold beard is he,
> Of azure foot and neck so ruddy?
> I've told the chief as you may see,
> My riddle well the wise will study."

Rasâlu disdained to answer. "Let it go!" said he. "I do not care for riddles." But Sirikap insisted on the answer. Then Rasâlu said, "What is that lying by your side?"

"It is my bow," answered Sirikap.

"And what do you do with your bow?" added Rasâlu.

"I shoot arrows with it," said Sirikap.

Then said Rasâlu, "Is not the thing you spoke of an arrow? See, here is one from my quiver; regard its four-feathered head, its blue steel foot, its ruddy shaft. And now, as you are answered, let me have the white-woven couch!"

But Sirikap was very wicked, and he continued to ask riddles, putting another, and saying, "There is a certain water in which trees are drowned to their summits, and in which the rhinoceros may bathe perfectly well. But in the same tank neither can we fill a pitcher nor can sparrows quench their thirst. What is it?"

And Rasâlu answered, "O uncle, no longer put me off, but let us play fair! Your riddle's answer is the dew, which is seen on the grass when the sun rises?"

But Sirikap was so wicked as not to be satisfied even yet, and he asked Rasâlu still another riddle, saying, "There are four husbands and sixteen wives, four wives to each husband, and all living under the same roof. I ask you, O Rasâlu, guess what it signifies?"

Then Rasâlu began to think Sirikap was not so clever as he was reported to be, and he answered, "Each thumb has four fingers, and your great toes have each four little toes, and that is your answer. A child might guess it. Had I a wager on this riddle, I should chop off your head. But I fear God! And now, as you are answered, give me the couch and let us get to business!"

"I cannot dispute your answers," said Sirikap. "Yet stay, it is now your turn, so put a riddle to me, and if I fail to give you the true answer, the white-woven couch shall be given you."

Then said Rasâlu, "Be it so—answer me this—

"Within your city-boundary,
  A wonder I did note:
A horse and sixty villages
  Were swallowed by a goat;
Then came a bald-head urchin,
  Of most capacious maw,
Who stooped him down and guzzled up
  The Râvi and Chenâ?"

"O," cried Sirikap, "that is quite impossible! It is even irreligious! Do not utter such impiety! Are you not afraid? Let us get out of the house, lest the roof fall on our heads!"

Then said Rasâlu, "Your riddles are all right, it seems, and mine all wrong?" And he told him the answer which compelled him to give in—and Rasâlu said to him, "See, you have not discovered the answer: grant me therefore the white-covered couch," and without another word Sirikap gave it to him.

But the Queen, who had been watching and listening, began to tremble with fear, until her husband went up to her and cheered her, saying, "Do not grieve—I shall cut off this fellow's head in a minute and send it over to you, because many others have come in like manner, but none have escaped my hands at last."

Then said Sirikap to Rasâlu, "Wherefore have you come to me?"

"It is reported," answered he, "that you are a tyrant, a man of blood, delighting in the slaughter of thousands of innocent men. Therefore have I come to your castle to challenge you to combat."

"Be it so," replied Sirikap. "Everything shall of course be ordered as you desire." Then said he again, "For you and me to fight together in public would be anything but creditable. Far better is it that you should come and play *chaupat* with me, and that the conqueror should cut off the loser's head."

To this proposal Râja Rasâlu willingly agreed, so the chess-board was brought, the lamp was lighted, and the two kings sat down to play.

As the game began, Sirikap chanted for luck, saying—

"Beneath this lamp's uncertain ray
Two kings contend in rival play:[1]
O changeful Game, change thou for me,
What Sirikap wills the same should be."

Hearing this charm, Rasâlu said, "That which you have now repeated is essentially wrong, since in your verse you have not mentioned the sacred name of God. What you should have said was this—

"Beneath this lamp's uncertain ray
Two kings contend in rival play:
O changeful Game, change thou for me,
What God decrees the same shall be."

With these words the game began. Râja Sirikap, repeating incantations over his dice, threw them, and Rasâlu lost Siâlkôt. Then Rasâlu waxed wrath, and in his anger he wagered all his servants, his goods and his whole kingdom, all of which were also won by Sirikap. The third time he staked his mare, Folâdi, and his parrot, Shâdi, which were also won by Sirikap: the fourth time he lost his arms: and the fifth and last time he lost his own life.

Then Sirikap sprang to his feet, and drawing his sword he prepared to cut off his rival's head. But Rasâlu said, "It is true I have lost my head, and you have a right to act as you please. Nevertheless I would look towards my own kingdom once more. Suffer me therefore to ascend for that purpose to the roof of your palace."

Sirikap consenting, Rasâlu went up to the palace-roof and began to gaze towards Siâlkôt, and as he gazed in sorrow he smote his hands upon his thighs and uttered a sigh.

Now the cat, with the two ribs, was concealed in his clothing, and when Rasâlu smote himself she cried out, upon which the King remembered her and rejoiced. "O you luckless little beast," said he, "you have not yet done me a service at all, but now let me try my fortune once more."

Coming down into the palace, he said to Sirikap, "By whom were you created?"

"By Him who created you," answered he.

[1] Literally, *Heads and houses are at stake*—a proverb

"If you really believe this," said Rasâlu, "permit me to try one more game in His name."

"Certainly," answered Sirikap, and the two kings again sat down to play.

Then Rasâlu exclaiming, "In the name of God," threw the dice and won back Siâlkôt. In the second game he won back his kingdom and all his subjects. In the third he recovered his horse and his parrot, in the fourth his arms, and in the fifth game he regained his own head.

The two kings were now quits, but Sirikap pressed for another trial, and the play proceeded. Fortune, however, had deserted him, and in the first game he lost his capital Sirîkôt, in the second all his kingdom, his furniture and army, and in the third his wife and children. Fiercely and warily he now contended for the fourth game, upon which he had wagered his head, and finding that he made no way, he cried out, "Harbansa, Harbansa!" when at once his male rat appeared on the scene. He stole in, and ran towards his master in response to the summons, but meanwhile Râja Rasâlu had brought his cat from his sleeve and set her down in the shadow of the lamp. Then as the rat approached to meddle with the lamp, the cat pounced upon him and swallowed him up. Sirikap in his despair now cried out, "Harbansi, Harbansi, look sharp, Harbansi!"

But the female rat, which had witnessed the fate of her mate, replied from a safe distance—

> "A curse to your service, O King,
> A curse to your handful of grain!
> I am off to the hills, and my teeth
> Shall nibble the herbage again."

The next moment the fourth game came to an end and Rasâlu was again the victor. Drawing his sword he approached Sirikap to smite off his head, but his opponent besought him saying, "You begged my permission to look towards your country and I gave it. You will allow me then, for the sake of God, to go and see my family, but first I would venture a game in the name of God as you did."

Rasâlu accepted his offer and the game was once more resumed, but again Sirikap lost. Then said he, "I would now, if you will permit me, go and bid adieu to my family, after which I will shortly return."

Rasâlu agreed, and the defeated King, going to his three daughters, said to them, "Put on your jewels, attire yourselves in royal array, and, presenting yourselves before Rasâlu, try to ensnare him with your beauty."

Now the names of his daughters were Chandei (Moonlike), Bhagdei (Fortunate) and Sûghrân (Wise), all three fair to look upon. Hastening to obey, they apparelled themselves gloriously in their best, adorning themselves with rich ornaments and bright jewels, and going to Râja Rasâlu they began to gaze on him and to parade their charms. But he heeded them not, neither did he gaze at them back, but he asked of them, "Where is Sirikap?"

"In fear of his life," answered they, "he has fled from the city."

"It does not matter," said Rasâlu. "Wherever he goes, I will search for him and find him out."

Going to the council of ministers, he inquired where their master generally sat. Some said, "He may be in his chamber of mirrors." Others said, "He may be in his subterranean dwelling." But the rest said, "He is a king, and he must have gone whithersoever it pleased him."

Then Rasâlu began to search the court and the palace; from chamber to chamber he passed; in some places he found miserable captives, in others the bodies of dead men and women, and in others precious stones and valuable ornaments, but nowhere could he discover Sirikap. Leaving the palace he went to the stables, and, as he looked and looked in every corner, his eye rested on a manger filled with litter which seemed to be alive.

"What is the matter," said he, "with this horse-litter that it swells and sinks and swells again?"

Going up to the manger he tossed out the litter, and there, crouching miserably beneath it, was found Râja Sirikap.

"Ah," said Rasâlu, "doubtless you are some mean fellow, since you have hidden yourself in this filthy place."

And he caught him by the neck and dragged him along to the chamber in which they had played, exclaiming as he went, "O villain, hundreds of heads you have smitten off in your time with your own hand and all for pastime, yet you never grieved or shed a tear. And now when the same fate is to be your own you sneak away and bury yourself in horse-dung!"

Now an event had occurred in the palace of which Rasâlu was not aware. Sirikap's wife, Ichardei, had given birth to a daughter, and the magicians and wizards had met Sirikap and told him, saying, "Sir, we have sought for the interpretation of this mystery, why ruin should have fallen on your house, and we find that all this calamity has been brought about by your infant daughter, whose destiny has crossed your own. She came in an evil hour. Let her now be sacrificed, and let her head be thrown into the river, and your crown and head will be secure."

And Sirikap had answered, "If my life depend on her, go, cut off her head, and mine may haply yet be saved." So a slave-girl was despatched to bring the infant to the magicians. And, as she carried it along from the apartments of its mother, she cried, while she caressed it, "O, what a pretty child, I should so like to save it!"

It was just at this moment, as she crossed the court, that Râja Rasâlu appeared from the stable, dragging Sirikap, and he thus overheard her remark. "Where are you taking that child to?" said he.

"This is the King's child, born twenty-one days ago," answered the slave-girl. "The Brâhmin soothsayers have declared that she is the cause of all her father's troubles, and now her head is to be taken off and thrown into the Indus to save further mischief."

When Rasâlu looked at the child he loved it, for it was very beautiful, so beautiful that the sun and moon felt ashamed in comparison, and he said to the girl, "Follow me!"

Having entered the chamber, he released his victim, who said, "Rasâlu, say now, what is your purpose?"

"I am going," answered he, "to cut off your head."

"For the sake of God," said Sirikap, "spare me and grant me my life, and in lieu of your wager take one of my daughters in marriage!"

"I want none of your daughters," replied Rasâlu. "I want only your head."

Sirikap then humbled himself more and more, pleading for his life and saying, "Sir, have mercy!" Also Ichardei came running from her chamber and threw herself at the feet of Râja Rasâlu in misery and distress, and begged him not to kill her husband.

"In the name of God, spare him!" cried she. At the same time the nurse came out, and taking the child, she laid her down also at Rasâlu's feet, and the child was shining in beauty like the moon. And Ichardei, prostrate, with head bared, prayed him to accept the child, saying—

"Oh, Rasâlu, take my daughter,
Take my loved one for your own,
Why, ah why commit this slaughter?
Leave the baby's sire alone!
If you, pitying my complaining,
Look upon her mother's tears,
I will gold advance, maintaining
Nurse and babe for fifteen years!"

At last Rasâlu, relenting, said to her husband, "You shall be spared on certain conditions. In the first place you will take an oath never to play villainous tricks at *chaupat* with any one again. In the next you will free all your captives. And in the third place you will draw five lines with your nose on a hot griddle."[1]

All these terms were accepted by Sirikap, who took the oath and released his prisoners, but when the red-hot griddle was produced he began to excuse himself—not to make the lines. But Rasâlu caught him by the back of the neck, and holding his nose to the griddle, he marked it with lines until his nose was singed to the bone, after which he loosed him and let him go. Then Sirikap, seeing himself in such a state of shame and disgrace, ran away into the wild woodlands, but by-and-by he returned once more, and lived for many years.

Meanwhile Râja Rasâlu, mounted on his grey mare, and ever followed by Shâdi, rode proudly away. With him, in a palanquin, escorted some way by a guard of honour, and accompanied by her nurse, travelled the little girl, the infant daughter of Sirikap, whose name was Kokal, or Koklâ, that is, the Sweet-cooing Dove. She it was who in after years, when she grew to woman's estate, became his hapless little Queen.

[1] Another version says that Sirikap was to "*bare his head*, and draw the five lines with his nose on the *ground*."

RÂJA RASÂLU

10. THE TREASON OF KOKLÂ

AFTER leaving Sirikap, Rasâlu, having dismissed his escort, and having travelled thence for twelve days, at last arrived at the hills of Khêrimûrti near Bûrhân, where he saw upon the height a beautiful castle surrounded by a fair garden which looked like the dwelling-place of a king.

"This," said Rasâlu, "is an abode worthy of living in, and here I resolve to remain."

"Sir," said his mare to him, "this is a palace which looks to me like the house of a giant. It is not wise to take up your quarters here."

"Let us abide," answered Rasâlu, "at least for a night. If we are molested we can then abandon it, but if not, I mean to occupy it, because it is a place after my own heart and I have no desire to leave it."

So there they slept in security, and no man or demon or any other creature intruded upon them for twelve years, and Rasâlu said, "Here there is no one to cause us alarm."

And in that lofty stronghold he dwelt, having strengthened it with walls and bastions all round and having cut out a flight of steps, eighty-six in number, from the garden beneath to the palace above.

When the child Koklâ was growing up, he ordered that the old custom of his people should be disregarded, and that the little Princess should be, not reared on vegetable food, but nourished also with flesh-meat every day. Her education was entrusted to the ancient nurse who had accompanied her from Sirîkot, and who was quite devoted to her. No other woman but herself was allowed to attend her, and no other woman but herself was permitted to enter the walls of the fortress. When with increasing years she became ill and was likely to die, the King said to her, "I have as much respect and love for you as for my own mother, and wherever it is your wish that your body shall be burnt, there it shall be done."

"Do not burn my body," said she; "lay me in the Abbâ-Sîndh."[1]

[1] Abbâ-Sindh—Father of Rivers, the Indus.

And when the day of her death came, her wishes were duly observed, and her body was committed to the river.

Râja Rasâlu was passionately fond of hunting. Leaving the child in the charge of the nurse to play with *mâina* and parrot, he was in the habit of visiting the woodland every day with bows and arrows to chase the wild deer. Rejoicing in his strength and in his skill as a marksman, he indulged in the sport either wholly alone or attended only by Shâdi his parrot. In the evening he returned with his spoil to the castle, when the feast was spread, and his minstrel-birds sang of his exploits and of the exploits of Vîkrâmâjît, as he sat with his little Princess on his divân, and fed her with venison. Her life was lonely with only a nurse to attend to her, but she had constant companions in eighty parrots, eighty-six *mâinas*, and eighty peacocks, who guarded her both night and day, and who, like all living things in those days, had the gift of speech. With them she used to converse, and to them she told all her little joys and sorrows.[1]

So passed the lives of King and Princess, until the old nurse died, and the little girl had grown into a woman and had become Rasâlu's Queen. They were very happy together, for the King was always a "good" man (which means in the Panjâb that he was faithful to the one lady of his choice, and that he never desired the companionship of another).

One evening, when he was in a merry mood, an odd fancy came into the King's mind, which was, that his young wife should accompany him to the chase. "I have eaten so much venison in my life," said she, "that, if I did go with you, all the deer of the forest would follow me."

But the proposal delighted her, and her spirits rose at the prospect of liberty, and of leaving the castle, if only for a day, to visit the wild trackless woodland.

"But," said she, "how do you kill the deer?"

"When I shoot my arrow at the deer," answered the King, "and when the deer feels himself wounded, he runs back and falls dead before my horse's feet."

The Queen was surprised to hear tell of this, and

[1] "Eighty-six *mâinas*"—a clever little bird of the *corvus* tribe, with yellow feet and bill. It is larger than a starling, and can be made to utter words and phrases in the deepest of notes.

she said, "How can it be? I should like so much to see it."

"And so you shall," answered he, "for to-morrow, Sweetheart, you and I will go hunting together."

So in the morning they set out unattended, the Queen riding on a pillion behind her husband, and they came to the wooded hillocks and grassy ravines where the deer love to wander. Soon the King loosed an arrow from the string, which wounded a doe, but the animal, instead of approaching them, ran forward half a mile, when she was overtaken and slain.

The Queen felt disappointed, for she had come to see a wonder, and she began to scoff. "You have not spoken the truth, sir," cried she.

"Why so?" asked Rasâlu.

"If no horse had been with you," replied the Queen, "you could not have caught this deer at all."

"The reason is this," said Rasâlu, "you have been sitting behind me the whole day, close to my body, and from touch of you one third of my power has left me."

Then the Queen flouted him again, and with a mocking laugh she said, "I know not whether I am a wife or daughter, but if touch has cost you one third of your strength, how will it fare with you for sons and daughters? Make way for me, and I will catch all these animals alive with my hands! You, O Râja, have killed a deer with an arrow from your bow, but, if you will allow me, I will bring a deer to your feet alive!"

"How can you do that?" said Rasâlu. "The thing is impossible. The deer will not come to you."

"No?" replied she. "But I can. You think yourself a hero, and I am a woman. Yet I am more than you!"

So the Râni dismounted and sat herself down among the rocks and the thickets, and lifting up her veil, she shook her *dâuni* (the pendant jewels of her forehead), and let them tinkle in the sun. Her eyes were filled with antimony, and her hands and feet were rosy with henna. So, when the deer saw her lovely face, which was shining like gold, they all came shyly up to her. Then said she to Rasâlu, "Come now, Râja, and catch as many of them as you please!"

"I will catch none of them," answered he, "nor are they worth the catching. Are they lovers of yours?"

Then came to her a great blue buck, Laddan by name, who was the king of them all. Boldly he came forward, for he had become like one without sense, beholding her beauty, and, disregarding the words of his dam, who entreated him not to venture, he ran and fell at her feet.

But Rasâlu waxed wroth, and catching the deer in both his arms, he raised him aloft, and hurled him to the earth, and made haste to kill him with his knife, laying the blade on his neck. But the Râni had compassion, and begged Rasâlu to let him go, and not to kill him, and she said—

"A king art thou of kingly race,
Strong is thine arm and keen thy knife;
By the Korân, O grant me grace,
And give this trembling deer his life!"

The Râja, listening to her words, spared indeed the deer's life, but he cut off his ears and his tail, and so let him go. And the deer, seeing himself thus dishonoured, and dripping with blood, reproached him with fateful words.

"O Râja Rasâlu," said he, "you are a monarch among men, and I am only a poor creature of the jungle. With your sword you have lopt off my ears and my tail; but know this that one day you yourself will be so gashed and slashed that until the Day of Judgment you never will heal you of your wounds again—

"O King, my ears and my tail you have lopt;
You have marred and insulted me sore;
But beware, for if ever by doe I was dropt,
The spoiler shall visit your door!"

The king-deer then departed, leaving the pair to themselves, but the Queen felt so vexed to think that her husband's power in spells and magic was less than her own. Nor was he less angry at the circumstance which had marred the glory of his life, one moment reproaching his wife, and another moment reviling the blue buck, but failing to see that the blame was his and his alone. And so the two returned to Khêrimûrti.

Meanwhile the blue buck was planning a bitter revenge. At the town of Atak (Attock) on the banks of the Indus a certain king named Hôdi had built a border-fortress on the top of a cliff which rises from the very margin of the river. This chieftain was noted for his love of pleasure, as well as for his passion for the pastime of the chase. Calling these things to mind, the blue buck said to himself, "Now I will betake me to the palace of Râja Hôdi, and I will graze in his garden, and, when the hue-and-cry is set up and he begins to follow me, I will run to the castle of Râja Rasâlu."

So he made his way to Râja Hôdi's, followed by all his friends, and entering the King's garden, he utterly destroyed it. These things the gardeners reported to their master, who, when he heard of the havoc which had been made, issued a notice, saying, "Whosoever shall kill *hîra haran* (the blue buck), whose name is Laddan, I will give him rich presents, a horse to ride on, and jewels to wear, and I will make him the commander of my army."

This notice was published all over that country, and it so happened that the news of it reached the ears of two shepherd-boys named Bald-head and One-eye, who said to each other, "Let us go and find this *hîra haran*, the blue buck."

So they searched and searched everywhere until they found him. Then Bald-head went privately to Râja Hôdi and made his report. "If you will come with me, O King," said he, "I will show you the blue buck." And the King loaded him with presents and accompanied him to the place.

Meanwhile, however, One-eye, who harboured a grudge against Bald-head, had hunted away the buck from that ravine into another. And when Râja Hôdi came and could not find anything, he became angry. "Where is the blue buck?" cried he.

Then spoke One-eye and said to the King, "This boy is known to be an idiot, he knows nothing whatever about the matter. He has been deceiving you, O king; but if you will take away his presents and give them to me, I will show you Laddan the blue buck, and no mistake."

So the King transferred the presents from Bald-head to One-eye, who took him to a distant ravine, and pointed out to him the game he was in search of.

As soon as Laddan perceived Râja Hôdi, he ran deliberately in front of him and led his pursuer in the direction of Khêrimûrti, all the time feigning a lameness in order to entice him more and more with the hope of eventual capture.

"Sir," said the wazîr, "do not pursue this deer, for I perceive there is some magic about him."

King Hôdi, however, refused to hear the voice of his wazîr, and galloping his horse he went straight for his quarry, leaving his attendants to shift for themselves. After a long run the blue buck sprang the river close to the palace of Râni Koklâ, and the horse of Râja Hôdi, roused by the chase, essayed and performed the same leap.

But the deer then disappeared into a cave and hid himself, and when the King came to the spot he was nowhere to be seen.

So Hôdi drew rein, and, finding himself in the midst of a garden of mangoes, he stretched forth his hand to pluck some of the fruit. But as he did so one of the sentinel-*mâinas* exclaimed, "Do not break the branches and do not eat the mangoes! This garden belongs to one who will punish intruders."

Râja Hôdi then observed that the trees grew beneath a fortress, but he could not see any means of approach. Looking up, he saw the plumage of the parrots gleaming from the eaves, and Râni Koklâ pacing the roof in her royal array. Then said he to the *mâina*—

"The parrots perch themselves aloft,
They dwell within the eaves;
But O that splendid lustre, soft
And bright as golden leaves,
Say, *mâina*, say, what beauty passes there,
Perchance some man, or is it maiden fair?"

"She is the wife of the King," answered the *mâina*, "and the King is away hunting the wild deer in the moors and woodlands."

Then one of the birds glanced down from above, and said to the Queen, "See, a man has entered the garden, and he is spoiling the fruit!"

"What is a man?" asked the Queen. "Is he a wild beast, or is he some other thing? Where is he? I want to see him—show me him! Heaven grant it is Râja Hôdi!"

The Queen looked down from the roof of her palace, and saw that some handsome râja was sitting on horse-

9

back in her garden, and that he carried a bow, and an arrow which weighed three pounds. So she cried out to him—

> "Ho, sir, beneath my palace walls,
>   Say who and what are you?
> Some skulking robber, rife for brawls?
>   Or are you champion true?"

And to her Râja Hôdi returned answer—

> "O Râni, thieves are clothed in rags,
>   True men are clean and white;
> For love of you, o'er flats and crags,
>   I kept my game in sight;
> And far from country and from kin,
>   He led me here fair lady's smile to win."

Then said the Queen—

> "What Râja's son are you,
>   And say what name you bear,
> Where lies your fatherland,
>   What city claims you there?"

The King answered her—

> "Râja Bhatti's son am I,
>   Hôdi is the name I bear,
> Udhè is my fatherland,
>   Aṭak is my city there."

Then thought Hôdi to himself, "Who is this woman in the midst of the wilderness? Is she a witch or some goddess? I must find out." So he addressed her and said—

> "Your father, who is he? your husband who?
> Where has he gone, the fool to troth untrue,
> To leave alone a lovely maid like you,
>   To pine from hour to hour
>   In lofty palace-tower?"

Hearing these words the Râni Koklâ, smitten with love, began to think of many things, and she answered him—

> "Sirikap, my sire, my lord's Rasâlu hight,
> Rings not the welkin with Rasâlu's might?
>   In lofty palace-tower
>   I sit in lonely bower,
> But he, who left his lovely maiden here,
> Ranges afar to chase the fallow deer."

Now when Hôdi heard the name of Rasâlu he began to grow sick with fear, and would fain have turned back. But love stronger than fear urged him on, and he said to the Queen, "Do you know who I am?"

"Yes," answered she, "I know you well, and I have been waiting for you ever so long, here, in this airy turret."

Then, seeing her meaning, Hôdi said to her—

"Running and walking in breathless haste,
From distant scenes I hied me,
Yet now the golden time I waste,
For I know no path to guide me;
O Râni, say, where lies your palace-road,
What steps will lead me to your bright abode?"

And to him the Queen replied again—

"Walking and running in breathless haste,
From scenes afar you hied you,
And now the golden time you waste,
For you know no road to guide you?—
Beneath the mangoes set your steed,
Your quiver to the pommel tie,
The steps that to my castle lead,
Among the mango-trees they lie;
Full eighty-six, nor less nor more,
Will bring you to my chamber door."

Râja Hôdi looked for the steps, and finding them he began to ascend. But, when he had gained the vestibule of the palace, one of the *mâinas* on guard stopped him, saying—

"Where have you lost your deer?
Where did your cattle go?
No right of road lies here—
You are now Rasâlu's foe!"

And turning to her companion, a parrot, she said, "The duty which is laid on us both by our dear master is to watch over the safety of the Queen, and we shall be false to our salt if we do not report to him the coming of this stranger."

By this time Râni Koklâ was growing impatient, and she was saying to herself, "Why does he tarry? why linger the steps of my Râja?" So she passed out of her chamber to inquire, and seeing that her favourite *mâina* was the cause of the delay she began to reprove her. But the *mâina* bravely replied, "What are you doing, admitting a strange man to these walls? If the King hear of this wickedness, he will strike you dead where you stand."

The Queen started and flushed with rage, but, restraining herself, she led Hôdi to the well which Râja Rasâlu had hewn out of the rock [and which was furnished with wheels and ropes and pitchers for drawing up water into the trough]. There they sat, and she gave him food and drink, and they entertained one another with delicious words.

Then Koklâ led the way to the hall of the King's chamber, but as she gained the doorway the *mâina* spoke again and said—

> "O hear me, parrot, let us fly—
> For hence we'll fly away!
> In this sad home can you and I
> Remain another day?
> The clustering grapes—ah! word of woe—
> Are pecked at by a wretched crow!"

The Queen instantly turned upon the *mâina*, but the parrot, eager to allay her anger, said to his companion, "O you senseless one! What harm is done if the man merely eats and drinks and goes away? What is Râja Rasâlu to us? Does not the Queen, our mistress, tend us and feed us with her own hands?"

"She does indeed," answered the *mâina*. "Still she has dishonoured her name, and done what she should not have done. And we are the servants of the Râja."

This speech of the *mâina* enraged the Queen still more, so much so, indeed, that she ran to the cage, and seizing the poor bird, she wrung her neck and cast her away.

But the cunning parrot, gazing at his friend's quivering body, said, "Ah, you silly chatterer, you have just met your deserts!" Then addressing his mistress he continued, "If you would but take me out of my cage, I should like to give the *mâina's* dead body a couple of kicks."

"Thank you, parrot," said the Queen, "you are loyal and true." And she opened the cage and let him out, when the parrot flew to the *mâina* and kicked her.

Meanwhile the Queen had closed the door and taken

Hôdi into Rasâlu's chamber, and there both he and she sat down together on a beautiful couch. Then the King, admiring her delicate beauty, said to her—

"A tiny mouth, a slender nose,
  A figure graceful as the fawn,
Two eyes as soft as opening rose
  When glistening with the dews of dawn—
O Queen, how dainty thou—so slim, so slight,
One little touch would surely break you quite!"

But Râni Koklâ answered and said—

"For joy the fletcher frames the arrowy dart,
For joy the blade is wrought by curious art,
And as in June the horn-tipt bow's unstrung,
And, all relaxed, within the chamber hung,
But, summer past, is pulled and pulled again,
Nor feels the force of unaccustomed strain,
So bounteous love, the more it takes and gives,
The more it charms us, and the more it lives." [1]

When night fell, they both slept on the one cot, and the Râni talked to the Râja and the Râja to the Râni, and all the sentinel birds, seeing this, began to weep, but none dared to utter a single word.

Now all this time the parrot was meditating an escape from the closed chamber, but he found no means of egress. At last, at dawn of day, he perceived a small aperture, and fluttering through it he flew on to the battlements.

"Alas! alas!" cried the frightened Queen to Hôdi. "What shall we do? The news has gone to Rasâlu!"

"Ah!" said Hôdi, with a deep breath. "But, O Râni," continued he, "if you will coax the parrot to return I think he will not disregard you, but come back to your house, and then we shall have no room for alarm, no cause for sorrow."

So the Queen looked out at a casement and cried through the lattice, in caressing tones—

"Rice with my nails have I cleaned for you ever,
Boiled it in new milk and chided you never;
Come to me, Pretty, return to me, Dear,
You are my Rânjha, and I am your Hîr!"

[1] During the summer-heat weapons of the chase are laid aside, to be taken down again in the cold season.

But the parrot was deaf to her blandishments; and spreading his bright wings, he answered her—

"You've killed my pretty *mâina* dead,
All widowed now am I;
If e'er by parrots I was bred,
Away to the King I'll fly."

With these words the bird mounted and flew far away, and he began to search for Râja Rasâlu among forests and hills and deserts, but unable to find him he finally stopped exhausted in one place.

Meanwhile Hôdi was in a fright, for when he saw the tell-tale parrot on the wing, fear seized upon him, and caring only for his own safety, he hastened out of the doors of the palace. But the Queen threw her arms about him and clipped him, and wept piteously, and Hôdi, to soothe her, wiped away her tears with his hands, and the black stain from her eyes discoloured his fingers. But though he wiped her eyes and embraced her again and again, he could not stop her weeping. Then, impatient to be gone, he tore himself away from her, and for his cowardice she regarded him with scorn, and cried, "What —you leave me?—

"Yes, yes, to me you leave the blame,
The taunt, the blow, the loss, the shame!
Methought some swan had fired my breast,
But out, thou crane, to run were best!
Oh hence! Had I thy spirit known,
Should craven lips have touched my own?"

Vexed by her taunts, Hôdi jeered, and cried back at her—

"The platter was laden with delicate fare—
My leavings are left, the table is bare:
The raiment so costly is tattered and old,
Scarce fit for a beggarman bitten with cold."

With these words he ran away from the place and made his escape. Coming to the river-bank, he went down to drink water, for he was thirsty, and there, when he had put down his hands towards the water, he saw on his fingers the black stain of the collyrium, and he drew them back, saying, "This is the only token of my love which I possess, and I must not wash it away." Thus speaking to himself he stooped down on his knees and drank like a goat.

Hard by there was an old washerwoman who, observing his action, said to his wife, "Who is that man drinking water like a beast?"

"Whether you know him or not," answered she, "I know him well."

"Tell me, then, who he is," said her husband.

"He is Râja Hôdi," answered the woman.

"O fool," returned the washerman, "did you ever see a Râja drinking water like that?"

"I am afraid," replied she, "to tell you the reason of it, lest, if I did, you should kill me."

"What a strange thing to say," said he; "as if I should kill you for telling me a good secret!"

"Take an oath!" said his wife.

"I take an oath of the God who created me," answered he, "that I will not harm you, if you will tell me why the Râja is drinking water like that."

Then his wife replied to him thus—

> "Last night, some wayward wife or daughter
> Enrocked him in her soft embraces;
> So, ox-like, stoops the King for water,
> For love to save love's piteous traces;
> She wept to part, he wiped her tears away,
> The sable stains his finger-tips beray."

The washerwoman, hearing this horrid scandal, became angry, and said to his wife, "No doubt you, woman, have been at the bottom of it; you have been the go-between; otherwise how could you know anything of the Râja's doings?" Thus saying, he took up his mallet and struck her on the back of the head, so that she fell senseless.

"A nice man you are," said she when she came to herself. "I told you what you asked for, and this was your return!"

Now Hôdi had stopped drinking to listen to their colloquy, and, feeling ashamed, he had risen, and was walking away without quenching his thirst. Then the washerman perceiving his anger, thought to himself, "In the morning this Râja will surely kill me." So he said to his wife, "Don't be offended; go to that Râja and bring him back to drink water; otherwise he will never leave me alone."

"That I will not," answered his wife. "By trusting you once I have already suffered enough, and if I bring the Râja back you will say I was his friend, as you have said already."

"Call him back," said her husband, "I will not touch you."

Then, yielding once more, she turned round to Hôdi and cried to him—

"Ne'er cleanse thy teeth with *âkh*, that blistering herb,
And feed not on the baneful flesh of snakes;
Caress not thou a stranger's beauteous boy,
For love will fill thy mouth with foul desire;
However needy, quaff no neighbour's curds,
Drink water rather—it is sweeter far:
Nor covet thou another's couch to win,
For know it never, never can be thine;
So wash away, O King—that stain is curst—
And come, in double handfuls slake thy thirst."

Râja Hôdi, seeing that she was a witch of infinite wisdom, took the woman's advice, and washing his hands he drank his fill. Then approaching the washerman, he said, "O washerman, this woman is not fitted for you, because she is wise, while you are a fool. You had better take a thousand gold pieces, and hand her over to me. I will cherish her like one of my children, and with my money you can marry another."

"Your pardon, sir," said the washerman, "this plan will never do."

So Râja Hôdi left them, and, passing on, he arrived at his own palace. There, choosing a solitary chamber in which stood an old couch, he laid himself down, and began with tears to remember and to lament for the Râni Koklâ.

RÂJA RASÂLU

II. FATE OF KOKLA

It happened, while all these disgraceful doings were going on at the palace of Râja Rasâlu, that the Queen's parrot, having recovered from his fatigue, resumed his search, and at last coming to Jhûlna Kangan in Hazâra he noticed some smoke rising up to the skies. So he flew towards it, and there he saw his dear master's horse picketed under a tree, and Shâdi the parrot sitting on the pommel of the saddle, while in the cool shade of the drooping foliage the King lay sleeping, close to the great cave on Mount Sarbân, near the village of Sarbâd.

Said he to Shâdi, "Wake up your Râja!"

"I have no authority to do so," answered Shâdi, "wake him yourself, since you are the Râni's messenger."

Then the weary bird, dipping his wings in the flowing stream, fluttered them over Rasâlu's face, and the drops fell upon him like soft rain, and he awoke, and seeing his wife's favourite sitting above him on the tree, he said, "Why have you left the house alone?"

Weeping, the bird made answer—

"The Râni killed my *mâina*-birdie,
 Cold it lies upon the floor,
And my reproaches unavailing,
 Only vexed her more and more;
Arise, arise, O sleeping Râja,
 Thieves have forced your palace door!"[1]

Hearing these sorrowful tidings, the King said—

"My *mâinas* number eighty-six,
 My peacocks tell, fourscore;
Well guarded thus, what thievish tricks
 Could force my palace door?"

"Alas!" answered the parrot, "what could the watchmen do?"—

"If goodmen rise at dead of night
 And steal their own possessions,
Then basely tax some luckless wight
 With guilt of their transgressions,
Or if the fence in evil hour
Perforce the barley-crop devour,
 How can the guard
 Keep watch and ward?"

Then Rasâlu arose, and said to his charger, "Now be wary and true, O Folâdi, and take me to my house in a moment."

"I will do so," answered the horse, "but never smite me with your heels."

Mounting, the King rode away towards Khêrimûrti; but in a fit of impatience he forgot his promise, and

[1] Among the Panjâbîs the term for a betrayer is "*thief.*"

plunged his spurs into the horse's side, when at once the animal came to a halt and was turned into a stone.

"Ah, you unfaithful one," cried Rasâlu as he leaped from the saddle, "O you unworthy friend, is this a time for perfidy?"

"Touch me again," said the horse, "and I shall never be able to carry you more—

"O spare your whip, your rowel spare,
Rasâlu, press me not at all;
If ever I was bred from mare,
I'll set you 'neath your castle-wall."

Saying these words, the gallant horse arose, and, taking her master on her back once more, in an instant she reached her destination.

The first act of Râja Rasâlu on dismounting beneath the mangoes was to ascend to his wife's chamber, where he found her lying fast asleep. Leaving her undisturbed, he went down again to the garden and said to Shâdi, his parrot, "Go silently and tenderly and bring me here the ring from off the Râni's hand"—and the bird at once went away and brought it.

Then the king, having tied it round his faithful comrade's neck, commanded him, saying, "Away now to Râja Hôdi! Tell him that Rasâlu has been killed in the forest, and that Râni Koklâ has sent you with this token of love as a sign for him to come and bear her away."

"I go at once, sir," answered the parrot, and taking wing, he flew towards Attock, and reaching the palace, he perched himself in one of the windows. There he was seen by certain of the servants, who said to each other, "See this parrot—it is tame—it looks like some royal pet!"

Overhearing their words, Shâdi answered them, "You are right, I am the companion of a king."

The servants went to the Râja and said to him, "There is a parrot sitting in one of the windows, who says that he has a message for you from the Râni Koklâ."

Râja Hôdi, hearing the name of Koklâ, sprang to his feet and came out instantly, and approaching the parrot, he said, "O faithful bird, what message have you brought for me?" Instead of answering, Shâdi began to shed tears.

"Why are you crying?" asked the King.

"Doubtless," replied the parrot, "you are an honourable man, to form a friendship and then to go away and discard it utterly!"

"What do you mean by that?" said Hôdi.

"This morning," answered the parrot, "the Râni on account of your absence was going to kill herself. I, seeing the dagger in her hand, implored her, saying, 'O wait until I return!' Then she gave me her ring, and bade me for dear life go quickly, and she is waiting for me. But if you do not go to her at once, she will destroy herself."

Hôdi, taking the love-token, said, "But where is your master Rasâlu?"

"God knows," answered Shâdi. "I have searched for him everywhere, but I was unable to find him. I think some demons or giants must have killed him and eaten him."

Râja Hôdi then called for his horse, and mounted, and rode away on the spot. And when they sighted the towers of Khêrimûrti, the parrot addressed him and said, "Let me fly in advance of you to inform the Queen of your arrival."

"Pray do so," answered Hôdi. And the parrot flew to the mango-trees and said to his master, "Your rival is coming. Make ready to meet him!"

When Râja Hôdi drew nigh, the King advanced to meet him and said to him, "Good-morrow, sir; will you walk up?"

Hôdi, on seeing him, became as still as a picture, and he began to make hundreds of excuses, saying, "I have come here by mistake. I did not know whose palace this might be, and I was coming to inquire. I hope you will excuse me."

"Nay," said Rasâlu, "your destiny has brought you here. It is better to betake you to your arms and to use them first on me."

"Sir," answered Hôdi, "I am not your enemy. I was unaware whose fortress this might be, so I was coming to inquire about it. I do not think there is any harm in inquiring!"

"Let this senseless talk go," said Rasâlu, "and use your weapons first! Otherwise you will say, 'Rasâlu smote me treacherously.'"

Hôdi, finding there was no escape from him, took an arrow from his quiver, and, putting it to his bow, he cried, "Now look out, my poisoned dart is coming!" and shot at Rasâlu.

But Rasâlu bent from his horse, and avoided the bolt, which, striking against the castle-walls, broke the stones into shivers. Then said the injured King—

> "O little, little bends the bow-string tight,
> But grandly bends the bow that bends to might;
> The wise man bends to shun the barbèd bolt,
> Who never bends at all is worse than dolt."

But King Hôdi, in fear and dismay, with his fate before him, groaned and said—

> "O little, little can I see of you,
> Rasâlu;
> A gathering mist obscures your form from view,
> Rasâlu;
> With knives of hardened steel my heart is riven,
> It burns like flames within the furnace driven,
> O hear, Rasâlu!"

Deaf to words and deaf to prayers, Rasâlu fitted one of his iron arrows to his mighty bow, and prepared to launch it. At first, to test his adversary's nerve, he grimly made a feint of shooting, when at once the quaking coward slipped behind a mango-tree.

"Ha!" cried Rasâlu, "you are behind the mango-tree, are you? Look out, your final hour has come!"

Drawing the bow to its utmost tension, he let fly the arrow, which drove through the trunk of the tree and pierced through the body of his foe, and fell four hundred yards beyond. So swiftly flew the fatal shaft, that Rajâ Hôdi never so much as felt it, and he said to Rasâlu, "You have missed!"

"I never missed in my life," answered he. "Shake yourself and see!"

And when Hôdi shook himself, he fell down senseless from his horse, and died beneath the mango-trees.

Then the King went forward sword in hand, and, dismounting, he smote off the traitor's head.

As the head rolled aside from the bleeding trunk, the lips of the dead parted, and the quivering tongue uttered the words, "Rasâlu, give me to drink!"

And Rasâlu, as in a dream, lifted his enemy's empty quiver from which the arrows had slipped, and filling it with water from a pool, he held it to the open mouth, and Hôdi drank, and when he had drunk he cried, "O birds, wheeling above me and cleaving the air with your pinions, go to the Queen, my Loved One, and tell her that Hôdi has drunk water from the hands of Râja Rasâlu!"

Then the soul of Râja Rasâlu rejoiced as he said to himself, "To-day I have brought my wife no venison. Yet she shall have venison daintier than ever she tasted before."

The headless corpse lay at his feet. Stripping it of its rich clothing and cutting open the body, he tore out the heart and took it with him to the castle, rolling aside the ponderous gate and closing it again with a giant's strength.

Having made his preparations, he went to the apartments of the Queen, and found her still asleep. "Arise, arise," cried he, "the hour is late!"

Lifting herself from her couch, she looked at him in amazement, for her conscience smote her, and she said to herself, "Does he suspect anything?"

Turning from the threshold and looking into the court, the King noticed that water had been recently drawn in the suspended pitchers of the well by means of the treadle, which was too heavy for the slender strength of his wife to move. There, too, stood his favourite hookah, close to the platform, which was befouled with spittle. Regarding his Râni with a sorrowful air, he said—

"Who has smoked my hookah, Râni,
Who his spittle here did throw;
Who the water lifted, Râni,
Wet's the trough with overflow?"

Then the Queen hastened to answer her lord—

"I have smoked your hookah, Râja,
I the spittle here bestrowed;
I the pitchers lifted, Râja,
And the water overflowed."

But in her mind she said, "Has the parrot betrayed me?"

Then the King looked about him and observed that both the favourite birds' cages were empty. "Ah!" said he, "I hear not the voice of your parrot, and the *mâina* greets not his master! Where are your friends?"

"The voice of the parrot is still," answered she, "and the *mâina* greets not her master, because they are roving abroad. I let out my friends for a flight, and they flew to the mango-trees."

But her mind misgave her, and she thought to herself, "Now the truth must come out!"

Then the King went to the walls and cried, "Miâmittû! Miâmittû!" and the parrot heard and replied from the mango-trees.

"Here I am," said he, "but my body shakes with fear. I dare not enter the palace."

He held out his hand and the parrot flew on to it. "You and the *mâina*-bird," said the King in reproachful tones, "were left by me to guard and protect the Queen. My confidence has been abused. All this evil has been going on, and you did not tell me."

"I could tell you the whole truth," answered the parrot, "but these days are not the days for truth. One of us told the truth, and now his head lies here, and his body there."

When the King saw the *mâina*-bird all ruffled and headless, he picked up the body and took it to the Queen. "Look!" cried he, "I left the *mâina* whole and well—what work is this?"

"He was killed by the parrot," answered she; "ask him—he dares not deny it." And as she spoke the words, she threw at the bird a threatening look.

But the parrot said, "Perhaps it was so; I may have killed the *mâina;* but did the King ever hear of such a thing in the world?" At the same instant he secretly pointed one of his claws at his mistress to signify that the *mâina* had been killed by herself.

After this the King entered his chamber, and as he gazed around him he noticed how the cushions and mats were disordered, and, here and there, scattered about, he saw the stones of his wife's broken necklace of rubies, which she had been vainly endeavouring to string. Then said he—

"Strange footsteps mark my floor, Râni,
My couch is all dispread;
Who forced my chamber-door, Râni,
What thief abused my bed;
What hand the necklace tore, Râni,
Who broke the golden thread?"

And again the Queen made answer—

"Soon as the *mâina* died, Râja,
My beads the parrot tore,
All scared I stepped aside, Râja,
And trod the polished floor;
O never ask me why, Râja,
Your couch is all dispread,
For none came here but I, Râja,
To rest upon your bed!"

But even as she uttered her excuses her heart sank within her, and she said to herself, "Alas, what next!"

Then the King, curbing his rage and his grief, cried, "Enough! Go, Râni, and see to the venison which is preparing in the cook-house, and bake me my bread." And he went out and sat down alone by the well.

When the Queen appeared with the smoking flesh and the cakes of bread, she laid them down on the floor, and the King looked at her and said, "Come, let us eat together once more!"

Like a woman, quite forgetful of her faults, she accepted his feigned kindness, and her spirits rose; but men are different—they nurse their thoughts and keep their suspicions warm.

Then the King put some of the bread to his lips, and said, "To-day my bread is tasteless!"

"Ah!" cried the Queen. "What food, dear Heart, have you brought me here? Methinks no venison was ever so dainty and sweet as this."

Pushing his bread away from him and rising up on the platform, the King answered her thus—

"What food is this so dainty sweet?
Alive he languished at your feet;
Now, dead and gone, he pleases still—
You eat his flesh,—nay, eat your fill!
But O! may she whose heart is proved untrue,
Ascend the funeral pyre, and perish too!"

At that, the bit dropped from the poor Râni's mouth, as

she said to herself, "Ah, I am betrayed, I am betrayed; he knows all! All is over!"

Then, with streaming eyes, she answered her lord—

> "I sit me down, and O you flout me sore,
> I get me up, and still you mock me more;
> Since then my suffering gaze nor help nor hope can spy,
> With him for whom you taunt me, Râja, will I die!"

Saying this, she sprang to her feet and ran quickly up the battlements, whence she beheld, lying far beneath her, the headless body of Râja Hôdi. Then, with a cry, she threw herself over; but before her body had reached the rocks below her breath had gone out of her, and so fell dead the Râni Koklâ.

RÂJA RASÂLU

12. DEATH OF RASÂLU

On witnessing the bloody and pitiful fate of his consort, Râja Rasâlu hastened in his amazement to the gate of the fortress, and passing swiftly out, he descended the rocky steps, and there, stretched by the very corpse of Râja Hôdi whose charger was still champing his bit under the mango-trees, he found the shattered remains of the luckless Koklâ. Strange and wan was the smile which still lingered on her lips, and full of pain and reproach the eyes which seemed to burn into his. Stooping over the dead body of the only woman whom he had ever really, truly, loved, the King is said to have then felt what it was to have loved and for ever to have lost. Taking her up tenderly, he carried her into the palace and laid her down. Both the bodies, his wife's and her lover's, he laid down side by side, say the bards, and he covered them over with the same cloth. Then he considered within himself, "But if I burn them, the disgraceful secret will be known abroad. No! at midnight I will carry them both down and throw them into the river."

Then, seeing the parrot, he said to him, "Your partner is dead and gone, so also is mine. Poor parrot and hapless king! See how the world is passing away!"

After this the King, being very weary, lay down and slept,

and forgetting the two bodies he did not wake until late in the night. It was almost dawn when he approached the river, bearing the dead on his shoulders. Just then he caught sight of the old washerman and his wife going down with a bundle of clothes. So he stepped aside to escape their notice, and dropped the two dead bodies into the river.

As he watched them drifting and sinking in the dark deep waters of the Indus, he overheard the woman saying to her husband, "It is not yet morning. To pass the time tell me a story!"

"What is the use?" answered the husband. "We have to get through the world somehow. Part of our life is over, and part only remains. We have no time to waste over stories."

"But," replied she, "it is not yet daylight, so tell me a tale while the night continues."

Then said the washerman, "Shall I tell you a true story, or some other one?"

"A true story," answered she; "something you have seen and known."

So the man began—

"Hear me, O wife! Not long ago, before I married you, I had another wife. She used to say her prayers five times in the day, and I thought her a treasure. Yet every night she absented herself from my house for at least an hour, until I began to wonder what was her motive. At last I determined to find out. The next time she went away, I followed her, because I said, 'Perhaps she goes out to her prayers, but I should like to see for myself.' I found she visited the grave of a fakîr, and that she prayed to him that I might become blind. When I heard this, I could not help feeling, 'Before my face she respects me, but how false she is behind my back! To-morrow I will be beforehand with her at the shrine, and she shall have her answer.'

"The next night I hid myself in the shrine, and when my wife came and prayed as usual I answered her, 'O woman, for a long time you have prayed to me, this time your prayer is answered. Go home and feed your husband with sweet pudding in the morning and with roast fowl in the evening, and in a week he will be blind.'

"I then got away home as fast as I could run, and

when my wife returned I asked her, 'Where have you been?'

"'I have been in the village giving out the clothes,' answered she.

"The next morning my wife said to me, 'Husband, see, I have here some buttermilk and oil, let me wash your head.'

"I accordingly undressed. But when my wife saw my body, she cried, 'Why, husband, how thin you have become! you are all skin and bone. I must feed you up.' To this I answered 'Good.' So my wife went and made me sweet pudding which I enjoyed. And in the evening she gave me roast fowl which I enjoyed too.

"After three or four days I said to her, 'Wife, I don't know what has happened, my eyes are getting quite dim.' Though she affected to console me, I could easily perceive that she was glad. After the seventh day I said to her, 'Wife, I am stone blind, I can't see a thing.' She, hearing this, set up a hypocritical howl, and going out she visited this saint and that, and offered up counterfeit prayers for my recovery.

"I now took to a stick and acted the blind man to the life. But one day my wife said to herself, 'This may be all a deceit; I must put his blindness to the test.' So she said to me, 'I am going out a-visiting; if I put some barley to dry, will you take care of it?'

"'How can I?' replied I. 'Still, if you will put it on some matting within my reach so that I can feel it from time to time, I will try.'

"This then she did, and I sat by it with my stick in my hand. In a short time I saw my wife slyly creeping towards the grain, and when she got near she felt it. Lifting my stick I gave her such a violent blow on the head that she fell almost senseless, crying out, 'Ah, you have killed me!'

"'Wife, wife,' protested I, 'how could I tell it was you? Did I not say I was blind? I thought there was a bullock or a goat here.'

"This quite convinced my wife that I must be entirely blind, and she continued to feed me as before.

"Now the truth was that she was intriguing with another man whom she used to visit, though at great risk, whenever she found the opportunity. This man she now introduced from time to time into my house. One day, when he was expected, she sought a quarrel with me to get me out of the way. 'Why don't you do something?' said she; 'you are always indoors. Get out, man, and stack some wood!'

"I abused her heartily for her speech and went out. When I returned I spied the man sitting in my chamber and said to myself, 'Aha, my friend is here!' My wife when she saw me coming told him to get into the great mat which was lying rolled up against the wall, and he did so. Going to the cow-house, where I knew there was some rope handy, I returned, groping all the way with my stick.

"'What do you want with that rope?' said my wife.

"Without answering I felt my way to the mat, and tying it up first at one end and then at the other I shouldered it, and said to my wife, 'This trouble which has fallen upon me is more than I can bear. I am now going as a pilgrim to Mecca, and this will serve me as a kneeling mat.'

"I then went out, but she followed me, entreating me to alter my mind. Don't go; don't leave your poor little wife!' implored she.

"But the neighbours said, 'Let the poor man alone. What use is he to you now?' So I got away from her.

"After I had gone two or three miles, the man inside the mat began to struggle and shake.

"'Shake away,' said I, 'you will have reason to shake soon. You think I am blind, but I am not.'

"I now approached a village, and the first thing I observed was a woman baking some bread of fine flour. When the cake was ready she took it inside to the corn-bin where her lover was hiding, and she gave it to him. Then she came out and began baking bread of coarse barley meal. Pretending to be a fakîr, I went up to her and said, 'Mother, make me some wheaten bread with a little butter.'

"'Where am I to get wheaten flour?' answered she. 'Do you not see how poor I am?'

"'Nay, but bake me some,' replied I.

"As we were disputing, her husband came up and said, 'Don't quarrel, woman, with fakîrs!'

"'I am not quarrelling,' said she, 'but this man is

begging for fine bread and butter. Did you ever get such a luxury?'

"When the husband heard this he was angry with me, and said, 'If a barley cake will suit you, take it. But if not, begone!'

"Then said I, pointing to the door, 'They who sit in corn-bins eat fine bread, but beggars mustn't be choosers.'

"'What's this about corn-bins?' cried he. 'This must be looked into.'

"So he went into the corn-bin, and there he found his wife's lover squatting among the grain and eating fine bread and butter. 'You are an honest man, O fakîr,' he cried out to me.

"But he was in such a rage that he drew his knife and would most certainly have cut the fellow's throat, if I had not caught him by the arm and checked him, and brought him out of the place.

"'Look here,' said I, opening my mat, and releasing my prisoner, 'here is another of them. Your fate is not different from mine, nor mine from other men's. Therefore do not kill, but let us both agree to make the best of a bad job, because you see, if Râja Rasâlu in his palace, great and mighty as he is, has the same misfortune as we, and yet bears it patiently, who are we that we should complain?'"

Filled with forebodings, Râja Rasâlu, who had overheard every word, now came forward and said, "I am Râja Rasâlu, the King of all this realm. Ask me for land and you shall have it, or if you want money take it, but tell me how knew you people that such wickedness was being done in my house?"

"And are you not aware," answered the man, "that women are by nature witches and soothsayers? They know or they find out everything, and they have been talking of the doings at Khêrimûrti for days."

Then the King took them both to the castle and gave them money, and to the husband he said, "You are a white-bearded man, old and venerable. Your years entitle you to respect. Therefore come and see me often, and let us converse together." And he sent them away.

He himself after this grew careless and morose, and he ceased to visit the field so often, leaving Folâdi to himself, his life being weary and his heart broken, thinking of his dead wife, of her black ingratitude, and of her dismal fate. Sometimes friends gathered about him in *darbâr* to counsel and to plan, and sometimes turn by turn they told him stories of kings of old, or passed the time in making up riddles. Frequently the old washerman visited him and brought him in news from without, and his favourite parrot strove to console him. But his kingdom was neglected, his conquests forgotten, many of his distant vassals forswore his service, his guards of parrots, peacocks, and *mâinas* mostly abandoned the palace, and in his vast fortress he lived, at least for a king, solitary and alone.

Meanwhile there were wise women at the town of Râja Hôdi who had guessed or divined the secret of Khêri-mûrti. One day Hôdi's brothers were riding past the village well when the women were drawing water for their households, and they overheard one of them saying, "Men value their darling vices more than life."

"What is that which you say?" cried one of the princes.

"I said," answered the speaker, "that men for a woman's love will sacrifice even life itself to gain their ends."

"But what do your words really signify?" said he.

"If the brothers of Râja Hôdi have any sense of their own," replied she, "they have no need to ask."

On hearing this, they galloped up to the palace of Râja Hôdi, and entering the court, they cried, "Where is Râja Hôdi?"

"Ever since the day on which he left the castle to pursue the blue buck," answered one of the attendants, "he has been paying visits across the river in the direction of the castle of Râja Rasâlu. Some days ago, he went out as usual, but he has not yet returned, and we know not what has become of him."

When the brothers heard these tidings they assembled their vassals from all parts, and addressing them, they said, "The King is a prisoner, or else he has been killed in the country of Râja Rasâlu. We must rescue or avenge him. Will you stand by us when we cross the river, or will you go back to your houses?"

Then answered they all with one voice, "Our heads be yours if we do not stand by you to a man."

Now the old washerman used to visit Râja Rasâlu day

by day, because the King delighted in his quaint stories and good sense. About this time he went up to the palace as usual and received his customary welcome. Said the King to him, "What news to-day?"

"Among the women of the village," answered the washerman, "there is a strange rumour, but it may not be true."

"Let me have it," said the King.

"I overheard them talking among themselves," replied he, "and they were saying that as Râja Rasâlu had cut off the head of Râja Hôdi, so his own head would also fall in three days."

When the King understood this he was greatly put out, and rising and pacing the floor, he said, "Have you really heard this?"

"Yes," answered the washerman, "the women have it so, but I know nothing about it."

"I have seen the day when I could singly and alone laugh my foes to scorn," said the king; "and still I have troops, if I can only assemble them in time."

Then he summoned his warder and bade him call out all his followers in the castle. But when they were drawn up, there was not a dozen men left to man the walls.

"Winning or losing a battle is in the hands of God," said he to the old washerman. "But what is one to do with a handful of men like this?"

Vigorously, however, the old warrior prepared for a siege. Something of his former spirit returned upon him as he directed one of his men to gallop out into the country to order his people to gather in strength and to bring in supplies for the defence of his castle at Khêrimûrti, and as he assisted with his own hands to repair the broken battlements and to close up the breaches. Hardly had he completed his task, when the hostile force appeared in sight. They were led by the brothers of Râja Hôdi, and were fully armed with every weapon of war. They swam the river or crossed it on skins; and like bees they swarmed round the hill and sat down beneath the walls of Khêrimûrti. Then passed mutual defiances between the opposing leaders, and the siege began in form. But Râja Rasâlu, though reinforced by fresh supplies of men, soon began to perceive that the struggle was a hopeless one, and that the end could not be far off. Resolving therefore not to be caught like a rat in a trap, but to sell his life as dearly as possible, he ordered his men to prepare for a sally. That night he piled up faggots in the chambers of Râni Koklâ, and with his own hand set the palace on fire, and, when the flames leaped up into the darkness of the midnight sky, the besiegers saw them and wondered.

The next morning he led his followers down the rocky steps, and, as he passed through the Queen's garden, he looked at the mango-trees, and cried—

> "O flushed with fruit, or bare of bough,
> Fruit may ye never form again,
> Dead is Koklâ, her place is void,
> And flaming red the fires remain!"

Then with a rush he descended to the plains and met his enemies hand to hand. There the battle raged with fury on both sides for seven days and seven nights. King Rasâlu fought like a lion, and many a foe went down beneath his mighty arm, never to rise again. At last his men were all of them killed, and the king himself, wearied out with the long fight, covered with wounds, and hemmed in by increasing numbers, was slain by an arrow nine yards long, which pierced his neck. And when the fight was over, his enemies smote off his head and carried it back with them in triumph to the castle of Râja Hôdi.

And thus, according to most of the story-tellers of the Upper Panjâb, perished their national hero Râja Rasâlu, having survived his might and outlived the fame and glory of his great exploits.[1]

[1] Some say that Rasâlu never died at all, but that he passed over or descended into the Indus, and that, like Arthur and other mythical characters, he is to come again.

[This concluding chapter, like the first of the series of the Rasâlu Legends, is partly made up from fragments collected from different villages.]

Collected from bards in the Rawal Pindi District, 1877–82.

X

OF THE WISE LUMBARDÂR

A LARGE earthen chatty, or jar, half filled with corn, was once standing in the courtyard of a farmhouse, when a horned sheep coming by thrust his head into it and began to enjoy himself. When he had satisfied his hunger, however, he found himself unable, owing to the size of the neck of the chatty, to draw forth his head again, so that he was thus caught in a trap. The farmer and his servants perceiving this were sadly perplexed. "What's to be done now?" said they. One of them proposed that the lambardâr, or village headman, whose wisdom was in every one's mouth, should be requested to help them in their difficulty, which was no sooner said than done. The lambardâr was delighted. He at once mounted his camel, and in a few minutes arrived at the spot. But the archway into the yard was low, and he on the top of his camel was high, nor did it occur to him or to any one else that the camel should be left outside. "I cannot get in there," said he to the farmer; "pray knock the doorway down!" and accordingly the arch was destroyed, and the wise man entered.

Having dismounted and gazed profoundly at the imprisoned ram, he suddenly exclaimed, "This matter is a mere trifle. Fetch me a sword." So the sword was brought, and taking it in his hand he cut off the animal's head at a single blow. "There," cried he, "is your sheep, and here is your vessel of corn. Take them away."

By this time the whole village had assembled, and every one began to murmur his praises. But a farm-servant, who was reputed cunning, observed, "But the sheep's head is still in the jar! *Now* what are we to do?"

"True," answered the lambardâr. "To you this affair seems hard; but to me the one thing is just as easy as the other."

With this he raised a great stone and smashed the vessel into a thousand pieces, while the people clapped their hands with joy. No one was more astonished than the farmer. It is true his gateway was ruined, his grain spilt, his jar broken, and his stock-ram killed. These things, however, gave him no concern. He had been rescued from a serious difficulty, and so the fame of that lambardâr became the envy of all the surrounding villages.

From Ghâzî.

XI

OF THE BANEYRWÂL AND THE THIEF

ONCE upon a time a little Baneyrwâl, holding his two fingers to his mouth, happened to look into a tub, and there perceived his own image reflected in the water. "Mother, mother," cried he, "there is a child in this tub begging for bread."

"Listen to that now," said the mother to her husband. "Look into the tub, man, and see if there is any one there."

So the husband looked in and at once exclaimed, "Wife, wife, there is no child; but I see an old villain of a thief, and when we are all asleep he will certainly jump out and murder us in our beds!"

Picking up a stone in the utmost alarm, the man hurled it into the tub, intending to strike the robber dead. Then he cautiously approached the tub once more, but failing to see anything but the tossing water, he said to his wife, "That thief must have been a very cunning rascal. He has escaped I don't know where, but he is not likely to trouble *this* house again."

From Ghâzî.

XII

OF THE TIGER AND THE HARE

A JUNGLE TALE

In a certain forest there once lived a fierce tiger, which was in the habit of hunting down the rest of the animals for mere sport, whether hunger impelled him thereto or not. All the animals, therefore, met together by common consent to consider their grievances. "Let us agree," said the jackal, "that one of us shall be chosen by lot day by day as a sacrifice to the tiger."

"All right," assented the others; "but first let us see the tiger, and let us offer him a petition."

So they all marched together to the tiger's den, and humbly besought him to refrain from indiscriminate slaughter, and to be satisfied with the animal which should voluntarily come to him day by day. "Do not hunt us poor fellows down," said they, "for one of us will always come to be devoured by you, and this plan will save you trouble as well."

"No, no," cried the tiger; "I shall use my claws and my teeth, and so eat my food."

"But," answered the animals, "God has said that we ought to live in hope."

"True," answered the tiger; "but he has also bidden every one to earn his own bread."

At last, after much argument, the tiger suffered himself to be persuaded, and made a solemn promise to remain at home in his den. Thenceforward every day an animal chosen by lot went to the den to be eaten. But when the hare's turn came, she flatly said, "I shall not go; I shall live my life." In vain the other animals tried to persuade or coerce her. Twelve o'clock, the tiger's usual feeding time, came and went, then came one, two, and three. At last the hare suddenly started up, and exclaiming, "Now I'm off!" she set out for the den. As she drew near she noticed the famished tiger tearing up the earth in fury, and heard him bellowing, "Who is this ridiculous hare to keep me waiting?"

"But I have an excuse," protested the hare.

"What excuse can you have?" demanded the tiger.

"To-day," said the hare, "it was not my turn to come at all. It was my brother's. I am thin, but my brother is plump and fat. My brother had started for your den, but on the way he fell in with another tiger which wanted to eat him, and, in fact, he caught him and was carrying him away, when I came up and said to him, 'This country is not your country, but the country of another tiger who will punish you.' To which the strange tiger answered, 'You go at once, and call that tiger of yours out, and then he and I shall have a fight.' So here I am, sir, sent to deliver his challenge. Come and kill the villain for us."

Full of rage and jealousy, the tiger said to the hare, "Lead on!" and the pair started forth to seek the rival tiger. As they went along the hare began to look alarmed and shrink back, and made as though she would have hidden herself in a thicket. "What is the matter now?" inquired the tiger. "What are you afraid of?"

"I am afraid," answered she, "because the other tiger's den lies close in front of us."

"Where—where?" cried the tiger, peering forward with searching eyes. "I see no den whatever."

"It is there—see!" answered the hare; "almost at your very feet!"

"I can see no den," said the tiger. "Is there no means of persuading you to come forward and show me the place?"

"Yes," replied the hare, "if you will please carry me under your arm."

So the tiger lifted the cunning hare under his arm, and, guided by her directions, he unexpectedly found himself at the edge of a large deep well. "This is the den I told you of," whispered the hare. "Look in and you will see the robber."

Standing on the brink and looking down into the clear depths, the tiger saw at the bottom the reflected image of himself and the hare, and imagining that he saw his enemy in proud possession of the fat brother, he dropped the nimble hare, which easily escaped, and with a roar he leaped down, where, after struggling in the water for many hours, he finally expired, and thus the forest was at last rid of the tyrant.

From Ghâzî.

XIII

OF THE GREEDY MONKEY

ONCE upon a time a monkey noticed some wheat which had fallen into a small hollow in a rock. Thrusting in his hand, he filled it with the grain, but the entrance was so narrow that he was unable to draw it out without relinquishing most of his prize. This, however, he was unwilling to do, greedily desiring to have it all. So the consequence was that he remained without any, and finally went hungry away.

From Ghâzî.

XIV

CONCERNING REPENTANCE

A CERTAIN priest asked one of his parishioners, "Which is the older, your beard or yourself?"

"I am the elder, of course," answered the man.

"Your beard seems to have changed," said the holy man, "for it was black before and now it is white, yet you are still the same. When will you begin to change—when cease to do evil and learn to do well?"

From Ghâzî.

XV

THE PREACHER CONFOUNDED

A Muhammadan priest, seated in his mosque, was once holding forth to some villagers on the torments of the life to come. When in the full flow of his eloquence, he observed one of his auditors, a poor farmer, weeping profusely.

"Ah, you sinner!" cried the preacher, interrupting his discourse, "you are crying, are you? My words have struck home to you, have they? You begin to think of your sins, do you?"

"No, no," answered the man; "I was not thinking of my sins at all. I was thinking of my old he-goat, that grew sick and died a year ago. Such a loss! Never was a beard so like the beard of my old he-goat as yours."

Hearing these words, the villagers began to laugh, and the priest took refuge in the Korân.

From Hazro.

XVI

STORY OF PRINCE AHMED AND THE FLYING HORSE

Once there was a king who had a son named Ahmed. He was only a youth, and his delight was to ramble about the bazaars of the town. There he became friendly with four other boys, the sons of a goldsmith, an ironsmith, an oilman, and a carpenter respectively. He used to work and play with them, and they became his companions. They were so clever that men used to call them the children of magic. By-and-by the vizier heard of these things, and said to the King, "Your son has chosen companions out of the very bazaars, four boys who are leading him to destruction." So the King sent a guard and had all the four boys arrested and thrown into prison. But the Prince intervened, and said, "Grant them a hearing; do not condemn them without a trial." When they were brought into the King's court, the little goldsmith said, "Give us time to clear ourselves from the charges of the vizier. After eight days we shall all appear again, and the King shall judge us." So they were reprieved for eight days, and at the end of the time they assembled to show their skill. The little goldsmith brought six brazen fish, which he cast into the King's tank, and they swam about, and the courtiers threw crumbs of bread to them, which they caught and devoured. The blacksmith brought two large iron fish, which swallowed up all the brazen ones. The oilman brought two artificial giants, which fought together on the plain until they were separated by Prince Ahmed. The carpenter brought a large wooden horse, furnished with a secret spring, and Prince Ahmed leaped on to its back; and when he had touched the spring, it mounted like lightning into the air, and was out of sight in a moment.

The King, who had been pleased at first, now flew into a rage, and seizing the carpenter, he shook him, and cried, "Villain, bring back my son!"

"O King, that I cannot do," said the carpenter. "Spare my life, and the Prince will return to you in all safety in two months."

The two months were granted, and all four boys were put into chains to await their death in case the Prince did not return.

Meanwhile the flying horse, having carried Prince Ahmed five hundred leagues, alighted on the terrace-roof of a magnificent palace, and there the Prince saw, reclining in the moonlight, a most beautiful young princess. Instantly he fell in love with her, and when she looked up and saw a handsome stranger standing by, she also fell in love with him. So the Prince and she went down into the palace together and had a talk, and when he left her he mounted his flying horse and flew to the top of a large *tâlli*-tree beyond the bounds of the palace grounds. There he disjointed his horse and hung the pieces to the branches, and, climbing down the tree, he lodged at the house of an old woman. But every night, when darkness had set in, he used to climb the *tâlli*-tree, mount his wooden horse, and fly to the palace roof. At last the Princess's confidential slave girl began to whisper the secret, and some one went to the King, and said, "Some thief pays nightly visits to the palace." So the King put on double guards, and every one was challenged going in and coming out, but still the rumour reached the ears of the King, "Some thief comes to your daughter's palace."

Then the King summoned his vizier and said, "No one but a woman is competent to unravel this mystery." So a wise woman was consulted by the King and the vizier, who advised that the stairs of the palace, to the very roof, should be covered with slime.

The next night, when Prince Ahmed arrived on the terrace and attempted to descend, he slipped down several steps, and, suspecting a trick, he made his escape, left his horse on the top of the *tâlli*-tree, and made for the hut of the old woman. The next morning he sent for a washerman, and gave him his soiled clothing to clean.

Meanwhile the King proclaimed, by beat of drum, that every inhabitant of the town should appear in the palace yard. The washerman, desirous of cutting a figure, donned the gorgeous clothing of the Prince, and when the people assembled, he was at once singled out, and then it was noticed that his coat was stained with slime. So the King called for the executioner, and cried, "String him up!" But the washerman fell on his face, and said, "My lord, I am only a poor washerman, and this clothing is not mine at all. It belongs to another, who sent it to be cleaned. Let the officers come, and I will give him into their hands."

So he took the officers to the old woman's hut, and there they found Prince Ahmed, and dragged him to the King, who ordered his instant death. Meanwhile, however, the Princess had sent a secret message to him, saying, "Offer the King a ransom. I will provide the sum, and save your life." But he sent word back, "No ransom shall I offer, but do you meet me in half-an-hour on the roof of the palace."

Then the soldiers dragged off the Prince to the *tâlli*-tree, and round his neck they put a halter, and they were just going to hang him, when he besought them, saying, "Please let me go up to breathe the air of the world for the last time;" and having bribed them with two gold mohurs, he began to ascend the tree. Having reached the top, where he was hidden from view, he quickly put the pieces of his horse together and flew to the terrace, where, seizing the Princess, he flung her into the saddle before him, and touching the spring he passed rapidly through the air in the sight of both King and people, and in a moment he arrived at his father's house.

After this the four boys were released from prison and made governors of provinces; while the Prince and the Princess, being married at last, lived together in the enjoyment of every pleasure.

From Torbela.

XVII

ADVENTURES OF NEK BAKHT[1]

Many years ago, when Nek Bakht was a boy, his father died, and he became King in his place. This lad took to hunting as his constant amusement, spending many days away from home. Now it was customary in that country for each courtier to follow singly his own game until he had brought it down. It was also the custom at the close of the day when all had returned from the field for the King to say, "Is there any king greater than I?" and for the ministers to answer, "None." The young King's daily pride, however, was one day brought low. He was following a deer, and he rode and rode till he was out of sight, when God ordered an angel to abolish space in such a way that in one moment the King found himself five hundred miles away in the territory of another king. He was now merely an ordinary mortal like any one else, but in a worse plight than most, for he was seized as a criminal. All that country indeed was in terror on account of a notorious robber, so that the gates of the city were closed at sunset and kept closed all night. Therefore when just before the time of closing Nek Bakht entered the city armed as he was, all the people cried, "Here is the

[1] Nek Bakht—Good Luck.

robber!" and banging the gates behind him, they unhorsed him, bound him, and carried him off to the King. And when the King heard what they had to say, he said, "Cut off his hands, and let him sit in the market-place." But some said, "What is the use of that?" Others said, "Better to hang him at once." So the King ordered him to be cast into prison, and he was taken to a cell. There he devoted himself to the study of the Korân, and one day he came to the passage, "God is almighty. He can set up and put down." This passage he used to deride whenever his vizier reminded him of it, but now it comes home to him, and he begins to weep bitterly. And when the jailor saw him thus he said, "O young man, you were just now reading and now you are crying. Why are you crying?"

"I am crying," answered he, "at my hard lot, and at the difference in my estate, comparing myself now with what I used to be."

"If you will tell me what you mean by that saying," said the jailor, "I will tell the King for you."

"If I do tell you," said Nek Bakht, "what good will it do? God has not sent me help, and how can you?" Then he said, "This part of the Korân I used to scorn when I was a King, for I said, 'Who can bring me down?' And did not my ministers tell me day after day that there was no king greater than I? Yet here are you, a poor man, earning a few pence daily, and here am I, and if you gave me two kicks, what could I do? Is it strange therefore to find me crying?"

Then the jailor went and told the King that his prisoner was not the robber at all, but Nek Bakht the great King. And the King began to feel afraid, because he used to be subject to the Prince's father, and he hastened to the prison with all his ministers, and begged pardon for his mistake.

"You are not to blame," answered the Prince, "but my own pride only. I have learnt a lesson."

"I am your vassal, as I was your father's," said the King, putting his hands together. "Be not therefore angry, nor bring armies to punish me."

"That I shall never do," said he. "But now, as I have been long absent from my people, give me an aid in men and horses to enable me to return, lest meanwhile some one may have seized my kingdom."

So troops and treasure were freely given, and Nek Bakht rode out at their head, and when he got nigh the border he began inquiring, "Who is the King?" and the people said, "The King was devoured by a wild beast;" others answered, "He has gone away, no one knows where;" while some others again said, "Wherever he is, he is chasing a deer." Thus he came, he and his army, close up to the capital, and his old wazîr rode forth to meet him, and recognized him as the lost King as soon as ever he saw him. "And how has my kingdom fared, since I went?" asked the Prince.

"As it was when you left it," answered the wazîr, "so is it now."

After that he entered his house, giving order that his own troops should receive those of his vassal and entreat them well. Then one day, when he sat on his throne, his wazîr said to him, "O King, you remember the day I used to say to you, 'God is Almighty, He can raise and He can abase'?"

"Yes," said the King, "I have experienced the full force of those words." The King also said, "Hunting I give up for ever. I will apply myself to other matters, and I will merely ride out day by day for exercise."

One day, as he was riding along the bank of the river, he observed an old woman stooping down by the edge of the stream, and going near, he saw that she was engaged in picking up bits of grass, tying them in small loose bundles, and throwing them on to the water, and he noticed that she kept watching them as they floated away. So he drew nearer still and said to her, "What are you doing?"

"Hush!" answered the wise woman. "I am reading fortunes."

"And whose fortune is figured in the last bundle?" asked the King.

"That bundle," said she, "carries the fortune of the King of this country, whose name is Nek Bakht."

Now it was seen that the handful of grass floated hither and thither among the currents, and that, after an uncertain course, it finally reached the opposite side. Then said the King, "That bundle has crossed to the further bank, but what is the meaning of it?"

"The King's life," answered the woman, "will be a long one, but full of troubles."

Then began the King to be sorrowful, and when he returned to the palace his countenance was altered, and his face downcast, so that the wazîr asked him what was the matter.

"Do not seek to know," answered the King.

"You are but a youth," said the wazîr. "Your father confided everything to me, much more should you."

"My life," said the King, "is to be like a bit of hay tossed about on troubled waters, no peace, no rest, but trial on trial."

"Nay," answered the wazîr, "who can tell that but God only?"

Then the King told him of the old woman, whom he found telling fortunes to herself by the river-side, and of the little bundles of dry grass, and what she said to him, to which the wazîr replied, "O King, all that is but fancy and illusion. If she could tell that, she would be a queen herself."

Some days after the King once more rode out, and as he approached the same spot he saw the old woman engaged in the very same thing. Again he addressed her, as before, saying, "Mother, what are you doing?"

"Just wait a minute," answered she. "Two spirits have come to me just now, for they want me to decide a case for them. Their names are Fate and Destiny.[1] Fate is saying, 'I shall cause the King, and the Princess of the Kingdom of Flowers, to meet.' And Destiny says, 'But what if I shall not allow you to do so?' 'I shall manage it!' cries Fate. 'Nay,' replies Destiny, 'you shall not, for when she comes to bathe in the river, I shall drown her there and so break your power.' Therefore," continued the old woman, "do you retire, until I have settled the business, which will take time."

So spake she to the King, who left her watching her wisps of straw, and went back moodier than ever to the palace. And the wazîr remarking his looks, said to himself, "Whenever the King rides towards the river now, he returns melancholy." And he said, "What is the matter?"

Then the King began again to relate to the wazîr his adventure of the day. "I found two voices, Fate and

[1] Fate—A ruthless objective Power, working capriciously from without. Destiny—A subjective Influence, impelling from within in obedience to law.

Destiny, contending together," said he, "and Fate has fixed it that I am to marry the Princess of the Kingdom of Flowers. And I am troubled, for what perils may I not have to go through, what anguish to suffer, before that can be!"

"O foolish King," said the vizier, "can even Fate accomplish the impossible? The Princess spoken of lives millions of miles away, and do what you will you can never meet."

Some days after, the King again rode towards the river, and again found the old woman there. This time she spoke first, saying, "O son, who are you?"

"I am merely the son of a khân," answered he.

"You have often come here," said she, "and as you do come so much, I now tell you that within fifteen days Nek Bakht will be married to the young Princess I told you about."

Then the King returned to the city more melancholy than ever, and calling his wazîr he began to tell him the day's woeful news. "Within fifteen days it is written that I must marry her," said he. "Since hearing that, I have been tormented, for how is it possible for me even to see her? Is space to be again annihilated, is the very earth to disappear again under my feet, are there more imprisonments in store for me, or what?" And he went in, distressed beyond words, expecting he knew not what misfortune.

Now it had so happened that in the kingdom of the Princess a decree had been in force for some time, ordering that all female children should be destroyed the moment they were born, and that any woman sparing her infant-daughter should be hanged. Only one woman had dared to disobey that cruel law, and only one little girl had been saved from death. For when she was born, her mother hid her so cunningly that she grew up to be eight or nine years old. One day she was playing about, when who should come in but the King. She tried to hide, but it was too late, and the King said to her mother, "Whose child is that?"

"If my life is spared," answered she, "I will tell."

"Take your life and answer," said he.

"Then I say," replied the woman, "this child is your own daughter."

"Ah!" cried the King. "So, after all, I have been disobeyed by you! But what to do now is more than I can say."

So he went off to his ministers and reported the matter to them. "Did I not order that all the little girls should be killed? How then do I find one of them living?"

Then the ministers put their heads together and considered, and, after much time spent in argument, they unanimously agreed on a verdict. So they sought out the King and advised him, saying, "Have the Princess shut up in a chest and thrown into the river." Then came the carpenter and made a box to fit the Princess, and her mother did not forget to line it handsomely and put food in it. And the child gets inside, and a man takes the box on his head to carry it to the river, and as it leaves the palace the mother goes to the lattice and looks and looks! But the man, who was a slave, had pity, and instead of putting earth in the chest to sink it as he was ordered, he sealed it round with dough, so that when it was committed to the current and went floating away, a great fish came and swallowed it up. And the fish having swallowed the chest, headed down the river, and it swam and swam and swam, until it came close to the very place where lived the old woman. And it was by this trick that Fate had his own way. For at that spot there was a back-water into which the fish turned, and in which it made so great a splash that the villagers soon saw it, and coming down with sticks and clubs tried their best to kill it. But while they were still engaged in that work, Nek Bakht himself came riding by, and urging his horse into the water he speared the fish, which was then dragged up high and dry. "Carry the fish to my cooks," said the King, "let them cut off the head and the tail thereof for the people, but the midst of the fish let them keep for the King's table."

As it was the King himself who gave the order, his order was at once obeyed, and the fish was taken to the royal kitchen. But when the chief cook took his knife to cut the monster open, he heard a voice which said, "Take care, I am a human being!" The cook looked very puzzled, but, thinking his ears had deceived him, he raised the knife again, when the same voice cried, "Take care, I am a human being!" Being more puzzled than ever, he called in one of his men and told him to listen, and again the same voice came from the inside of the fish. Then that man who had been called in said to the chief cook, "That fish must have eaten something!" So they went very carefully to work, and in the very centre of the fish they found no box at all, but a beautiful little lady. The wonderful news was at once despatched to the King, who ordered the girl to be brought to him, and who asked her, saying, "Who are you?" She, however, being a very wise girl, thought it best not to say too much, so she only told a little of her story, and the King sent her away, putting her under charge of some of his handmaidens. But within a few days the wazîr himself said to the King, "The girl is very handsome. Why not marry her?" And the King did so, and called her Dilârâm,[1] and the fifteen days were completed.

When the wedding was over, the King suddenly bethought himself and said, "This is the day I was to have married the Princess of the Kingdom of Flowers. But no, it has not been so, and it is not so, and now I must go and see the old woman."

So he rode down to the bank of the river, and there the old woman was working her spells as usual. "What is your business now?" said he.

"Have patience, O sir," she answered him. "Fate and Destiny have again come to me, and they are talking of the same thing. Listen and you will hear what they say!"

And the King listened and heard the voices. Fate said, "Those two I am going to marry together." "No, no," said Destiny. Suddenly Fate cries, "But I have married them already!" Thereupon both voices addressed the old woman and said, "You stand umpire between us two! Go at once to the palace and see which of us is right!" And all the time the King was standing a little way off, listening to the dispute. Then said the woman, "Agreed! I will go, but first let Fate declare by what means he brought the marriage about."

"I managed it so," said Fate.—"I drove the King of that country to a fury when I led him to the chamber in which the Princess was, so she was shut up in a box, she was thrown into the river, and I caused a great fish to swallow her up, and to bring her to this very lake; and the fish was opened, and then the Princess stepped forth

[1] *Dilârâm*—Heart's-ease.

to marry the King, and she did marry the King. Go and see for yourself!"

At this moment the King advanced quite close and said, "What tidings to-day, O old woman?"

"Only what I have already told you," answered she. "I am now going to the palace to find out particulars."

"No need," said Nek Bakht. "Your prophecy has come true, it is all fulfilled, and the King has married the Princess."

"Really?" said she, "is it really true?"

"Yes," said the King, "all is finished and over this very day."

"Alas! alas!" then said the woman. "I am sorry for it."

"Sorry?" said he. "But where is the cause for sorrow?"

"Alas!" said she again, "I am sorry because the young King's mother is a sorceress and so also is that princess. Now that there are two of them, what will become of him?"

So the King turned back more miserable than ever. "I cannot kill my wife," said he to himself. "It would be no use, for my mother is also a witch." And as he drew nigh to the city the wazîr met him, and observing his disturbed countenance, asked him the reason. So he tells him all his new trouble, and how not only his young wife is a witch, but his mother also. The wazîr was grieved. "O foolish King," said he, "this your mother lived with your father for many a year, and never was such a thing ever heard about, and as for your wife, she is yet but a child. What can she know of magic?"

Nevertheless the King believed the words of the old woman, and going into a chamber apart, he lay down. By-and-by his mother came to him and said, "O son, why are you so sorrowful? Cast your eye on your fair young Queen, see how beautiful she is, and how truly she loves you!"

"Leave me," said he to his mother. "I am not well. To-morrow we shall see."

"God will make you well, my son," said his mother. And she left him there. But a little after he looked out, and saw his mother and his wife working spells at a *pipal* tree, and he felt afraid.

Some time passed away, until one day the King was minded to ride to the river again. He did so and found the old woman at her old occupation, watching her bundles of dry grass. Just then her two spirits, Fate and Destiny, were again conversing one with the other. Says Fate, "In a kingdom beyond the sea lives another princess, and in four days Nek Bakht will go there and marry her." "Yes, that indeed will happen," replies Destiny, "but in the meantime he will have trouble enough."

Having heard so much, the King came forward and said, "Old woman, what occupies you now?"

"The same old thing," answered she. "I am only acting the part of arbiter between the two powers, and sifting the true from the false. As for the King, poor man, for him I grieve, for in four days he will be far away and married again, and still he will be vexed by plaguing cares."

These words sounded in the ears of the King like a sentence of Death, and so beset him all the way home, that he took no heed of his mare, where or how she was going. And when, in the bazaar, a certain woman bearing two water-pitchers on her head came by, he knocked against her, and as the shock overbalanced her, down fell the pitchers and the water was wasted. As she was only a poor woman she lost her temper and cried out, "He is jumping his horse in the street, and he calls himself a king, and yet he does not know the tricks they play in his own house, fine as he is!"

On hearing these words the King woke up and touched bridle, but the woman had passed on. She entered a house and closed the door, but the King followed, and said to an attendant, "Set a mark on that house for me!" And a mark was set on it that the King might know it again. Then he went on, and the wazîr saw him and said, "O King, before you used to look sorrowful, but to-day the very colour has left your face! What new trouble has come to pester you now?" The King beckons to the vizier to come near to him, and he tells him the story of the woman whose jars he had broken and whose water he had spilt. "Her words were strange," said he. "Who made her so hardy to seek to undo me thus?"

Presently the King again spoke and said, "Let us both disguise ourselves and sally out, let us go to her house!" So both dressed themselves up as fakîrs, in old garments of many colours, all shreds and patches, and with bowl and staff went forth. The woman took them for mendicants, and said to them, "Shall I give you flour, or would you like some cakes?"

"We will have neither," answered the wazîr, "but we'll just come in and have a smoke, and a talk about something we have in our minds."

So they entered, and as they squatted over the hookah, the woman looked at them and at once recognized the King. "I suppose you have come for explanations," said she.

"Some women are wiser than others," answered the King.

"In two days," said she, "the daughter of the King of a certain land is to be married, and her name is Azîz.[1] With the King of that land your wife and mother intrigue, and in a moment they can be with him. They go and come the same day. How do they do it? They sit on a *pîpal* tree, and the *pîpal* tree carries them there and back."

"Can these things be?" said the wazîr, and the King remembered how he saw both the rânis doing magic to a *pîpal* tree hard by the palace, and he said, "That *pîpal* tree I know."

"Well," said she, "if you doubt my word, have a hole made in the tree, and sit in it, and you will go too."

Then they went away and no one knew them. And when Nek Bakht got back to the palace, he ordered his wife and mother to remain in their own apartments, and he shut them in. Then he called a cunning carpenter who made a chamber in the tree, and it had a door to it, and when the door was closed, no one could see the difference, for it looked the same as the rest.

Now as soon as the two days were up, he was lying on his bed, when he overheard his wife and mother talking. "The hour has come," said they, "let us start now!"

"Your husband the King is asleep," said the elder Queen. "Here, take these magic mustard-seeds, and drop them on the King's breast. They will sprout, and the roots will fasten him down."

So Dilârâm Begam took the mustard-seeds and went into the chamber where the King was feigning sleep. And

[1] *Azîz Begam*—Beloved Lady.

she said, "Alas, this is my dear, dear husband! I will not sprinkle his breast with them, but only drop them round the edges of his bed." When she returned, her mother said to her, "Have you done it?"

"Yes, it is done," answered the wife.

"Come along then," said her mother. "First let us bathe and dress, and then go to the *pîpal* tree, when by the power of God and magic the *pîpal* tree will fly."

Now, when they had gone to the bath, the King arose, and creeping through the branches of the mustard-trees he got to the *pîpal* tree first, and entering into the chamber, he closed the door and kept quiet. By-and-by came the ladies and got on the top of the tree. And they uttered magic words over a red thread, and tied it round the tree. Then they addressed the tree, and said, "By order of God and magic, ascend!" And the tree, with leaf and branch, and with its roots attached, flew off to the city of the kingdom over the sea, where it settled in a place outside the gates. Then both mother and wife got down and hastened away. Nek Bakht also opened the door of his chamber and came out and followed them, and he saw that they made for the King's palace, which they entered by a wicket, and then the door was closed and they were lost to view.

As he stood there awhile, he heard the sound of music and tom-toms, and presently a marriage-procession swept by. "What wedding is this?" And some one told him it was the wedding of the King's daughter, the Princess Azîz. So he joined himself to the party and passed in with the rest.

Now, it so happened that the bridegroom was the ugliest man in the whole world. His party knew well how ugly he was, and that the bride's party would tease him about his ugliness and give him no rest. So they all decided that he should be married by proxy, and that he should not appear at all. "Let us choose out some handsome youth," said they, "to represent him, and then he will escape the flouts and the jeers of the girls." And when they looked round and saw Nek Bakht, they all declared for him, and begged him to go through the ceremony, which after much persuasion he at last consented to do, and he looked most handsome, so that none of the courtiers could touch him. The people, too, were astonished, and they ran and said to the King, "So handsome is the bridegroom that no one can look at him, nay, when he showed himself to the bridesmaids, they all swooned away for very trouble."

This news heard also his mother and his wife, for they were then with the King, and the mother said to the wife, "Go, child, and see him. Surely he cannot be more handsome than Nek Bakht!" And the girl went to have a peep, and she saw them both, the bride and the proxy bridegroom, going through the ceremony. And she gazed and gazed as they dropped their rings into a bowl of milk, and saw the bridegroom take out his ring and put it on the finger of the bride, and the bride take out her ring and put it on the finger of the bridegroom. And she went back and said, "So handsome is he that I can see no difference between him and Nek Bakht. The one is the very image of the other."

By this time the ceremony was over, and Nek Bakht, having played his part, walked out before King and courtiers and wife and mother, unrecognized, and, remembering the counsel of the old woman, determined to hasten to the *pîpal* tree. So, turning to the wedding-party, "Here, take these trappings, I am off!" said he, and leaving with them his wedding garment, he ran to the tree first, shut himself in, and bided events. Towards evening came his mother and the Princess Dilârâm his wife. Nor did they suspect anything, but they got on the top of the tree as before, and pronounced the magic words, "By the order of God and magic, ascend!" when at once the tree rose and in a single breath it reached their home and sank into its own place. Entering the palace, the ladies went to the bath, while the King escaped to his own room, and forcing his way through the mustard-trees, lay down on his bed and feigned sleep. The first thing the Queen-mother did, when she returned from the bath, was to light a candle, and then she went into the King's room, where she saw with horror that the mustard-seed had been sown on the edges of the bed, and she noticed the opening in the mustard-trees through which the King had crept. Going to her daughter, she cried, "All's up! You have worked foolishness. O how wrong you have been! It was Nek Bakht himself and none other, who was with us at the wedding, for who else in the whole world could face Nek Bakht for beauty?" Then she hastened back again to the King's chamber and peeped through the leaves, scanning her son's appearance and the colour of his hands. "It is only too true," said she when she got back. "All his fingers are red with the stain of the henna. Now, if we do not contrive something, he will kill us both."

"O what shall we do?" said the wife.

"There is one way and one only," answered she. "Leave it to me and you will see!"

So she takes water of magic, and throws it over the face of her son, and at once he becomes unconscious. And all the time she keeps upbraiding her daughter and saying, "It is all your doing, disobedient one. Why did you not sow the mustard-seed on his chest as I ordered?" She then takes a silk thread from her hair, and, with mutterings, ties it round her son's ankle, and he turns into a peacock, and they take the peacock and set it loose in the garden.

Some time after this the Queen-mother went to the old wazîr and said, "Where is the King? He must have disappeared again." Search was made for him, but he was not to be found, and the wazîr governed, thinking he would again return as at the former time.

Now in the kingdom over the sea there was commotion as soon as it was discovered in the morning that the mock bridegroom was not the real bridegroom after all. The ugly Prince had not a chance, as the Princess spurned him from her, and bade him begone. Then she looked at the ring on her finger, and saw it was a signet ring engraven with the name of Nek Bakht, and she told the King, who got into a rage and sent messengers everywhere through the world to look for the kingdom of Nek Bakht. And the messengers set out. But the Princess built a large caravanserai and invited merchants from every part to put up there. And over the gateway she built herself a bower in which she dwelt, for she hoped by that means to hear all the foreign gossip and to get tidings of the runaway bridegroom. It so happened about that time that a company of merchants visited the capital of Nek Bakht. Before leaving, these people stole the peacock from the King's garden, and brought it back with them to the very *serâi* in which lived the Princess Azîz, who, when she saw the peacock, gave them their price and bought it, and the bird became her companion. One day when the rain was falling, she called the peacock to her, and laid it in her lap. As she was caressing it, she caught sight of the red thread which bound its foot, and taking a knife she severed it, when in a moment the peacock disappeared and she saw Nek Bakht standing before her, no longer a bird, but a man. Then was she glad; and her father ordered general rejoicings and gave Nek Bakht an army and sent him back to his own country. So Nek Bakht set out, taking the bride with him, and so journeyed home.

One evening, as the party was approaching a certain tree, two large white kites were seen wheeling round about them. At last they flew to the tree on which they settled. Then said the Princess, "Do you see those kites? They are your mother and your wife, who by the power of magic have learnt everything that has happened. Give me the order and I will destroy them."

"How can you destroy them?" said the King.

"Nay, speak the word and I will do it," answered she. "You will see how, and it will save trouble in the end."

So Nek Bakht gave her leave, and she at once changed herself into a black kite, and flew off. Then ensued a fierce encounter between the black kite and the two white ones, and in the struggle they came tumbling to the ground, when the King ordered them, all three, to be killed on the spot, which was at once done by a soldier.

Then the King went home and lived a still more melancholy life than ever. Finding no rest, he again consulted the old witch of the river-side, and found Fate and Destiny wrangling together as usual. Says Destiny, "He will live long." "Not so," replies Fate, "and moreover he is doomed to die a violent death," which came to pass in an earthquake which swallowed up King, wazîr, and palace, and so ends the story.

Told by Mullâh, of the caste Pâveh, at Hazro, in the Râwâl Pindi District, January 1881.

XVIII

OF THE MAN AND THE BEAR

ONE day, when the river was in flood, a certain dark object was seen floating down the stream. Thereupon a poor man, mistaking it for a log of wood, plunged into the water, and, swimming with vigorous strokes, seized it with both his hands. When too late, he discovered that he was clasped in the shaggy embrace of a brown bear. "Ho!" cried his friends from the shore, when they saw him drifting, "let the log go! let the log go!"

"Just what I am trying to do," answered the unhappy man, "but the log won't let *me* go!" [1]

This, with the following four, from the Chach Plain, 1877-80.

XIX

OF THE MISER AND THE GRAIN OF WHEAT

A GREAT miser was once sitting on a precipice and dangling his feet over the edge. Hunger having become insupportable, he took out his small bag of parched grain and began to toss the food, grain by grain, into his mouth. All at once a single grain missed its destination and fell to the bottom of the ravine. "Ah, what a loss!" cried he. "But even a grain of wheat is of value, and only a simpleton would lose it." Whereupon he incontinently leaped down from the rock to recover his precious morsel, and broke both his legs.

[1] Logs of deodár are frequently floated down the Indus from the Himalayas. During floods many of these logs are washed away from the "timber-yards" far up the mountains. For every log regained the villagers receive a reward of four annas from the owner. Each log bears its owner's mark.

XX

OF THE BANEYR MAN AND THE MILL

A BANEYRWÂL came down to the Indus, where he saw a water-mill at work. Said he to himself, "People say that God is known by His wonderful ways. Now, here is a wonderful thing with wonderful ways, though it has neither hands nor feet. It must be God." So he went forward and kissed the walls, but he merely cut his face with the sharp stones.

XXI

OF THE FARMER, HIS WIFE, AND THE OPEN DOOR

ONCE upon a time a poor farmer and his wife, having finished their day's labour and eaten their frugal supper, were sitting by the fire, when a dispute arose between them as to who should shut the door, which had been blown open by a gust of wind.

"Wife, shut the door!" said the man.

"Husband, shut it yourself!" said the woman.

"I will not shut it, and you shall not shut it," said the husband; "but let the one who speaks the first word shut it."

This proposal pleased the wife exceedingly, and so the old couple, well satisfied, retired in silence to bed.

In the middle of the night they heard a noise, and, peering out, they perceived that a wild dog had entered the room, and that he was busy devouring their little store of food. Not a word, however, would either of these silly people utter, and the dog, having sniffed at everything, and having eaten as much as he wanted, went out of the house.

The next morning the woman took some grain to the house of a neighbour in order to have it ground into flour. In her absence the barber entered, and said to the husband, "How is it you are sitting here all alone?"

The farmer answered never a word. The barber then shaved his head, but still he did not speak; then he shaved off half his beard and half his moustache, but even then the man refrained from uttering a syllable. Then the barber covered him all over with a hideous coating of lamp-black, but the stolid farmer remained as dumb as a mute. "The man is bewitched!" cried the barber, and he hastily quitted the house.

He had hardly gone when the wife returned from the mill. She, seeing her husband in such a ghastly plight, began to tremble, and exclaimed, "Ah! wretch, what have you been doing?"

"You spoke the first word," said the farmer, "so begone, woman, and shut the door!"

XXII

OF THE FOUR PALS

ONCE upon a time a crow, a jackal, a hyena, and a camel swore a friendship, and agreed to seek their food in common. Said the camel to the crow, "Friend, you can fly; go forth and reconnoitre the country for us." So the crow flew away from tree to tree until he came to a fine field of musk melons, and then he returned and reported the fact to his companions. "You," said he to the camel, "can eat the leaves, but the fruit must be the share of the jackal, the hyena and myself."

When it was night all four visited the field and began to make a hearty supper. Suddenly the owner woke up and rushed to the rescue. The crow, the jackal, and the hyena easily escaped, but the camel was caught and driven out with cruel blows. Overtaking his comrades, he said,

"Pretty partners you are, to leave your friend in the lurch!" Said the jackal, "We were surprised. But cheer up; to-night we'll stand by you, and won't allow you to be thrashed again!"

The next day the owner, as a precaution, covered his field with nets and nooses.

At midnight the four friends returned again, and began devouring as before. The crow, the jackal and the hyena soon had eaten their fill, but not so the camel, who had hardly satisfied the cravings of hunger when the jackal suddenly remarked, "Camel, I feel a strong inclination to bark."

"For heaven's sake don't," said the camel; "you'll bring up the owner, and then while you all escape I shall be thrashed again."

"Bark I must," replied the jackal, who set up a dismal yell. Out from his hut ran the owner; but it happened that while the camel, the crow, and the jackal succeeded in getting away, the stupid hyena was caught in a net. "Friends! friends!" cried he, "are you going to abandon me? I shall be killed!"

"Obey my directions," said the crow, "and all will be right."

"What shall I do?" asked the hyena.

"Lie down and pretend to be dead," said the crow, "and the owner will merely throw you out, after which you can run away."

He had hardly spoken when the owner came to the spot, and seeing what he believed to be a dead hyena, he seized him by the hind-legs and threw him out of the field, when at once the delighted hyena sprang to his feet and trotted away. "Ah!" said the man, "that rascal was not dead, after all."

When the four friends met again the camel said to the jackal, "Your barking, friend, might have got me another beating. Never mind, all's well that ends well; to-day yours, to-morrow mine."

Some time afterwards the camel said, "Jackal, I'm going out for a walk. If you will get on my back I will give you a ride, and you can see the world." The jackal agreed, and, stooping down, the camel allowed him to mount on his back. As they were going along they came to a village, whereupon all the dogs rushed out and began barking furiously at the jackal, whom they eyed on the camel's back. Then said the camel to the jackal, "O jackal, I feel a strong inclination to roll."

"For heaven's sake, don't!" pleaded the jackal; "I shall be worried."

"Roll I must," replied the camel, and he rolled, while the village dogs fell on the jackal before he could escape, and tore him to pieces.

Then the camel returned and reported the traitor's death to his friends, who mightily approved the deed.

XXIII

THE STORY OF LALL, THE IDIOT[1]

THERE once lived an idiot named Lall, who on the very day of his birth lost his father. It is an old saying that a boy-child who has no father is a king, for he can do just what he pleases. And this was doubly true of Lall, because he had so little sense that it was useless even to attempt to control him.

In the same town lived Lall's aunt, his mother's sister, who was also a widow with an only daughter. Her his mother used to visit from time to time, and on these occasions she would say, "Sister, you have a daughter. Shall not our children marry together?" To which the sister would answer, "What! marry my daughter to an idiot? What would happen then, I wonder? No, sister, this cannot be." To this the poor mother would reply, "You are my own sister. If you won't give your daughter to wife to my idiot son, who in the world will?" And then the aunt would relent, and say, "Well, I suppose, as you are my eldest sister, I must. Come once again, and we'll see if we can settle it."

At last it was all arranged, and, in accordance with the

1 *Lall* (pronounced Lull) means "a fool;" *Lalla* is "a little fool."

usual custom, Lall's mother sent to the boy's betrothed presents of clothes and trinkets. Poor Lall began to visit the house, too, and the people in the street, when they knew he was engaged, were quite civil to him, saying to each other, "Don't you know this is Widow Hîra's son-in-law?"

Now, it is considered an unworthy thing for a youth to be always haunting the house of his betrothed, and frequent visits are always discouraged. But Lall, being an idiot, and having been well fed on the occasion of his first visit, had no regard for people's prejudices, and in short used to visit his aunt every day in the week.

One day he was on his way to the house as usual, when a girl, drawing water from the well, saw him, and cried, "O Lalla, come here, and help me to carry this vessel of water!" She was by no means so big as Lall, who was active and strong; but when he came up she began to smile wickedly at him and to joke him about his sweetheart. Thereupon Lall gave her a great push, which toppled her over into the well, and as there was no one near to rescue her the poor thing was drowned.

When the lad arrived home his mother said to him, "O Lall, where have you been again to-day?"

"I have been to the same place," answered Lall; "and I have had plenty to eat."

"Lall," said his mother, "you should not go there so often now that you are betrothed. The girls will all begin to make fun of you, and who knows what you may be doing?"

"What fun will the girls make of me?" replied Lall. "One of them did so to-day, and I caught her by the neck and threw her into the well. And she's as dead as a stone, I can tell you;" and Lall quite laughed at the capital joke he had played her.

"Ah, what fatal news is this?" cried the distressed mother. "Now this lad of mine will be hanged."

Without a moment's delay the idiot's mother ran out, and as it was getting dark she escaped observation and came to the well. With the greatest difficulty she managed to get out the body, which she carried to the river, and, tying a large jar full of sand to the neck of it, she threw it into the water.

On her way back she saw the dead body of a he-goat

lying in the road. This she lifted on to her shoulders, and taking it to the well, she dropped it in. Then she returned to her own house.

She now began to reflect that, as her idiot boy was certain to chatter to every one about the trick which he had played the unfortunate girl, her precautions ought to be increased. So she took a box of sweetmeats and scattered them all over the court of the house. Then she cried out to her son, who had gone to bed: "Get up, Lall—get up, boy! the sky has been raining sweetmeats!" No second invitation was needed for Lall, who loved sweetmeats with all his heart. He sprang from his bed, and, rushing out just as he was, gathered up every one of them, cramming his capacious mouth again and again.

By this time, however, there was a great commotion at the house of the missing girl. Messengers were sent everywhere to look for her, but they all returned no wiser than they went. All night long the search went on, and in the morning some said, "The poor girl has been made away with for her trinkets and bangles, and they have hidden her body."

Now, Lall had risen early, intending to visit the house of his cousin as usual. Going up the street, he noticed an unusual stir, and he stopped and asked, "What is all this noise for?"

"O Lall," said one, "Gaffer Laiya's little girl went out to fetch some water, and now she is nowhere to be found."

"Is that all the fuss?" answered Lall. "I caught that girl by the neck, and threw her into the well. Haven't you looked for her there?"

Some of the bystanders, with the girl's father, hearing this, seized him, and took him along with them. "Come along, Lall, and show us," said they.

On the way one cried, "When did you kill her, Lall? When did you kill her?"

"What, you stupid people?" said Lall. "Why, of course, I killed her last night before the sky began to rain down sweetmeats."

"What a fool this fellow is!" then became the cry. "What is the use of our wasting time over him?" But others said, "No, let us go and see. Perhaps there is something in it."

When the crowd arrived at the well, the girl's father said, "Let Lall go down and bring up my daughter."

"All right," cried Lall; "give me a rope, tie it round my waist and let me down. I'll soon find her for you."

So the people brought a stout rope, and Lall was lowered into the well, which was very wide, though not very deep—like all the wells of that country.

When Lall, who could swim like a fish, found himself in the water, he looked round him, but could perceive no signs of the dead body. Then he gave a dive down into the well, and coming across something at the bottom, he examined it, and rose once more to the surface.

"Hi!" cried he, looking up the well and addressing the distracted father, "has your daughter two horns?"

"Bring it up, bring it up, Lall!" cried the poor man, "and let us see it."

Down into the water Lall dived again, and after an interval which seemed like eternity he again came to the surface. "I say," cried he to the father, "hasn't your daughter four legs?"

On hearing this, some said, "What's the use of bothering here with this silly fool?" But others cried out to Lall, "Bring up the body, Lall, there's a fine lad! bring it up and let us see it."

Lall dived down for the third time, and was longer out of sight than ever. At last he appeared once more, and looking up to the eager faces, he cried, "Hi, uncle, has your daughter a long tail?"

Then many of the people got very angry. "Why don't you bring it up, you idiot!" they cried, and they threatened to brain him with stones. The boy now hastily disappeared for the last time; but if he had been as other people, he would have felt the father's tears, as they dropped into the well, worse even than stones. This time he remained under water a longer period still, until the people began to imagine he was drowned too. But at last he appeared again, and holding up high over the water the head of the old he-goat, he cried to the unfortunate father, "See! isn't this your daughter?"

This caused the greatest disorder and confusion among the people, because, while some were bursting with rage, others seemed bursting with laughter, and no one knew what to say or where to look. "Ah, what stuff this is!"

said one of the serious ones; "and what precious time we have wasted over this wretched idiot!" Then some were for throwing in the rope, and leaving the lad to drown. But the father said, "No! he is only a poor idiot—let him go." And so Lall was pulled roughly up and sent about his business.

While all this was going on, Lall's poor mother—half out of her wits with fear and apprehension—was giving away bread in charity, and offering up her intercessory prayers at all the shrines in the place on behalf of her boy. And overjoyed was she when she received him once more safe and sound, because, though he was only an idiot, he was the very light of her life. Yet she did not spare him when she got hold of him again, and often she reproached and reviled him with, "Ah, you little fool! you have lost your sweetheart, and who'll marry you now?" For her sister had lost no time in coming to her and saying, "A pretty to-do in the town, and all about your idiot of a son! No more sweethearting at my house if you please, sister! I have had enough of it, and, in short, my daughter is promised now to somebody else." So the match had been broken off, and poor Lall's love-making came to an end.

Some time after this Lall was loitering about the street, when a passing soldier laid hold of his arm and said, "Here, lad, carry this vessel of butter for me, and if you are smart I'll give you three halfpence." This quite delighted Lall, who was as strong as a horse, and taking up the vessel, with an "All right, I'll carry it," he swung it on to his shoulders. The vessel was a large jar of earthenware, and the butter was in a liquid state, like oil.

As Lall strode along the road, followed by the soldier, his busy brain began to build up castles in the air. "How lucky am I!" said he to himself. "This fellow is going to give me three ha'pence, and what shall I do with it? I know. I'll go into the market and buy a hen with it, and I'll take it home and feed it; and the hen will lay eggs, and I shall have a fine brood of chickens. And I'll sell them all for what they will fetch, and when I have sold them I'll buy a sheep. After a bit the sheep will have young ones, and when I have also sold them, I'll buy a cow. And when my cow has young ones I'll buy a milch buffalo; and when my milch buffalo has young ones, I'll sell her and I'll buy a mare to ride on. And when I am riding my mare the people will all stare at me, and say, 'O Lall! Lall!' and the girls will nudge each other, and say, 'Look at Lall on his beautiful mare!' And when I have a mare of my own, I shall not be long making a match with some fine girl with a pot of money; and I'll get married, and I shall have four or five nice little children. And when my children look up to me and cry, 'Papa, papa!' I'll say to one, 'O you little dear!' and to another, 'O you little darling!' And with my hand I'll pat them on the head, one by one, just like this.' Suiting the action to the word, Lall, in total oblivion of the jar of butter, lowered his hand, and made several passes in the air as if patting his children's heads; but as he did so, down fell the unlucky jar, which was broken into a thousand pieces, and all the precious butter ran about the street.

The soldier now ran up in a furious passion. "Ah, you villain," said he, "this liquid butter was the King's! Come along, I am going to the King, and you shall be punished. Five rupees all pitched into the street!" So he seized Lall and took him along with him.

They had not gone many yards when they saw a mule coming towards them, and some distance behind him a buniah running and shouting, "Hi! my mule is running away, my mule is running away! Will some one give him two cracks with a stick and stop him?" Hearing this, Lall lifted his staff and smote the mule so heavy a blow on the head that he fell to the ground quite lifeless. When the buniah came up, he cried, "Ah, you villain, you have killed my mule, and you shall go before the King!"

So the buniah, in high indignation, joined company with the soldier, and all three went on towards the King's court.

As they were walking along they came up to a little hut, or hovel of grass, by the roadside, in which lived a very old man and a very old woman. Here the three sat down to rest, and Lall, being thirsty, had a drink of water. Then the soldier and the buniah said to the old couple, "Do you know who this is? This is Lall!" When the old woman, who was of a whimsical turn, heard that, she said—

"O Lalla, do tell us the story of how Lanka was

captured, and how Dehsâr, the ten-headed god, was killed."

"Now, woman," answered Lall, "don't be teasing me. Don't you see what trouble I am in?"

But the old lady was not to be denied. "Now, do tell us, Lall," said she. "Now hear, O soldier," then replied Lall, "and hear you, O buniah! This old woman wants to know how Lanka was taken, and how the ten-headed god was killed. I can show her this far better than I can tell her, and if I do not show her she will not believe me."

Saying this, the stupid lad sprang up, and, seizing a hatchet which was lying by, he cut off the old man's head at a single blow. "This," cried he, "is how the ten-headed god was killed."

Then he caught up some dry grass, set a light to it and fired the hut, which in a moment was enveloped in flames. Nor would the old woman have escaped being burnt to death if Lall had not dragged her out of the place. "And now," said he, "this is the way that Lanka was taken."

Then was the old woman sorry she spoke, but her rage was greater than her grief, for she swore in the most dreadful manner. "But, you villain!" said she, "I'll tell the King, and you shall be hanged." And she joined the soldier and the buniah to add her accusation to theirs.

Away started the party once more; but before coming to the King's court they passed the shop of an oil-seller. Here Lall halted and said to the soldier, "Look, my hair is so rough and untidy that I am not fit to go before the King. Let me enter this shop and smooth down my hair with a little oil." To this the soldier consented, and Lall entered the shop, which was kept by another old woman. All round there were shelves, and on the shelves stood large earthen vessels quite full of oil. Said Lall to the shopkeeper, "Mother, I have a few cowries here; let me have a little oil for my hair." And he gave her two or three cowries. Then the woman took an iron spoon and brought the boy a little oil from one of the vessels. Lall held out his hand for it, and she poured it into his palm; but Lall was so silly that he let it all run out between his fingers, and it dropped on the floor. Then said he, "I bought a few cowries' worth of oil, and even that small quantity has slipped away!" But spilt oil is a sign of good luck, and the woman thought she would cheer him up by saying, "O boy, you are in luck to-day; you have certainly escaped something dreadful!"

When Lall heard the woman speaking thus, he began thinking to himself, "I have spilt these few drops of oil, and I am in luck, and perhaps have missed some great misfortune or other. But if I spill all the oil in the shop I shall bring far more luck on myself and luck on everybody else as well." So he lifted his heavy staff, and laying on the chatties with the utmost violence, he smashed them to atoms, and let out so large a quantity of oil that it covered the ground and ran out at the door.

"Hulloa!" cried the soldier, who was sitting outside; "what, more mischief here?"

Presently out came the old shopkeeper, fuming with rage, and crying, "Ah, you villain of a thief, we'll see what the King will say to this!" And she joined company with the other complainants, and all went forward and entered into the King's presence.

The King was at this time in his court hearing cases and administering justice. When he saw Lall and his four accusers at the door, he called them forward to his judgment-seat, and bade them state their business. The first to speak was the soldier. "O King, I hired this man," said he, "to carry five rupees' worth of ghee for your Highness' kitchen, but he dropped it in the street, and it was all wasted."

Then the King turned to Lall and said, "What is your name?"

"My name is Lall," answered the lad. "This soldier is complaining about his pen'orth of ghee; but if the King will lend me his ears, I will state the case truly."

The King nodding assent, Lall proceeded: "I agreed with the soldier to carry his butter for three ha'pence. As I went along I began to think what I should do with so large a sum. I would buy a hen and hatch chickens and sell them. Then I would buy a sheep and have lambs and sell them. Then I would buy a cow and have calves and sell them. Then I would have a milch buffalo and have baby buffaloes and sell them. And lastly, I should buy a fine mare and go riding among the girls and choose me a wife, and get children four or five. And I was just fancying myself in the midst of them, petting them and tousling them, and I merely took down my hand from the jar to pat their dear little heads, when crash! down came the jar, and all the butter ran away. But was I to blame, O King, seeing I lost so much myself?"

When the King heard this he perceived that Lall was a merry fool, and he began to laugh. As fools were his delight, he felt very well inclined to him, and, turning to the soldier, he gave sentence thus: "Soldier, for the sake of three pice this poor fellow has lost his all, and, in short, ruined himself, for he has lost his fowls, his sheep, his cows, his buffaloes, his mare, and even his poor unhappy children; while all you have lost is five rupees. Stand aside; he is forgiven. I dismiss the case."

The King then called forward the next accuser, upon which the buniah advanced and gave his evidence thus: "This miserable man, my lord, whom I have never injured, struck my mule with that staff of his and killed it."

"Did you kill this buniah's mule, Lall?" asked the King.

"Yes, I did," answered Lall; "but, O King, let the buniah witness whether he did not tell me to do so, crying out again and again, 'O traveller, traveller, give my mule a couple of cracks!' I merely struck his animal once."

"Soldier, what have you to say to this?" the King then asked. "Is Lall's statement true or false?"

"My lord, it is true," answered the soldier.

"Then," said the King to the buniah, "this misfortune is surely no one's fault but your own. Ho, guard, give this false witness half-a-dozen stripes and turn him into the street!"

So the unfortunate buniah was led off in disgrace.

Then the poor old woman whose house was on fire began her pitiful story: "This man, O king, both cut off my husband's head and burnt up my house. I ask for justice."

"Can this be possible, Lall?" asked the King.

"Yes," answered Lall, "it is true enough. But she asked me again and again to give her the story of the death of the ten-headed god, and to show her how Lanka was taken, and I merely obeyed her."

As the old woman could not deny this, Lall continued, "I thought it was best to explain to her properly how it was done, for deeds are always better than words, and so I showed her properly in order that there might be no mistake."

To the woman the King then said, "As this appears to be the case, the prisoner must be acquitted. Be more careful another time, and meanwhile my servants will provide you with a dwelling." So this case also was dismissed.

Then lastly the oil-seller came forward and accused Lall of having wantonly and maliciously smashed the whole of her oil vessels and spilt the oil, thereby ruining her for ever. "Did you do this thing, Lall?" said the King.

"Yes, O King, I did," answered Lall.

"And why did you?" returned the King.

"I went into the shop to buy four cowries' worth of oil to oil my hair before coming into your Highness' presence; but the oil ran away between my fingers, and the woman told me how lucky I was to have spilt it, and I thought to myself, 'If spilling a little of her oil brings me luck, spilling the whole of her oil will bring me and her and every one else luck.' So I spilt it as much for herself as for me."

Then the King, addressing himself to the woman, said, "Woman, you must have known this poor fellow was an idiot, and you should have been more careful of your speech. It is quite evident that he broke your vessels of oil because he thought you were not strong enough to break them for yourself. He wished you to have all the luck in the world. But the original fault lay with yourself."

So the King, greatly amused, dismissed this case as well, and ordered the prisoner to be discharged.

Lall then joyfully betook himself home to his mother, who said, "Lall, Lall, I have been in the greatest agony of mind about you! What became of you?" And to his mother Lall told all his adventures from first to last. And when she had heard them through, she said—

"My Lall does everything upside down;
God brings it together as right as a crown."

Told by Mûllâh, a villager of Hazro, May 1880.

XXIV

THE LOVE STORY OF MÎRZA AND SÂHIBÂṆH[1]

In a city by the Chenâh,[2] known by the name of Gûlvâllâh, lived Râja Khîva of Jhang, whose daughter was called Sâhibôh. By caste he was a Syâl. Up to the age of twelve his daughter did little else but attend the village school, kept by the kâzi at the village mosque, where she learned her lessons. And the man to whom her father had betrothed her was Tâhâ Khân of the tribe of Chandan.

Away on the banks of the Râvi, dwelt the tribe of the Kharrals, among whom there was a certain man of the name of Dâdu Khân, who had a son named Mîrza. And of all that tribe Mîrza's uncle, Ibrâhîm Khân, was the ruler and chief.

Now Mîrza was passionately fond of sport, being reckoned a mighty hunter. He was a roving blade, always on foot or in the saddle, but he was wild and eccentric, and said by the people to be half mad. One day he was away hunting, and exactly at noon he reached the outskirts of the town of Jhang Syâl. The girl, Sâhibôh, was then bathing in the river, attended by her sixty maidens, and she said, "How is it that at this hour of the day a horseman comes riding here?" Then Sâhibôh, standing knee-deep in the water, cried aloud—

"O rider of the dark-grey mare,
Why stand you burning there
Beneath the noon-tide glare?"

But Mîrza only looked and looked, and then he answered her thus—

"The sun is the sun of my country too,
Never shade in my fate can exist;
My business, O maiden, to-day is with you,
But the rest—let them live as they list!"

After this, Mîrza said, "I have come far in the sun, give me some water."

The first time he asked her, she answered, "This water

[1] Throughout this story, in deference to my village story-teller, I spell the heroine's name exactly as he pronounced it—*Sâhibôh*.

[2] Otherwise the Chenâb.

is the water of Jhang Syâl, it is the water of love, and you will not like it."

He spoke to her a second time, "Give me some water to drink!"

And the second time she answered, "This water is the water of Jhang Syâl, it is the water of love, and you will not like it!"

Then said he—

"What brings twin spirits face to face?
  Sure, Fate alone can bring;
We eat and drink, just as we please,
  But God controls the string.
By Râvi's banks I drew my breath.
  O women's hearts beware!
No lover dreads the dart of death,
  Though his grave be yawning there!"

Then said Sâhibôh to one of her companions, "Go you and take him some water!" The girl filled a brass vessel and took it; but her thumb was in the water as she carried it, and when he saw that, Mîrza said, "Your thumb is in the water, I cannot drink it!"

The girl went back and repeated that speech to Sâhibôh. Then said Sâhibôh to another girl, "You take him some water, but hold the lotah on your palm!" The girl took it, but a whirlwind swept along, and threw dust and shreds of grass into the vessel. And Mîrza said, "I cannot drink it. This water is full of dust and the shreds of grass."

The girl went back to Sâhibôh and threw down the vessel, saying, "The man says that, unless Sâhibôh herself gives him to drink, he will die standing where he is!"

Then Sâhibôh, standing knee-deep in the water, cried aloud—

"O you, with your mare so glossy and grey,
  And your necklet of amber flowers,
With your quiver of arrows so green and so gay,
  And the pearls dropping from you in showers!
Have you heard of our khâns?—men mighty are they!
    And I bid you beware,
    Lest they come for your mare!
Better drink, if you're wise, and go on your way!"

But Mîrza only looked and looked, and then he answered her—

"My camels roamed, from Râvi's banks they strayed,
And for your own Chenâb methinks they made!

I looked both east and west, but, still bereft,
To Khîva's town I come, for that alone is left!
Of Dâdû Khân I am both son and heir,
And Mîrza is the name men call me there.
But what my crime, O matchless maiden say,
That Khîva's khâns should take my mare away?"

Then Sâhibôh carried the water and gave to him to drink herself. And when he had drunk, she laid aside the lotah, took the bridle, and said to her friends, "You go on with your bathing, and I will show the traveller the road." So she went along with him through the jungle, and taking him to a *jhand* tree,[1] she said, "Get down from your horse, please!" And, when he had dismounted, they both sat down in the deep shadow, and they were talking and talking and talking, until at last evening surprised them, and Mîrza said to himself, "It is dusk, and I have far to get back to my home." She tried to detain him, saying, "It is now too late, stay, be my guest!" But he said to her, "Within ten days I will come again," and so he mounted his mare, and galloped away.

Ten days had well-nigh passed when, starting once more, he came to Jhang Syâl, and round the town he went, looking for his beloved. But he looked in vain. So he went to the house of an old woman, and, tying up his horse, there he rested. Then said he to the woman, "Come and show me the place where Sâhibôh lives."

"No," answered the woman, "stay you here! First I will go to Sâhibôh, and tell her you have come, and ask her if I may bring you there or not?"

"If she ask you who has come," said Mîrza, "say it is her cousin, the son of her mother's sister."

So the old woman started off, going to the house of Sâhibôh, to whom she gave the message, and Sâhibôh said, "Where has he come from?"

"He says he comes from the Râvi," answered the woman, "and he says he is son to your mother's sister."

Then said the girl, "Go back and find out if that is really so, and bring him—bring him quietly—bring him quietly here!"

[1] An acacia (*Prosopis Spicigera*) sacred to marriage, before which a sprig from it is ceremonially cut off by the bridegroom. This *jhand*-tree incident, therefore, constituted an informal marriage betwixt the twain, Mîrza and Sâhîbâṇh.

So back the old woman went to Mîrza, and she led him forth. But said he to her, "What about my arms and my horse?"

"Bring all!" answered she, and so he did. But Sâhibôh had ordered that he was to be kept outside for a while, and to her mother she spoke, disclosing her mind—

"Friendship, O Mother, with men,
And close to the heart a throe!
Sad lovers bear their love,
As trees bear the rending snow!
What does the earth want most?
It cries for the showers of heaven;
And the kneaded bread cries "salt,"
To season and sweeten the leaven!
As the holes in a sieve, as the stars above,
So many in number the pangs of love!"

"O daughter!" answered her mother, "for twelve years you have been learning from the priest! You have been promised to the tribe of Chandan, who number twelve thousand men, and what strange thing is this you are prating about? It is a bad word and nothing less, that you are saying, my child. God forbid that it should be so!"

Now all the time Mîrza was standing in the street, watching her through some stacks of fuel, as she sat winding her thread on the top of the house. In the enclosure below the mother was sweeping up the dust, and, suddenly looking up, she caught sight of him peeping, and it seemed to her that his eyes burned like coals of fire. So she put down her broom and came out to the street, and at once she recognized him as her sister's son, for she had heard tell of his beauty and his famous grey mare. Now Mîrza's mother, like herself, had been a girl of Jhang Syâl, so she said to him, "Why should the son hide in the village of his mother's family? What, peeping are you? But your eyes are peering eyes—eyes that are bloody eyes—and covetous eyes—eyes quick to pounce; inwardly calculating, outwardly too cunning to betray the secrets behind them. What, the old murder have you forgotten?" Then she bade him enter.

Now in the courtyard there was a mango-tree, and under it she set a cot, and told him to sit down. Then she went away, and Sâhibôh came down and sat with him and talked. In the afternoon the mother came back, and with her eyes she made signs to her daughter to bid him begone, since her father and brothers would be coming in from the fields. All this Mîrza saw and understood, and rose at once. As he was mounting, Sâhibôh caught hold of him, saying, "You are my guest. I will hide you somewhere, but stay you must!"

But he, supposing that already the girls of the town must be talking about them, said, "For your own sake I go, but within ten days I will come again!" So, though she pulled and strove, he mounted and rode off. And from the house-top she watched him as long as he was in sight. Then she folded up her mat and down she went into the court, taking her spinning with her, and saying—

"O Mîrza Khân, have I sent you away?
And what in the world is left for me,
What is now left me to hope or to see?
With my coloured bobbins I idly play,
As I sit alone, 'neath a shady tree,
In the shade of my father's mango-tree!

My little brother, he ran to my side,
'Come sing me a nursery song!' he cried;
So I sang him a song, but all the time
The name of Mirza slipt into the rhyme.

O Mîrza Khân, O Mîrza Khân,
Ease to the smart,
Peace to the heart,
Comes with the name of Mîrza Khân!"

Then, overpowered with grief, she fainted away. Many were the doctors who were summoned, but none could understand her complaint. Lastly came the priest, who taught her her lessons, and he felt her pulse. Never before could he take this liberty, much as he wished, being in love with her himself, but now he could and did, and he said to her mother, "An evil spirit has frightened her, yea, one of the great demons!"

"Spend what you please on medicine," said the mother.

"This kind cannot be driven out under four hundred rupees," said the priest.

"Spend anything you like," said she, "only cure her!"

"Well," said the priest, "the hour is past for a cure to-day. It is too late! But to-morrow something may be done!"

But to himself he was saying, "To-day she was ready with her four hundred rupees. To-morrow she may give eight hundred." And he went away home. But he was unable to sleep, vexed that he had not taken the four hundred rupees. The night was as long as a year to him. In his concern he rose at midnight instead of at dawn, and cried the *bhang*,[1] and the good men of the place all got up and came to the mosque for their matin-prayers. A long time kept he them waiting, and even, when at last he came, it was still too early. And when he opened school, his mind was in such a state, thinking of the four hundred rupees, that he taught the wrong lessons, and always his eyes kept wandering to the door, and he was saying to himself, "Now some one will come!" and ever and again, "Surely now some one will come to call me to Sâhibôh's house!"

Now, by the morning, Sâhibôh had recovered, and she got ready to go to the mosque for her lessons, and as she was washing her hands she said to her mother—

"In the river Chenâh I was bathing, mother,
And O how my heart was quaking!
Then came to me Mîrza and showed himself, mother,
A veil from before him taking!—
If you are my mother, I beg and I pray,
O keep my purdah[2] for ever, for aye!"

So saying, she went to the mosque. But when the priest saw her coming, he got frantic with rage, thinking, "What was the matter with the vixen yesterday that she should be so well to-day? I have lost my four hundred rupees!" Then said he to the children. "Cut rose-slips, and beat Sâhibôh well, whether she knows her lessons or not!" Hardly had she entered when she noticed his anger, and expected her beating. But, thought she to herself, "I can save myself, if I can but give him a hint that Mîrza Khân is my friend." So she said to him—

"With switches beat me not, O master mine,
Nor yet with cruel blows inflame my blood—
All learning, and the power to learn are gone!
I am enflamed with love! I slept and slept,

[1] The Muezzin.

[2] Keep my secret. The *pardâ* is the curtain fencing off the secret, or women's quarters of the house. It is also the mantle which hides the face.

But love awoke and stirred within my breast—
To praises ever listening, love arose!
In that dark cloud that darts the fiery flash,
'Tis there, yea, there resides my Mîrza Khân!"

Then the kâzi jumps up in a flurry, he is tying and tying his turban on, he is going to Sâhibôh's! So off he hastens, and he says to her mother, "O Mother of Sâhibôh, Sâhibôh will not learn!"

"O priest," answered she, "wherefore not? why will she not learn?"

"She is in love with Mîrza Khân," said he. "Some day you will be thinking this love has been brought about by me, for, mark my words, she will not remain in your house. To-day, or to-morrow, she will be off with him!"

"O kâzi," said her mother, "leave me now and go! When she comes home, I'll give her a dressing."

So the priest went away, and when Sâhibôh came in, her mother was heating the oven, and having the oven-stick in her hand, she gave her daughter several strokes on the back, and the girl answered, "I have checked Mîrza Khân from coming to our street, and yet you, my own mother, even you must taunt me! Two have been learning the same lesson, and into the very marrow the lesson has sunk. But if you are my mother, O keep my purdah!"

Time passed, and Mîrza came riding over again, but, fearing scandal, he thinks to himself, "It is best not to go to the house." So he rides on to the shop of an apothecary, near which were assembled a number of people, and he stands looking on.

Now that very day Sâhibôh had opened out her hair, and she said to her mother, "Go, please, Mother, and bring me some oil for my hair, for I feel ashamed to go out like this!"

"I am old," answered her mother. "Go, bring it yourself!"

So she took a little vessel, and, with her hair all loose, she went for the oil herself. There, at the shop of the apothecary, stood Mîrza Khân on his mare, and she saw him; and when Mîrza saw her, he said to the apothecary, "What do you make by your sales?'

"Four or five rupees a day," answered the man.

"Take ten rupees," said Mîrza, "and give me up the

shop to myself, and let me bargain with this girl!" So he sat in the shop and received her there, and the apothecary locked the door and went away. Towards evening the man came back, and he opened the door and said, "It is late now; therefore get away home!" So Sâhibôh went home, and home also went Mîrza. But when Sâhibôh reached her house, her mother beat her again, saying, "It was morning when you went for the oil—where have you been all these hours?"

"You sent me out for oil," answered she, "and I went to the shop of the apothecary. Three men were there, one a Brâhmin, and the other two Jats.[1] But they knew not how to balance the rod, or to weigh out the silk, and so I made bargains for them. After this, I saw Mîrza Khân playing. Oil I bought not, but love was there, and there in abundance!"

Now Mîrzâ had promised to come again after three or four days to a certain private place outside of the town, where Sâhibôh had a garden-lodge. And Sâhibôh, being an only daughter, her father was fond of her, and he let her go there, only saying to her, "The place is outside the town, and not over safe. Take therefore with you your sixty playmates for company!" So away they all went, and the time came, and Mîrza did not appear. Now she had slung swings from the boughs of the trees, and so at first she was glad, expecting him, but now she was sorry, seeing that he was some days behind his time. At last, on the fifth day, he came, and she saw him coming and turned her back. Mîrza Khân, supposing she had not seen him, came in front of her, but again she turned her back. He was puzzled, but thinking again to himself, "Perhaps she has not seen me," he came in front of her again, and again she turned her back to him. Then said he to himself, "O, she is angry with me!" and, so thinking, he turned his horse's head as if for home. When he had gone some way, however, he said to himself, "But I never asked her why she is angry!" So he retraced his steps, but she turned her back on him again. Then spoke he to her and said—

[1] *Jat*, a tribe among the Hindus. All these dark figures of speech are in verse. Though commonly current, and well understood by the people, they are not explainable in English.

"In Khîva's town the *tâli*[1] trees are grown
A forest vast and deep; and in the shade
Are tied his countless mares, to tighten up
Whose silken girths press on as many grooms;
But Khîva's matchless daughter decks herself
With amulets, careless of aught beside.—
O Sâhibôh, deign from the folds of your *chadda*
One glance to throw me!
Look at me patiently standing before you,
Do you not know me?"

Saying this, he turned his horse's head away once more. Then thought Sâhibôh to herself, "Now he is going in earnest!" and she made a bound and caught hold of his horse's bridle, "for," thought she, "he will never come back any more!" And she said to him—

"I bore in my hand a basin of curds,[2]
And went to the river;
My tresses I washed in the rush of the river,
Framing the words,
Using the curds,
Then the river rolled on and the curds were all gone,
But love lies for ever and ever.
O Mîrza, cut me with your knife,
Nor deem that I shall feel the pain,
Then will you know no blood can flow,
So full of love's my every vein!"

"And now come in," said she, "and see my house!" and she took him through the garden and into the pavilion, which they entered, and he thought, "It will be wonderful if I escape the eyes of so many girls!" Thinking of the danger of discovery, and fearing to stay too long, he said to her, "Now show me over the house!"

And Sâhibôh took him by the hand, and she led him in saying, "Come, I will go with you myself!" But soon one of the maids met them, and, addressing Mîrza, she said—

"Thou stranger youth, so tall, so slim, so straight,
What business brings you to my lady's gate?
Look elsewhere thou—this darling is bespoken!—
Would'st thou an anguished mind, and a heart broken?"

[1] *Tâli*, in Hindustân proper called *sîsam*—an acacia producing an excellent timber, very handsome and hard, sometimes called the Indian mahogany.

[2] Curds are used by the Panjâbi women for washing the hair.

Mîrza Khân felt vexed at the words of the girl, and he answered her—

> "No one can cross another's path unless
> By *kismet* driven. Ours is the bread and ours
> The limpid draught, to leave or take at will,
> But only God Himself can hold the string—
> Does trouble ask before it deigns to come?
> Or Love request before it pierce the heart?
> And, if my love has bound me wrist to wrist,
> Will Love consent to force, and set me free?"

Then said he to Sâhibôh, "Now let me go!"

"You told me to have the house made ready," said she. "For you I have had it prepared, but for you to stay, not that you should come and leave again so soon!"

Then Mîrza, thinking to himself "What is best to be done?" sat down again, and all the maidens in the place flocked round about him; and Sâhibôh said to them, "Is there any one in the whole world to compare with this man?"

"He is so fair," answered they, "he is so delicately made, that you can see the water as it trickles down his throat."

And they were all delighted at his coming, and begged him to remain. And he looked round on them all, but, wherever he looked, his eyes always came back to Sâhibôh.

That night Sâhibôh kept him with her, and all the night long she and her handmaids sat up to admire him.

Now in the morning Sâhibôh's mother went to him, and warned him, saying, "O Mîrza Khân, be it known to you that my daughter has been promised and betrothed in a very great tribe! Stay nigh, if you like, for eight days, but after that begone, and take care never to come after Sâhibôh again, lest the tribe come down and sack the town!" And to her daughter she said, "Now, go you to your books!"

And Mîrza said to Sâhibôh's mother, "For fifteen days I have learnt nothing. Let me go to the mosque and learn too!"

Now the priest kept his boys outside the mosque, while the girls sat within. So the woman answered, "Yes, you go too, but sit with the boys, don't go in with the girls!"

So Mîrza went to the school, and sat outside among the boys, and he said to the priest, "You teach all the boys of your own town. I am a stranger. Why do you not teach me too?"

Then the priest came to him and said, "What stranger are you?"

"I come from the Râvi," answered he. "I am a nephew of Khîva Râja. Teach me quickly, I pray you!"

And the priest said to Mîrza Khân, "Look over all you have learnt before, and when you can say it by heart, I will give you something else." So, first uttering the name of God, Mîrza began, and kept on repeating, "Sâhibôh Syâl! Sâhibôh Syâl!" The priest, hearing him uttering these words, was astounded, and he said to himself, "What gibberish has this fellow got hold of!"

While all this was going on, the girls within the school were calling out, "Priest, priest, come and give us our lessons!" But Mîrza said to him, "No, no, give me my lesson first, before you go!" And when the priest went in, thinking some madman had come to his school, he first called up Sâhibôh, and to her he said, "Now let me have your lesson!"

Now this priest had a stick for the boys, but for the girls he kept a whip. So when Sâhibôh answered him, "In the name of God, Mîrza Khân, Kharral of the Râvi! Mîrza Khân, Kharral of the Râvi!" the priest cried out, "What are you doing, you madcap? For twelve years I have taught you, and what stuff is this you are jabbering?"

"Am I not saying my lesson?" said the girl. "Only that I remember, and that only I repeat. I am not saying anything strange, am I?"

Then the priest caught her one crack with his whip, and he hit her again, and then he hit her a third time, when, with a bound, in sprang Mîrza, and, seizing him, hurled him out of the door. All the pupils were astonished, and they wondered, saying among themselves, "What has this farmer of a fellow done to our priest? He has thrown him out, and so belaboured him, that half his breath is out of his body." Then they tried a rescue, but Mîrza said, "No, no, why should I loose him? He has been beating one of the girls as if she had been his wife!"

"She is not my wife," answered the priest, "no, but she is my pupil, and has been so for twelve long years!"

"True," said Mîrza, "you have beaten your pupil. But is that any reason for beating me too?"

"Liar!" cried the children. "Who has beaten you?"

"I am telling lies, am I?" said Mîrza, and drawing up his jacket he showed them the three livid marks of the whip along his bare back. So all began to say, "This priest has beaten the girl, but the lad has the marks. How is this? Ah, it is some love-affair!"

After these things, the priest made up his mind what to do, and writing a letter he sent it secretly to Tâhâ Khân, and the words of the letter were, "Mîrza Khân is in love with your betrothed, and will take her away. Get ready your wedding-party, and in eight days come and marry her. Take heed to yourselves! Otherwise he will carry her off." Then he went to the girl's father, Khîva Khân, and told him too, saying, "Such is the state of affairs; all these things occurred at the mosque."

Then Khîva and the girl's mother took Mîrza, and said to him, "You are a Kharral, we are Syâls. We cannot mate ourselves with you, and besides the girl is already promised. So go away home, and do not come any more!" Thus Mîrza was dismissed from Jhang Syâl, and mounting his horse, he rode rapidly away. But Sâhibôh was at her place on the house-top, and she saw him go, and thence she again watched him long, till he was no longer in sight. Still she watched, and at last her mother came up, crying, "Come down! Come down from the house-top! Wouldest go and kill thyself?"

The girl gazed at her mother and answered her thus—

"And come you so to me, and Mîrza Khân
Driven out? But what is left me now in all
This house to look upon? Ah me, ah me,
The spine of the black snake is snapt in twain!
My little cot I press to my embrace
And weep the while. The roof-post of the house
I strain unto my aching breast, and cry—
'O Mîrza, spring like a tiger, swoop like a hawk,
Come back, come back to Jhang Syâl!'"

But Mîrza Khân rode on, and reaching his home, he threw himself on his bed, nor thought of house, or horse, or arms any more, being weary of heart.

Now the priest's letter reached the Chandan tribe in safety, and they called together their twelve thousand armed men, and prepared for the start on the eighth day. This news one of her companions gave to Sâhibôh, who was lying, dry-eyed with sorrow, but in fear of her father. And she thought to herself, "If I could only get a runner to go and tell Mîrza!" (She became so ill that her mother was minded to send for the priest again, but her daughter said to her, "Why ask the priest about me? Do you not know my illness that you should ask the priest? Are you so simple as all that?"

When the priest came, he brought with him his books. And he made pretence of opening his books to consult them, but all the time reading out verses of his own. "In the book," said he, "I read sweet food; all will come right at last; five hundred-weight of vermicelli, with ten fowls, and she will recover."

And Sâhibôh thought to herself, "My love is away at the Râvi, and the priest is plundering like this!"

Then the priest turned another leaf, and said, "From death Sâhibôh is set free. She has been stung by a bitter sting. Five tons of flour with five buffaloes, in the name of God give to the priest!")[1]

Again Sâhibôh thought within herself, "My love is away at the Râvi. I will go tell my mother myself, and she shall know my complaint." And to her mother she said, "When you sent me to the bazaar for oil, did I not tell you they knew not how to hold the scales, or to weigh out the silk? Instead of selling honey, they measured out love. Generally people, when they cry, cry tears, but lovers cry blood. With what a lance has Mîrza struck me through, that in my veins no blood is left remaining! Either let Mîrza come and see me, or to-day I die!"

Then her mother grew very angry. "Deceitful girl," said she, "when will you learn your duty?" And she also wrote a note to the tribe of the Chandans, bidding them come at once and take her daughter away. And in these words it was she wrote to them, "The daughter of Khîva, Sâhibôh, Tâhâ Khân's betrothed. Come and take your dhoolie. Ask peace from God!"

Then Sâhibôh also wrote a letter, and she put it in a little box, and she launched the box on the river, so that it might float away to her lover. And thus she wrote to him, "A letter Sâhibôh has written to Mîrza Khân. If

[1] The part between brackets probably belongs to a variant.

you are sitting, rise; if you are standing, come quickly. Tâhâ Khân's wedding-party is coming with numbers of men. No footmen are to be seen—all are riding on horses. I shall have to go to the Chandan, and then what will you do?"

Now Mîrza Khân was so stricken as to be ill, and in grief of heart he had gone walking to the river. "I will go to the river," said he, "I will drink of the water of the stream which flows down from Sâhibôh, and that will console me!"

So he had his cot laid by the river-side, and there he lay, and one day, as he lay, he saw a casket coming floating down the stream. In wonder about it, he sent out a servant to fetch it, and when it was brought in to him, he saw there a lock, and in the lock a key. So he opened the box, and found the letter within. "What is this?" cried he, and he read the words. Then went he to the khân, his uncle, and threw the letter and his turban down on the earth before him. The letter his uncle read, and to the people he said, "Take up my nephew's turban, and put it again on his head!"

"Nay," said Mîrza, "not until you promise me your aid against the Syâls!"

"They are stronger than I, those people," answered his uncle. "Take from me money, as much as you please, —take, if you like, the weight of the girl in gold, but I cannot go fight against the Syâls."

Still he pleaded, Mîrza Khân refusing to don his turban, until the khân became sorrowful, and going up to him, he put on him his turban himself, saying to him—

"O kinsman, our warriors are always at hand,
They muster in swarms on the banks of the Râvi;
The Râvi river is a river of love,
It fills up the heart with the odour thereof;
Like a turtle of gold is your Sâhibôh Syâl,
And a golden peacock, my nephew, are you!
The flower of the Râvi shall meet the Syâls,
They shall fight and o'erwhelm them, so great is their strength;
Whilst I, even I, Ibrâhîm, see the day,
What host shall dare come to take Sâhibôh away?"

But when the mother of Mîrza heard of this compact, she took away her son's horse and his arms, and laid orders on him not to stir abroad, but to remain at home.

And to Ibrâhîm Khân she said, "For mercy's sake, do not give him this help! Give him the prettiest girl of the tribe, but never go to Jhang Syâl."

Then were numbers of damsels, the loveliest of the tribe, brought before Mîrza, with a dancing girl or two to divert him, but he could not be induced to regard them, or even to look at them, but he turned to his friends, and said, "Sâhibôh only do I praise, Sâhibôh alone will I marry, nor shall I marry any one else who is not her very counterpart. Sâhibôh is daughter to Khîva Râja. She was born on a Tuesday; one year old was she and she drank her mother's milk (for the last time); when two years old she was clad in lovely garments; when four years old she wore her bangles; when six years old she went running among her girl-companions; when eight years old she began to step on her toes; when ten years old she walked so as to be heard; when eleven she began to develop strength as a young buffalo runs up a hill; at twelve she was the complete woman, and looked bright as a polished keen-edged sword. And when she was a woman, all the young khâns began to take note of her beauty and made haste to win her—

"In plaits, like twisted snakes, low hangs her hair;
Her brow is like the moon; curved as the point
Of Hosain's scimitar her well-cut nose!
How black her eyebrows!—lo, they terrify
Like serpents, and her lashes pierce the heart!
(O, beautiful is Sâhibôh!)[1]

Handfuls of rings adorn her ears, they fight
Like pairs of rival starlings! Daintiest buds
Of jasmine are her dazzling teeth—what hand,
What master's cunning fingers, fashioned them?
(O, beautiful is Sâhibôh!)

Thin is the fragrant betel-leaf, and thin
Her fragrant lips, distilling sherbet meet
For lovers,—oh, stoop down, stoop down and sip!
(So beautiful is Sâhibôh!)

What wonderous apple, praised of all the world,
With Sâhibôh's chin may men compare? Her breasts,
Two round *surâhis*,[2] like ruddy rubies shine!
(O, beautiful is Sâhibôh!)

[1] *Sâhibâṇh*—a noble (gentleman's) bride.
[2] Spherical water-bottles of terra cotta.

A goblet is her navel-pit—behold
Where pass her thronging lovers round and round!
(O, beautiful is Sâhibôh!)[1]

In velvet slippers hide her tiny toes,
And, as she moves along, with measured steps
And dainty tread, more dainty far than tread
Of snow-white pard, how gracefully she goes!
(So beautiful is Sâhibôh!)

Stained are her heels with henna rosy red,
So that, where'er she goes, she colours red
The very ground she walks on! Who of all
Her maiden-friends can rival her in charm?
(O, beautiful is Sâhibôh!)—

"Call you these girls beautiful? They cannot compare even with her handmaidens—How can I marry them?—You are all in league to deceive me!"

Then said all his brethren, "We have done for Mîrza Khân the best we can. If he will die, die he must!"

And all the girls, when they saw them forsake him, lifted up their hands and prayed for him. "Mîrza Khân," said they, "by all means go to Jhang Syâl, and may God be with you! On your shoulders sling your green bow! There is no man like you, no one so brave, and no one so handsome there!"

Then they went their ways, and he sought out his mother, saying, "Give me my horse and my arms!"

"Your arms," said she, "I cannot give—keep still!"

"Why can you not give me my arms?" said he. "Is it not better for me to die there than here? Do you want me to die at your gate?"

"O my son," said his mother, "it is madness for you to go there! They are a most mighty tribe. Yet hear me! If go you must, never shall I regard you as son of mine unless you bear away Sâhibôh five *kos*[2] before you are killed yourself."

So his mother handed over to him his arms, and Lakhi[3] his mare. Then thought Mîrza of God, and having com-

[1] Compare with this the Song of Songs iv. 1–6; v. 10–16; and vii. 1–10; and especially vii. 2—, "Thy navel is like a round goblet that wanteth not liquor." The wine-cups of the old world were often shallow saucer-like vessels, and it should be noted that, among oriental women, whether trousers or skirt be worn, the garment is tightly bound round *below* the navel, which is exposed often to view.

[2] Five *kos*—about eight miles.

[3] *Lakhi*—beautiful.

mended himself to Him, he mounted and galloped away, and at once arrived at Jhang Syâl. There he saw the twelve thousand Chandans. But, he being alone, the people said, "Who is this coming alone?" So he passed to the house of the old woman, who said to him, "Why do you not join the wedding-party?" And he answered her, "Let me stay here, I pray you!" But she would not, so he handed her money, five-and-twenty rupees, and then she gave in, saying, "By all means, but are you that same Mîrza Khân? Why, O foolish one, have you come to your death? If your body were in tiny bits, and every bit a body, you would not be a match for all the people here."

"Old woman," said he, "I have come and I am here. Only do something for me, if you will. Go tell Sâhibôh that Mîrza has come!"

So away she went, and Sâhibôh gave her a hundred rupees, and said to her, "Now manage to bring him to-night. To-morrow he will be cut to pieces; only let me see him to-night!"

"But how contrive?" said the old woman. "Now look you! Give me some of your beautiful robes, something in which to disguise him, and I will bring him dressed up. Let me have ample—enough to cover himself, his horse and his arms!"

So Sâhibôh handed her an immense cloak, fifty or sixty yards of cloth, which same cloak receiving she went her way. And first she set before Mîrza some food, for he was in need of it. Then she bade him mount Lakhi, his grey mare. His sword and his bow were slung over his shoulder, and he bent low in the saddle, leaving exposed to gaze only the ears and the tail of his horse. Hundreds of steeds were hitched about, which began to neigh, and to break from their ropes, and the old woman made pretence, crying, "O you grooms, take care, the daughter of the wazîr is coming to visit Sâhibôh!" So she led him safely through the gateway of the Lodge of Mirrors, telling an attendant to tie up his mare somewhere close by, and thus, having seen him well into the house, she went her way home.

Now all Sâhibôh's maidens took him for some princess, and Sâhibôh said to him, "How is it you come so late? All these people are now here, and what can you do alone?

You will be killed, Mîrza Khân! The remedy for one is two, and the remedy for two is four, but here we have thousands!"

Mîrza laid his hands on his moustache, saying to her, "Only listen to me! Keep cool! Do not lose your presence of mind!"

"You tell me to keep cool," answered the girl. "Ah—

"For you I am risking my life,
For you I am beckoned away,
Only dare to be mine, Mîrza Khân,
Be mine, O be mine but to-day!"

Drink, drink, O my Heart, of the cup,
By the side of your hand as it lies—
Let us drink the sweet poison of love,
The moment of destiny flies.

Long, long e'er we met you were kin,
As soon as I saw you, how dear!
Too far have we gone for regret,
The sugar is mixed with the *khîr*![1]

O, beware, Mîrza Khân, it is I,
Khîva's daughter, who's stolen your heart!
If you die, die with me, Mîrza Khân,
Even death shall not tear us apart!

Yet, O but to live till to-morrow,
And O to be with you till then!
This night is our last, my Belovèd,
We shall never be happy again!"

Then Mîrza took the girl in his arms and kissed her wet cheeks, and spoke to her—"All this," said he, "you have been saying and well I understand, but I too am ready, so hear also me—

"Now has the lover his bundle of perils tied up,
His destiny daring!
The flesh on my body has shrunk and dried up,
My bones are all staring!
If my head is to fall, fall it must,
Can Fate be evaded?
But for ever with thee are my love and my trust,
Till life shall have faded!—

"But, O Sâhibôh, all can be arranged if your maidens can only be made to sleep. Give them some wine!"

[1] *Khîr*—rice boiled in milk, and sweetened with sugar, a favourite dish, especially at *weddings*. Here a proverb—The deed is done, the die is cast!

Then Sâhibôh called out to her companions, "Now, O Girls, make merry, since to-morrow I go!" and she served out beakers of wine, saying, "Give them wine and call it sherbet!" And so tiny cups were passed round, and all the girls grew drowsy. But one of them, suspecting a trick, smelled something in it, and, instead of draining her goblet, she poured it into her bosom. Now this girl was loved of Sâhibôh the most.

When midnight came, Sâhibôh got up to see, and found them all asleep excepting the one, who said to her, "The wine was drugged by me, but surely I am your friend. Why should I drink, seeing that I wish you well?" And to Mîrza Sâhibôh spoke, saying, "Rise, it is time for us to go!"

Then Mîrza got up, and answered her, "Before Tâhâ Khân and all the chiefs, women are dancing and lanterns are gleaming. All are engaged in revelry. Yes, now is the time!"

So he saddled his mare, but he pulled so hard that the girth-strap broke, and Sâhibôh said, "Mîrzâ, I sneezed, and the girth of Lakhi has broken! Either a king will lose his crown, or a prince will be killed!"

"You speak as a woman," answered he. "Leave all to God, and come, mount behind me!"

So she got on the mare, and when she was seated, the girl who had drunk no wine, rose and took the bridle, saying, "Long have I eaten your salt, nor will I leave you now, until I have seen you safely out of the place." Then the great cloak was thrown over both the lovers, and the girl led them forth in their disguise.

As they passed along, Mîrza said, "Hear me, Sâhibôh! I want, before leaving, to see your betrothed, Tâhâ Khân."

"Oh, for mercy's sake, don't!" cried she. "Are you mad? Let us get on!"

But Mîrza persisted, riding by the place where music and dancing were being kept up all the night through, and he cried aloud, "Look out, and hear me! I am Mîrza Khân, and I am taking away Sâhibôh!"

At once the whole company rushed for their swords, but the girl at the bridle called out, "Nay, listen, ye people! This is merely a mad fakîr. He is mad, and always he repeats the same thing. You are a forest of men, innumerable, and the man has received presents accordingly, this horse and a cloak to cover him. How should Mîrza be here?" Then was heard the voice of another woman, "O yes, he is a madman. Let the mad fakîr go!" So all the men sat down again.

Then came Mîrza to another party of revellers, while Sâhibôh was protesting, saying, "O fool, to say such things! You will ruin all!"

"Look at Tâhâ Khân!" said Mîrza.

"Come along, Mîrza Khân!" answered she. "I have looked at him enough. Tâhâ Khân is thinner than a buffalo and blacker than a griddle. A basketful of bread he devours, and he gobbles a whole chatty of *dâl*.[1] Yea, he is bald, and has large feet! Is that a fellow to look at? Let us haste away!"

Then cried Mîrza, "O you people, whether awake or asleep, here am I, Mîrza Khân, taking away Sâhibôh!"

At once the men rushed to their arms, and again the girl cried aloud, and said, "O you people, hear me! This is only the mad fakîr. He spake the same words to the other party, and he speaks them again to you. Regard him not!"

So the men sat down again, keeping quiet, and Mîrza passed on, while the girl returned to the house.

Now it so happened that as the lovers were passing along the village street, a certain Brâhmin pundit was sitting in his house reading a book. This man, glancing up, saw Mîrza's leg gleaming from beneath the long cloak, so at once he made his way to Khîva Khân, and said to him, "I have just seen something like magic."

"Keep still, keep still!" said Khîva.

"I will tell you what that was," said the Brâhmin, and opening his book, he feigned to read—

"In the town of Khîva Khân,
I perceive a mighty stir,
Dame Jimiâb[2] has swooned,
Her house is in a whirr!
With the Kharral Mirza Khân,
Your Sâhibôh, O the grief,
She's gone off with Mîrza Khân,
The bastard and the thief!"

Now at the distance of five *kôs* from Jhang Syâl there

[1] *Dâl*—peas, food, victuals. [2] *Jimiâb*—Glory of the Land.

was a certain shrine before which Mîzra Khân used to halt and pray, saying, "O Panj-pîr,[1] if ever I succeed in bringing away Sâhibôh, passing here will I tarry and rest!" To that spot the two lovers now came in their flight, and Mîrza spake, saying, "O Sâhibôh, this is the place of my vow!"

"There are twelve thousand of the Chandans in pursuit," said she. "Do you want to die? Let us get on!"

"I have an oath," answered he. "Come down, lay your knee beneath my head, and here let me rest for one half-hour!"

It was then close to dawn, and Sâhibôh said, "In half-an-hour the morning will be on us. What are you thinking of?"

But Mîrza dismounted, and lifted her down, and he laid his head in her lap, and so fell asleep.

Meanwhile Khîva Râja, with Tâhâ Khân, and some maids, had betaken themselves to the house of Sâhibôh, and there they saw her sixty companions lying heavy with drunken sleep, and they wondered where Sâhibôh could be. "All these are her maidens," said they, "but where is herself?" So forthwith arose a great tumult, and many more came running up, crying, "Say, what is the matter?" Then a rumour went round, and all began to say, "Mîrza has carried Sâhibôh away!" And the news flew through the town, and the Syâls and the Chandans began saddling their horses, and there was a great stir.

But all this time Sâhibôh was on the watch in the place of the shrine, and soon she began to hear the noise of the pursuit, so she tried to rouse Mîrza, crying, "Get up! get up! for God's sake get up!"

But the only answer given by Mîrza was, "Let me sleep!"

Then she looked at his arms. "He has only one hundred and forty arrows," said she to herself, "only that at the utmost, and what good is that? One arrow of his can kill but three or four, while his horse is good for a hundred *kôs*. No resistance, therefore, but flight alone will serve us." Then again she thought within herself, "All these horsemen are coming, and the foremost among them will be my own two brothers, they will be the first to be killed, and all the people will curse me, and say,

[1] *Panj-pîr.* Five Pirs—The five Apostles of Muhammad.

'Not only has this woman gone off with her lover, but she has killed her brothers as well.' Now, if I could do anything by which I could get at his arrows and throw them away, that would be best!" So she rolled up her *chadda* (mantle) and gently transferred Mîrza's head to it. Then, taking the arrows, she threw them all out, and, having put back the empty quiver, she laid his head in her lap once more.

By this time the pursuit was close, the Brâhmin having betrayed them, and as Sâhibôh saw them rushing onward she woke up Mîrza. Then Mîrza rose and looked back, and, lo, his foes were at hand. So he threw his quiver over his shoulder, not missing the arrows, and, with his sword girded on his thigh, he mounted Sâhibôh and himself, and prepared to start. And of his foes Dârâbâdshâh refused to follow, but Khîva Râja and Tâhâ Khân pressed him sore. Then said Mîrza to Sâhibôh, "Shake yourself, Sâhibôh!" and Sâhibôh shook herself, and it came to pass when Lakhi heard the jingling of Sâhibôh's jewels of silver and gold, the good mare leaped the wall of the shrine, and got away from them all. But Tâhâ Khân taunted him, crying out, "Now, sir, be brave, and quit you like a man, nor turn a woman's back to your foes!"

Then Mîrza drew rein, and looked at his quiver, and he saw no arrows there, but one only. And he said to Sâhibôh, "You have done wrong, O Sâhibôh, to empty my quiver! But for you I might with this have killed Hanîshamîr and Lakmîr, and your father's grey horse, and the others I could have sent among the rest of the Syâls. But now, though the mare is eager to close and my enemies taunt me, I am all unarmed." Nevertheless, he took the single arrow, and, fitting it to his bow, let loose, crying, "Come on, O ye Syâls!" and the arrow found out the two brothers, Hanîshamîr and Lakmîr, who were galloping well in advance with lance and sword, and it brought them down, having pierced the breast of the one and lodged in the thigh of the other. By this time the host was closing in upon him, and the air was rent with the sound of their music. And Mîrza said, "Mîrza is but one, he is alone! If I fall, I fall alone, one against many." Now Lakhi, his mare, was accustomed of old to rush into the midst of battle, and as now she rushed among the advancing warriors, Mîrza Khân drew his sword, and fought for four hours, cutting down every man whom he encountered, until his hand swelled and stuck to the hilt. At last, after five hundred and fifty of the party of the Syâls had been killed or disabled, came Khîva Khân himself, crying, "Truce!"—and he said to Mîrza, "Why have you killed my troops, O Mîrza Khân? Why have you slain my sons? Let us now have peace!" But he spake deceitfully, for even then, while they were parleying, Tâhâ Khân rode up, and hit Mîrza with his lance on the back of his head, so that his turban rolled off and fell to the ground. And Mîrza, turning to Sâhibôh, said, "A curse to the love of women, whose wisdom is in their heels! They profess friendship; anon they betray! My turban has fallen, my head is bare. Mîrza alone, unaided, dies here, and no brother or friend beside him!"

Then Khîva, who was hiding a dagger in his hand, said, "Surely you have killed enough, and why now kill yourself? I will give the Chandans another girl, and you can take Sâhibôh away. Give me then, O Mîzra Khân, the right hand of peace!" And when Mîrza stretched forth his right hand, the old man smote him through the body, so that he fell dead. Then, seeing his daughter, he at once took her up behind himself, and starting for home, left Mîrza's bleeding body on the ground.

Now when the Syâls, returning with Khîva to Jhang, arrived at a spot within three *kôs* of the town, Sâhibôh looked back, and she saw the crows gathering round the body of Mîrza Khân. Then, seeing a dagger hanging from her father's saddle, she drew it, and plunging it into her side, she fell. And when Khîva looked round and saw the blood, he said to the chiefs of the Chandan tribe, "Now see, friends, and do not say I kept not faith! This girl has killed herself!" So the party rode on, leaving her lying there. On opposite sides of the vale lay the bodies of these two hapless ones, and the blood of Mîrza from the one side, and the blood of Sâhibôh from the other, flowed down the slopes, and mingled in the hollow between. And all the people, when they saw it, said, "Oh, we did wrong to kill two such lovers as these!"

But Sâhibôh, before dying, laid her hand on her wound, and a raven came and sat hard by. And she took out pen and some paper, and dipping her pen in the blood, she wrote on the paper and said, "O Raven, take this letter to Ibrâhîm Khân, Kharral of the Râvi!" And the writing was this, "Mîrza and Sâhibôh have been killed at the crooked *tâlî* tree. Tell Pîlo, the poet, to make such verses on this mishap, that the story will last till the day of judgment!"

So the raven went and took the letter, and Ibrâhîm Khân read it, and he told Mîrza's mother, saying, "Your son lies dead five *kôs* out of Jhang Syâl. Do you want the body brought in?"

"If he has really fallen there," answered she, "yes—certainly—send for the body!"

Then the chief of the Kharrals summoned his men to the number of twenty-four thousand sabres, with their twelve thousand horses, and twelve thousand buffaloes with pierced noses. Having all mounted, they set forth, and by-and-by reached the crooked *tâlî* tree, and there they found the mare standing by the body of Mîrza, and his body was shining like the body of a martyr. And all that multitude grew sorrowful, and taking the bodies of Mîrza and Sâhibôh, they laid them together in the one dhoolie which they left at the *tâlî* tree under a guard, and so continued their march to Jhang to fight the Syâls. As for the Chandans, they still abode in Jhang, for they claimed the body of Sâhibôh, saying to Khîva, "Where have you left her body? Give us her body that we may bury it among our own people?"

To whom Khîva replied, "When she was alive I gave her to you. Now, dead, she lies out there. Go fetch her yourselves!" But they feared to go, knowing the Kharrals were there.

Then met the opposing forces, and, in the fight which ensued, seven hundred more of the Syâls and Chandans fell on the field, until, pressed beyond measure, Khîva Râja craved a peace. "Take my town," said he, "take what you please for the life of Mîrza Khân!"

But the Kharrals answered, "For you no peace! Our sorrow for Mîrza will never abate, until we have burnt your town about you!" So the fight went on, until, in the town of the Syâls, not one stone was left upon another. In the end, Khîva and his wife Jimiâb were taken, and sent away to the Kharral country, and the victors put a man of their own in Jhang.

So Khîva and his wife were led away, and when they

reached the crooked *tâlî* tree, they halted there, and said to the guard, "Now tell us true, are these indeed the bodies of Mîrza and Sâhibôh?"

"Yes," answered the men, "these are really they."

"Then," said Khîva and Jimiâb Mâi, "it would be well for both our tribes to build their tombs here at the crooked *tâlî* tree, since that tree is the boundary between us. So shall we be friends for all the time to come!"

But Ibrâhîm Khân said, "No, their shrines shall be made in the Kharral country, and there only shall they rest!"

So they took the two bodies home, and there they made their shrine, and there, in the same tomb, they lie unto this day.

After this, Ibrâhîm Khân said to Khîva and Jimiâb, "You are now alone, you have no children, and at Jhang there is always trouble. Abide you here!"

"O son," answered Khîva, "let us go back! Give me but bread to eat and clothing to put on, and let me die at Jhang!"

"Very well!" said Ibrâhîm Khân. So he gave them horses, and sent them back, and made them tributary.

Told at Ghâzi on the Upper Indus, on the night of 3rd September, 1883, by Sharaf, son of Kesar, of the village of Kûri, District of Râwâl Pindi.

XXV

OF THE SAINT AND THE PILGRIM

THERE was a certain saint, by name Abûl Hassan, whose power and sanctity were noised all over the country. One day a pilgrim came from a distant land for the sole purpose of seeing him, but when he called at the house he found that he was absent. "Where has he gone?" inquired he of his wife. Now, the saint's wife was a hard woman, bitter and peevish in speech, and instead of answering the question, she began to abuse her husband with unmeasured violence, so that, hearing her words, the pilgrim lost all faith in the holiness of the person he had travelled so far to see. As he left the house, he said to some of the neighbours, "This saint of yours—where is he?" They answered, "He has gone to the hills to gather sticks."

"Though I no longer believe in him," said the pilgrim to himself, "I will at least look upon his face before I return."

So he set out forthwith for the jungle, but he had not proceeded far when he met the holy man face to face. His wood was borne before him by a tiger, and in his hand, instead of a whip, he carried a live snake. Then the pilgrim fell at his feet and said, "At the reproachful words of your wife my faith decreased, but I now believe that verily you are a saint indeed. Pray forgive me!"

"He who will use invincible patience," answered the saint, "especially with a shrew of a wife, shall command the very tigers, and they will obey him, for patience is rewarded of God. But a scolding wife can no man tame, seeing she is the very fiend himself."

From Ghâzî.

XXVI

ON THE LOVE OF MONEY

A MISER once found his way into the bazaar to buy bread. The weather was unusually warm, and as he trudged along the perspiration gathered round the coin, which was closely clutched in his hand. Arresting his steps, he gazed at the moist piece with a fond eye and said, "I won't spend you then. Weep not, dear friend; we shall not separate, after all—I will starve first!" So he restored the money to his bag, and begged for scraps from door to door.

XXVII

ON CHARACTERISTIC PRIDE OF THE BANÉYRWALS

A POOR man of Banéyr, unable to support himself in his native mountains, set out for Hindustân to seek his fortune, and there rose to the rank of nawâb. One of his poor relations, hearing of his good fortune, determined to visit him. So he went to the bazaar, and with a few annas bought one pound of sugar as a neighbourly present for his former acquaintance. After a long journey he arrived at the palace, and found the nawâb in the midst of his fine friends. But though he winked and nodded and beckoned to him to step aside for a friendly greeting, and to receive his pound of sugar, his efforts to engage the great man's attention were quite unsuccessful. At last, perceiving that his unwelcome visitor was about to open his mouth, the nawâb said to one of his attendants, "Conduct this poor stranger to my store-room, where my bags of sugar are laid up, and there let him sit down and eat his fill." Then he caused a letter to be written to his native village sternly forbidding any more of his poor ill-clad kinsmen to trouble him with their objectionable presence.

From Aṭtock.

XXVIII

TALE OF THE FALSE WITNESS[1]

A JUNGLE TALE

A CARAVAN of merchants came and pitched for the night at a certain spot on the way down to Hindustân. In the morning it was found that the back of one of the camels

[1] This story is intended as a satire on the universal practice prevailing among the natives of India of getting up false cases and procuring false witness in courts of law.

was so sore that it was considered inexpedient to load him again, and he was turned loose into the wilderness. So they left him behind. The camel, after grazing about the whole day, became exceedingly thirsty, and meeting a jackal, he said to him, "Uncle, uncle, I am very thirsty; can you show me some water?"

"I can show you water," said the jackal; "but if I do, you must agree to give me a good feed of meat from your sore back."

"I do agree," replied the camel; "and now show me the water."

So he followed his small friend until they came to a running stream, where he drank such quantities of water that the jackal thought he was never going to stop. Then, turning to the jackal, he invited him to his repast. "Come, uncle," said he, "you can now make your supper off my sore back."

"Nay," answered the jackal, "you forget. Our agreement was not that. It was, dear nephew, that I should have a meal of your tongue,[1] not of your wretched old back. This you distinctly promised if I would take you to water."

"Very well," replied the camel; "bring forward your witness to prove your words, and you can have it so."

"My witness I have handy," said the jackal, "and in two minutes he will be here."

So, going to the wolf, he pitched him a lying tale, and persuaded him to bear false witness. "You see, wolf," remarked he, "if I eat his tongue he will certainly die, and then we shall both have grand feeds, and all our friends can come and feast as well; but no one could possibly touch the flesh of a sore back." So the two made their way to the camel, and the jackal, appealing to the wolf, began, "What was the bargain? Did he not agree that if I would take him to water he would give me his tongue?"

"That was the bargain, most certainly," asserted the wolf, "and the camel agreed. Sitting behind that rock, I overheard the whole affair."

"Be it so," said the camel. "As you both delight in lies, and have no consciences, come along, Mr. Jackal, and

1 "Sore back" in Panjâbî being *chîgh*, and tongue *jîb*, there was sufficient similarity of sound to suggest prevarication.

devour my tongue." With which words he lowered his long neck until his head was on a level with his diminutive foe. But the latter then said to the wolf, "O friend, you see what a morsel I am! I am much too weak to pull out that enormous tongue. Could you not seize it and hold it for me?"

Then the wolf ventured his head into the camel's mouth to pull forward the tongue, but the camel instantly closed his powerful jaws, and, crushing the skull of his enemy, shook him to death. Meanwhile, the jackal danced and skipped with glee, crying out—

"Behold the fate of the false witness! behold the fate of the false witness!"

From Ghâzî.

XXIX

STORY OF THE KING AND THE PARROT

In former days, when birds possessed the gift of speech, and were as intelligent as the wisest statesmen, there lived a certain king who took much pleasure in a favourite parrot. It was the greatest delight of his life to caress her, to converse with her, and to feed her with dainty scraps from his own hands as she stood perched on his royal knee, while the lovely-plumaged bird, coyly reciprocating the king's attachment, manifested her love for him in a thousand endearing ways and by the prettiest of speeches.

One day, in the warm early spring-time, just as the tender willows by the mill-stream were beginning to put on their bright clothing of green, the parrot addressed her petition to her master in these words—

"O King, it is now a long time since I left my home. Give me leave to fly away and visit the well-loved spot once more."

But the King refused her request, not finding it possible

to part with her. It was only after many solicitations, extending over many days, that at last he granted a very sorrowful permission.

"Go, dear bird," said he, "and visit your own native clime. When six months have fled, then come back to me once more, and when you come, remember to bring me some sure token that your love has never diminished."

"Absent or present, O King," answered the parrot, "I shall love you still the same."

So the King and his favourite had a most tender parting, with many a sweet little kiss to be remembered by them both thereafter. And then the parrot spread out her golden wings and started for her own home, flying from tree to tree and from hill to hill for many a league.

But the King, who knew the direction of her flight, had commanded some of his courtiers to follow her and to observe her doings. It was a long and a weary journey. One hundred miles at least did the courtiers travel through the woods. At last they came to a barren plain, quite destitute of vegetation, over which the wind howled dismally. At the end of this plain their further progress was barred by a mighty river, which they could by no means cross over. As they were preparing to retrace their steps they noticed a few solitary trees growing near the brink of the water. On the drooping branch of one of them was built a nest, and upon the nest, to their joy and surprise, sat the King's favourite parrot; while ever and anon a gust of the keen wind would come and rudely bend the fragile bough with its precious burden and dip it into the chilly water.

Having noticed these things, the courtiers once more returned to the palace, and reported to the King all that they had witnessed. Naturally the King was astonished that a bird so wise and sensible, able to command the most beautiful lodging and the daintiest food, should prefer exile in a desolate place amid want and privation. But, as he had a thoughtful and sagacious mind, he began to reflect on a circumstance so extraordinary, and at last, addressing his court, he said—

"This is only an instance of a true instinct. Be it ever so poor and humble, its own proper home is what the heart of every living creature must yearn after the most, and it is the will of God that the parrot should love her poor wet nest of sticks on the blown willow before all the palaces in the world."

The six months had nearly expired when the parrot, having reared and forsaken a vigorous brood of young ones, prepared to set out for the King's palace. But first, remembering her promised love-token, she visited the beautiful Garden of the Fairies, and from an enchanted tree which grew in the middle of it she selected two small rosy apples, and then continued her flight. Having arrived at court, her presence was at once announced, and she was welcomed with every manifestation of joy. Then she presented her two apples, as tokens that her love had never suffered diminution during all her weary absence. But the King, full of suspicions, as kings are so apt to be, eyed them askance, and to test the virtues he threw one of them to his favourite hound. The dog greedily devoured it, but scarcely had he done so when the poor animal was seized with horrible convulsions and expired in agony. Without a moment's consideration the King rose up, anger darting from his eyes, and, seizing his unfortunate parrot, he instantly wrung her neck. This done, he ordered that the remaining apple should be cast out.

Now, this apple was endowed with magic power, and as it happened that, when it was thrown from the casement, it fell into the King's garden, it soon began to grow; and though it did not grow so high as the clouds, it quickly became a goodly tree, bearing quantities of fruit. It need scarcely be said that no one about the palace ever dreamed of approaching it. Indeed, the King had issued a law that no one should go within fifty yards of it, and on account of its supposed deadly qualities it was known far and wide as THE TREE OF DEATH.

The King's garden was very large and extensive, and in one of its remote corners, just behind the royal stables, there stood a lowly hut in which dwelt an old sweeper and his wife, whose business it was to keep clean the stalls. They were both very miserable, being poor, aged and infirm. One night, as they were meditating on their sad and forlorn condition, the sweeper said to his wife—

"See how wretched we are! Life has become intolerable. As we have now lived too long, let us eat some of the fruit of the Tree of Death, and so die together."

This was no sooner said than done, and the man or the

woman, one or the other, went out and plucked the forbidden fruit, and they made what they believed to be their last meal of it. But lo! now a miracle, for these two old creatures, instead of instantly falling down dead as they expected, became suddenly endowed with youth and beauty, and into all their limbs began to flow a feeling of renewed vigour and strength.

Early the next morning down came the master of the horse, and when he perceived two persons whom he supposed to be perfect strangers in the royal garden he demanded of them who they were, and by what means they had entered.

"We are not intruders," answered they. "We are the two poor old sweepers who have lived in this hut this many a day. Being weary of living, we have eaten of the fruit of the Tree of Death, hoping to die; but, by the blessing of God, instead of dying, we have both become young again."

When the master of the horse had heard this wonderful account he was surprised, and, commanding them to follow him, he ushered them into the immediate presence of the King.

"These two persons," said he, "have strange tidings for you, O king."

So to the King they related all that had befallen them, having first of all fallen on their knees and implored his pardon for their transgression of the laws.

At first the King was so incredulous that he felt inclined to order them forth to instant execution; but at the request of his master of the horse he spared them, in order to test the truth of their statement.

Calling one of the most aged of his nobles, he bade him go forth and gather some of the mysterious fruit which had wrought such miracles. The old courtier instantly hobbled away, and when he returned he held in his hand a small basket of the tiny rose-red apples.

"Behold, sire," said he; "I have obeyed your command."

"Now eat!" exclaimed the monarch. And the old man, not without many misgivings, proceeded to eat one of the shining morsels. Then, indeed, the mind of the bewildered King became satisfied, when before his very eyes he saw his wrinkled servant gradually assuming the lineaments of a glorious youth. It was small wonder that this mighty potentate forgot the dignity of his position, and, rising from his seat, sprang forward to taste so delicious a repast. The whole of the court was permitted to follow his example, and in a single day all the lords and ladies of the palace who had passed the heyday of their strength and beauty became young and blooming once more.

The King now sent for his diviners and soothsayers to interpret for him so singular a wonder, and to explain the mystery of the apple which had killed his dog. Having arranged their enchantments and worked their various spells, they one and all agreed that the first apple had been licked by a serpent, which had lain hidden in the tree of the Garden of the Fairies, and that its venomous saliva, adhering to the fruit, had caused the death of the dog, but that the parrot was in no way to blame. We may feel quite sure that the King, who was noble and generous at heart, had reason then to mourn over the fate of his beloved bird. He made what amends he could, for he erected in her honour a magnificent shrine, where she was ever afterwards adored as a saint, not only by his own subjects, but by pilgrims from all parts of the known world. And the Tree of Death became the Tree of Life.

Told at Ghâzî by a bard, Christmas 1879.

XXX

OF THE OLD WEAVER AND THE CAMEL'S FOOT-PRINTS

One night a camel trespassing in a weaver's field left there the marks of his feet. In the morning the owner brought to the spot the oldest weaver in the village, expecting that he would be able to explain what manner of animal had trodden down his corn. The old man, on seeing the footprints, both laughed and cried. Said the people, "O father, you both laugh and cry! What does this mean?"

"I cry," said he, "because I think to myself, 'What will these poor children do for some one to explain things to them when I am dead,' and I laugh because, as for these footprints, I know not, no, I know not, what they are."

From Ghâzî.

XXXI

OF GRÎBA, THE WEAVER

At the village of Bhurân lived an old weaver named Grîba, who, for a wonder, was shrewd enough. It happened that Habîb Khán, the lambardâr, laid a tax on the weavers' houses at the rate of two rupees for every doorway. When Grîba heard of this, he tore down his door, and, laying it on his shoulders, carried it off to the khân's. "Here, khân," said he, with a profound salaam, "I have heard you want doorways, so I have brought you mine. I also hear you want the side-walls, and I am now going to fetch them, too." Hearing this, the khân laughed, and said, "O Grîba the weaver, take back your door; your tax is paid."

From Hazro.

XXXII

THE ADVENTURES OF ÎSARA AND CANÎSARA

Some years ago there lived two merchants, a Hindu and a Muhammadan, who were partners in the same business. The name of the Hindu was Îsara, and the name of the

Muhammadan was Canîsara. They had once been extremely well off, but hard times had come upon them, their business had declined, and they had gradually sunk into poverty.

One day Canîsara came to the house of Îsara and said, "Lend us something—some money, or some grain, or some bread—we have absolutely nothing to eat."

"O friend," answered Îsara, "you are not in worse plight than we are. We are quite destitute of everything. What can I give you?"

So Canîsara's visit was fruitless, and he returned empty-handed as he had come.

After he had gone, Îsara said to his wife, "All we have is a brass plate and a single brass cup. As the plate is of value, put it for safety into a net and hang it from the roof over our beds; and put some water in the plate, so that if Canîsara comes into the house to steal it when we are asleep, the water will spill on our faces and we shall awake."

That very night Canîsara, who knew of the brass plate, determined to make an effort to become possessed of it. So, long after the inmates were in bed, he visited the house of Îsara, and, softly lifting the latch, stole into the apartment. There, in the faint light of the moon, he saw the plate hanging in a net over the beds, but, being a cunning fellow and suspecting a trick, he first put his forefinger through the net and discovered that the plate contained water. To avoid detection, he now took up some sand, and, with the utmost care, dropped it gradually into the plate, until the whole of the water was absorbed. Having accomplished this, he slowly abstracted the plate from the net and made off with it.

On his way home he considered that his wisest course would be to hide the plate for a short time until he met with an opportunity of selling it. Going, therefore, to a tank, he waded into it some distance, and buried it in the mud, and in order to mark the place he stuck in a long reed which he had plucked on the margin. Then, perfectly satisfied with his success, he went home and got into bed.

The next morning, when Îsara awoke, he missed the plate, and cried, "O wife, Canîsara has been here. He has stolen the plate."

Going at once to his friend's house, he searched it high and low, but returned home no wiser than he was before. As the day was far spent, he went out to the tank for his accustomed bath. When he arrived at the edge of the water, he observed the solitary reed nodding in the wind, and said, "Hallo! this was not here yesterday. This is some trick of Canîsara's." So he waded into the water, and had the satisfaction of discovering his missing plate, which he carried home to his wife, but he left the tell-tale reed undisturbed.

After a day or two Canîsara came down to the tank, and wading out to his reed, began to grope among the mud for the brass plate, but he groped in vain. "Ah!" groaned he, "Îsara has been here." Vexed and disappointed, he returned to his house and smoked his hookah.

Canîsara now visited his partner once more, and said to him, "Friend Îsara, we are both as badly off as we can be. Let us now go together to some other country, and let us take our account-books with us, and see if by hook or by crook we cannot make some money." To this proposal Îsara agreed, and the two friends set out on their travels.

After a weary tramp they arrived at a city in which a rich merchant had recently died, and by inquiry they found that, his body having been burnt, his remains had been duly laid in a certain place. Then Îsara, by tampering with the ledgers which he had brought with him from his own home, concocted a tremendous bill against the defunct merchant, ingeniously running up the amount to forty thousand rupees. When night set in, the two friends went to the place of sepulture, and dug out a chamber, in which Canîsara hid himself, while Îsara covered him over with sticks and earth, and, in short, managed his task so well that in the morning no one would have suspected that the ground had been disturbed at all. Îsara, armed with his account-books, went presently to the house of the sons of the dead merchant, and said to them, "Both your father and your grandfather were in debt to the house of which I am a partner. The total sum due to us is forty thousand rupees, and payment is requested without more delay."

The sons at first attempted to brave it out. "Not a

farthing do we owe you," said they. "Why was not this monstrous claim sent in before?"

"The claim is true," replied Îsara, "and the money is owing in full. I appeal to your dead father. Let him be the judge. I cite you to appear with me at his grave."

The two sons, thus solemnly charged, accompanied their pretended creditor to their father's grave. Now, the dead man's name was Bâhnûshâh.

"O Bâhnûshâh," cried Îsara, "thou model of honour and probity, hear and answer! Are you indebted in the sum of forty thousand rupees to the house of Îsara and Canîsara, or are you not?"

Three times was this appeal made with a loud voice over the grave, and in answer to the third appeal Canîsara spoke in a sepulchral tone from the bowels of the earth: "O my sons," cried he, "if you are faithful to my memory, leave not this weight of woe on my soul, but pay the money at once."

The sons were overwhelmed, and, dropping on their knees, promised to fulfil the request of the dead. They then returned home, and taking Îsara into their counting-house, paid him over the sum demanded, and presented him with a mule in addition to carry away the burden. Îsara, who was beyond measure enchanted with the success of his stratagem, forgot in the full flow of his happiness to return for his partner, and having mounted the mule and ensconced himself in comfort between the saddle-bags, he made haste to get out of the town.

By this time Canîsara, beginning to tire of being pent up in his dark, narrow lodging, was thinking to himself, "Strange! Why does not Îsara come back with news?" And, unable to bear the suspense any longer, he burst open his frail tenement and entered the town. Going to the house of the deluded merchants, he inquired for one named Îsara, and learnt that he had just received the amount of the debt, and had departed. "There he goes," said they, "on yonder mule." Following with his eyes the direction indicated, he saw Îsara astride of the mule going up a neighbouring hill, and occasionally belabouring his stubborn animal with a cudgel. "Ha! ha!" laughed Canîsara, "so Îsara is leaving me in the lurch." And he began to follow him.

Now, as Îsara jogged along he saw a handsome gold-embroidered shoe lying upon the road; but he was too proud in the possession of his newly-acquired wealth to regard such a trifle as an odd shoe, however embroidered, and he continued his way without dismounting. When Canîsara arrived at the spot, however, he picked up the shoe, and a happy thought striking him, he ran at the top of his speed round by some rocks along a by-way and joined the main track again some distance ahead of Îsara. There he laid down the shoe in the middle of the road, and hid himself in a bush.

Îsara, riding up as happy as a king, turned a projecting corner of the road and at once espied the shoe. Reining up his mule, he gazed at it and cried, "Ha! here's the fellow of the shoe I left behind—the same pattern and everything." And, dismounting, he picked up the shoe, tied his mule to the very bush in which Canîsara was in hiding, and ran back as hard as he could go for the supposed fellow. The moment he was out of sight Canîsara got out from the bush, mounted the mule, and rode off at a full pace.

Now, Îsara, of course, looked for the fellow-shoe in vain, and, what was still harder to bear, he returned to the bush to find his mule gone. "Ha!" cried he, "Canîsara has been here!" And he hastened on foot towards his own village.

Meanwhile Canîsara was also pressing on with all speed. He arrived at his home in the middle of the night, and without a word to any of his neighbours he unloaded the mule and drove it away into the forest. He then summoned his wife, and the two between them carried the bags of money into the house and buried them under the mud floor. But being afraid of unpleasant questions if he met Îsara just then, he absented himself from home, charging his wife not to reveal the fact of his arrival.

Îsara, by no means despairing, arrived at his own house and related his adventures to his wife, who agreed with him in his opinion that the money had been taken by Canîsara. "And what is more," said Îsara, "he has buried it in his house."

The next night the wife of Îsara invited the wife of Canîsara to spend a few hours with her, and during the interval Îsara visited the house of his partner and successfully dug up the money, after which he restored the floor to its former appearance. Taking the hoard to his own house, which he entered after the departure of Canîsara's wife, he buried it in like manner under the floor of his chamber. He then went off and hid himself in an old dry well, directing his wife to bring him his food at a certain hour every day.

By this time Canîsara had ventured to return to his home, and choosing a proper time for the purpose, he dug up the floor of his house, stopping now and then to chuckle with his wife over the success of his stratagem. But, alas! the money was nowhere to be found, and he laboured in vain. "Ah!" cried he, throwing down his spade, "Îsara has been here!" Then he considered within himself, "Îsara has taken away the money, but instead of looking for the money I shall now look for Îsara himself."

Canîsara now watched in the neighbourhood of Îsara's house night and day, and observing that his wife always went out at the same hour, he began to suspect that she must be taking her husband's food somewhere. So he dogged her footsteps at a safe distance, and discovered that she made for the old well. There he watched her from behind a boulder, and saw her take bread and buttermilk from under her veil, and lower the food with a piece of string down the well. After a time he noticed that she drew up the empty vessel, and, with a few words to the person below, returned to the town. "Ha, ha!" laughed Canîsara, "Îsara is here; he is down that well! But where can the money be?"

That night Canîsara made up some atrociously bad bread, and the next day he disguised himself as a woman in a long red cloth, and taking with him the bread, a vessel, and a piece of string, he went out to the well and lowered down the food.

"O, you cursed woman!" cried Îsara in a rage, "what bread is this you have brought me?"

"O husband!" answered Canîsara in feigned tones, "you rail at your poor wife, but what am I to do without money?"

"You wretched woman!" said Îsara, "you know that under the floor of our old house there are bags and bags of money! Why can't you take a rupee occasionally and buy me decent victuals?"

Canîsara, having heard quite enough for his purpose, pulled up the empty vessel and took himself off. He passed the real wife on his way into town, and going straight to the house, he abstracted the whole of the money, and carried it to his own house; but this time he buried it in the garden.

Meanwhile, Îsara's wife, having arrived at the well, let down her husband's food. Îsara, when he saw the suspended vessel again bobbing in front of him, cried out, "Hullo! you here again? It is not half-an-hour since you were here before!"

"What are you talking about?" answered the woman. "I have not been near you since this time yesterday."

"Ah!" exclaimed Îsara with a groan, "is it so? Then Canîsara has been here, and we are undone again!"

So he climbed up by the loose masonry and came out of the well. "Now let us go home," said he, "and look after the money." When he came to his house it was too evident that the place had been rifled, and having plied his shovel to no purpose, he rushed off to the house of Canîsara. His wily partner, however, was nowhere to be found, nor with all his searching and digging could he light on the slightest trace of the lost treasure. At last, baffled and disappointed, he went back to his wife and got her to lay him out as if he were dead, and to bewail him after the custom of his people. Then came the neighbours bearing bundles of wood, and a funeral-pyre was erected to burn his body. Canîsara, hearing of these lugubrious preparations, said to himself, "All this, I fear, is only some trick of my old friend;" and he went to the house and asked permission to view the body. "This merchant who is dead was a friend of mine," said he. But they drove him out of the place, saying, "No, no; you are a Muhammadan."

Îsara was now carried out of the house on a stretcher and laid on the top of the funeral-pyre, while blankets and clothes were held round to keep off the gaze of the multitude. Just as the torches were applied, and the smoke began to envelop him, and while the confusion was at its height, he slipped out of his shroud, and, taking advantage of the darkness, he managed to escape from the scene unobserved. His first act was to go again to the house of Canîsara, feeling satisfied that he must by that time have ventured to return; but the latter, full of suspicion and in dread of his life, still kept out of the way. So Îsara's search was a complete failure. "I cannot find the money," said he; "but Canîsara I am determined to hunt out, and then we shall have an account to settle."

Canîsara now resolved to feign death in his turn. "Îsara has not deceived me," said he; "but if I can deceive Îsara, I will return some night, dig up the money, and be off to other parts." So first of all a rumour was circulated that he was very ill; then it was asserted that he was dead; and his wife, to keep up the deceit, laid him out and bewailed him with shrieks and moaning cries. When the neighbours came about, they said, "Alas! it is poor Canîsara!" And they ordered his shroud and carried his body to the grave. There they laid it down upon the earth, close by the tomb of an old hermit, for the customary observances, and Îsara, who had followed the mourners, contrived to get a peep at his friend's face, saying, "This poor man, as you know, was a crony of mine." Having satisfied his doubts, he climbed into a tree, which was near the grave, and waited there until, the rites being completed, the body was laid in its chamber. As soon as the company had dispersed, night having now set in, Îsara got down from the tree, crept to the old tomb, and, lifting up the slab, dragged out the body alive and laid it down by the edge of the grave. Just then the noise of approaching footsteps and subdued whispers caught his attention, and he again got into the tree, wondering what this interruption could be.

The party which now approached was a gang of notorious robbers, seven in number, one of whom was blind of an eye. Catching sight of the body in the old tomb, they examined it with great care, and exclaimed, "See, this must be some famous saint! He has come out of his grave, and his body is perfectly fresh. Let us pray to him for favour and good luck!" So they one and all fell down on their knees and besought his assistance. "We are pledged to a robbery this night," said they. "If we are successful, O saint, into your mouth we shall drop some sugar." The one-eyed man, however, said, "As for me, I shall tickle his throat with some water."

Having made their vows, they all set out for the town, robbed a rich man's house, and returned, each one bearing his own bag of money, to the graveyard. They now dropped morsels of sugar into Canîsara's mouth in accordance with their promises; but when it came to the turn of the robber of the one eye, he trickled in some vile water. Poor Canîsara had accepted the sugar with stolid indifference; but the disgusting water, tickling his gullet, nearly choked him, and he began to cough most violently. Precisely at this moment Îsara, who had been an absorbed observer of the scene, suddenly shrieked out in menacing tones, "Never mind the fellows behind; catch the rascal who is standing in front!"

These unexpected words sounded in the robbers' ears like the voice of the black angel, and imagining themselves in the midst of evil spirits, they took to their heels and incontinently ran away, leaving their bags of money behind them by the open grave.

The dead Canîsara now sprang to his feet, crying out, "Ha! ha! Îsara is here, and I have caught him at last!" And as the latter had descended from the tree, the two friends embraced each other most cordially. Picking up the seven bags of gold, they entered the old tomb, where they managed to light one of the little earthenware lamps belonging to the shrine, and by dint of drawing the feeble flame close enough, they poured out the glittering heaps, and proceeded to settle their accounts. They were, however, unable to agree about a balance of a single farthing; and their words began to run high, each of them asserting his claim with tremendous warmth.

By this time the robbers, having come to a halt, deputed their one-eyed companion to return and look for the money. One-eyed men are proverbially cunning, and this one was determined not to impair his reputation. Creeping quietly along, he arrived at the tomb as the dispute was in full career; but, alas! he was seen; and just as his head appeared through one of the holes in the wall, Canîsara suddenly snatched off the fellow's old turban, and, handing it to Îsara, cried, "Here, then, is your farthing; so now we are quits!" The robber, drawing back his head with the utmost despatch, ran as fast as his legs could carry him to his confederates, and told them, "The number of demons in that old tomb is so immense that the share of each of them comes to only a single farthing! Let us get away, or we shall all be caught and hanged!" So, in a great fright, they left the place on the instant, and never returned again.

Then said the wily Canîsara to the wily Îsara, "With the forty thousand rupees which I possess already, my share of this capture is one bag, and these other six bags are therefore yours."

The two friends were now equally rich; and returning to their homes, they bought lands and houses, and defied poverty for the rest of their days, living together with their wives and children in the utmost happiness and in the enjoyment of every blessing.

Told at Ghâzi, Upper Indus, 1880.

XXXIII

THE STORY OF PÛRAN BHAGAT[1]

KING SÛLWÂHÂN (Sâlivahân) reigned in Siâlkôt in the Panjâb. In course of time he had a son named Pûran, whose mother's name was Ichrân. When Pûran was born the King sent, as usual, for the astrologers and the family priest to make his horoscope, and, as it was written in his forehead, so was it read by them, for they told the King that he was not to see his son for twelve years. Therefore poor Pûran, as soon as he was born, was confined in a tower. Having come out of one solitary cell he was sent into another, with attendants both male and female and provisions of all kinds, for twelve years. There he had governors to train him, professors to teach him the use of the bow, and learned men to instruct him in affairs both civil and military. When he was six years old the pundits gave him lessons in the sacred books. By the time he was twelve he was fully equipped in every kind of knowledge and equal to the discharge of all worldly affairs. Then the order came that he might leave his tower and visit his father. And when Pûran heard it he was much pleased, and, getting together innumerable

1 *Bhagat*—a devotee, a saint.

presents, he set out to see his father, who was waiting impatiently to receive him. Well pleased was the King to see his son Pûran at last; and he distributed largess and alms, and gave presents to the pundits and Brâhmins, as cows, buffaloes, horses and elephants. And to Pûran was given a seat near to the throne on the right side, where he sat and ruled the court.

Now the King beholding his son, and observing that he was now nearly grown, issued strict orders to his servants and courtiers to look out for a wife for him. "As God has granted to me this jewel," said he, "I should see that he is married." But Pûran refused that honour, saying, "I do not care for marriage, neither do I value it. I desire to see the world, and devote myself only to the service of God. Of your grace, please do not lay trouble upon me, nor chain and shackle me with your own hands. O sir, hold me not back from the ways of virtue!"

The King, hearing these words from Pûran's own mouth, became displeased, and said, "So, you are my son, and you have the power to disobey me?"

But the wazîr, observing his state of anger, said, "Sir, you will please excuse him; he is only a boy; what can he know about marriage? When he comes of age, he will not want telling, he will then go wooing himself. You need not feel concerned about his marriage."

Then the King's anger was appeased, and he said no more.

Now the King himself had not long before married a new wife, a girl named Lûna, of the caste of the leather-dressers, who was very handsome, and who, when adorned, looked like the moon. And it came about at this time that the King said to Pûran, "Go now and pay your respects to your mother and the other Queen, your step-mother, for they are also anxious to see you, and be careful that you disobey not this order!"

So Pûran rose accordingly, and taking with him all his servants male and female, he went to the King's palace to pay his respects to the two queens. Many were the presents which were borne by his attendants, and many the jewels and the ornaments which he wore on his own person, and which doubled and trebled his beauty. His earrings were shining like stars in the sky, the diamonds in his necklet were glittering brilliantly, his hand-rings were right noble, and it cannot be expressed how greatly his looks were enhanced by their display.

Having arrived at the place, Pûran made inquiry from the attendants where the palace of his mother stood, and where the palace of his step-mother, and each was pointed out to him. And he said, "It is better that I should pay respect to my step-mother first, because my real mother knows that I am her son, and that to her I am always bound in honour and obedience."

Having so said to his attendants, he went towards the palace of the Râni Lûna, passing in without difficulty and having confidence that a kind and tender reception awaited him. But scarcely had he entered the chamber, when this lady, having looked on his youth and beauty, became suddenly enamoured, the fires of love were kindled into flames which issued from her body, and losing all sense of modesty, she fixed eyes of eager desire upon him. Pûran, unwitting of danger, meanwhile advanced towards her, and, having reached the place where the Râni was seated, he folded his hands together, and, prostrating himself, made his salutations. But instead of returning a dignified answer, she also humbled herself, paying him the respect of an inferior, which when Pûran saw, he was astounded, and he thought within himself, "Alas, it was fated that I should be brought in here!" Râni Lûna, on the other hand, was thinking that to be with him would be to bathe in the sacred waters of the Ganges, and that to be loved by him would be Paradise itself, and she promised herself that she would be one of the lucky women of the world if Pûran would comply with her wishes. In short, such was her state of melancholy and distress that she could not longer control herself, but broke out openly into speech.

"Why say 'Mother, mother!' to me?" cried she. "I am not your mother! Never were you born of womb of mine, then why call you me 'Mother'? You are my equal in age, and in person we are worthy each of the other; your love-darts pierce my heart, and words cannot tell all that I suffer for love of you!"

Then in his shame Pûran said to her, "Never must you use any such words to me! Was such friendship between mother and son ever yet heard of? And how will the world speak ill of us if we meditate this thing! I am your son! As a mother you must embrace me and think of me!"

But Râni Lûna, throwing away the wheel of shame, caught hold of him by his coat, and pulled him towards her, saying, "Come, sit with me on this royal couch! Behold in me, not a woman, but some fairy, entitled to make offers to you, and begging you to accept them. But you, whether you are man or eunuch I know not, seeing you display no manly attribute. O dear friend, come and sit down to please me!"

Then Pûran regarded her sternly, and with rough language spoke. "Mother, you are mad! Your husband is my father! Me you should think of as a son born of your own bosom. If we were to commit this folly, earth and sky would vanish away! Oh, come to your senses! In the name of God, do not be mad!"

"I shall kill you!" cried Lûna. "Yea, I will cause you to be killed by your own father, if you deny me again! Here am I standing before you, like a poor beggar for an alms, and you, because you are stern and stout-hearted, care not a jot for my prayers, which in fact you disdain. Were you born of me? Have I given you milk out of my breasts! By what law, by what reason do you call me 'mother'? Why will you slay yourself? why lose your own life?"

"Please take note and be careful to remember," said Pûran, "that I will not touch your couch, nor put a foot on it, and that from this moment I will not allow even my eyes to turn towards you! And now, I care not if I am killed or not!"

So saying, he wrested his clothing out of her hand, and fled the place, saying, "At least I will not die laden with sin so unnatural and so dreadful!" But Lûna, when she saw him going, cried out, "Very well—look out!—This day I will drink your blood!"

That evening, before the arrival of Râja Sûlwâhân, Râni Lûna, taking off all her jewels and ornaments, some of them breaking, some of them twisting, laid them aside, and lighted no candles in her palace, but went into a solitary room, and there, wrapping herself in an old torn dress, sat in grief. And when the Râja entered the palace she instantly came to him crying bitterly, and sat down with him. The King asked her of her trouble, to which she replied, "Ah, do not ask me! Ask rather your son who has been fed like a stallion from the stall, and has burnt up my heart. Keep him by you—you had better—but let me go away!"

The King, hearing this, was enraged, and ordered Lûna to explain herself, and to disclose everything whatsoever he had done to her. "If he has spoken unbecomingly to you," said he, "if he has used harsh language to you, tell me of it! Verily I will hang him. What value is such a son to me? If he has done evil to you to-day, will he do less to me when he comes to manhood?"

"See my body, see my jewels," cried the Râni, "look at my couch, these are the signs of his violence! I spoke to him as a son, but he did not treat me as a mother!"

Then she brought out her jewels. "This was broken, when he twisted my arm," said she, "and when I withstood him, he rushed from the palace!"

At these tidings the King's heart was aflame with rage, he was weltering in troubles caused by his own son. The whole night he passed counting the stars and thinking about him. But when morning broke, he rose and, after taking his bath, he ordered his doorkeepers and his other attendants to summon his wazîr and to bring Pûran before him. "If they ask the reason," said he, "say there is work for them." Then those servants went to the wazîr, and told him, and afterwards sought out Pûran, to whom with folded hands they spoke. "Your father calls you!" But Pûran, at the rehearsal of their message, understood well enough the reason of the summons, and he said to himself, "I know all about this affair. But I do not care; let me see what comes of it!"

When Pûran came into his presence, the Râja said to him, "You have plunged me into rivers of trouble! Would God you had been killed at your birth! Behold what you have done in the house! Get out of my sight, lest I cut you to pieces! When I asked you to marry you refused, and now you would choose your mother for wife, would you?"

Pûran wept bitterly. And he said, "Father, it is not in my power to tell you, still less to make you believe, what has come to pass. Do not lose your senses, I pray, that you should blame me for such a crime. If you would judge me truly, and see whether I am guilty or innocent, take a chaldron of oil and heat it well, and when the oil is hot like unto fire, put my hand into it, and if my hand burn, let punishment light on me, but if not, then you still can act as you please!"

On hearing these words, the King was the more incensed, and said, "Instead of asking pardon, instead of atoning for your crime, you contradict me! I have seen every sign and every proof of what you have done!"

Then the King ordered the executioners to take him and to kill him. And that order, when it passed, caused a great disturbance in the palace and in the city all round. All was disorder, and the King began to reprimand his wazîr, too, saying, "It is you who are at the root of all my troubles!" But when Ichrân, Pûran's real mother, heard of it, she came running to the Râja, breaking her jewels and throwing dust on her head, and crying, "What anger have you against my son Pûran? You are in the power of Râni Lûna, and therefore must you kill the innocent boy!"

"Away with him!" said the King. "And you, you wretched woman, be off! Otherwise you shall go with him! Your son is an unlucky son, born on some luckless day, who, having come into the world, has caused me all this disgrace. He is no shame to yourself, nay, he is no good at all. I know perfectly well the mischief he has wrought!"

"Sir," answered the Râni Ichrân, "it is not true. You should consider well. Why have you taken leave of your senses? How do you know that the Râni Lûna has spoken the truth? For her only you are losing the Faith!"

The King, however, would hear no more, but ordered the executioners to obey his command forthwith, saying, "Go out into the jungle with him, and cut off his hands and his feet!"

Hearing the sentence, Pûran paid him his last farewell with respect, and started under charge of the executioners.

And Pûran said, "I am as one without strength, with no power to explain what I am suffering, and there is no friend of mine who can tell me what fault I have done that I should suffer so much. All I can think is that it was written in my forehead that I should be judged a thief through Râni Lûna my step-mother!" And though Râni Ichrân interceded for him again, pleading for his life, and saying, "Do not kill your son! Who now will call you father!" the Râja closed his ears, refusing to be entreated; nay, in his fury he again charged the executioners, saying to them, "Go at once and obey my orders! You will cut off his hands and his feet, and then kill him like a goat!" And so the executioners caught Pûran, and away they went with him.

Now it came to pass, as they were taking him out of the city, that Râni Lûna sent a letter to him secretly, saying, "If you will agree to my request, I will stand security for you, and lay the blame on another servant. Think of it! There is still time. Why lose your life for nothing?"

But Pûran spat on the letter and told her, "I do not wish to save my life weighed down by the burden of such a crime. Even if I live thousands of years, it is still appointed unto me once to die!" Then, with a deep sigh, he said, "May God visit you, as you have dealt by me! Unnatural is the crime which you have fastened on me. Whatever has come upon my head, that I will bear, but my mother will die with the sorrow of it!"

Then Pûran besought his executioners to stop for a moment at his mother's palace, and his request was allowed, and Pûran and his mother Ichrân met once more, and bade each other their last farewells, resigning all hope of ever meeting again. Then she returned, crying and beating her breast, and saying, "For a slight offence, Pûran Baghat, my son, is going to be killed innocently!"

And the executioners, having taken him some distance into the jungle, cut off his hands and his feet, and, throwing him into an old ruined well, came back with a cup full of his blood to the palace of the Râni Lûna, who rejoiced to see it.

Twelve years passed over, when the Gûrû Gôrakhnâth was pleased to order his disciples to go on a tour with him, and, having started, they reached Siâlkôt, and pitched their tents not far from the ruined well into which Pûran had been cast by the King's executioners. Halting there, he ordered one of his disciples to go and fetch some water, but when the man had thrown his line and lotah (brass vessel) in hopes to reach water, he peered down and saw a man in the well. The disciple was frightened at the sight, supposing it was a spirit or a demon, and ran back to his *gûrû*, and explained what he had seen, saying, "Gûrû Sâhib, as soon as I had reached the well, and was about to draw up water, I saw to my great surprise a man sitting in the well. If you will please come yourself, you will be satisfied that this is so. I cannot tell if it is a man, or a spirit, or some evil ghost!"

The *gûrû*, hearing these words, went to the well, and with him went all his followers. And when they reached the well, all the rest kept silence, while the *gûrû* spoke and asked, "Who are you? What is your name? How came you in here?"

Then Pûran, crying bitterly, answered and said, "After lapse of twelve years I have seen a human face again! I also am a man, you can see that for yourself, if you like! But if you feel any pity for me, you will kindly take me out, and then I will tell you my history."

The *gûrû* therefore ordered his disciples to take Pûran out, which was accordingly done. And when Pûran came to the surface, the *gûrû* was greatly pleased when he beheld his beautiful shape, and he said, "O God, have mercy on him!" Then ordered he his disciples to carry him tenderly to his tent and to set him down.

And he asked him, saying, "Where is your home, O child? What is your name and your father's name? How comes it that your hands and feet are cut off? Explain to me everything."

And Pûran answered, "Our real country is Ujjain, the land of the Râja Vîkrâmâjît, and to this side came our ancestors and settled in Siâlkôt. My name is Pûran, son of Sûlwâhân, and Râja Sûlwâhân having cut off my hands and my feet, threw me in here. So far I tell you, but I can tell you no more, unless you lay your injunctions on me, and then, if you do, I will explain further to you!"

The disciples, hearing this, said to him, "Happy should you be, and well content, that you have met Gûrû Gorakhnâth! He is the beloved of God, and his worship has been accepted by the Almighty. You can ask what you please of him!"

Then Pûran began his hapless story, not forgetting his father's kindness, and the *gûrû* heard him attentively. And Pûran said, "When I was born every one loved me, and my father fed me with love and caresses. After twelve years I came forth from my tower, and my father, when he saw me, ordered his minister to arrange a marriage for me, but I refused the favour designed me. Then, in a short time, he ordered me to go and pay my dutiful respects to my mother and step-mother. But when I entered the palace of Lûna you may think what she was about to do, for, losing the wheel of shame, she tried to subdue me with love, but I, drawing my clothes forcibly away from her, ran out of the palace. Then, in the night, she made my father believe what she pleased. And when the Râja heard it, without further consideration he ordered the executioners to take me and kill me, and so, having brought me here, they cut off my hands and my feet, and left me in this old well."

Then Gûrû Gorakhnâth was pleased exceedingly to hear this history of Pûran, and taking a vessel, he threw handfuls of water over him, and remembered God, and prayed for him, that He would see fit to grant him his lost limbs, and lo, his prayers were heard, and Pûran was made whole again.

Then Pûran, seeing that he was restored, offered his thanks to the *gûrû*, and begged him to make him one of his disciples; but the *gûrû* answered, saying, "Rather you must now return to your own home, and see your father again."

"Much I may not say," said Pûran. "Only do you please accept my petition and grant me *jog*. Having pierced my ears, O sir, insert the stone earrings with your own hand!"

"*Jog* you must not think of," answered the *gûrû*. "The performance of *jog* is beyond you. You will have to suffer hunger and thirst, to bear trials with patience, and to renounce the world. You will have to leave behind all the pleasures of sense, and to enter upon a life most difficult to pursue."

But Pûran, folding his hands, persisted, saying, "I will obey your orders, I will accept all your directions. Show me kindness, then, and make me one of your slaves. I will strive my utmost, and do whatever service you impose."

At last the *gûrû* granted his prayer, and having shorn off some of his hair, he pierced his ears with his own hands, and put the *muṇdrâ* (stone earrings) in them, and so Pûran became a *jogî* or fakîr.

Two days passed, and the *gûrû* then ordered Pûran to go to the palace of the Râni Sundra,[1] and bring thence food for the brotherhood. As he was going, the other disciples said among themselves, "Let us see now of what sort he will be when he returns!"

But Pûran took no notice, but having asked the *gûrû* to lay his hand upon him, and having uttered the name of God, he started for the house of Sundra. The *gûrû* also said to him, "Take care, you must treat every one, man and woman alike, as brother and sister. This alone is the way to win the world!"

"Sir," answered Pûran, "if it had been my desire to enjoy the world, I should have listened to Lûna, or I should have followed my father's direction to marry; or again, when you bade me return to my house, I should have gone, if I had hankered after pleasure. Be assured, therefore—I have no worldly desire at all!"

With these words he went on his way, and came to the palace of Râni Sundra, and there, speaking with a loud voice, he begged for alms, which were sent out to him by a female slave. But Pûran said, "My business to-day is not with slaves, nor from them have I come to take alms. You will please go and tell the Râni to come herself, and give me the alms."

The slave fell in love with him the moment she saw him, and, without a word in answer, she went in and told the Râni all he had said, adding other words of her own. "Râni," said she, "you are always admiring your own beauty. Look at this fakîr who is sitting before your house, he is a thousand times handsomer! You can come and see for yourself!"

The Râni went to one of her palace-windows and looked out. And when she saw his beautiful face, instantly she too fell in love with him, and she said to the slave-girl, "Go and call the fakîr in!" So the girl came once more to Pûran and gave her message, saying, "Please come in, the Râni wants you!"

But Pûran answered, "It is not the custom of fakîrs to enter houses. Go tell the Râni to come out and give me whatever alms she has to give herself!"

When the Râni heard that, she opened her caskets, and filling a tray with rich jewels, she took them out herself to

[1] *Sundar*—beautiful.

the fakîr, and said, "Please accept them, so shall I esteem it a favour! Yea, I should be fortunate if you would accept myself and my house as well!"

Pûran, however, did not consent, but, taking from her all the jewels, he returned to the *gûrû*, and told him the things which had befallen him.

Now the *gûrû* was astonished to see him again, and he asked him, saying, "Who gave you all these precious stones?"

"The Râni Sundra herself gave them to me," answered Pûran.

"These stones," said the *gûrû*, "are of no use to fakîrs. You must look upon them as common pebbles of the public road. Better go and return them!"

So the next day Pûran set out again for the house of the Râni Sundra, who was eagerly waiting for him, and who, when he arrived, received him with pleasure. Pûran paid his compliments to her, and said, "You will please take back the jewels. My *gûrû* is not pleased. But if you have bread, or any other victuals in the house, pray bring them!" The Râni then set to work and prepared various cakes and sweetmeats with her own hand, and, laying them in dishes and trays, she ordered her servants to carry them to Gûrû Gorakhnâth. Then said she to Pûran, "Come, I will go see the *gûrû* myself!" So she went with him, and her servants bearing loads of food followed after, and so came to the *gûrû*, to whom she offered her respects, laying all her offerings at his feet. Round about stood the whole band of the disciples, who came together at that sight, and she threw looks at them all, and no one of that company persevered in virtue saving and except the *gûrû* and Pûran only.

Now her coming pleased the *gûrû* greatly, and he said to her, "What boon do you wish?"

"By your kindness and grace," answered she, "I have in my house all I desire—servants, horses, elephants, female attendants—nothing is wanting but your goodwill and the grace of God."

Then said the *gûrû* to her again, "What boon do you wish? Ask without fear!"

Then the Râni, standing in the midst of them, looked round on all his disciples, and she chose Pûran as worthy to be the boon she desired. And the *gûrû* consented, accepting her request, and laid his orders on Pûran to go with her. Pûran kept silence, not wishing to gainsay his *gûrû*, but, rising, he went with the Râni Sundra, and accompanied her home. And when they came to the palace, the Râni said, "I am one of the fortunate women in the world, and blessed is my lot. To-day I have obtained my desire through the kindness of the Gûrû Gorakhnâth, yea, such a bargain have I made this day, that no one else in the world will ever make the like of it again!"

Pûran, however, was not so pleased, for as they drew nigh the house, he was in mind to run away, and ere they reached the door he begged the Râni to allow him to go into the jungle for a space. And the Râni, consenting, ordered two of her female slaves to attend him. But having gone some distance from the city, he ran for his life, saying to the slaves, "Go tell your Râni that Pûran has gone away!" Those attendants therefore went back to the Râni, and explained to her all that had happened in the jungle. The Râni, hearing the news, fell senseless, and began to cry and to beat her breast, saying, "If I had known you would have played me this trick, never would I have allowed you to go to the jungle. Hardly had I known the bliss of looking at your face, when, like an enemy, you left me in all this woe. Ah, dear one, I have no power over you at all, and for you alone I go to my death this day!" Then she went up to the top of the palace, and looked long into the jungle, but no sign of Pûran was to be seen anywhere round. Failing to find him and despairing of his return, she threw herself over and killed herself, and her death was mourned by the whole city.

Pûran, on the other side, leaving that place, came to Tillâh, where his *gûrû* was then abiding, who, when he saw him approaching, straightway understood that he had left the Râni Sundra. And he spoke angrily to him, saying, "You have not acted in accordance with my wishes!" But Pûran wept before him, and said, "I told you, Gûrû Sâhib, that I have no desire for worldly pleasures, and yet, notwithstanding my words, you bade me marry a wife."

Then, understanding it all, the *gûrû* felt pleased, and took him into favour.

The next day the *gûrû* said to Pûran, "Now go to

Siâlkôt and see your father!" Instantly Pûran obeyed, and coming to Siâlkôt, he entered an old garden of his own, which for want of water and care had dried up, and in that garden he tarried, and the moment he entered the garden, all the trees and the flowers, which had died down to the earth, instantly revived and put forth blossom and leaf, and all over the city went the news, that the garden that had been dry for many years was now as green as before. And people wondered and said, "Who has come here that the garden is so green again?" And multitudes came to see him, and whosoever came received whatever he needed.

And it came to pass that some one made report of the miracle to Râja Sûlwâhân and Râni Lûna, who, when they heard of it, also went to see the strange fakîr. And the people cleared the way and told him, saying, "Here are the Râja and Râni come to see you!" When Pûran heard that, he got up, and offered his respects to them both, receiving them humbly.

And the King said to him, "Sir, I have come to see you, but you have laid weight of obligation on my head to receive me with ceremony thus!"

"How came you here, and why do you visit me?" said Pûran. "Please say!"

"You seem to be a sage and a friend of God," answered the King. "All I need is a son, if, in your kindness, you will grant the boon."

"I think," said Pûran, "that you had a son, and that somebody, taking him into the jungle, killed him like a goat. Will you tell me how he died?"

Hearing these words, the Râja wept bitterly, and answering, said, "Yes, sir, there was once a son in my house, born of the Râni Ichrân. When he was young, I ordered him to go and visit his mothers, and he, seeing his step-mother, Râni Lûna, and throwing all shame and virtue aside, wanted to deal injuriously with her."

"O sir," said Pûran, "beware how you speak! Your son was innocent, but not so his mother!"

Then turning to Râni Lûna he said, "Râni, will you explain now how it all happened? God will give you a son, but first you must truly confess your fault. Only beware and do not prevaricate!"

"Alas," said the Râni, "mine alone was the fault and

not Pûran's! Not he, but I, I only was to blame! When he came to my palace, I, at sight of his lovely face, begged him to be my friend. But Pûran refused, and I then said to him, 'If you will not be mine, something worse shall happen to you.' So, after that, beguiling the Râja, I caused him to be made away with."

Great was the astonishment of the Râja on hearing these words. "O wretched woman," cried he, "then it was your deed that lost me my son, and you it was who wrought the mischief, by which Pûran, my son, went out of my hands!"

When Pûran saw them both crying, he could not restrain himself, but, weeping too, he said to the Râni, "Lûna, let the past go! That which was written in his destiny has come to pass!" Then giving a grain of rice to the Râja, he ordered him to give it to his Râni, "for then," said he, "by the grace of God, there shall be a son in your house again; but trouble shall be his portion such as that which Râni Lûna brought on Pûran, and through trouble like his shall he die."

In the meantime, Râni Ichrân, Pûran's real mother, heard of the wonders that were being wrought, and she said to herself, "Let me also go there, and beg healing for my eyes!" So she started for the place, but her eyes were dim from much weeping, and scarcely could she see where she was going. And as she was stumbling, Pûran turned, and saw his mother coming to him in her trouble, so he got up, and ran to her, and bringing her to his shed, he questioned her, saying, "Mother, what has happened to your eyes?"

"Ah, sir," said she, "the loss of my son Pûran has blinded me."

"You should not weep for him," said Pûran, "neither should you lament him. He who has once died can never again come back. Rather pray to God, and He will give you your sight!"

She, having recognized his voice, then said, "Son, from what side have you come? Where was your birthplace, who was your father, what fortunate mother brought you into the world? If I could see, soon should I find out who you are. But your voice tells me you are Pûran. Am I right or not?"

"I am disciple of the Gûrû Gorakhnâth," answered

he, "and *jogî* by profession. My ancestors were men of renown in Ujjain. I am a son of the Râja Sûlwâhân, my name is Pûran, and *Pwâr* (Râjpût) is my caste!"

His mother, hearing these words, became happy, light once more visited her eyes, she embraced her son, and all her trouble and sorrow vanished away.

Now the Râja, when he saw and heard all these things, became ashamed, and he began to mourn over his own folly. But Pûran looked at him, and said, "Sir, let it go, for, as it was fated to be, so has my destiny brought it to pass." And as Lûna was also thinking and lamenting over all she had said to him, he spoke to her as well, saying, "Think no more of the past! Regard me as your own son and forgive me! Not so much your fault is it, as the fault of my father, seeing he did not inquire into the matter." Then the Râja, with folded hands, cried, "O God, forgive me, for I alone am the root of all my son's misfortunes! What answer shall I make to Thee, O God, hereafter?"

After these things, Pûran said to them all, "Now go back to your house! There live happily, and let me return from whence I have come!"

"Sir," said the King, "go not away again! Come home with me, take the keys of all my palaces, and of all my treasuries, and be king of the land instead of me, for, if you leave me now, the parting will surely kill me!"

But Pûran refused his father's request, and then his mother Ichrân begged him to come and live for a time near her. But that too he refused, saying, "From this place, when a child, I was taken away into exile. How then shall I show my face now before the people! But I give you my *gûrû* as a surety, that I will come and see you again. Do not therefore urge me with speech, but allow me to go!"

Having so spoken, Pûran got up to leave them there, both the Râja and his mother, and to his father he said, "Treat Lûna as your queen, and also take care of my mother!" So having started from that place he came once more to Tillâh, and there paid his compliments and his respects to the Gûrû Gorakhnâth, as also to all the brethren of the order, explaining the strange events which had passed between his parents and himself. And the *gûrû* was greatly pleased to hear it, and to see him again, and he blessed him, saying, "May God guard you and keep you happy!"

Told at Murree, July 1881, by Gharal, a story-teller.

XXXIV

THE STORY OF THE KING AND THE FOUR GIRLS

THERE was once a king who, during the day, used to sit on his throne and dispense justice, but who at night was accustomed to disguise himself and to wander about the streets of his city looking for adventures.

One evening he was passing by a certain garden when he observed four young girls sitting under a tree, and conversing together in earnest tones. Curious to overhear the subject of their discourse, he stopped to listen. The first said, "I think of all tastes the pleasantest in the world is the taste of meat."

"I do not agree with you," said the second; "there is nothing so good as the taste of wine."

"No, no," cried the third; "you are both mistaken, for of all tastes the sweetest is the taste of love."

"Meat and wine and love are all doubtless sweet," remarked the fourth girl; "but in my opinion nothing can equal the taste of telling lies."

The girls then separated, and went to their homes; and the King, who had listened to their remarks with lively interest and with much wonder, took note of the houses into which they went, and, having marked each of the doors with chalk, he returned to his palace.

The next morning he called his wazîr, and said to him, "Send to the narrow street, and bring before me the owners of the four houses the doors of which have a round mark in chalk upon them." The wazîr at once went in person, and brought to the court the four men who lived in the houses to which the King had referred. Then said the King to them, "Have not you four men four daughters?"

"We have," answered they.

"Bring the girls hither before me," said the King.

But the men objected, saying, "It would be very wrong that our daughters should approach the palace of the King."

"Nay," said the King; "if the girls are your daughters, they are mine too, besides which you can bring them privately."

So the King sent four separate litters, curtained in the usual manner, and the four girls were thus brought to the palace and conducted into a large reception-room. Then he summoned them one by one to his presence as he required them. To the first girl he said, "O daughter, what were you talking about last night when you sat with your companions under the tree?"

"I was not telling tales against you, O King," answered she.

"I do not mean that," said the King; "but I wish to know what you were saying."

"I merely said," replied she, "that the taste of meat was the pleasantest."

"Whose daughter, then, are you?" inquired the King.

"I am the daughter of a Bhábrá," answered she.

"But," said the King, "if you are one of the Bhábrá tribe, who never touch meat, what do you know of the taste of it? So strict are they, that when they drink water they put a cloth over the mouth of the vessel, lest they should swallow even an insect."

Then said the girl, "Yes, that is quite true, but, from my own observation, I think meat must be exceedingly pleasant to the palate. Near our house there is a butcher's shop, and I often notice that when people buy meat none of it is wasted or thrown away; therefore it must be precious. I also notice that, when people have eaten the flesh, the very bones are greedily seized upon by the dogs, nor do they leave them until they have picked them as clean as a lance-head. And even after that, the crows come and carry them off, and when the crows have done with them, the very ants assemble together and swarm over them. Those are the reasons which prove that the taste of flesh-meat must be exceedingly pleasant."

The King, hearing her argument, was pleased, and said, "Yes, daughter, meat is very pleasant as food; every one likes it." And he sent her away with a handsome present.

The second girl was then brought in, and of her the King inquired likewise, "What were you talking about last night under the tree?"

"I said nothing about you, O King," answered she.

"That is true, but what did you say?" asked the King.

"What I said," replied she, "was that there was no taste like the taste of wine."

"But whose daughter are you?" continued the King.

"I am," said she, "the daughter of a priest."

"A good joke, forsooth," said the King, smiling. "Priests hate the very name of wine. Then, what do you know of the taste of it?"

Then said the girl, "It is true I never touch wine, but I can easily understand how pleasant it is. I learn my lessons on the top of my father's house. Below are the wine-shops. One day I saw two men nicely dressed, who came with their servants to buy wine at those shops, and there they sat and drank. After a time they got up and went away, but they staggered about from side to side, and I thought to myself, 'Here are these fellows rolling about, knocking themselves against the wall on this side, and falling against the wall on that: surely they will never drink wine again!' However, I was mistaken, for the next day they came again and did the very same thing, and I considered, 'Wine must be very delicious to the taste, or else these persons would never have returned for more of it.'"

Then said the King, "Yes, O daughter, you are right; the taste of wine is very pleasant." And, giving her also a handsome present, he sent her home.

When the third girl entered the room, the King asked her in like manner, "O daughter, what were you talking about last night under the tree?"

"O King," answered she, "I made no reference to you."

"Quite so," said the King; "but tell me what it was you were saying."

"I was saying," replied she, "that there is no taste in the world so sweet as the taste of love-making."

"But," said the King, "you are a very young girl, what can you know about love-making? Whose daughter are you?"

"I am the daughter of a bard," answered she. "It is true I am very young, but somehow I guess that love-making must be pleasant. My mother suffered so much when my little brother was born that she never expected to live. Yet, after a little time, she went back to her old ways and welcomed her lovers just the same as before. That is the reason I think that love-making must be so very pleasant." [1]

"What you say," observed the King, "cannot, O daughter, be justly denied." And he gave her a present equal in value to those of her friends and sent her, also, away.

When the fourth girl was introduced, the King put the same question to her, "Tell me what you and your companions talked about under the tree last night."

"It was not about the King," answered she.

"Nevertheless," asked he, "what was it you said?"

"Those who tell lies, said I, must tell them because they find it most agreeable," replied she.

"Whose daughter are you?" inquired the King.

"I am the daughter of a farmer," answered the girl.

"And what made you think there was pleasure in telling lies?" asked the King.

The girl answered saucily, "Oh, you yourself will tell lies some day!"

"How?" said the King. "What can you mean?"

The girl answered, "If you will give me two lacs of rupees, and six months to consider, I will promise to prove my words."

So the King gave the girl the sum of money she asked for, and agreed to her conditions, sending her away with a present similar to those of the others.

After six months he called her to his presence again, and reminded her of her promise. Now, in the interval the girl had built a fine palace far away in the forest, upon which she had expended the wealth which the King had

[1] The caste of the professional bard (*mirāsi*) is very low. Their women are generally "dancing-girls."

given to her. It was beautifully adorned with carvings and paintings, and furnished with silk and satin. So she now said to the King, "Come with me, and you shall see God." Taking with him two of his ministers, the King set out, and by the evening they all arrived at the palace.

"This palace is the abode of God," said the girl. "But He will reveal Himself only to one person at a time, and He will not reveal Himself even to him unless he was born in lawful wedlock. Therefore, while the rest remain without, let each of you enter in order."

"Be it so," said the King. "But let my ministers precede me. I shall go in last."

So the first minister passed through the door and at once found himself in a noble room, and as he looked round he said to himself, "Who knows whether I shall be permitted to see God or not? I may be a bastard. And yet this place, so spacious and so beautiful, is a fitting dwelling-place even for the Deity." With all his looking and straining, however, he quite failed to see God anywhere. Then said he to himself, "If now I go out and declare that I have not seen God, the King and the other minister will throw it in my teeth that I am base-born. I have only one course open, therefore, which is to say that I have seen Him."

So he went out, and when the King asked, "Have you seen God?" he answered at once, "Of course I have seen God."

"But have you really seen Him?" continued the King.

"Really and truly," answered the minister.

"And what did He say to you?" inquired the King further.

"God commanded me not to divulge His words," readily answered the minister.

Then said the King to the other minister, "Now you go in."

The second minister lost no time in obeying his master's order, thinking in his heart as he crossed the threshold, "I wonder if I am base-born?" Finding himself in the midst of the magnificent chamber, he gazed about him on all sides, but failed to see God. Then said he to himself, "It is very possible I am base-born, for no God can I see. But it would be a lasting disgrace that I should admit it. I had better make out that I also have seen God."

Accordingly, he returned to the King, who said to him, "Well, have you seen God?" when the minister asserted that he had not only seen Him, but that he had spoken with Him too.

It was now the turn of the King, and he entered the room confident that he would be similarly favoured. But he gazed around in dismay, perceiving no sign of anything which could even represent the Almighty. Then began he to think to himself, "This God, wherever He is, has been seen by both my ministers, and it cannot be denied, therefore, that their birthright is clear. Is it possible that I, the King, am a bastard, seeing that no God appears to me? The very thought is confusion, and necessity will compel me to assert that I have seen Him too."

Having formed this resolution, the King stepped out and joined the rest of his party.

"And now, O King," asked the cunning girl, "have you also seen God?"

"Yes," answered he with assurance, "I have seen God."

"Really?" asked she again.

"Certainly," asserted the King.

Three times the girl asked the same question, and three times the King unblushingly lied. Then said the girl, "O King, have you never a conscience? How could you possibly see God, seeing that God is a spirit?"

Hearing this reproof, the King recalled to mind the saying of the girl that one day he would lie too, and, with a laugh, he confessed that he had not seen God at all. The two ministers, beginning to feel alarmed, confessed the truth as well. Then said the girl, "O King, we poor people may tell lies occasionally to save our lives, but what had you to fear? Telling lies, therefore, for many has its own attractions, and to them at least the taste of lying is sweet."

Far from being offended at the stratagem which the girl had practised on him, the King was so struck with her ingenuity and assurance that he married her forthwith, and in a short time she became his confidential adviser in all his affairs, public as well as private. Thus this simple girl came to great honour and renown, and so much did she grow in wisdom that her fame spread through many lands.

XXXV

OF THE PRETENTIOUS MULE

A CERTAIN mule, having a good opinion of himself, began braying pretentiously, so that every one stopped to say, "Who is that?" A traveller, passing by at that moment, said to him, "O sir! pray tell me what was the name of your mother?"

"My mother's name was Mare," answered the mule, with a louder bray than ever.

"And what was your father's name?" continued the inquisitive traveller.

"Be off!" answered the mule—"be off! None of your insolence, if you please! You are growing a little *too* familiar!"

XXXVI

OF THE FROG AND THE FARRIER

A FARRIER was once engaged in shoeing a fine Arab horse at the door of his smithy. Just then a frog came hopping up, and, thrusting out one of his feet with a consequential air, he cried, "Ho, farrier, shoe me, too!—shoe me, too!"

XXXVII

OF THE FOUR FOOLISH WEAVERS

FOUR poor weavers were once sitting together by the wayside, and when a traveller rode by and threw them four pence, intending by his act of charity that each of them should take as his share a single penny, one of the weavers, nimbler than the rest, picked up the whole of the four pieces, and said, "These pence are for me." Each of his companions preferred precisely the same claim, saying, as they fell to quarrelling, "Nay, these pence were for me."

Just then, a second traveller, coming up, asked, "What are you four weavers making such an ado for?"

"These four pence were thrown to me," answered their possessor; and so answered each of the others.

"You stupid people!" said the traveller, "there are four pence, and four claimants. Why do you not divide the money, and take a penny apiece, instead of falling out over them?"

"I take all or none," said the man who had secured them.

Then said the second traveller, "But the person who gave them to you is not yet out of sight. Run after him, and ask him which of you is to have them."

All the four weavers instantly rose and ran after the first traveller; and when they had overtaken him, they cried in a breath, "O traveller, say to which of us you gave these four pence!"

The traveller looked at them, and seeing that they were weavers, he answered, "First, let me know which of you is the greatest fool, and then you shall be told for whom I intended the pence."

The fellow who had grabbed the money cried, "I am an exceeding great fool, and if you will listen, I will prove that I am." He then related the following story:

"When I was first married, I went one day to my father-in-law's village to pay him a visit, and to keep me in countenance I took with me as a companion our village barber. While we had still some little part of our journey to perform, the sun went down, and darkness began to set in. You must understand that I am moon-blind, which makes it very difficult for me to distinguish anything after dusk. Well, as we were going along, we approached a great pit full of water; and as the road seemed black and the water looked white, I naturally imagined that the water must be the road. Full of this idea, I walked straight to the bank, and in another minute I was floundering about up to my neck. When the barber saw this, he said, 'Hullo, friend, where have you gone to?'

"'Wait a minute,' answered I; 'I shall be with you presently.'

"I said this because I did not wish to appear such a fool as to have walked into the pond except with a purpose, and I was equally ashamed to confess that I was moon-blind, but I felt anything but comfortable in my desperate struggles to regain the bank. The barber, however, cried out with a loud voice, 'Help, help! a man has fallen into the water!' and three or four men, hearing his cries, rushed to the spot, but before they arrived I managed to scramble out myself. One of the new-comers then said to me, 'How were you so unlucky as to tumble in?'

"'Oh,' answered I, 'I didn't tumble in—I jumped in. This barber argued that there was not much water here, so I jumped in to show him the real depth of it.'

"The men laughed at me, and went away, while I waited to wring the water out of my dripping clothes.

"As the barber had gone on ahead, I made haste after him; but it so happened that as we entered the village all the cattle were coming in from grazing, and, the barber passing down the street close to a bullock, I missed him, nor could I tell which way to turn. In this dilemma I said to myself, 'I cannot possibly see my way. I had better take hold of a bullock's tail, and when he reaches his home I'll ask his owner the way to my father-in-law's house.' So, seizing a bullock's tail, and holding on to it with a tight grip, I walked patiently along.

"Meanwhile the barber had reached the house, and finding that I had not followed, he turned back to look for me, and was rather astonished to find me holding a bullock's tail.

"'What are you doing with that bullock's tail?' said he.

"As some villagers were standing within earshot, and

I was afraid of being laughed at, I did not mention that I had lost my way, but I began to abuse the barber: 'You wretched fellow!' answered I; 'you say this fine bullock is only worth five rupees! Feel him! Any one with half an eye might see he is worth twenty-five at the least.'

"This speech must have impressed the villagers, because one of them said, 'What a clever weaver!'

"I then followed the barber without further mishap to my father-in-law's, where we were welcomed, and a bedstead was brought forward for us to sit on.

"In the courtyard where the family was assembled there was a young buffalo, which ever and anon came up to the barber and me, and sniffed at us, and sometimes it licked us, besmearing our cheeks with a tongue like a painter's brush, though we remonstrated and tried to keep it away.

"My mother-in-law now brought us out some bread which she had just baked, and having laid it down between us, she said, 'Come, eat your bread;' after which she went in for some butter. At this moment the buffalo-calf again approached us, and the barber hunted it back with his stick. He had scarcely sat down again when my mother-in-law arrived with the liquid butter, and began to pour it over the bread. It was very dark, and as for me, I was unable to see the least bit in the world; but hearing the trickling of the butter, and believing it was the buffalo at the food, I gave my mother-in-law so sharp a back-hander that she was sent sprawling on the ground, and all the butter was wasted. Being, for a wonder, a woman of the sweetest temper, she picked herself up without a word of blame, and, taking her vessel, went meekly back to the house.

"A few minutes afterwards said the barber to me, 'I hope that was not your mother-in-law whom you hit, but I think it was!'

"Having finished eating, I said, 'Barber, put this bread aside,' and, lying down, we went to sleep.[1]

"Some hours must have passed, when I was awakened by the clinking of money at some distance, and, imagining there was a robber somewhere, I got up to listen.

[1] In the hot weather people bring their light beds out of doors and sleep in the courtyard.

Then, rising, I tied one end of my long turban to the bed, so that I might be able to guide myself back when I wished to return, and proceeded in the direction of the sound, allowing my turban to glide gradually through my hands. Almost immediately I found myself at the doorway of the court, and, looking out, I stood for a moment with cocked-up ears, listening to every sound. As the chinking was not repeated, I pulled at the turban in order to find my way back, when, as I imagined, the whole piece of stuff came towards me, the fact being that the mischievous buffalo had taken advantage of the occasion to bite my turban in two. 'What shall I do now?' thought I. 'I shall be found out to a certainty, and every one will call me the blind man.' This thought distressed me exceedingly, since a blind man is an object of pity and scorn, but, groping here and groping there, I did my best to retrace my steps. Suddenly my shins struck sharply against the edge of a bedstead, and in another instant I was lying prone across my old mother-in-law, whom I nearly crushed, and who, lifting her head, yelled out, 'Murder! What wretch are you, coming about here?' I answered her, 'Mother dear, when you were giving us the butter, I thought, as it was so dark, that your young buffalo had come to steal the bread, and I hit without looking. But as I am afraid I must have struck you, I have just come over to apologize to you.'

"My mother-in-law was pleased, and answered, 'Son, go back to bed; I forgive you.'

"'Nay, mother,' said I, 'you come as far as my bed with me, just to show that you really forgive me, and that you bear no malice. This kind of forgiveness does not suit me.'

"So the good-natured old lady accompanied me back, and I spent the rest of the night undisturbed.

"And now," continued the weaver, "did you ever hear of such a fool as I am? And am I not entitled to the four pence?"

The second weaver here interposed, and said, "It is true you are pretty foolish, but I am more so. O traveller, when you hear the story of my adventures, I think you will admit that the four pence properly belong to me!

When I went to pay the accustomed visit to my father-in-law after my marriage, I determined to travel in style. So I borrowed a horse from one neighbour, arms from another, and jewels from another. Thus mounted, adorned, and accoutred, I set out, and every traveller that passed me stared and said, 'What a respectable weaver! What a rich, respectable weaver!' On the road I was caught in a storm of rain, and I had to take shelter at a certain village. When the rain was over I started again, but, owing to the delay, it was so late when I approached the village of my father-in-law that I thought to myself, 'If I enter the village now no one will see me, but if I wait till the morning and enter then, every one will say, 'What a grand son-in-law that neighbour of ours has managed to get!' This reflection induced me to pull up at the door of a poor fakîr, and to ask him for a night's lodging. 'Welcome!' said the fakîr, and I dismounted and salaamed him. Then said the fakîr, 'What business has brought you this way to-day?'

"'All I wish,' answered I, 'is just to rest here for the night. To-morrow I shall continue my journey.'

"'But,' said the fakîr, 'it is the custom at this village for travellers first to report themselves to the watchman before resting.'

"'Surely you do not take me for a thief?' protested I. 'All I want is leave merely to sit down and wait.'

"'I don't know,' answered the fakîr; 'there have been thieves about lately, and if you are not careful you will get into trouble. I do not mind allowing you to remain if you will put on my clothes and go round and beg some bread for me.'

"'But I don't know how to beg,' said I. 'Pray be so good as to permit me to remain.'

"'Out of my doors!' cried the fakîr, and he bundled me out into the cold. Then said I, 'All right; if you will allow me to stay, I will go and beg for you.'

"So the fakîr took charge of my clothes and all my other property, and gave me his rags and his begging-bowl and bade me make haste. As I was changing, I said to myself, 'I will beg at every house except my father-in-law's.' Scarcely had I gone ten steps, however, when the fakîr cried after me, 'Remember, you are to bring scraps from every house in the village, or else in this place you shall not remain. I know the bread of every one of them, so beware!'

"This was a caution I had not expected, but I made the best of my way into the village in my disguise, and having begged at every other house, I stopped in doubt and perplexity at that of my father-in-law. On the one hand, I was afraid of the fakîr, and on the other I was afraid of discovery. At last the former feeling prevailed, and I entered the courtyard. Now, my father-in-law had lately taken up his store of wheat out of the ground, and the recent heavy rain had filled the empty pit with water. Avoiding the danger, I took up my station in front of the house, and cried, 'For God's sake, give me some bread! For God's sake, give me some bread!'—after the usual style and manner of fakîrs. It was horribly dark, and the strong wintry wind was so bitterly cold that I felt perished. My mother-in-law, hearing my cries, said to my wife, 'Take a little bread out to that poor fakîr.' And my wife, lifting some dry sugar-cane to serve her as a torch, lighted it, and with the light in one hand and the cakes in the other she came out into the veranda. The moment I saw her I said to myself, 'If I go too near her, she will recognize me;' so as she advanced I stepped backward, and the more she advanced the more diffident I became, until suddenly I fell plump on my back into the pool of water. Then cried my wife, 'Oh, mother, mother, this poor fakîr has fallen into the pit! and he is sinking, he is sinking!' And so great a stir did she make, that my mother-in-law, and my father-in-law, and several of the neighbours, came rushing together and surrounded the pit, crying, 'What has happened?' Half dead with cold, and shivering in every limb, I was dragged out of the water by my father-in-law, who said, 'Oh, fakîr, fakîr, where do you live?' but I was in such a state that the chattering of my teeth was the only reply of which I was capable. Then said my father-in-law, 'This poor fellow will die of cold, and his blood will be on our heads. Light up a fire for him, and let us warm him.' This was no sooner said than done, but as I began to revive, the people, by questioning, found me out, and one of them slyly remarked, 'This man is very like your son-in-law, neighbour.'

"'Yes, yes,' answered I, gasping; 'I am, I am.'

"'But what on earth,' asked my relations, 'happened to you that you had to beg your bread?'

"'The truth is,' answered I, 'I came riding to this village on a mare; and as it was late when I arrived, I put up with a fakîr, living hard by the road. But he was a churl, and he compelled me to take round his bowl for bread before he would lodge me, and that is how I came to find myself here before the morning.'

"'What a misfortune!' cried my father-in-law. 'That fakîr has not been in the village more than a day, and who knows what sort of a character he is! Run, my son, and see whether he is still there, for my mind misgives me.'

"The son made haste to the hut, but the cunning fakîr had mounted my mare and decamped at a gallop, carrying off all my jewels, my money and my clothes. Then did my mother-in-law most unjustly reproach me with bitter words, 'A precious wiseacre for a son-in-law! You would not come straight to the house, lest no one should see and admire you. Does no one see you now, you silly! and when to-morrow comes you will be the gazingstock of the whole village.'

"And now," continued the second weaver to the traveller, "this man says he is a fool, but is he one-half such a fool as I am?"

Then said the third weaver, "That these two fellows are fools no one can deny. It may be that I am not quite so foolish; but you, O traveller, shall judge, and if you think me worthy of the four pence, I hope I may receive them.

"On the occasion of my visit to my father-in-law's house, whither my wife had gone before me, the village barber bore me company; and on our arrival my mother-in-law put out a bedstead for us, and said, 'Sit down.' Down we sat; and she then said, 'You must be hungry?' The barber answered, 'Yes.' So she brought a pound of uncooked rice and some brown sugar, and mixing them together, said, 'Eat this.' Then she sat down to her distaff just in front of us, and began spinning her thread. The barber's whetted appetite waited for no second invitation, and he fell to; but I was ashamed even to touch the food with my mother-in-law looking on, and I took never a grain of it.

"'This is very nice food,' remarked the barber; 'why do you not eat some of it?'

"'I don't feel inclined,' answered I.

"My mother-in-law then got up, and said to me, 'Son, you are not eating!'

"'No,' said I; 'I am not hungry.'

"She then looked vexed; and going to the other women of the house, she said, 'I gave the lad some rice, thinking he would relish it after his long journey, but he will not touch it.'

"As soon as she had turned her back on us, however, I took advantage of the circumstance to pounce on the rice like a hungry hawk, and, taking up a double-handful, I crammed it all into my mouth, intending to eat prodigiously. If she had only remained away a little longer I should have swallowed my mouthful; but, to my great annoyance, she returned at the critical moment, and sat down again at her distaff, looking straight at me all the time. I kept as quiet as a mouse, not daring to move my jaw, while my cheeks were bursting with the quantity of sugar and rice which I had stuffed into my mouth. After looking at me fixedly for some seconds, she said to herself, 'This lad was all right a little time ago, when I left him. What has happened to his face to be all swollen up in that way?' Then she rose, and approaching me, she said, 'O son, are you ill, or what's the matter, that your face has become swollen so frightfully?' As my mouth was so full, it was not in my power to utter a syllable, and I stared at her mutely. The old woman, now seriously alarmed, began shrieking, 'Oh, help! my son-in-law is ill. He is ill—he is dying! See what a dreadful face he has!'

"The barber, who was not a very intelligent man, but, if anything, decidedly stupid, said to her, 'For goodness' sake don't make such a noise. These are nothing but simple tumours, and I'll cure your son in a jiffy.'[1]

"'Oh, if you will only cure him,' said she, 'of this horrid disorder, I have a couple of milch buffaloes in my house, and the one we intended for my son-in-law I will give to you—you shall have it, you shall indeed, if you will only cure him!'

"The barber, taking out his lancet, made a deep gash

[1] Barbers in India are also surgeons—barber-surgeons, in fact, as formerly in England.

in each of my cheeks, and immediately the rice and the dissolved sugar began to ooze out.

"'You see the blood,' said he, 'which is oozing out?—and those white things are maggots! If I had not been at hand to cure your son, those maggots would have eaten up into his brain and killed him.'

"My mother-in-law was profuse in her acknowledgments, and at once presented him with my milch buffalo; but as for me, I lost my buffalo, and had both my cheeks cut open into the bargain.

"And now," said the third weaver, in conclusion, "judge whether I am not a greater fool than either of these fellows."

"It must be admitted," observed the fourth weaver, "that all these three men are consummately silly; but now hear me, for I venture to think I am the biggest fool of them all.

"When I went to visit my father-in-law, I also invited our village barber to accompany me. We rode on borrowed horses, and my wife was carried in a doolie. When we arrived at the house, we were made heartily welcome, and as an omen of good luck on our happy union, my good father-in-law, according to the usual custom, poured abundance of oil into the stone socket in which turned the lower hinge of the door. Then he gave us seats of honour in the midst of his guests, and called for supper. Now, my mother had given me the strictest orders to be on my good behaviour, and to show my respect and good breeding by eating as little as possible. When, therefore, my friends invited me to the repast, I affected an indifference to food, and said, 'I will eat by-and-by.' My friend the barber, however, went boldly forward, and as boiled rice was a delicacy we seldom partook of, he proceeded to make a hearty meal. Then said my mother-in-law, 'Why do you not eat, son? Come and have your supper.'

"'I do not feel hungry just now,' answered I.

"When the meal was over, the plates were removed, and my portion was put on one side. Then, as it was time for bed, we all retired, my friends to the courtyard and the barber and myself to the house-top.

"After we had lain down, the barber said to me, 'Why did you not eat any food?'

" 'I was hungry then,' answered I, 'but I am more hungry now. Go and ask them to let me have my food here.'

" 'Let us first see,' replied he, 'whether there is a hole in the roof.'

" We looked and found that there was one large enough for a man to pass through, for it was one of those houses in the roofs of which such holes exist in order that the grain, laid on the roof to dry, may be shovelled back into the little household granary below.

" Then said the barber, 'Let us take some of the cording off this bed, and I can lower you down. You will find your food on the shelf.'

" Tying the cord round my waist, he lowered me into the chamber beneath, and finding my plate of rice on the top of the corn-bin, I sat there and ate it. When I had finished I said quietly, 'Pull me up!' The barber, however, did not pull. Again and again I called to him, 'Pull me up!' but without avail. Tired of calling, I sat still where I was.

" Now, it happened that some stranger had arrived at the house just then, and that my brother-in-law had said to my wife, 'Go into the house and bring out that plate of rice for him.' My wife, therefore, opened the door from without, and began feeling about for the plate. At last her hand touched mine, and she uttered a shriek, crying, 'There is an evil spirit in the house! Help!' Then said I to her, 'Don't run out, and don't make a noise; you will be heard.' But without stopping to consider, she rushed out, and my mother-in-law instantly shut the door and put the chain up.

" The disturbance roused up the barber, who, looking down, said, 'What is the matter? Do you wish to come out?' I begged and begged of him to pull me out as quickly as possible. 'I will only pull you out,' answered he, 'on condition that you hand me up a chatty of flour.' With this request I at once complied, and he took the vessel of flour and then pulled me up to the roof.

" Meanwhile my father-in-law had sent for the village priest to exorcise the evil spirit from his house. The priest, arriving, sat by the doorstep, opened his book, and began to recite appropriate verses. Then said he, 'Some spirits are white, and some spirits are black. The spirit which has entered your house is a white one, and a tough customer he is likely to prove. How much will you give me if I drive him out for you?'

"'Here,' said my father-in-law, 'are five rupees.'

"'Good!' replied the priest. 'He shall be driven out, but he must be killed as well. Arm yourselves with sticks and stones, and when he makes a rush give it to him well!'

"Opening the door, the wily priest now entered the house. But the truth was he knew nothing whatever about evil spirits, and when he caught sight of the bright round disc of light cast by the moon on the floor as it shone through the hole in the roof, he was struck dumb with fear and astonishment, and remained rooted, half dazed, to the spot. Just then the barber peeped down and saw him, having overheard all that had passed in the yard below. Seizing his vessel full of flour, he emptied the whole of it over the priest, who was just under the hole. Nearly suffocated, and imagining himself pursued by ten thousand furies, the wretched man rushed for the door, but was set upon the moment he appeared by the party watching outside. 'Hold, hold!' cried he; 'don't beat me, I am the priest!'

"'Nay, you are an evil spirit,' answered they; 'our priest is not of this colour.'

"So they killed him, and cast his body out of the courtyard, and went to sleep. When morning came, however, they saw that he was really the priest, and no evil spirit at all; and they were in a fright, and were brought up to answer for the mishap; nor did my father-in-law escape under a heavy fine.

"And now, sir," continued the fourth barber, "do you not agree that I am the greatest fool of all?"

"You are all such a rare collection of fools," answered the traveller, "that though the four pence were intended for equal division among you, you shall now have four pence apiece," saying which he gave them more money, and continued his journey.

Told at Ghâzi by a villager of the Chach Plain, November 1879.

XXXVIII

OF THE KING AND HIS DAUGHTERS

THERE was once a king who had several daughters. To the first he said, "How do you love me?" "I love you as sugar," said she. To the next he said, "And how do you love me?" "I love you as honey," said she. To the third he said, "And how do you love me?" "I love you as sherbet," said she. To the last and youngest he said, "And how do you love me?" "I love you as salt," said she.

On hearing the answer of his youngest daughter the King frowned, and, as she persisted in repeating it, he drove her out into the forest.

There, when wandering sadly along, she heard the tramping of a horse, and she hid herself in a hollow tree. But the fluttering of her dress betrayed her to the rider, who was a prince, and who instantly fell in love with her and married her.

Some time after, the King, her father, who did not know what had become of her, paid her husband a visit. When he sat down to meat, the Princess took care that all the dishes presented to him should be made-up sweets, which he either passed by altogether or merely tasted. He was very hungry, and was longing sorely for something which he could eat, when the Princess sent him a dish of common spinach, seasoned with salt, such as farmers eat, and the King signified his pleasure by eating it with relish.

Then the Princess threw off her veil, and, revealing herself to her father, said, "O my father, I love you as salt. My love may be homely, but it is true, genuine and lasting, and I entreat your forgiveness."

Then the King perceived how great a mistake he had made, and there followed a full reconciliation.

XXXIX

OF THE WIDOW OF BANÉYR

THERE was a widow of Banéyr who had two sons. They had cut the harvest of their little ancestral field, and their two bullocks were treading out the grain, when suddenly the sky became overcast and a storm of rain swept by. The poor silly woman instantly caught a certain familiar insect, a friend to man, and, running a needle and thread through it, hung it up to a neighbouring *bér*-tree as a charm to drive away the unwelcome shower. At the same time she addressed God in the following words, "O God, my boys are but children, and in this thing are innocent. But Thou art a white-bearded man. Didst Thou not see that this rain was not wanted for threshing out my wheat?"

XL

OF THE GARDENER'S WIFE, THE POTTER'S WIFE, AND THE CAMEL

A GARDENER'S wife and a potter's wife once hired a camel to carry their goods to market. One side of the beast was well laden with vegetables and the other with pottery. As they went along the road the camel kept stretching back his long neck to pilfer the vegetables. Upon observing this, the potter's wife began laughing, and jested her friend on her ill luck. "Sister," said she, "at the end of the journey there will not be a single vegetable left; you'll have nothing whatever to sell!"

"It is true you are luckier than I am," answered the gardener's wife, "but, remember, the first to win are the last to lose!"

When they arrived at the market-place the camel-man

ordered his animal to kneel down, but the weight on one side was so much greater by this time than the weight on the other that the camel gave a lurch as he got on his fore-knees and crushed the pottery between himself and the earth, so that most of it was smashed, and what was not smashed was cracked. So it ended that the gardener's wife had something, at least, to sell, but the potter's wife had nothing.

XLI

OF THREE SILLY WEAVERS

There were three weavers, all brothers, who lived in the same village. One day the eldest said to the others, "I am going to buy a milch buffalo." So he went to a farmer, paid for the buffalo, and took it home.

The second brother was quite touched at the sight of it. He viewed its head, its horns, and its teats, and then said, "O brother, allow me to be a partner in this beautiful buffalo." Said the elder, "I have paid for this beautiful buffalo twenty-two rupees. If you wish to be a partner in her, you had better go to the farmer and pay him twenty-two rupees too, and then we shall have equal shares in her." This then he did.

Shortly after the third brother came in and said, "O brother, you have allowed our brother to be a partner with you in this beautiful buffalo; won't you let me take a share too?"

"Willingly," answered the other; "but first you must go to the farmer and pay him twenty-two rupees, as we have done."

So the third brother did likewise; while the farmer chuckled, saying, "This is a fine thing, getting all this money for my skinny old buffalo!"

The three brothers now agreed that each one of them should have a day's milk from the buffalo in turn, and that each should bring his own pot. The two elder brothers had their turns; but when the third day came, the youngest said, "Alas! what shall I do? I have no pot in my house!" In this perplexity the eldest remarked, "This is a most difficult business, because, you see, if you milk the buffalo without a pot, the milk will be spilt; you had better milk her into your mouth."

His ingenious solution of the problem was at once adopted, and the youngest brother milked the buffalo into his mouth.

Going home, he was met by his wife, who asked, "Well, where is the milk?"

"I had no pot," answered the man, "so I had to milk the buffalo into my mouth."

"Oh, you did, did you?" cried she; "and so your wife counts as no one? I am to have no milk? If I am not to have my share of the milk, in this house I refuse to remain." And she went off in anger to the house of her mother.

Then the three brothers went together to the head-man of the village and complained, begging him to order the woman to return to her husband.

So the head-man summoned her and said, "O woman, you may have your share of the milk, too, just the same as your husband. Let him milk the buffalo into his mouth in the morning and you milk it into yours in the evening."

"Then why," cried she, "could not my husband have said so himself? Now it is all right; and, besides, I shall be saved all the trouble of setting the milk for butter." And she returned to her husband's house immensely pleased.

XLII

ON A WEAVER'S STUPIDITY

ONCE upon a time a certain weaver, who owned a little ancestral field which he had no time to reap, wove a piece of cloth, and taking it to the village blacksmith, he said,

"Here, friend, accept this gift, and make a sickle that shall cut my corn of itself."

When the blacksmith had finished the work, the delighted weaver took the sickle and laid it quietly at the edge of the ripe corn, saying, "O sickle, mow my field!" Then he went home, but in the evening he returned, for he said, "Perhaps the job is done; so let me now go and see how much of my harvest my new sickle has mown." When he arrived at the spot he found the corn undisturbed, and the sickle lying idly by. But, taking it in his hand, he perceived that it was exceedingly hot, since the sun had been playing on it the whole day, and he said to himself, "My crop would have been all cut down; but, alas! my sickle has fever."

So he went to the blacksmith and said, "My sickle has done no work because fever is heavy upon it, and so I crave some medicine."

"Take a long string," answered the ready smith, "and having tied your sickle to the end of it, dip it into the well, and the fever will leave it." Then the weaver did as he was bidden, and the sickle recovered and became cool, and he took it home with him and joyously hung it up.

Now, it happened that very night that the weaver's old mother fell ill of a violent fever, and that the heat of her body was such that she kept tossing about and was like to die. So her sagacious son, saying to himself, "Aha, I know the medicine!" immediately carried her out to the well, and having tied a rope round her body, he lowered her in, plunging her repeatedly into the cold water until she really breathed her last. Then he drew her forth, and said, "Now my old mother's fever has left her!" So he bore her home, and put her sitting up in a corner of the chamber before a spinning-wheel, saying, "Now my dear old mother is going to spin." There he left her, going himself out to his work. And when he returned in the evening he looked at her, and her mouth hung open, and her teeth protruded, and great brown ants were crawling about her gums. So the weaver said, "My clever old mother is eating oil-seeds (*thil*), and laughing away like anything." And with this he began to laugh too, and he laughed and laughed so heartily that he brought all his neighbours together, who, seeing his error, reproved him, saying, "O foolish one, your mother is not laughing, but dead!" And having so spoken they carried her forth and buried her.

XLIII

OF CERTAIN DELUDED WEAVERS

It was long ago, when the Durânis had subdued the country, that there was a certain small village inhabited only by weavers. As the Durânis spoke in Persian, and the weavers only knew Panjábî, it happened that, when the new officers appeared to collect the revenue, the poor villagers were unable to explain their grievances, but had perforce to sit still and submit to all the exactions possible. Then the weavers summoned a meeting of their people, and agreed that they would all put ten rupees each into a common stock for the purpose of despatching two of their number to Kabul to purchase a supply of the language of Persia. This was no sooner said than done, and two old grey-beards from among their tribe, whose wisdom had become the common admiration, set out on the long journey past Peshawur and through the dark Khyber Pass to obtain the coveted gift. At every village they made the anxious inquiry, "Have you any Persian for sale?" and from every village, because they were seen to be weavers, they were hooted away, or passed contemptuously by. They had arrived at the town of Jâlâlâbâd, and were about to enter the gates, when they met a man who was both clever and cruel. "We would buy some Persian for our village," said the poor weavers. Then said the man to himself, "These fellows are great fools, but let me see if I cannot please them and secure their money too." So he answered them, "Here, come with me, and hand me over a fair price, and I will provide you with two jars full of the most excellent Persian." So he took them home for the night and gave them some supper.

Now, it happened that it was the time of year when wasps have their nests hanging from the beams, so this wretched man put sweet-stuffs into a couple of jars and then filled the jars with black wasps, and, having tied them down, he sold them to the travellers, saying, "Be careful not to open these jars on the way, lest the Persian escape, but keep them safely sealed, and when you arrive home call your friends together on a Thursday, and, entering all together into a dark chamber, close the doors, undress your bodies, and then, opening the jars, let every man among you take his share and be satisfied."

These foolish men then left for India, and having arrived at their own village, they called their neighbours together and told them the good news. So they all hastened into a dark chamber, and, when they had closed every aperture, they divested themselves of their shirts and opened the jars. The imprisoned wasps flew instantly forth, and stung them severely, while, groping here and there from their attacks, the deluded weavers kept crying, "Where is the door? Where is the door?" At last the door was found, and an escape was made into the open air, but when they looked at each other in the light of day, scarcely could they recognize each other by reason of their swollen features. One of them, having missed his mother, who had been one of the party, cried to some bystanders, "Has no one seen my mother?" "Your mother," answered they, "has run away, and gone with quantities of Persian, which was sticking to her fast." So, searching high and low, they found the poor old thing, but she was all swollen, and she became ill and took to her bed.

After this sad experience the weavers of the village determined never more to meddle with Persian, but to leave that tongue for those who were cunning to master strange languages.

XLIV

A TALE OF A KING AND A FARMER

One day a certain king, having called his ministers about him, mounted his horse and rode out into the fields. There he halted before an old farmer, who, though bowed with the weight of many years, was toiling in the furrows. So he beckoned to him to rein in his oxen, and said to him, "Old man, why, in God's name, did you not do it?" And the old man answered, "Sir, I did it; but it was not God's will." Then said the King the second time, "Why did you not do it?" and the man answered as before.

And the third time the King repeated the same question, and the old man answered to the like intent.

Then the King, continuing the conversation, said, "And who in the world is it, with whom you country folk do your business?" And the old man answered, "With the King himself."

"But if no king comes," asked the monarch, "what then do you do?"

"We trust to the favour of the King's prime minister," answered the man.

"And if there is no minister?" said the King.

"We then depend on the Prince," answered the man, "if the Prince be worthy."

The King then turned his horse's head towards the city, saying to the old man, "Some one may come to you desiring vehemently to know the meaning of this our conversation, but my will is that you do not tell the secret under a heavy sum."

With these words the King rode home, and, calling his vizier, he said to him, "You heard my conversation with the old ploughman, and you heard the nature of his replies. Now tell me the interpretation thereof."

And the vizier was confounded, notwithstanding his reputed wisdom, and he said, "O King, I know well the words which were spoken, but I know not the meaning of them."

So the King said to his minister, "Under penalty of a

heavy fine, and of dismissal from your office, you will bring me the meaning within twenty-four hours."

Then the vizier went sadly away, but as he approached his house the thought occurred to him that he would visit the old husbandman. So he took with him heaps of money and sought him out, and said, "O father, tell me the mystery of the words which passed between you and the King." And the old man answered, "Not under three thousand rupees dare I divulge the secret." So the minister counted out the money, and gave it into his hand, three thousand rupees all told, in bright silver coins. Having received the money, the old man explained thus—

"When the King asked me, 'Why did you not do it?' he meant, 'Why did you not marry in your youth, for then you would have had sons to plough for you, and you would never have been compelled to plough yourself now in the time of old age.' My reply was, 'I did marry, but it was not the will of God that sons should come to me.' The King by his second question meant, 'Why did you not marry a second wife?' and my answer was, 'I did so marry, but again it was not the will of God that sons should be born.' And the King's third question was, 'Why did you not marry the third time?' and my reply was to the same tenor as before. After this the King asked me, 'With whom do you have dealings, you people of the soil?' and my answer was, 'With the King,' for with us the King of all the year is the month of July, when the rain comes in abundance, and our fields are well watered, and the earth is loosened, and our seed germinates and shoots forth. Then said the King, 'But if there is no King, what then?' and my answer was, 'If July is in drought, then we trust to August,' which, as being the next best month for the farmer, is like the King's minister; and when the King, continuing, asked me, 'But if there is no minister?' I answered, 'We trust then to the young Prince,' which is the month of September, when we sow the crops that are to ripen in spring. This is the explanation of the words."

So the minister went away satisfied, wondering at the wisdom of the old man who could interpret the dark sayings of the King, and at the wisdom of his master in divining the hearts of his subjects.

XLV

OF A CREDULOUS WEAVER

A VILLAGE weaver went out to cut firewood. Climbing a tree, he perched upon one of the branches, which he began to hew off close to the trunk. "My friend," said a traveller passing below, "you are sitting on the very limb which you are cutting off; in a few minutes you and it will both fall to the ground." The weaver unconcernedly continued his task, and soon both the branch and himself fell to the foot of the tree, as the traveller had foretold. Limping after him, the weaver cried, "Sir, you are God! you are God, sir! you are God! What you prophesied has come to pass."

"Tut, man, tut!" answered the traveller. "I am not God."

"Nay, but you are," replied the weaver; "and now pray, O pray, tell me when I am to die!"

To be rid of his importunity, the traveller answered, "You will die on the day on which your mouth begins to bleed," and he pursued his way.

Some days had elapsed, when the weaver happened to be making some scarlet cloth, and as he had frequently to separate the threads with his mouth, a piece of the coloured fibre by chance stuck in one of his front teeth. Catching sight of this in a glass, and instantly concluding that it was blood, and that his last hour was at hand, he entered his hut and said, "Wife, wife, I am sick! in a few minutes I shall be dead; let me lie down, and go, dig my grave!" So he lay down on his bed, and, turning his face to the wall, closed his eyes, and began deliberately to die. And, indeed, such is the power of the imagination among these people, that he would have died without doubt if a customer had not called for his clothes. He, seeing the man's condition, and hearing of the prophecy, asked to examine his mouth. "Ah," said he, "what an idiot are you! Call you this blood?" and, taking out the thread, he held it before the weaver's eyes.

The weaver, as a man reprieved from death, was overjoyed, and, springing to his feet, resumed his work, having been rescued, as he imagined, from the very jaws of death.

XLVI

OF THE BANEYRWAL[1] AND HIS DROWNED WIFE

THERE was once a sudden flood in the Indus which washed away numbers of people, and among others the wife of a certain Baneyrwâl. The distracted husband was wandering along the banks of the river looking for the dead body, when a countryman accosted him thus, "O friend, if, as I am informed, your wife has been carried away in the flood, she must have floated down the stream with the rest of the poor creatures. Yet you are going up the stream."

"Ah, sir," answered the wretched Baneyrwâl, "you did not know that wife of mine. She always took an opposite course to every one else. And even now that she is drowned I know full well that, if other bodies have floated down the river, hers *must* have floated up."

XLVII

OF THE PRETENTIOUS FROG

A CERTAIN frog, after several ineffectual attempts, managed to climb to the top of a clod of earth close to the puddle in which he was spawned. "Ah!" cried he, casting one eye at some cattle which were grazing near, in the hope that they would burst with envy, "what a grand sight have I! I see Kashmîr! I see Kashmîr!"

[1] Baneyrwâl—a Banéyr-wâlla—a Banéyr-fellow—an inhabitant of Banéyr.

XLVIII

THE ADVENTURES OF ALPHÛ AND SHARPHÛ

THERE was once a farmer who had two wives, one of whom was wise and the other foolish. The son of the wise wife was named Alphû, and the son of the foolish one was named Sharphû. The foolish woman was of a disposition so perverse, suspicious, and contradictory that she invariably followed a course exactly opposite to that which was recommended to her; and this trait in her character soon became known to her sister-wife, who, if she desired at any time a favour from her, requested her, above all things, not to grant it.

One day the wise wife fell ill, and perceiving that her end was approaching, she sent for her rival, and thus addressed her, "Come close to me and hear my last words. I am very ill, and like to die, so I have sent for you to give you some advice before I go. You know what my son is, and what he requires. When I am no more, send him daily to the plough, and let him labour, and feed him with hard fare. With your own son you should deal differently, and I recommend you to send him every day to the school, where he may learn, and remember to clothe him cleanly and to feed him well."

The foolish wife answered her, "Very well, your wishes I shall attend to;" and very soon after her rival breathed her last, and was buried in the little cemetery close by the tomb of the village saint.

The foolish woman then began to consider her dying words. "I see," said she, "she wanted my son to be sent to school, and her own son to be at large over the farm doing the work of the fields. Exactly! she would like my son to get a good thrashing from the surly priest every day of his life, while her own escaped free. Very likely! but I shall do no such thing."

So she called the two boys, and said to them, "You, Alphû, from this day forward are to attend school and learn your lessons; but my son Sharphû shall go to the field and do the work of the farm."

Sharphû was not sorry to escape the rod, nor did he complain that his food consisted only of cakes made with water, for that had been ever his accustomed fare. On the other hand, Alphû, who was of a serious turn, had no reason to complain that he had to go to the mosque day by day and learn reading, writing, and arithmetic, especially as his cakes were made up with sugar and butter, and as his clothing was always clean and respectable. Thus the two lads spent their days, until, in a short time, Alphû had so far progressed in knowledge that he was employed to collect the revenue of his district, while Sharphû grew more and more awkward and stupid.

One day it happened that Sharphû broke his plough, so he threw the broken pieces over his shoulder and carried them into the village to be mended by the village carpenter, with whom he left them. After this he said to himself, "It must be near dinner-time; I shall now go home."

For once he was at home before his brother, who had generally come and gone before he appeared. The cakes for both brothers were standing in a pile in a wooden platter, and as he squatted down beside them, he said, "Mother, let me eat my bread and get back to the field, or else the bullocks may stray and get lost."

"Your bread is ready," said she, "and so is Alphû's. Your cakes are those at the top, and in the other dish you will find some onions. Eat, son, but do not touch the cakes of your brother."

But when Sharphû saw how rich and dainty was the food provided for Alphû, he naturally murmured against his mother's partiality. "Here am I working hard," said he, "and see what poor food I get, while Alphû, who does nothing but sit at the *hûzrâ*,[1] has sugar and butter." So he laid his own cakes aside, and ate Alphû's. Then said he, "Mother, I am going to the *hûzrâ*—I can do collector's work as well as Alphû; let him go to the field—I plough no more."

When Alphû came in, his mother said to him, "O my son, my other son came in and has eaten your dinner. He has left the plough with the carpenter, and the bullocks he has left in the field; and he says you will be able to do his work for the future. But you are hungry, so I'll send the servant to the field to-day, and make you some more cakes, and to-morrow you can begin the work of the farm."

[1] *Hûzrâ*—the general guest-house at a village (*hûjrâ*).

"Not at all, mother," answered Alphû. "My brother may do my work if he pleases, and I will do his. But you need not send the servant, because I am ready to go at once."

Without another word the lad set out, and receiving the plough from the carpenter, he made his way to the field, where he yoked on the two bullocks, ploughed for the rest of the day, and in the evening returned home.

Meanwhile the silly Sharphû had gone to the *hûzrâ* and taken a seat there. He had not even changed his clothes, but dirty as he was, and with his rough blanket on him, he appeared in the meeting place at an hour when all good farmers were hard at work in their fields. By-and-by one of the officers of the Government treasury arrived with a man carrying a load, and addressing the village watchman, whose post of duty is always the *hûzrâ*, he said, "Give me a fresh man to carry this load on to the next village." The watchman looked for one in vain. "Every one is out in the fields at work," said he. Upon hearing this, the officer, who had no knowledge of Sharphû, replied, "But here is a man—why not give me him?"

"Me?" cried Sharphû; "but I am one of the village landlords!"

"Ha, ha!" laughed the officer, "you look like one!"

Saying this, he gave poor Sharphû two blows with his stick, and compelled him to carry the load, not only to the next village, but to the village beyond as well, for the treasury was distant several stages.

In the evening the wretched Sharphû, aching in every limb, came back to the house.

"Hullo!" cried Alphû, "where have you been? You are late—what became of you?"

"Oh!" answered Sharphû, "I was sitting at the *hûzrâ*, when a fellow came up and beat me with a stick, and forced me to carry a heavy load about ten miles."

"How unlucky!" replied Alphû. "Never mind; to-morrow you will be more fortunate. See, this is the revenue which I have been collecting for the Government. As you are now to be responsible for my work, you will have to set out with this money to-morrow, and hand it over to the Tahsîldâr." And so saying he counted over into his brother's hands the full amount.

In the morning Sharphû rose early, and taking some dry flour for his journey, he deposited in the same napkin with the flour the rupees which he had received from Alphû. He then put the burden on his head and started for the Tahsîl.[1] About mid-day he arrived at a certain village, and going to the house of a baker, he said to the woman, "Mother, bake this flour for me." Taking the flour, she remarked its weight, and inquired, "Is this flour of yours sifted or unsifted?"

"Sifted or not sifted," answered he, "I want it baked. Sift it if you like; if not, cook it as it is."

The woman then took the flour away and baked it into tasty cakes, which he enjoyed, after which she gave him a bed to sit down upon, and a hookah to smoke, and entertained him with every civility.

In the morning Sharphû bethought him of the money, and exclaimed, "Here, you! my money was all in that flour I gave you. Give it up!"

"Did I not ask you," answered the woman, "if your flour was sifted or not sifted? However, I have your money safe enough. But until you tell me two stories this way, and two stories that way, not a single piece shall you have."

This she said only to try him, and to discover if he was a man of mettle or merely a fool. Poor Sharphû was quite confounded. "But I don't know any stories at all," said he, "so how can I tell you two stories this way and two stories that way?" Then he thought to himself, "What am I to do? This money is lost to me. Well, at any rate, I'll go and have a look at the Tahsîl at least; I am not going to turn back now." So he continued his journey penniless as he was, and went on to see the Tahsîl.

As he was walking along he came to a well or pool of water, at the edge of which grew a fine melon-plant, and Sharphû noticed that some of the melons were floating on the surface of the water. So he said, "I'll tell the officers at the Tahsîl that I saw melons growing in a well, and that will astonish them."

Having rested and drunk, he went on once more, and presently he saw a deer in a thicket scratching his ear with one of his hind-feet. Just at that moment a hunter, who

[1] Tahsîl—the district court-house and Government treasury. Tahsîldâr—the native magistrate in charge.

had been in pursuit, fired his matchlock, and the ball pierced both the foot and the ear, and struck one of the animal's horns. "Ah!" cried Sharphû, with a long breath; "here's a wonderful thing. I'll go and tell the officers at the Tahsîl that I saw a bullet pierce a deer's foot, then his ear, and then his horn! All the same bullet! This will astonish them still more."

Some distance further on there was a snug nook under the roots of a thorny tree in which a bitch had laid her pups. One of the pups had crawled out into the open, and a kite had swooped down and carried it off. As Sharphû came to the spot he heard the yelping of the creature, far above his head, but knew not how to explain it. "Ho, ho!" said he, "here's another wonder! I'll go and tell the officers at the Tahsîl I heard dogs barking in the air, and that either God keeps them, or else there is some country or other overhead. This will astonish them most of all."

On reaching the Tahsîl, he entered the quadrangle, and going into the office, where the Tahsîldâr was busy with some clients, he cried, "I have a petition, I have a petition!"

"Well," said the officer, "what is your petition?"

"I wish it to be written down that I saw melons growing out of a well," said Sharphû.

"Who is this madman?" asked the Tahsîldâr, and at a signal the servants hunted him out of the place.

Sharphû, abashed, but by no means disheartened, now thought to himself, "One thing I have told, and two others remain. Angry or not angry, they shall listen." So he returned and cried out, "Another petition, another petition!"

"Tell it quickly, and be off," said the Tahsîldâr.

"Let it be recorded," said Sharphû, "that I am the man who saw a single bullet shot from a gun which wounded a deer in the foot, the ear, and the horn."

On hearing this nonsense, the Tahsîldâr fell into a rage and ordered his attendants to seize unhappy Sharphû by the shoulders and to thrust him out, which accordingly they did, adding abuse to their violence and saying, as they drove him away, "Take care you do not venture back here again!"

Sharphû, however, notwithstanding his evil treatment, determined that the third wonder should not be lost to the world for the want of telling. So he had the temerity to appear before the Tahsîldâr once more, crying as on the former occasion, "Another petition, another petition!"

"Wretched idiot," said the Tahsîldâr, "if you have a petition why cannot you state what your petition is, and have done with it once for all?"

"I am the man," answered the undaunted Sharphû, "who heard dogs barking in the sky!"

"Give the fellow a beating," said the Tahsîldâr, "and beat him well, that he may trouble me no more."

The attendants needed no second bidding, but arming themselves with their slippers, they thrashed the unfortunate petitioner within an inch of his life and cast him out with ignominy.

Sharphû now decided to return to his own village. When, after a weary journey, he appeared at the door, his brother accosted him, and said, "Sharphû, have you paid in the revenue?"

"No, indeed," answered Sharphû; "I put the money among my flour for safety, but the baker's wife at such-and-such a village refused to return it unless I told her two stories this way, and two stories that way, so I had to go on without it, and on my way I saw melons growing in a well, and I saw a man who wounded a deer in the foot, the ear, and the horn at one shot, and I heard dogs barking in the sky; and I told these wonderful things to the Tahsîldâr and all his men, but they beat me and drove me away."

When Alphû had heard this statement a smile stole over his face. "So, so," said he, "you will be the lambardâr, eh, and I am to be the husbandman? Look here! one of the bullocks has fallen ill. Take this money in the morning and go buy another, and I'll try my luck with the baker's wife. Perhaps I shall be able to tell her two stories this way, and two stories that way."

Before starting, Alphû bought a large number of common brass finger-rings and secreted them in the bag of flour which was to serve him for the journey. Arriving at the house of the baker, he addressed the woman, and begged that she would bake some cakes for him.

"Has your flour been sifted, or not sifted?" asked she.

"I know not," answered Alphû; "but you may sift it if you think proper."

As she was sifting she caught sight of the rings, and perceiving that Alphû's eye was upon her, she remarked, "There are some gold rings in it."

"Yes," answered Alphû, "there are lots of those rings in a bush by the roadside. I picked just a few as I passed, and put them among the flour for safety."

"But whereabouts is the bush?" she inquired anxiously.

Alphû mentioned the spot, and in a few minutes she suddenly observed, "I have a little work to do now, and I must leave you, but I will return and finish the cakes for you in a short time." So she started off, running as soon as she had reached the path, to look for the wonderful bush which bore gold rings.

During her absence her husband came in, and, missing his wife, he said, "O guest, my wife was here a few minutes ago; where has she gone to?"

"I don't know," answered Alphû. "A strange man came by just now and looked in. He passed the door twice and made signs, and your wife went out and followed him."

The husband was laden with a couple of bundles of wood, and hearing this news, he threw them down, and, taking up the bamboo-stick on which they had been suspended from his shoulders, he strode out of the house to look for his missing wife. He soon found her returning quickly from her fruitless search after the rings, and when he met her he said, "Where have you been?"

"I have had some work to do," answered she.

"But," said he, "the man who made signs to you—where is he?"

"I saw no man," protested she, "nor did any man make signs to me."

Not believing her, he lifted his bamboo and thrashed her soundly, after which they sulkily returned to the house together.

Meanwhile Alphû, who had noticed the baker's little girl playing in the enclosure, had slipped out of the house and had met one or two of the villagers. "What is the name of the village," asked he, "where the lad lives to whom the baker's little daughter is betrothed?"

"The village of Jâbbî," answered one, "four miles distant."

"That will do," said he; and he had returned and was

sitting quietly in the house when the baker and his wife entered, and when the latter, still crying from the effects of her chastisement, resumed her baking.

In the morning he rose up early and went to the *hûzrâ*, where he happened to meet a traveller who was going to that very village of Jâbbî. Having ingratiated himself with him, he said, "When you get home, go to the house of the lad to whom this baker's daughter is engaged, and do not forget to tell his friends that his little betrothed was sent to the stack to bring some dried cow-dung for the fire, and that most unfortunately a snake leaped out and bit her, and that she is dead. And say, too, that he and his friends are to come here quickly to show their sympathy with the family."

After this Alphû went back to the house and said to the baker's wife, "Do you not know that the lad to whom you have betrothed your daughter is dead? He was sent out yesterday to gather sticks, and some wolves set on him and tore him up."

"But where did you hear of all this?" asked the astonished woman.

"Oh!" returned Alphû, "I met a traveller just now who was going along the road in the greatest haste to give this news to other relations elsewhere, and he asked me to let you know."

When the wife of the bread-seller heard these doleful tidings, she at once started forth for Jâbbî. But by this time the former news had also reached Jâbbî, and the other woman was also at that very moment leaving her house for the purpose of demanding an explanation from the mother of her son's betrothed. Half-way between the villages the two women met, and she of Jâbbî at once began abusing her friend in unmeasured terms. "You horrid hag!" cried she, "why did you send my little daughter-in-law to the dunghill for fuel in order to be bitten by a snake?"

"Hold your abominable lying tongue!" retorted the other, "and tell me what devil bade you turn out my daughter's betrothed among wolves?"

And with these words the two indignant mothers fell on each other fist and claw, and fought like furies; while scraps of clothing and wisps of hair lying about attested the violence of their rage. At last, wearied with the struggle, they both sat down for breath, when the woman of Jâbbî suddenly said, "But my son is alive and well, thank God!" to which the other replied, "And my daughter is also alive and well."

Then came explanations, and the end of it all was that the two antagonists composed their differences, took some food together, embraced each other tenderly, and parted for their respective homes.

When the baker's wife arrived at her house, she flew at Alphû and said, "So it is you who have been causing all this trouble and bother to me!"

"I have not done anything, mother," answered he quietly, "so very wrong. I have merely told you two stories this way. But if you do not give me up the rupees my foolish brother left with you, I shall have to tell you two stories that way!"

The woman, hearing this, began to feel afraid, and going in, she brought out the money, which she handed to him, and glad was she to see her visitor's back.

Alphû now hastened on to the Tahsîl to pay in the sum which he had recovered. The Tahsîldâr, who had been wondering that the money had not been brought before, received him kindly, and in the course of conversation remarked, "I am told that it was a brother of yours who came here the other day. If so, he was a very stupid fellow."

"Yes," answered Alphû; "his mother is stupid, and so also is he."

"He told me," said the Tahsîldâr, laughing, "that he had seen pumpkins growing out of a well. Just think of that!"

"And why not?" replied Alphû. "The pumpkins might easily have been resting in the water. But my brother, not being clever, had omitted to observe that the plant was really growing at the edge of the water."

"But," said the Tahsîldâr, "he also told me he had seen a stag wounded in the ear, the heel, and the horn, and I know not where, with a single bullet."

"Even that may be true," answered Alphû; "but he did not understand the thing. I presume the deer was lying in a particular position, or scratching his ear, or something."

"Possibly," said the Tahsîldâr; "but you cannot so

easily explain his saying that he had heard dogs barking in the sky."

"Why not?" answered the brother. "Are there not vultures and kites about in abundance, and do they not sometimes pounce down upon puppies? But my brother, you see, is not very clever, like you and me, and could not explain himself."

After paying in the money, Alphû returned to his own village. Entering the house, he said to Sharphû, "Where is the bullock I sent you for?"

"I looked for a bullock all over the country," answered Sharphû; "and as I could not find one, I bought a buffalo instead. As I was passing through a certain village, some fellows cried out, 'Hi! sir, where did you bring that fighting ram from?' As the whole of them averred that my buffalo was a fighting ram, I left it with them, for I thought to myself, 'My brother was angry with me before, because I failed to pay in the revenue, and now, if I take him this buffalo, and it turns out to be a fighting ram, he will be still more angry.'"

Alphû was unable to hold his anger when he heard of this new loss, and he spake such bitter words to his brother that the latter left the house and took himself off altogether.

Poor Sharphû now determined to seek his fortune elsewhere, and he went forth he cared not whither. On and on he travelled, and after a long journey he came to a village, and rested for the night at the *hûzrû*. He there heard of a certain Mughal who lived in those parts, and who owned all the country round. "He will employ you," said the watchman; "he never refuses a poor beggar anything."

The next day Sharphû walked up boldly to the Mughal's door and offered his services.

"Work you shall have," answered the great man solemnly, "but I have a playful fancy which I always indulge when engaging a new servant. If you will agree to the condition, well; if not, begone."

"I agree to anything and everything," said the hungry man.

"Be it so," replied the Mughal. "My stipulation is this: if my servant gets angry I pull out his eye, and if I get angry he pulls out my eye. Besides this, your daily quota of work must be performed. It is not very much. You have only to plough six acres of land every day, to fence it with brushwood, to bring in game for my table, grass for my mare, and firewood for my house; and you are also to cook my food."

In the morning Sharphû drove his bullocks afield, and began to plough the stony hillside. Mid-day came, and he had not finished half an acre. Becoming very tired, he let the bullocks go, and, quite unmindful of ploughing and fencing and hunting and grass-cutting, he lay down and slept under the shade of a tree. After a time a one-eyed slave-girl brought out some bread to him. It was tied up with several tight knots in a bit of calico, and she said to the man, "My mistress bids me tell you that you are to take out your bread from this cloth without unloosing the knots."

"If I am not to loose the knots," cried he, "how am I to get out the bread?" and he gave the parcel back to her, saying, "Take it away, take it away!" So the slave-girl took the bread back again to the house.

When evening came he drove home the bullocks, but took no game, no grass, and no wood. As he was tying up the animals for the night, out came the Mughal, and asked him, "Have you ploughed the six acres of ground?"

"No," answered he.

"Have you brought in some game?"

"No," answered he a second time.

"Grass for my mare?"

"No," once more said the man.

"Firewood for my house?"

"No, I have not," replied again the deluded Sharphû, warming up.

"What!" cried the Mughal; "you lazy rascal, have you done no work at all?"

"How can I do all that work," answered Sharphû, "when I am all alone?" and he began to curse and to swear.

"But the stipulation?" said his master. "I made a stipulation, and you are angry, are you not?"

"And why shouldn't I be angry?" said Sharphû.

"If you are angry, give up your eye," returned the Mughal, and with this he seized poor Sharphû, threw him on to the ground, plucked out his eye, and sent him about his business.

Sharphû now set his face towards his own home once more. "I have had enough of playing the gentleman," said he; "I will go back to my father's fields, where I was happy, and never leave them again." As he entered the house, Alphû looked at him, and saw that he had lost an eye.

"How did you come to lose your eye?" asked he.

"I went to work as a servant to a Mughal," answered Sharphû; and then he related his adventures, and the cruelty of his master in depriving him of an eye.

"But," remarked Alphû, "you were going to be a lambardâr. Is this all you have been doing?"

"I made a mistake," answered Sharphû; "forgive me, and now I will be a servant to you, if you will but allow me food and clothing."

"Very well," said Alphû, "you carry on the work of the farm for our mother. As for me, I have other work; and first I must visit the village where you were robbed of your buffalo."

So he handed over charge of the place to his brother, and prepared for his journey. First he bought a sleek young mule and furnished it with gay trappings. Then he engaged a fine servant to attend on him, giving him certain directions which he was to carry out exactly. When all was ready, and he himself had put on his best clothes, he set out and came to the village of the robbers, where he took a seat in the *hûzrâ*, and all the robbers came about him and received him with great respect. They also gave him refreshments, and lodged him well, and on account of his appearance took trouble to oblige him.

In the morning, when the place was crowded in the usual way, Alphû called his servant and said to him, "Go and do your business!" and the robbers observed that, as the servant removed and broke up the mule's dung, he took therefrom numbers of rupees. This astonished them, and they began to plot among themselves how they should obtain possession of so valuable an animal.

The next morning the servant went through the same performance; for in truth, in accordance with his directions, he had put the rupees there himself overnight. But the robbers knew nothing of the matter, and they said one to another, "An animal like this we should persuade our guest to part with." So one of them asked Alphû, "Sir, will you take the price of this mule and sell it to us?"

"I will not sell her," answered he.

"Nay," said they; "take, if you like, four thousand rupees and let us have her."

"No, no," again answered Alphû. "This mule is my kingdom, and pays me tribute every day; whereas if I accepted ever so large a sum for her I should soon spend that, and then I should have nothing."

Seeing they could not prevail on him to sell, they brought some of the most respectable men of the country, and at last Alphû was persuaded to part with his mule for four thousand rupees, and having received them he returned towards his own village.

On the way to his house he passed a certain bazaar, where, seeing two live hares exposed for sale, he bought them both, and took them with him. These he tied up in his house, and then rested for the night.

The next morning he gave one of the hares into his wife's charge, saying to her, "I expect three or four strange men will come here seeking for me to-day;" and he gave her the most careful instructions how she was to act with regard to the hare and to the visitors. Then he took the other hare, and on leaving the house he said, "Tell them they will find me at the well in the field." Meanwhile, she began preparing dinner for six.

Now, when the robbers discovered, as they soon did, that the wonderful mule declined to produce rupees for them, they were indignant, and four of them banded themselves to set out and seek for Alphû. "Whenever we find him," said they, "let us kill him." When they arrived at his house, and had inquired after him, his wife said, "He has gone to the well;" and as soon as they had turned their backs she brought the hare, which had been left in her charge, out of the house, tied it at the door, and went on with her cooking.

Alphû was seated on a bedstead by the well, and when he saw the robbers approaching he rose up, received them politely, gave them seats, and offered them a hookah. Then, while engaging them in conversation, he took out his hare, gave it two slaps, and said to it, "Go and tell my wife to prepare supper for six." The hare immediately scampered off, and by-and-by it escaped unseen into a field of sugar-cane. The robbers were amazed at Alphû's proceedings, and said among themselves, "Let us not kill him now; let us first see what will come of this."

After a time Alphû invited the four men to come and sup with him, and they accompanied him home, where they were still more amazed to see the very same hare, as they supposed it to be, tied up at the door. Then they said to each other, "This hare must be a very good sort of animal to have; let us see if we cannot get possession of it."

Alphû now invited them to sit down, and messes were laid for six, which was also a surprise to the robbers, who exchanged looks. In the middle of the meal Alphû said to his wife, "Give this guest some more bread;" but instead of bread she brought him water. Feigning anger, her husband struck her so severe a blow that she fell to the ground as if dead. Then said the robbers, "Alas! what have you done? This crime will be fastened on us, and we shall all be hanged!" But Alphû took down a handsome crooked stick, which he kept in a silken cover, and tapping his wife's head with it three times, he said quietly, "Rise, rise!" and at once the woman got up, smiled, and again sat down as if nothing had happened.

The amazement of the robbers had now reached a climax, and they said to each other, "We must contrive by all means to get possession of this stick too, so that if any of our people die we shall know what to do."

Supper over, they all retired to the cool shade of the garden, and sat down on bedsteads. Then said the robbers to Alphû, "Are you willing to part with your hare and your magical stick?"

"No," answered he. "What should I do without them? My hare is my messenger. And as for the stick, you know a man cannot restrain himself always, and it is well to be on the safe side. Besides, I sold you my mule, and I lost by the transaction."

As their arguments availed nothing, the four robbers left him and returned the next day in company with the most substantial men of their tribe to assist them in their efforts at negotiation. "Name," said they, "a price for these articles." The more he refused, the more persistent they became, and the upshot of it was that Alphû affected to fall into a great rage, and cried, "Here, take them away, you may have them as a gift!" and that they, feeling ashamed of their importunity, forced upon him two thousand rupees, and carried away both the wonderful hare and the still more wonderful stick to their village in the hills.

On reaching their homes, one of the robbers, who was more wealthy than the others, bought out his comrades and took both the prizes to his own house, where he carefully tied up the hare in his chamber, and deposited the stick in the corn-bin, which was the safest place he could think of. That done, he sat down in the midst of his family with a contented heart.

The next day he would go out ploughing. So he took up the hare, and said to his wife, "When I want my dinner, I will send you this hare to let you know. If she tells you to prepare for one, you will prepare only for myself, but if she tells you to prepare for more, you will know that guests have come."

Having arrived at the field, he tied the hare to a stump and went on with his ploughing. At noon, feeling very hungry, he ceased working, loosed the hare, and, giving it two smart slaps, he let it go, saying, "Away, tell my wife to bring me out my bread quickly." But the hare, glad of its liberty, soon escaped into the jungles.

In the evening the robber returned to the house in a great rage, and said, "Wife, why did you not send me out my dinner?"

"I was waiting for your orders," answered she.

"But I sent you the hare!" said he.

"No hare ever came to me," replied she.

Notwithstanding, the duped husband visited all his rage on his wife. Lifting a heavy stick, he killed her on the spot, and not content with that, he killed also his children for attempting to save her.

When his rage began to cool he was seized with terror, and, rushing to the corn-bin, he brought forth his magic stick, and began tapping the heads of all the corpses one after another, saying, "Rise, rise!" But he tapped in vain: not a movement, not a turn of the eye, was visible. Then he called in his neighbours and friends, and because all the people of this village were notorious for their robberies, and even murders, they became frightened, and they said one to another, "Never have we been so over-reached! We only seized a single buffalo of that man's, and he has robbed us of six thousand rupees, and brought about all this terrible misery and bloodshed. Therefore, let us have no more to say to the villain, but let us remain quiet, lest worse befall us."

As for Alphû, he kept good watch for ten or twelve days; but as none of his enemies seemed inclined to molest him again, he at last said to his brother: "I have avenged you on that tribe of róbbers, and now I must go and visit your friend the Mughal."

When he was leaving the house he spoke to his mother, saying, "I may be absent one month, or I may be absent twelve months; but I shall not return until I have paid off old scores, and settled with him in full. Meanwhile Sharphû must take care of the property."

Then he disguised himself like a poor servant in old worn-out clothes, and with his staff in his hand he journeyed to the Mughal's village, where he stopped at the *hûzrâ*.

"Does any one want a good servant?" inquired he.

"Yes, I do," answered the Mughal, who happened to be present. "But stay," continued he, "I always make one stipulation, and if you would serve me you must accept it."

"And what is that?" asked Alphû.

"If you get angry," answered the Mughal, "I pull out your eye, and if I get angry you pull out mine."

"Agreed!" said Alphû; "and what work do you expect?"

"Every day," replied he, "you will plough six acres of land and fence it, and bring in to me from the jungle game for my table, grass for my mare, and firewood for my house, and you will cook my dinner for me."

"All this I agree to, and even more, if you like," said Alphû, with assurance. And he accompanied the Mughal home.

The next morning a pair of bullocks and a plough were made over to him, and he was sent to the field. He began his labour by ploughing all round the six acres, and by ploughing twelve furrows in the middle. Next he made up four bundles of brushwood and set them at the four corners of the field. He then tied up his bullocks to a small acacia tree, and spreading his cloth on the ground, he lay down and went to sleep.

About noon the one-eyed slave girl brought his bread to him, tied, as before, by several knots, in a napkin.

"My mistress," said she, "bids you take out your food without untying the knots."

Alphû received the napkin, tore a hole in the bottom of it, and thus took out the bread. While he was eating it he observed that one of the house-dogs had followed the girl. This little creature was a great pet of her mistress, and her name was Lâûnghî. When the girl was going away he contrived to detain the creature by throwing scraps of bread to her, after which he quietly caught her, slipped a rope round her neck, and tied her up to the tree.

Towards evening he went to an old dry well in the neighbourhood, where he found a little grass—about a mouthful—and he cut it, saying, "This will do for my master's mare." As the forest was several miles off, and he had no mind to travel so far afield for firewood, he broke up the yoke and the plough into several pieces, saying, "This will do for my master's fire." Then he took the little dog and killed her, after which he skinned her, and said, "I shall now have a rabbit for my master's dinner."

Having completed his arrangements, he went home, and the Mughal meeting him, asked, "Have you ploughed the six acres?"

"Yes," answered Alphû.

"And have you fenced them?"

"Yes," answered he again.

"And brought in some game?"

"Certainly," said Alphû; "see, here it is!"

"And grass and firewood?"

"Of course!" once more replied the undaunted servant.

"Then," said the Mughal, "make my dinner quickly."

Alphû went away, lighted a fire, set on the pot, and made an excellent stew of poor little Lâûnghî.

As soon as his dinner was served the Mughal sat down, and, in accordance with his usual habit, he called for the little lap-dog. "Lâûnghî! Lâûnghî!" cried he. But he whistled and called to no purpose. Then said Alphû, "Lâûnghî won't come!"

"And why will she not?" asked the Mughal.

"How can Lâûnghî come to you," answered the man, "when you are eating her?"

"What?" cried the Mughal angrily; "would you dare to put a dog before me?"

"Are you not getting angry with me?" said Alphû meaningly.

"No," answered the Mughal; "I am not getting angry. Here, take this food and throw it away, and cook me something else!"

"What shall I cook?" asked Ulphû.

"Flesh-meat will take too long," said the Mughal, "so make me a little *satthû*" [parched grain prepared as a porridge].

"Nay!" said the servant; "I will make you up in no time a nice little curry."

"All right," said the Mughal, "but remember to put a couple of cloves in it."

Alphû, who was a good cook, then made a delicious curry with spices and sauces, and when it was ready he went into the garden and caught a frog, which he tied by the leg to a stool in the kitchen. After this he served up the dinner.

"Did you put some cloves in it?" asked the Mughal.

"Yes, certainly," answered Alphû; "I caught two of them in the garden. One I put in the curry, and I tied the other by the leg to a stool. If you haven't enough, I can go and fetch the other, and put that in too." Then thought the Mughal to himself, "This is a very tricky fellow. I should like to see what he has been doing." "Go!" exclaimed he, "and bring me that thing you have tied by the leg to a stool."

Alphû left the room, but soon returned, holding up the frog between his finger and thumb, and saying, "This is the other clove which I caught in the garden."

The Mughal then became very angry.

"What! are you getting angry?" cried Alphû. "If so, give me up your eye."

"No, no," said the Mughal hastily; "I am not getting angry. I am only asking, why you put a frog in my food?"

"I know not what you call a frog," said Alphû. "In my country we call these things 'cloves.'"

The incensed Mughal thrust away his plate, saying, "Here, remove this rubbish; I won't eat it—eat it yourself." Nor did Alphû wait to be told a second time; for he took the food, and, squatting down in a comfortable corner, he devoured it all himself.

In the morning the Mughal got up, and began cooking his own breakfast. "In the future," said he to Alphû, "you cook no more food for me. Go, take your bullocks and your plough, and do your six acres!"

"And how am I to do them," answered the imperturbable Alphû, "when I have neither plough nor yoke?"

"But," said his master, looking amazed, "I gave both into your hands only yesterday!"

"Quite true," said Alphû, "but I broke them up and used them as firewood to cook your dinner with."

The Mughal, purple with rage, now rose and stamped with his foot. "Did you ever hear," cried he, "of any one who used his plough for firewood?"

"Are you getting angry with me?" retorted Alphû. "If so, give me up your eye!"

"No, no," protested the distracted Mughal, "I am not getting angry. Go away to the carpenter, and order another plough forthwith, and, in short, get out of my sight."

While a new plough was being made, Alphû had two days of comparative idleness; and on the morning of the third day he resumed his labour. The Mughal also visited the field; and when he saw the one furrow all round the six acres, and the twelve furrows in the middle, with the forlorn bits of brushwood at the four corners, he again waxed wroth, and asked, "Is this the way farmers plough and fence their land in your country? Now attend to me. I perceive that you are more than I can manage. So leave me sharp, and get away to your own place!"

"Not so fast," answered Alphû. "If I had had anything to do at my own house, why should I have come to serve you? We stipulated that if one of us got angry, he was to give up his eye to the other. And now you are angry, since you are turning me out of your service. So give me up your eye!"

"Nay, I am not angry," answered the Mughal. "I am merely pointing out that you should not behave like this."

The Mughal then bent his steps towards his home, leaving Alphû at the plough. As he walked along he could not help thinking of the story of the two men on the bank of the river: how they saw something black floating down the stream, which they imagined to be a blanket; how one of them said to the other, "You can swim; go out, and see what it is;" how he went, and seized it, and how it was a bear which caught him; how the man on the bank cried, "If you can't bring in the blanket, let it go!" and how the other replied, "I wish to let the blanket go, but the blanket won't let me go." "Yes," said the Mughal aloud, "before, when I took servants, I conquered them easily, and took their eyes from them; but this fellow is not to be baffled; and what is worse, he has caught me in his grip, and I can't get rid of the rascal."

It happened some time after this that the Mughal's wife died, and that he wished to visit a distant village for the purpose of bringing home another wife. So he saddled his mare, and, taking Alphû with him as his servant, he went on his way. By-and-by they approached a village, and, as it was late in the day, the Mughal said, "Let us enter the village, and lodge there for the night."

"Let us rather stay here," advised Alphû. "Why should you run the risk of infection and no end of vermin in a strange village? On this spot some travellers are already encamped, and with them we shall be safe."

The Mughal, who, as a man of substance, was of a corpulent habit, dismounted heavily from his mare and tied her to a tree. A fire was then made, and cakes were prepared for supper, and having eaten, the Mughal covered up his head in his robe and went to sleep while Alphû watched.

Alphû now began thinking to himself, "This Mughal takes care never to get angry, or, at least, he denies that he does, so I must make another attempt to surprise him, and this time I may perhaps succeed." So he got up quietly and went to some cattle-drovers who were also halting in that place, and said to them, "My master has a fine mare here. Give me a price for her and take her off somewhere, but tie up in her place the most vicious bullock which you have in your herd. I will answer for it that in the morning you shall receive it back again, besides which you can thrash my master well for a robber, and compel him to make you compensation."

The cattle-drovers began to laugh at the drollery of this advice, but, finding he was in earnest, some of them sprang up, singled out a wild bullock, and tied it in the place of the mare, which they sent away somewhere else. After this, Alphû lay down and slept.

Some time before daylight the Mughal awoke, and cried, "Alphû, Alphû, saddle the mare!" Alphû, pretending zeal, fussed about for a few minutes, and then said, "Sir, the mare is saddled and ready." It was too dark for the Mughal to see what manner of animal it was which he was about to mount, nor had he time to do so, for the moment he approached he was tossed on the bullock's horns and thrown on his back. "In the name of heaven!" cried the poor man, "what's this? Has my mare grown a pair of horns in the night?" Then, calling his servant, he said, "Alphû, O Alphû, look here, and tell me quickly what animal is this!"

"If it is not your mare," answered Alphû, "what can it be?"

By this time morning began to break, and up came the cattle-drovers in a body. Seizing the bewildered Mughal, they belaboured him well with goads and sticks, saying, "Thief, you have stolen our bullock!" The Mughal retaliated, hitting out with his staff, or butting at them with his head, while he called out repeatedly, "You are the thieves; you have stolen my mare, you have stolen my mare!" Then they thrashed him again, and finally seized him by main force, saying, "Come along, we'll take you to the justice!"

All this time Alphû was holding his sides laughing immoderately. "You are my servant," remonstrated the Mughal; "why have you not taken my part?"

"How can I?" coolly replied he. "How do I know where you have sent your mare? And if you have stolen this bullock the case is worse. I will do your work for you, but you must not expect me to throw myself into a well for you."

As the herdsmen were shuffling and urging the unlucky man to come on, Alphû asked him, "Why did you bring that bullock here and tie it up to our tree?"

When the Mughal, in his shame and anger, heard this,

he thought to himself, "If my own servant is going to witness against me I am lost!" So he addressed himself to his persecutors, and said, "Take your bullock away, and, see, here is some money for you to leave me alone. You have stolen my mare, but never mind."

"Nay," retorted they, "you have caused us trouble and loss of time. You must go to the court."

"Ah," groaned the Mughal, "these fellows are too much for me! They out-do Alphû himself."

At this stage Alphû came forward and interfered, handing the men their bullock, and ten rupees out of his master's purse, and sending them away whispering and laughing.

Then said the Mughal to Alphû, "My mare is gone and my honour is gone too. Let us return home, and I'll buy another mare, and we can set out again. Here, pick up the saddle and let us be off!"

"Do you call this thing a saddle?" answered Alphû. "I call it a basket, and in the old hut which you have given me to live in I have a dozen of them. If you want some more I can supply you with plenty, but I am not going to carry this one all the way home."

Said the Mughal, again becoming excited, "Do you say you have baskets like this in your house? Are you aware that this basket, as you call it, cost me fifty rupees?"

"Well, pick it up yourself," answered Alphû, "I won't. If you like to carry such a wretched thing, do so."

"What!" yelled the Mughal, growing infuriated, "did I not hire you as a servant?"

"Are you getting angry with me?" asked Alphû quietly.

"No, no, not at all, not at all," replied the Mughal, recovering himself. "I was merely observing that this was a saddle, and not a basket."

The Mughal then picked up the saddle himself, and the two ill-assorted companions began their return journey. "Look here," said the Mughal, "it will be a disgrace for me to be seen carrying a saddle into my village. I will carry it within a mile, and to save the scandal do you take it then."

"Well," answered Alphû, "do you carry it within a mile."

When they arrived at the place indicated, the Mughal said, "Now you carry the saddle."

"Nay, that I will not," answered Alphû.

"Why not?" said his master, astonished. "You said you would."

"I did not say I would carry the saddle," said Alphû. "I said you might carry it, and I said that I had plenty of baskets of the same pattern."

Then the Mughal again began to flare up.

"Are you getting angry with me now?" asked Alphû. "If so, give me up your eye."

"No, no," answered the Mughal, "I am not getting angry. I am merely pointing out that a servant should obey his master."

"If the thing were worth carrying," said Alphû, "I might take it for you; but an old basket, never!"

The Mughal, who would not for shame be seen entering his village bearing a saddle on his head, was fain to take it down, lay it on the ground, tie a piece of string to it, and in that manner to make for his house by the shortest possible path, dragging the unlucky saddle behind him.

Having arrived home, the Mughal borrowed another mare from a neighbour, and the next morning he started very early, so as to reach his destination on the same day. His dignity would not permit him to travel without a servant, and he was compelled to take Alphû with him again. They were within a mile of the village, when the Mughal sent on his servant in advance, saying, "I shall rest here and bathe. Do you go on and request my friends to prepare my dinner for me."

On reaching the house, Alphû gave the people his master's message, thus, "My master sends his respects to you, and wishes you to know that in a little while he will be here. Meanwhile, he would have you prepare some dinner for him."

They were all delighted at the intelligence, and began their preparations. But Alphû surprised them by saying, "Of course any food will do for me, as I am only a servant. But my master is indisposed, and he has asked me to say that for two days he has been taking only the food which his doctors have prescribed for him, and which he must adhere to."

"What kind of food, then," asked they, "would he like?"

"You will take," answered the man, "one pound of the common country soap and dress it with assafœtida and spices into a kind of porridge. It is the only thing my master will touch."

When the Mughal arrived, all his new wife's relations came forward to receive him, and they gave him the seat of honour. "I am very tired," thought he, "and very hungry, and when I have had a good dinner I shall go to sleep." The food came, and the aroma which assailed his nostrils was a trifle compared with the flavour of the first spoonful. He was amazed, and nearly beside himself with rage and disappointment, but shame kept him silent. At the same time he perceived his mischievous servant eating wholesome food close by, and eyeing him with a malicious twinkle. To make matters still worse, his host pressed him cordially to make a good meal for the credit of the house, which he was compelled to do to avoid offending them. Then, pleading fatigue, he retired to another chamber and lay down. In the middle of the night he became very sick, and complained of horrible nausea and pains and spasms. Calling his servant, he said, "Come along with me outside; I am ill."

"Nay," said Alphû, "if we go out now, we shall be arrested by the watchman and locked up as thieves. If you are sick, I will bring you the vessel, and in the morning I can take it out before any one is astir."

Before morning the Mughal ordered his servant to throw out the vessel. "I am coming," answered he. And whenever the Mughal called him he answered in like manner, "I am coming," but he came not. At last daylight appeared, and the Mughal, for very shame, had to rise to take away the odious thing himself. He covered it with the sheet which he had thrown over his head, and, stepping out in the cold, crossed over towards the jungle.

Hardly had he left the room when his friends came in and inquired for him.

"The food you gave him last night," said Alphû, "did not agree with him at all, and he is so angry that he has started for his home. Some of you go and persuade him to return. He is just outside. He will make excuses, but never mind them, bring him back."

One or two therefore followed the Mughal, and overtook him before he had time to disencumber himself of his load. "We apologize," said they, "if the food was not to your liking. Do not part in anger, but come back with us."

The Mughal protested that he was merely taking the morning air; but they would listen to no excuses, and, as they laid hold of his arms in order to add a friendly violence to their arguments, the vessel which he held dropped out of his hands on to the stones and was broken. The poor man was covered with confusion, and his anger getting the better of him, he rushed back to the house to revile his servant. "Ah, villain," cried he, when he saw him, "would you play your tricks on me in a strange house?"

"Are you getting angry with me?" answered Alphû. "If so, give me up your eye."

"No, no!" said the Mughal, dancing and almost speechless with rage; "I am not angry—not at all. I would merely point out to you that your conduct is infamous." And he once more subsided.

He then went and called for his mare, and when his friends again entered the room he said, "I must return to my home at once, as I am not well." So he put his new wife into a palanquin, mounted his mare, and all three left for their own village.

They were within a short distance of the village, when the Mughal looked back and saw that the bearers of the palanquin had lagged far behind. "Go quickly back," said he to Alphû, "and hasten up my wife. Make her fly, so that she may be there and here in the same moment, as darkness is rapidly falling."

Alphû hastened back and said to the bearers, "Strange bearers are not permitted to enter this village, so set down the palanquin and return to your homes; other bearers will be here presently."

The men obeyed him, and, as he was considering what he should do next, he saw a party emerging from a wood, who told him that they had just been burying a young girl of the village, who had died of a fall from a swing. A thought came into the mind of the wily Alphû. Bidding the bride get out of the palanquin, he took her into the wood and bound her securely to a tree. "If you utter a sound, or make the least noise until you are released," said he, "I will put you to death." He then went on to the newly-made grave, and began to open it. A foot and a half below the surface he came to the narrow chamber, and, taking out the body, he chopped off one of its legs. With this in his hand he hurried to his master.

"What in the name of heaven is that?" exclaimed he with starting eyes.

"I am your servant," quoth Alphû, "and I have merely obeyed your orders. You told me to hasten on your wife so fast that she might be there and here in the same moment. That is exactly what I have done, for she is there, and she is also here." And he held up the ghastly object before the astounded Mughal, who, crying out, "Villain, you have undone me; you have destroyed me, and you have killed my wife!" rushed at him savagely.

The two men instantly closed and rolled over and over, while their excited voices mingled together, Alphû crying, "You are angry at last; you are angry at last!" and his master screaming, "Yes, yes; I am angry!" But Alphû, being younger and stronger, soon prevailed over his obese antagonist, and while he nearly throttled him with one hand, he plucked out his eye with the other. After this he got up and shook himself, and, returning to his own village, he said to his brother, "Now, Sharphû, I have reckoned in full with the Mughal, and exacted eye for eye —see!" and he threw down the Mughal's eye before him.

From this time the two brothers lived together on the family estate very happily, nor had Sharphû ever again a wish to abandon his own proper work.

As for the Mughal, his bride was discovered and restored to him. But he reformed his manners and turned over a new leaf, for it was never afterwards heard that he plucked out the eyes of any of his servants again.

Told by a bard at Hazro, February 1879.

XLIX

OF THE SON WHO REPROVED HIS FATHER

A CERTAIN villager died, and, as his body was being carried along to the grave, his little son, who was walking in front, began to address the corpse, and to say, "Father, they are taking you now to a very narrow house. There will be no sleeping-mat for you there, nor any light; there will not be even the smell of bread, nor a single cup for you to drink from."

Another boy, of about the same age, who was also in the procession, overheard these words, and said to his father, "They are taking this body, then, to our house?"

"Nay, boy," answered the father, "not to our house, but to the grave."

"But," replied the child, "the dead man's son says it is to our house, for we have no sleeping-mats, nor any lights, we have never any food to eat nor water to drink, and our house is also both dark and narrow. I think it *must* be going to our house."

L

OF THE THIEF AND THE POOR MAN

A THIEF broke into a house in the hope of finding something worth stealing, but, unfortunately for him, the house was the home of a man who was miserably poor. When the thief entered, the owner was lying awake, sadly wondering where in the world his next meal was to come from. He neither moved nor spoke, but quietly looked on while the thief was feeling along the bare walls, and rummaging his slender property, trying hard to discover something to carry away. At last, as the fellow was leaving the room empty-handed, the poor man grinned aloud with mocking laughter. Turning round in a rage, the startled thief exclaimed, "What! you are laughing, are you? And do you call yourself the owner of a house?"

LI

OF THE TRAVELLER AND HIS CAMEL

Once upon a time, a traveller, coming along the desert road with his laden camel, stopped to rest during the noontide heat under a shady tree. There he fell asleep. When he awoke he looked at the camel, and, finding to his sorrow that the faithful companion of all his journeys was dead, he thus apostrophized him—

> "Where is the spirit fled, ah, where
> The life that cheered the weary ways?
> Couldst thou not wait one hour, nor spare
> For me, thy friend, one parting gaze?"[1]

LII

CONCERNING THE TWO FRIENDS

Once upon a time a dog and a cock were sworn friends. But a famine fell on the land, and the dog said to the cock, "There is no food for me here, so I am going away to another country. I tell you this that you may not blame me and say, 'This dog was my friend, but he left me without a word.'"

"O dog," answered the cock, "we are sworn friends.

[1] This well-known verse comes naturally to the lips of a Panjâbî when he receives news of the death of a friend.

If you go I go. Let us go together, and as you are a dog, you can forage for us both, since if I venture about all the village curs will set on me and eat me up."

"Agreed!" said the dog. "When I go for food you shall hide in the jungle, and whatever I find I will fetch to you and we'll share and share alike."

So the two friends set out. After a time they saw a village, and the dog said, "Now I am going forward to prowl for food; but as for you, you must remain here. But first of all, if anything should happen to you when I am away, how shall I know it?"

Said the cock, "Be this the signal—whenever you hear me crow three times, at once hasten back to me."

So for some time these two creatures lived happily, the dog bringing in supplies every day, while at night he rolled himself up beneath the tree in the branches of which the cock sat safely at roost.

One day, in the absence of the dog, a jackal came to the tree, and, looking up, he said to the cock, "O uncle, why, pray, are you perched so high? Come down and let us join in evening prayer together."

"Most willingly," answered the cock; "but first it is necessary that I should cry the bhángh,[1] that all good Musalmans may hear and come too."

So the cock began to crow lustily, until the dog in the distant village heard his note, and said to himself, "Alas! something has happened to my dear old friend; I must trot home at once."

So he started for the jungle, but when the jackal looked round and saw him he began to sneak off, upon which the cock remarked, "O good nephew, this is merely a pious neighbour coming to join us. Pray do not leave us! At any rate, stop for prayers!"

"Alas! uncle, I would stop with pleasure," answered the jackal, "but the fact is I have—in short, it just occurs to my mind that I forgot to perform my ablutions.[2] Farewell." And, quickening his pace, he disappeared.

[1] The Mussalman cry to prayers in the Panjáb is called the bhángh, and so is the crow of a cock.

[2] I have been compelled to altar this phrase, which in the original is too coarse for polite ears. It is a most bitter satire on the excessive punctiliousness of the stricter Muhammadans in the matter of ceremonial washings.

LIII

STORY OF THE YOUNG MAN AND THE SNAKE

THERE was once a farmer who was extremely poor. It happened that when his poverty was greatest a son was born to him, and this son was such a lucky child that his father speedily became quite as rich as he was before poor, and obtained a great name over all the country.

After a certain time the farmer thought to himself, "I must get my son betrothed somewhere. I was poor once, but I am now rich, and my son is lucky. It is right that he should be betrothed to the daughter of some rich man like myself."

It was long before he found a suitable match, but at last he betrothed the boy to a girl who lived in a distant town. The ceremony came on, much money was spent, many guests were invited, and much food was given away. In short, the betrothal was splendid.

The son had scarcely grown to manhood when the father died, leaving him in the world alone.

The parents of his betrothed, when they heard the sad news, felt very sorry for him, and at first they would have brought him to live at their own house. But the mother said, "He is old enough now to come and take our daughter home with him, so let us send for him that he may do so. No friend like a good wife."

A messenger was accordingly sent off, and the lad, when he received the invitation, dressed himself up in his best, and, mounting his mare, set off.

On the way he came to a lonely jungle, in which he saw a mungoose, and a snake of enormous dimensions, engaged in deadly combat. He reined up his horse to look on. The mungoose soon began to wear out his adversary, and to inflict such wounds as would have put an end to its life in a short time. Seeing which, the boy considered to himself, "When two are contending, it is an act of charity to separate them." So he tried to separate the combatants, but every time he failed, as the mungoose again and again sprang upon his adversary in spite of him. Finding he could not prevail, he drew his sword and dealt the warlike little mungoose his death-blow.

After this he went on again, but he had not proceeded far when he found that the snake had rushed round and intercepted him. Then began the boy to remonstrate.

"I did you good service," said he. "Why, then, have you pursued me?"

"It is true," answered the snake, "that you saved me from my enemy. But I shall not let you go. I shall eat you."

"Surely," replied the lad, "one good turn deserves another. Will you injure me because I assisted you? In my country we do not deal with each other thus."

"In these parts," said the snake, "the custom is different. Every one here observes the rule of returning evil for good."

The boy then began to argue with the snake, but he argued in vain, for the snake was determined to eat him. At last he said, "Very well, snake, you can eat me, but first give me eight days to go about my business, after which I shall come back."

With this request the snake complied, saying, "Be it so; in eight days you must return to me."

The snake, which had coiled himself round about the boy's body, now released his hold and suffered him to depart, so he rode on once more and completed his journey.

All his friends were very glad to see the young bridegroom, and especially his little wife, and at his father-in-law's house he remained for several days. But as he was always downcast and sad, they asked him, "Why are you so sorrowful?" For six days they asked in vain. On the seventh they spoke to their daughter. "Is he angry? What is the matter with him?" But she also asked him in vain.

When the eighth day came, he said, "Now let me go home." The father and mother then gave the daughter her portion, and, having placed them both in a bullock-cart, they sent the young couple away.

So the two travelled until they had left the village far behind them. Then said the lad to his wife and to her servants, "Return now back again to your own home. As for me, it is decreed that I shall die on the way."

All the servants, being alarmed, at once returned, but his young wife said, "Where you fall, I shall fall. What am I to do at my house?" So she continued to accompany her husband.

When he arrived at the spot appointed, he dismounted and called forth the snake.

"I have come," said he, "in accordance with my promise. If you wish to eat me, come and eat me now!"

His wife, hearing his ominous words, descended also, and came and stood by her husband's side. By-and-by a dreadful hissing sound was heard, and the snake crawled out from the jungle, and was preparing to devour the unfortunate boy, when the girl exclaimed, "Why are you going to eat this poor youth?" The snake then told her the whole story, how he was fighting with a mungoose, and how her husband interfered and killed his adversary; "and in this country," continued he, "our custom is to return evil for good!"

The young wife now tried all the arguments she could think of to divert the monster from his purpose, but he was deaf to her pleadings and refused to listen to them. Then said she, "You say that in this country people do evil in return for good. This is so strange a custom, and so very unreasonable, that I would fain know the history of it. How did it all come about?"

"Do you see those five *tâlî* trees?" answered the snake. "Go you to them and cry out to them, 'What is the reason that in this country folks do evil in return for good?' and see what they will say to you!"

The girl went and did as she was bidden, addressing her request to the middle of the five.

The tree straightway answered her, "Count us! We are now five, but once we were six—three pairs. The sixth tree was hollow, having a vast cavity in its trunk. It happened once upon a time, many years ago, that a certain thief went and robbed a house, and that the people followed him. He ran and ran and ran, and at last he came in among us. It was night, but the moon was shining, and the thief hid himself in the hollow *tâlî* tree. Hearing his pursuers close at hand, he besought the tree, saying, 'O tree, tree, save me!' When the *tâlî* tree heard his miserable cry it closed up its old sides upon him, and hid him in a safe embrace, so that the people searched for him in vain, and they had to return without him. When all pursuit was over, the tree once more opened and let him go. Now, in this old *tâlî* tree there was sandal wood,[1] and the thief, when he went forth, had the scent of sandal wood so permanently fixed upon him that wherever he was, and wherever he appeared, he diffused a delightful fragrance. It so happened that he visited the city of a certain king, and a man passing him on the road suddenly stopped, and asked him, 'Where did you get this beautiful scent?'

"'You are mistaken,' answered the thief; 'I have no scent.'

"'If you will give me this scent,' said the man, 'I will pay you its value.'

"Again the thief answered, 'I have no scent—none.'

"Then the man, who was shrewd and intelligent, went his way to the King and told him, 'There is a stranger arrived here who possesses a most wonderful scent. To your Highness, perhaps, he might be induced to give it up.'

"The King then ordered the thief into his presence, and said to him, 'Show me the scent you have.'

"'I have none,' said he.

"'If you will give it up to me quietly,' said the King, 'you shall be rewarded. If not, you shall be put to death.'

"When the thief heard this he got frightened, and said, 'Do not kill me, and I will tell the whole story.' So he told the King how his life was preserved in the heart of the *tâlî* tree, and how the scent of sandal wood had never left him since. Then said the King, 'Come along and show me that wonderful tree of which you tell me.'

"Arriving at this very spot, the King instantly gave orders to his followers to cut the tree down and to carry it to his palace. But when the *tâlî* tree heard his order, and when it understood the reason of it, it cried aloud, 'I have saved the life of a man, and for this I am to lose my own life. For the future, therefore, let it be decreed within this jungle that whosoever dares to do good, to him it shall be repaid in evil!'"

The girl, having heard this doleful story, returned once more to her husband's side.

"Well," said the snake, "have you consulted the *tâlî*

[1] There is a superstition that *tâlî* or *sîsam* trees in old age develop sandal wood.

tree? and do you find that our custom here is even as I told you?"

She was compelled to admit that it was so; but as the monster advanced to his victim, she wept and said, "What will become of me? If you must eat my husband, you must begin by eating me!"

The snake objected to an arrangement so unreasonable. "You?" cried he. "But you have never done me the smallest good. You have not even done me harm. How, then, can I be expected to eat you?"

"But if you kill my husband," replied she, "what's left for me? You acknowledge yourself that I have done you no good, and yet you would inflict this injury upon me."

When the snake heard these words he stopped, and began to grow remorseful, especially as she wept more copiously than ever. That the boy must be eaten was certain, but how should he comfort the girl? Wishing to devise something, he crept back to his hole, and in a few minutes he returned with two magic globules or pills. "Here, foolish woman," said he, "take these two pills and swallow them, and you will have two sons to whom you can devote yourself, and who will take good care of you!"

The girl accepted the pills, but, with the cunning natural to a woman, said, "If I take these two pills, doubtless two sons will be born. But what about my good name?"

The snake, who knew not that she was already wed, hearing her speech, became exasperated with her. "Women are preposterous beings," cried he, and he crept back once more to his hole. This time he brought out two more pills, and when handing them to the disconsolate girl he said, "Revenge will sweeten your lot: When any of your neighbours revile you on account of your sons, take one of these pills between finger and thumb, hold it over them, rubbing it gently so that some of the powder may fall on them, and immediately you will see them consume away to ashes."

Tying the former pills in her cloth, the girl looked at the other pills incredulously, and then, with a sudden thought, she gently rubbed them over the snake, saying with an innocent air, "O snake, explain this mystery to me again! Is this the way I am to rub them?"

The moment an atom of the magic powder had touched the snake, he was set on fire, and in another instant he was merely a long wavy line of grey dust lying on the ground.

Then with a glad face the little wife turned to her husband and said, "Whosoever does good to any one, in the end good will be done to him; and whosoever does evil to any one, in the end evil will be done to him. You did good, and, lo! you are rewarded. The snake did evil, and evil befell him. All things help each other. The Almighty brings everything to rights at last."

After this the two went on their way to their own home, where they lived in happiness and contentment for many a year.

LIV

STORY OF THE WEAVER AND THE THIEVES

THERE were once three notorious thieves who had a friend who was by trade a weaver. At this man's house they were accustomed to meet to plan their nocturnal expeditions, and to divide their ill-gotten gains, and he used to entertain them with water and bread and tobacco in return for various trifles which were occasionally assigned to him. One night these thieves stole four buffaloes and drove them to the weaver's, who was astonished when he saw so rich a capture enter his yard, and who said, "You three go off for a single day and you bring back four buffaloes. Next time you must take me with you."

"No, no," answered his friends; "we will present you with one of these buffaloes, but you must not come out with us."

"I don't want this buffalo," said the weaver. "I should like to have something of my own earning."

The three thieves then took away the buffaloes and hid them in a cave, and when they next went out for spoil the weaver went with them.

This time they betook themselves to a large city, and determined to break into a thatched house which seemed a likely place for plunder. The thieves therefore said to the weaver, "You look about for a long pole, so that we can raise the thatch and get in." The weaver looked everywhere but was unable to find one. Seeing, however, that the people of the house were sleeping outside in the enclosed space, he went to them and woke them up, vociferating, "We are just going to break into your house, my good people! So lend us a pole to raise up the thatch." All at once they jumped up in a fright, yelling out, "Thieves! Thieves!" and the four house-breakers scampered off through the darkness in various directions and escaped.

After a time they met in a certain place, and the thieves said to the weaver, "Friend, you must not come with us again. You will get us into trouble and we shall be all hanged. You remain in this place until we return."

"This time," answered the weaver, "I shall be more careful, so don't be afraid, and take me too." So all four set out together again.

After prowling through a street or two they came to a house and made a hole through the wall. The three thieves said to the weaver, "Do you stop outside and keep watch, and we will enter and hand out the things to you." The thieves then crawled through the hole and disappeared. A long time seemed to elapse, and at last the weaver said to himself, "Those fellows must be hiding all the best things for themselves," and he crept in after them.

He now found himself in complete darkness. Beginning to grope about, he happened to put his hand into the fire-place which was on the floor, and he found that the embers were still glowing. So he blew them up, and, seeing close by him some vermicelli and sugar, he put them into a vessel and began to boil them.

Now, it so happened that the wife of the good man of the house was sleeping on her low charpoy, or bed, next to the fire-place, and as she turned herself in her dreams she stretched out her arm over the side, and her hand, palm uppermost, came between the weaver's nose and his pot of vermicelli, where it rested. He, imagining that she was asking him for some of his mess, ladled out a spoonful boiling hot and clapped it into her hand. At once she uttered a piercing shriek, which roused up her husband, while the weaver, without a word, escaped into the rafters of the low roof, and the three thieves, who had just that moment entered laden with booty from another room, hid themselves in corners.

Now, it must be understood that the weaver's name was Kâdrâ, a word which in that town signified "God." Hardly had Kâdrâ got into the rafters, when the husband, who had risen in a fury, smelt the vermicelli and the sugar, and found that cooking was going on. "Ah, you slut!" cried he to his wife, "you have been making this nice stuff for some friend of yours, have you? and you thought I was asleep!" And, taking up a good stick, he thrashed her soundly.

The poor woman, raising her eyes to the rafters, cried through her tears, "Kâdrâ (God) knows whether I have done this thing or not. I appeal to Kâdrâ!"

The weaver, who had come from a village where the word Kâdrâ was not used in that sense, thinking himself accused, and imagining that the woman was staring up at him, began to protest, saying, "Why am I to have all the bad name? The other fellows are a good deal worse than I am. Look where they are hiding in those corners!"

Hearing these mysterious words issuing from the roof, and discovering that there was a band of thieves in his house, the astonished husband took down a sword and mounted guard over the hole in the wall, while the cries of "Thieves! murder!" uttered by himself and his wife quickly roused up their neighbours, who presently entered in all haste, and, seizing the four confederates, carried them off to gaol.

The next morning the three thieves and the unhappy weaver, all bound together, were brought up before the King and accused of house-breaking and robbery. The King, with a solemn air, opened his law-books, but, as he was some time examining them, the weaver cried out, "O King, if I am to be hanged, pray hang me at once, and let me get back to my work. I am only a poor weaver, and as the sun is getting hot, my thread which was put out yesterday will all be dried up and spoilt."

The King, who loved a joke, whether intended or not, was so amused at this speech of the weaver that he ordered his release, but the three thieves he sentenced to imprisonment, and they were taken back to gaol.

LV

STORY OF THE TRAVELLER AND THE OILMAN

ONCE upon a time there was a certain traveller who was riding a mare. After a long march he came to a village and lodged at the house of an oilmaker. It happened that during the night his mare had a foal; but in the morning, when he was preparing to resume his journey, his host came out and seized the foal, saying—

"This foal is mine. My oil-press had it last night."

"Nay," said the traveller, "it is mine. My mare has been in foal for months."

"And my oil-press," replied the oilman, "must have been in foal for months, too."

As they were unable to agree, they went to the court and laid the case before the King. When each of them had made his statement, the King, after some consideration, at last addressed the traveller and said, "Your mare could not possibly have had this foal, because, you see, it was found standing by the oil-press."

So in his wisdom he gave a verdict in favour of the oilman, and sent the parties away.

The owner was very sorrowful indeed when he saw his foal led off by the grinning oilman, nor was his mare less so at being so cruelly parted from her young one. In vain he urged her forward. She turned her head perpetually, and tried hard again and again to trot back to her quarters of the night before.

While the poor man was in this predicament, a jackal met him and said, "What is the matter with your mare, and why are you so sad?" Then the traveller told the jackal the story of the foal, and how the King had awarded it to the wrong party. "Cheer up," said the jackal. "Only promise to keep me safe from the village dogs, and I will get you back your foal."

The traveller, who was overjoyed to hear the jackal speak thus, at once replied, "I will engage to keep you perfectly safe if you will help me to recover my foal."

"Very well," said the jackal, "put now a cloth over me, and when you take me into the court, set me up in some conspicuous place where the King will not fail to see me, and the rest you may leave to me."

The traveller did as he was directed. He dressed the jackal up in a red cloth, which covered his head, and set him in the court-house.

When the jackal, who was sitting as still as a mouse, perceived that the King was looking in his direction, he fell suddenly down on his side. No sooner had he recovered himself than he fell down on his other side. Again, having sat upright once more, he fell flat on his face.

The King, noticing this extraordinary proceeding, called out, "Send and ask that child why she is falling down here, and then falling down there, here, there and everywhere in the court-house." When the attendant approached and put the question, the jackal answered, "That is a secret which I can only impart to the King himself. Take me quite close up, so that the King may hear, and I will tell it."

The jackal was now conducted forward to the steps of the throne, and the King, seeing he was a jackal, began to question him.

"Why are you come here to play your jackal-tricks?"

"If my life is spared," answered the jackal, "I will tell you all."

"Take your life and speak," said the King.

Then the jackal replied, "Last night, O King, the sea caught fire, and in order to put it out I was throwing water over it with a sieve the whole night through. Not a single wink of sleep did I get, and I am now so tired that I tumble down first on one side and then on the other, and sometimes I fall forward on my face, so weary am I with all my exertions."

"You silly jackal!" cried the King; "did any one in the world ever hear of the sea taking fire? And even if it did, would any one throw water on it with a sieve?"

"And, O King," retorted the jackal, "did any one in the world ever hear of an oil-press bearing a foal?"

When the King heard that, he began to bethink himself, and after some moments he said, "Call the traveller and the oilman once more. The jackal is right—it must have been the mare which had the foal. Therefore, take away the foal from the oilman and give it to the traveller."

This was accordingly done, and the traveller, in gratitude and gladness, carried the jackal safely to the jungle, where he put him down and made him a low salaam, saying, "O jackal, it is to you I owe the restoration of my foal, and your wisdom I shall ever remember!"

LVI

OF AN UNFORTUNATE JACKAL

In the month of October, when the crops are ripe and the jackals are accordingly frisky and well fed, some of these little animals found some loose papers on the ground, and agreed to elect a lambardâr. To the one elected they handed the manuscripts, saying, "Hold these in your pad wherever you go, because they are the authority by which you shall govern us."

"Kings have crowns," remarked one of them, "and our lambardâr should also possess some ensign, mark, or decoration, so that all may recognize him."

"Tie this basket to his tail," suggested a sly fox.

So the new lambardâr was invested with his papers, and adorned as well with an old basket fastened securely to his tail. Just then a pack of dogs broke in upon them, and the jackals scampered off to their holes. The lambardâr's new decoration, however, that wretched basket, caught in the entrance, and he was unable to advance. "Come in," cried the other jackals from within; "come in, Mr. Lambardâr."

"Thank you," answered the lambardâr; "but you have done me too much honour, and your royal ensign holds me fast."

"Oh!" said they, "show the villains your papers."

"Precisely what I have done," replied he; "but they are such barbarians, these village dogs, that they cannot even read."

In another minute the dogs had dragged forth the wretched lambardâr and despatched him.

Thus [added the story-teller] honour and rank bring peril and loss.

LVII

TALE OF A WEAVER AND A WATER-MELON

ONCE upon a time a poor country weaver visited a town, where he saw a quantity of water-melons piled up one above the other in front of a grain-seller's shop.

"Eggs of other birds there are," he said, "and I have seen them; but what bird's eggs are these eggs? These must be mare's eggs."

So he looked at the grain-seller, and said, "Are these eggs mare's eggs?"

The man instantly cocked his ears; and perceiving that he was a simpleton, answered, "Yes, these eggs are mare's eggs."

"What is the price?" inquired the countryman.

"One hundred rupees apiece," said the grain-seller.

The simple weaver took out his bag of money, and, counting out the price, bought one of the melons and carried it off. As he went along the road, he began to say to himself, "When I get home I will put this egg in a warm corner of my house, and by-and-by a foal will be born, and when the foal is big enough, I shall mount it and ride to the house of my father-in-law. Won't he be astonished?"

As the day, however, was unusually hot, he stopped at a pool of water to bathe. But first of all he deposited the melon most carefully in the middle of a low bush, and then he proceeded to undress himself. His garments were not half laid aside, when out from the bush sprang a hare, and the weaver, snatching up part of his clothing while the rest hung about his legs in disorder, made desperate efforts to chase and overtake the hare, crying out, "Ah, there goes my foal! Wo, old boy—wo, wo!" But he ran in vain, for the hare easily escaped, and was soon out of sight. The poor weaver reconciled himself to his loss as best he could. "Kismet!" cried he; "and as for the egg, it is of course of no use now, and not worth returning for, since the foal has left it."

So he made the best of his way home, and said to his wife, "O wife, I have had a great loss this day."

"Why," said she, "what have you done?"

"I paid one hundred rupees for a mare's egg," replied he, "but while I stopped on the road to bathe, the foal jumped out and ran away."

"Ah, what a pity!" cried the wife; "if you had only brought the foal here, I would have got on his back, and ridden him to my father's house!"

Hearing this, the weaver fell into a rage, and, pulling a stick out of his loom, began to belabour his wife, saying, "What! you would break the back of a young foal? Ah! you monster, take that, and that, and that!"

After this he went out, and began to lament his loss to his friends and neighbours, warning them all, "If any of you should see a stray foal, don't forget to let me know." To the village herdsmen especially he related his wonderful story: how the foal came out of the egg, and ran away, and would perhaps be found grazing on the common-lands somewhere. One or two of the farmers, however, to whom the tale was repeated, said, "What is this nonsense? Mares never have eggs. Where did you put this egg of yours?"

"I put my egg in a bush," said the weaver, "near the tank on the way to the town."

"Come and show us!" cried the farmers.

"All right," assented the weaver; "come along."

When they arrived at the spot, the melon was found untouched in the middle of the bush.

"Here it is," cried the weaver; "here's my mare's egg. This is the thing out of which my foal jumped."

The farmers turned the melon over and over, and said, "But what part of this egg did the foal jump out of?"

So the weaver took the egg, and began to examine it.

"Out of this," cried one of the farmers, snatching back the melon, "no foal ever jumped. You are a simpleton, and some rogue has choused you out of your money! We'll show you what the foals are."

So he smashed the melon on a stone, and, giving the seeds to the weaver, said, "Here are foals enough for you;" while the farmers themselves, amid much laughter, sat down and ate up the delicious fruit.

LVIII

THE STORY OF THE PRINCE AND THE WAZÎR'S SON

PART I

ONCE upon a time there was a certain Prince who was strongly attached to the son of his father's wazîr, so that the two youths became inseparable companions. On one of their hunting excursions, when they had ridden far away into the wilds, the Prince, weary of the long chase, and suffering from intense thirst, cried, "Oh for some water now, from tank or pool or well! Where shall I find water in this wilderness, destitute of a single village?"

Hard by there happened to be growing a clump of trees, and to them the two friends rode, and there they dismounted. And because the Prince's distress increased, the wazîr's son spread his mantle under a tree, and said to his master, "Rest you here awhile, and let me go and look for some water." So the Prince lay down, and the full foliage of the tree screened him from the burning sun; for trees are not like men: they endure upon their own heads piercing heat and driving rain, yet the wayfarer's head they shelter and protect.[1]

Having searched awhile, the wazîr's son at last found some water in a lonely garden. In the garden there was a well, with a flight of steps leading down to the water's level. So he descended and filled his vessel. On his way

[1] This is a very favourite figure among the people of the Panjâb.

up, as he was bearing the water, he saw painted at the top of the staircase the portrait of some princess. Her hair was all loose and flowing. In one hand she held a lemon, and with the other she was lightly drying her dishevelled tresses. She was so exceedingly handsome that the wazîr's son thought within himself, "If the Prince now should chance to see this likeness, he will cause me infinite trouble, for he will bid me bring him the Princess herself." So he took some earth, and mixing the water with it, he made clay, and smeared it all over the picture, obscuring it from view. Then he descended once more, and having filled his vessel a second time, he returned to the Prince, and gave him to drink. Having drunk the water, the Prince's strength revived, and, standing up, he said, "Now I shall go and examine the garden for myself."

"The garden is a wilderness in the midst of a wilderness," said the wazîr's son. "It is wild and desolate. Who knows what things may abide there? Let us avoid it, for to remain in it cannot be safe. Let us rather mount and begone."

"Nay," replied the Prince, "I have a fancy to see it."

So they both went to it, and entered within it, and the Prince was delighted with the massive walls and the grandeur of the trees. After walking about it for some time, they at last came to the well, and, the Prince leading the way, they began to descend. Gazing about him, he said, "These walls are beautiful, excepting just here. Who has been spoiling these lovely designs with a vile coating of mud? Wash off this mud, and let us restore the colour once more."

"That is a thing we cannot do," answered the wazîr's son. "And why? The garden is the owner's, and this is surely not our business, but his."

The Prince, however, paid no heed; but he went down, brought up some water in a broken vessel, and threw it against the wall until the earth was all washed off, revealing the likeness clearly and distinctly. Then the Prince sat him down opposite to the picture, and looked at it. Long time he looked at it, and at last he said, "Now life to me is nothing. Until I meet this lady, whoever she is, I shall be miserable; and if I do not meet her, here I shall die."

The wazîr's son was sore perplexed. "Who knows," said he, "when this drawing was made? She may have died ages ago, and where then shall we look for her?"

"If she be dead," answered the Prince, "then I die too. When I hear the fatal tidings, 'She is dead,' that moment shall be my last!"

Again the Prince said, "If any one deems himself my friend, he will bring me this Princess." And with these words he lay down prostrate from sorrow.

Once more the Prince looked up, and said, "If from your heart you are really my friend, you will go quickly and bring me this Princess."

The wazîr's son then began to consider within himself, "If I do not attend to the Prince's orders, I shall bring ruin on myself and my father the wazîr, too; and if I leave him here and return alone, the King will slay me; and it may be he will slay my father as well, and my father and mother will load me with reproaches, saying, 'See what a son was ours, who could not save himself, and who ruined us!' To return to my home alone, therefore, is not to be thought of."

He then endeavoured to rouse up his master, saying, "Let us at least go to the next village, and ask to whom this well belongs."

"I cannot quit this beauteous face," answered the Prince. "I am sick to the heart for her, and here I am determined to stay for ever."

At last the wazîr's son left him, and set out alone. After riding some distance, he came to a town, where he met a man to whom he said, "Whose is the garden in the wilds in which there is a well? Is it a prince's or a merchant's?"

"That garden in the wilds," answered the man, "a merchant made, and he dug the well for the sake of charity; and he used always to keep a servant there, and his order was, 'Whenever a traveller comes, give him food; to a Hindu, uncooked; to a Mussalman, cooked—and I shall pay for all; but let no one go empty away.' That good merchant, however, is dead; and his sons were worthless, and they turned off the servant, and now they do not go there even themselves, lest they should be expected to entertain strangers."

"I should like," said the wadîr's son, "to see that son of the merchant who is the least worthless of them all."

So the man took the wazîr's son to the merchant's house, where he found in possession the eldest son.

"Does the garden in the wilderness belong to you?" asked the youth.

"It is mine," answered the son.

"And the garden-well, too?" asked the other.

"That, too, is mine; both are mine," answered he.

"Then, who are they," continued the wazîr's son, "who built the well?"

Then the man told him that the builder of that well was a man who dwelt in a town some distance away; and when he heard that, the wazîr's son at once went there, and after two days' journey he arrived, and finding the builder, he said to him, "Did you build that well?"

And the man took him in and showed him hospitality, and kept him there for the night, and told him, saying, "Yes; that well was built by me."

Then said the wazîr's son, "What portrait was that which you painted on the wall?"

"The well was mine," answered the man, "but the portrait was the work of my elder brother, who lives in another village."

Now, the person who spoke thus was himself a very old man, and the wazîr's son began saying to himself, "The brother of whom he speaks must be of immense age. Can he be living still? How unfortunate this is!"

Nevertheless, he started for the next village without delay, and soon discovered the house to which he had been directed. But, to his surprise, the owner seemed far younger than the man he had just quitted, and when he looked at him he began to think, "This man cannot possibly be the elder brother. He must be some one else." Nevertheless, his host bade him enter and, seeing he was a stranger, he put down a bed for him, and entertained him liberally. The wazîr's son, however, did not mention the object of his visit that night, and when morning came, he said to himself, "I suppose the elder brother is absent from home, and I must wait until he return." Yet he made no communication to his host, though he was the very man he sought.

The next night the man, whose politeness was now satisfied, said to him, "On what business have you come to my house?"

"I have come," answered he, "to inquire concerning a well in a certain garden in the forest owned by a merchant. I have heard that you built it. Is that so?"

"Yes," answered the man, "it was I who built the well."

"And was it you," continued the wazîr's son, "who drew the likeness on the wall?"

"No," said he. "The well I built, but the likeness was painted by another brother still older than I, and he lives elsewhere."

Learning the name of the place, the wazîr's son once more set off on his search; and finding the town, he inquired for the house. "Mine is the house," answered the first person whom he accosted.

Now, this man seemed still younger than either of the other two, a strange circumstance which astonished the wazîr's son more than ever. But, accepting his invitation, he went to his house, and in the evening his host said to him, "What business have you come upon?"

Then said the wazîr's son, "That I will tell you presently. But I am strangely puzzled. You look quite a young man. Have I turned mad, or are you mad?"

"Any information I can give you," returned the other, "shall be at your service."

Now, his wife was at that time very poorly, yet he bade her, saying, "Go, wife, to the top of the house, and fetch me down an apple which you will find on a shelf." Though she was so feeble, yet without a word she instantly arose, and, going up to the house-top, she brought down the apple and gave it to her husband. Having taken the apple from her hand, he said, "Now go up again and bring me down another apple which is also there." Instantly the wife again obeyed her husband and presently returned with the other apple. "There is a third apple," then said he, "haste, and bring that too." She went as she was bidden, but she found no more, so she came down and said, "There is no third apple there."

The man then turned to the wazîr's son, and said, "By this have you understood anything?"

"I have understood something," answered he, "but not all. Go on with your story."

Then said the builder to the wazîr's son, "Ever since that excellent wife of mine has come into the house, my life has been easy and happy. The youngest of my two brothers, who looks so aged and worn, his wife does not obey him, neither does she regard him, and what is the consequence? He is the most miserable man alive. Worse than a hundred diseases is the disease of anxiety. When he asks for water, she answers, 'Get up, and fetch it for yourself.' If he asks for bread, it is the same thing. Since the day on which that woman took up her abode in my brother's house he has not had a moment's happiness, and his anxiety has eaten him up. Therefore it is that he has grown so aged in his appearance. As to my other brother, his wife obeys him in part, but in part only. Sometimes, indeed, she makes her husband's heart happy, but at other times she renders him wretched. And that is the reason he does not age so rapidly as the other. And now, O friend, tell me the object of your journey."

"About the well in the forest-garden—was it you who built it?" answered the son of the wazîr.

"As to the garden, I know nothing," said the man. "I built the well, but at that time there was no garden. After the well was built, some one else must have made the garden."

"But who drew that beautiful likeness?" asked the wazîr's son.

"That likeness?" said he. "Why, I drew it myself."

"And where did you see the original of such a face as that?" said the wazîr's són.

"What would you do with her?" replied the other. "To begin with, you could not gain her."

"My Prince," said the wazîr's son, "after looking on that picture, has fallen into desperate illness, and there he lies, and he declares that if I obtain that Princess I shall save my life, but that if not I must die."

"But no one may visit her," said the mason. "If a man dare even so much as to look up at her windows, the King, her father, takes out his eyes, and whosoever points towards the house loses his hand."

"And if the King's orders are so exceeding strict," said the wazîr's son, "how on earth were you able to draw her?"

"I happened to be in the city where she lives," replied he; "and as I was crossing the river in a boat, the current drove me under her palace walls. I did not dare to look up, but in the smooth water beneath I saw reflected her likeness, as she sat at her casement. In one hand she held a lemon. With the other she was playing in the tresses of her flowing hair. Having my colours with me, I at once sketched her portrait exactly as she appeared."

Then asked the wazîr's son the name of the town, and, bidding his host farewell for the time, he hastened away. On the road he came to a wood, in which some little boys were grazing their cattle. But they had caught a tortoise, and were playing with it, beating it with sticks and kicking it like a ball. Seeing this cruel sport, the wazîr's son became sorrowful, and exclaimed, "Look how everything that has breath suffers when beaten about!" So he begged them to let the creature go. "If you are so fond of the tortoise," answered they, "give us five rupees and take it." So he gave them the money, and took the tortoise; and when he had come to some water he set it at liberty, and let it go.[1]

After that he went along, and at last he came to the city in which lived the beautiful Princess. Then thought he to himself, "I am a man, and the King's orders are so dreadful, what shall I do? I will disguise myself as a woman, and in that character it will be easier for me to find her. Even if I knew some woman here, and confided my plans to her, the secret that some one is after the Princess would be sure to leak out, and then I should be killed. My best plan is so to manage that no one may suspect, while at the same time I succeed in my object." So he went and bought some jewels, and then he dressed himself up as a woman, adorning himself with the jewellery. Having so done, he went once more into the bazaar, and bargained for a supply of bangles, and having procured a rich variety, he put them into a basket, and went crying them up and down the city among the palaces of the nobility. And as he cried, "Bangles; who'll buy bangles?" he looked so exceedingly handsome that many a purchaser called him in to fit on his bangles. But his prices were so exhorbitant that the commoner folk were unable to buy. Two days he cried his bangles, and on the third day he chanced to find himself under the palace of the Princess, and as he cried, "Who'll buy my bangles?"

1 This incident of the tortoise is an interpolation from one of the legends of Râja Rasâlu.

the Princess heard him and looked out; and when she saw him, that he was so handsome, she sent a slave-girl, and called him in, and said to him, "Fit some of your bangles on my arms." So he began to try on some bangles; but he delayed and delayed as much as possible, almost till the evening, because some he wilfully broke, while others were too large, and others, again, too small; and the more the Princess regarded him, the more she felt some secret attraction towards him. At last, however, she was suited, and then, because he was so beautiful, the Princess bade him attend on her every day and sell her some bangles. Joyfully the wazîr's son took his leave, and the next day he returned again; and so he kept coming and going for some time. At last the Princess said to him, "You break an enormous number of bangles. When you go back in the evening, is not your master angry with you?"

At these words he grew very thoughtful, for he knew not what to say or how to tell her who and what his master was. At last he answered her, "I am only a traveller from a distant town, and in your town I am a stranger." After that he added, "My husband is very ill. When I left him to-day he was nearly dead, and who knows if I shall now find him alive?"

After these things the Princess took so great a fancy to the beautiful bangle-seller that she kept him near her constantly; and one day she said to him, "Even if your husband does die, you can stay with me, and then you need not sell bangles any more. I am a king's daughter, and here there is plenty of everything. Eat what you like and dress as you please."

Three or four days passed by, and then the wazîr's son went to the palace, and said, "My husband is dead!" The Princess, finding him free, ordered a slave-girl to take his basket of bangles and cast them into the river; after which she said to him, "Now throw off your mean garments, and array yourself in beautiful clothes like mine." So the wazîr's son retired; and when he had dressed himself up, he returned to the Princess, who took up a mirror and looked at herself and then looked at him; and as she did so, she thought within herself, "This bangle-seller is even handsomer than I am."

One day the Princess became very sorrowful and began

to cry. Her maidens said to her, "O Princess, why are you crying?" But she answered them never a word. But when the wazîr's son spoke to her, she began to disclose to him her grief, even her whole heart, which never before had she confided to any one. "In my heart I have one sorrow," said she. "I now wish to marry, but I have told my father I shall marry only the man I love. I told him this because who knows where he might get me married, or what the suitor might be like? But I would have a husband as handsome as myself. And when I look at my face in the mirror, and where I see you not less beautiful than myself, I weep, for I think what a wonder of the Almighty it would have been if you had been a man instead of a woman. What a peerless pair we should have made!"

"But do not cry, Princess," said he. "Have patience. If this is all your grief, Providence will grant your wish. I mean to have a husband as handsome as yourself. I know a certain town, and in it there is a holy shrine. Whoever goes there and prays and gives an alms ever attains his desires."

"Two thousand rupees shall I give in charity," cried the Princess, "if one of us two can become a man."

After some days the Princess again spoke to the wazîr's son, and asked him more about the shrine. "You must have patience for a time," answered he, "for I fear to speak much on account of the King, your father."

"Whatever I ask my father," answered she, "he never denies me." Again she said, "Tell me all your mind."

The wazîr's son then disclosed the secret to her, and said, "Now I am turned into a man."

Now when the Princess heard those words she was glad, and said to him, "Listen! if I steal away with you the world will reproach me. But do you so contrive matters that the King himself shall tell us to go, since we cannot get off without his permission. Here, take these four thousand rupees. Go at once, and, resuming your proper dress, purchase merchandise and bring it into the city for sale."

Then the wazîr's son, naming the day of his return, set forth, for he went to a distant town, changed his clothes on the way, and, having bought servants and horses and rich stuffs in abundance, he came back to the city and took up his abode in a superb mansion. There the Princess came to see him disguised as a man, and when he had presented himself at the court, she said to the King, "Let this be the day of my marriage, and let my choice be the new merchant."

When the King heard that he was pleased, because he looked on the rich merchant with the utmost favour. "O my daughter," said he, "you have permission to marry when and whom you like. So let it be." Then the King sent for the merchant and made a great feast, and the ceremony of marriage was performed with splendour and with general satisfaction.

Now, as soon as the wedding rite was over, the wazîr's son, under pretence of visiting the shrine for the purpose of distributing doles, mounted his horse, and, taking his bride with him, he at once rode away to the garden and the well in the distant wilderness, where he had left the Prince and all their substance. And he said to the Princess, "Whatever my faults in the past may appear, O Princess, forgive me for all!" She forgave him, and presently they arrived at the well, and to the Prince the wazîr's son said, "The Princess has come." As soon as the Prince looked at her face he was glad, but he did not speak to her then. Presently the wazîr's son again said to the Princess, "I have used deceit with you from the first. Will you forgive me? I went to you for the sake of this Prince, my lord and master. I am only his servant, and, besides, I am also his friend."

The Princess accepted her fate, saying, "My father gave me to you. You are now my master. Therefore, give me away to whomsoever you please."

The wazîr's son then brought the Prince, and he put her hand into his, and the Prince and Princess, charmed with each other, exchanged vows of eternal fidelity. And when all this was done, the whole party returned once more to the Prince's own court, where, in the presence of the King and Queen, the real nuptials were celebrated, being attended with unusual rejoicings in all parts of the kingdom.

THE STORY OF THE PRINCE AND THE WAZÎR'S SON (*continued*)

PART II

AFTER these things the Prince showered on his friend abundance of favours, for he enriched him and gave him villages and lands, saying that he loved him before all men, and feeling sure that if he bade him go and do anything, however difficult, he would do it. In consequence of all this, it soon happened that the wazîr's son became an object of envy to many of the other courtiers, who, seeing him always next to the Prince, riding or walking, or playing at chess, plotted how they might destroy him. Among the rest there was one man, named Baglâ, whose jealousy found expression in deeds as well as words, for he promised to give a large sum to any one who could sow distrust between the Prince and his favourite. "Let me make the Prince angry with the wazîr's son," said he, "and then, when he is King, he will kill him, and I shall be wazîr instead." In order to compass his ends, he looked out an old woman suitable for the purpose, and, when he had found one, he said to her, "See, here is money; do my bidding as I shall direct." And when the old woman understood his drift, she said, "Get me four bearers and let them bring me a rich litter, and bid them do whatever I deem necessary." So the men were provided and the palanquin, and when the old woman had dressed herself in fine array, she entered, telling the bearers, "When I lower my hand, set the litter down, and when I raise my hand, lift it up and bear me away." Then she covered her face with her veil, and she was borne to a place which the Prince and his friend had to pass when riding to tennis. Here her bearers set her down, in obedience to her desire, and beckoning to the Prince, she signed him to come near, as though she had a petition to offer. But the Prince sent the wazîr's son, who approached, and she beckoned him nearer, and laid her hand on his neck, and drew him towards her, and made as though she were whispering to him something of importance. But she spoke not a single word. Having thus accomplished her design, she entered, gave the signal, and instantly her bearers lifted her litter and bore her away.

Then said the wazîr's son to himself, "The woman has not uttered a syllable. What message, then, can I give the Prince?" When he returned, therefore, his face was troubled, for he knew not what to say.

"What did the woman want?" inquired the Prince.

"I know not," answered he, "for she did not even speak."

The Prince felt annoyed. "Some secret, I suppose," said he to himself. "All right, Sir Wazîr, keep it to yourself."

The next day the woman returned in exactly the same way, and did precisely the same thing, and when she had gone, the Prince again said, "Well, what was her message to-day?"

"Not a word did she utter," answered the wazîr's son.

Then the Prince began to get very sorrowful. "Now see," said he, "what happens. This man no longer confides in me." And he began to harden himself against his friend.

The next day the wretched woman came again, and repeated exactly the same performance, and again the Prince sent the wazîr's son to receive her petition; but she said nothing, going off suddenly just as before. Once more, also, the Prince asked his friend the object of her mission, saying, "What did she say?" And once more the wazîr's son was compelled to answer, "Not a word."

"Is it such a secret that you cannot tell me?" cried the Prince in a rage.

"I have no secret," answered he, "for I have received no communication. The woman must be mad, I think."

Then the Prince became still more angry than before, and, dismissing his favourite, he bade him begone to his house. He also himself threw down his bat, and went to the palace, where he met the King, his father, who, when he saw him, addressed him, but the youth answered not, for he was speechless with rage.

"O son," said the King, "has any one presumed to affront you? If so, cheer up: he shall die immediately."

"My wazîr," answered the Prince, "is no longer the same man to me that he was. He is now nothing to me, and worse than nothing. Never shall I have peace of mind again until he is slain, and a bowl of his blood brought to me for testimony."

"Is that all?" said the King. "Be of good cheer, my son. Consider him dead already, for he shall die at once."

Then the King went forth to his own house, and summoned his executioners, and ordered them to seize the wazîr's son, and to carry him into the forest, and to behead him, and to bring back his two eyes and a cup of his blood. So, having caught the unfortunate youth, they led him away.

Now, as they were preparing to despatch him, he said to them, "Hear me speak one word, since what I say may be of service to you hereafter. You have been told to kill me. But if you kill me, to-morrow you will find that the Prince will be saying, 'Bring back my wazîr—bring back my wazîr!' Then what will you do? He will certainly avenge my death on yourselves. Follow good advice: kill something else, and take the blood of that."

Three of the men who had been sent then said to the fourth, "This young wazîr seems in a fright for his life. He does not talk as if he wished to lose it."

"Let us be cautious," answered the fourth, who was wiser than his fellows. "This is a great man and he speaks truly, for, being a wazîr's son, he knows all things. I have a tame deer. Let us kill that and carry its eyes and its blood to the King."

To this they all agreed, but they said, "Let us, however, detain this man somewhere so that he cannot escape, lest all become known and evil befall us."

So they hid him and fed him, and in his stead they killed the deer; and the eyes and the blood they took to the Prince, who, when he saw them, was glad, and said, "A man who would turn his back, let him die the death." But the eyes and the blood he gave to be thrown away.

Some days elapsed and then Baglâ, the plotter, came forward and petitioned for the office of wazîr. "Very well," was the answer, "you can be wazîr." So he was appointed, and forthwith began to attend the person of the Prince.

One day the Prince went out to snare partridges, and took with him his new wazîr. When tired of the sport, since the birds were shy and refused to be decoyed, he thought he would like to bathe.

"Shall I bathe to-day, or not?" said he to Baglâ.

"If you would like to bathe," answered he, "you will do well to bathe; but if you would rather not bathe, it will be best to leave the bathing alone."

Then thought the Prince to himself, "Here is an answer for a wazîr! If my old friend had been by my side, he would have advised me distinctly which to do, the one or the other."

Some time after he said to his wazîr, "Shall we go hunting to-day, or shall we not?"

"To hunt is good," answered he, "and not to hunt is good. I should hunt to-day if I felt thereto inclined, but if I felt otherwise I should not hunt on any account."

After hearing this, the Prince's mind reverted still more to his former favourite, and he thought with a sigh, "My old minister was different. He would have advised me freely one way or the other. This fellow, however, is such an owl—where could I have found him?"

Once more they went out hunting, and as they rode along they saw a beautiful Princess in a boat, and she, when she saw the Prince, began to make signals to him. First she pointed to her breast, then to her head, and lastly she laid her hand upon a vessel which stood beside her.

"What mean those signs?" asked the Prince of the wazîr.

"You have two eyes, O Prince," answered the man, "and I have two eyes. You see, and I see. But what the lady means you cannot imagine, and I can't."

This reply set the Prince thinking more than ever, and he thought to himself, "As for this fellow, he is not worth keeping." He became so vexed and sorrowful that on his return home he dismissed his minister altogether, and from grief of heart he went and lay down on his bed and became very ill. His father, having been informed of his illness, went to his chamber to see him. "O son," said he, "what is now the matter?"

"Nothing," answered the Prince, "but I wish back my wazîr; and if I cannot have him back, I am willing myself to die the same death."

"Courage, my son," said the King. "I will look to it myself, and straightway he shall be restored to you."

Then the King went out and called for his hangmen, and said to them, "Produce the wazîr's son on your lives!"

"O King," answered the men, "you ordered us to kill him. If, then, we had spared his life, our own lives would have paid the price. Where in the world are we to look for him now?"

"If you do not find him and bring him here instantly," cried the angry King, "I shall have you killed precisely in the same way as he was killed."

Then the men went forth, saying to themselves, "How fortunate for us! What a mistake we should have made but for the wisdom of the wazîr!" And forthwith they went, and, delivering him out of prison, they brought him to the King, and the King took him to the Prince, who at once began to amend.

For a time these two friends were a little strange and distant with each other, but soon their old habits revived, and they were to be seen as much together as ever. One day they went out hunting, and as they approached the river the Prince began telling the wazîr's son about the mysterious signals which had been made to him by the beautiful Princess. "What," asked he, "did she mean by those signs?"

"When she put her hand towards her forehead," answered his friend, "she meant that her name was Chûshmâ Rânî, or the Eye Rânî; when on her breast, she meant to say, 'If you visit my country, my heart shall be yours'; and when she touched the bowl, she intended you to understand that the name of her home was Lotah (a bowl)."

"Is it even so?" said the Prince. "Then let us set off instantly and see her."

"Alas!" answered the wazîr's son, "how much pain and trouble the other Princess cost us; and who knows how much more we may suffer from this!"

"We are to die but once," replied the Prince gaily. "Let us, therefore, go and seek her."

In vain the young minister endeavoured to dissuade his master from the rash enterprise. A prince's will is like the whirlwind or the torrent, which will not be denied.

In a few days their preparations were completed, and both companions set out on their travels once more. In due time they came to a certain town where they found a noble garden stocked with all manner of trees. "Let us spend the night here," said the Prince. But the woman in charge refused her consent. "You wish to stay here," said she. "But Chûshmâ Rânî also comes here, for this garden is hers, and if she find you here she will be angry, and her anger will fall on me." Then the wazîr's son rejoiced and he bribed her, saying, "Prepare us a place, and, here, take for your trouble these four gold coins."

So the woman set to work to prepare them a lodging in the garden. All day long she was thus engaged, and when evening came she sat down and cried bitterly. Seeing her, the wazîr's son said, "O woman, what is the matter, and why are you weeping?"

"Every day at twelve o'clock," answered she, "it is my duty to prepare three hundred and sixty necklets of flowers, and to take them to the Princess. Now it is evening, and how shall I perform my task? I am undone!"

"Bring hither the flowers," said the wazîr's son, "and let me prepare them for you."

So he began to thread the flowers, and he made such beautiful garlands as had never been seen by the gardener's wife before. After all was ready he said to her, "Which necklet will the Princess herself wear, do you think?"

"All those on the top," answered she, "she divides among her young companions, and the last of all she keeps for herself."

When the wazîr's son heard that, he wrote an exquisite letter and attached it to the lowest necklet in the basket, and in the letter he told the Princess that the Prince of the River had come to see her. So the woman carried them all to the Princess, and laid them before her as usual. When she had examined a few of them, she said, "O woman, who made these necklets?"

"A sister of mine has come from the country to see me," answered she. "I gathered the flowers, and my sister wove the necklets."

The Princess declared them beautiful, and began to distribute them to her maidens. The last she took up and put round her own neck, but observing the note, she opened it and read it in haste. Then she turned to the woman and said, "Do you still say your sister wove these flowers? do you speak the truth?" The woman fell down at her feet and confessed that some merchants had come and lodged in the garden. So the lady pencilled a note and gave it to the woman, saying, "Go and give this message to the merchant who made my necklet." And the woman went and delivered it to the wazîr's son, who read the message to the Prince. "It is my custom," ran the note, "to exact implicit truth from all my suitors. The man who fails in this respect is at once seized by my attendants and thrown from my windows into the street. I have asked my father a favour, and he has granted that I may marry only him whom I see and like. Let me know how many followers you have with you, that I may send them all needful supplies. Also come to my house and visit me."

"This is a strange letter," said the Prince.

"It is the inconsequent letter of a woman," answered the wazîr's son. "But, come, make haste! Tell her you have come absolutely alone, but beware, see that the couch has been properly arranged before you sit down. She will put you to the test. If the cushions are wrongly placed, still you must sit at the head of the couch, and, as the head is always slightly higher than the foot, here, take this lemon and lay it on the couch, and, as it moves, so it will tell you which is the head and which is the foot."

So the Prince set off, while the wazîr's son, to forestall mischance, went to the bazaar, where he found a long train of camels laden with cotton. This cotton he secured, and induced the merchants to set it down for him close to the walls of the palace, and he saw it laid beneath the apartments of the Princess, and then he said, "My master, who is a rich merchant, is absent on business, therefore leave the cotton here on approval while I go and seek him, and meanwhile give us the refusal of it in consideration of this payment if we do not complete the bargain."

Meanwhile, the Prince had arrived at the palace, and had been received with favour. The lemon revealed to him the real head of the couch, and he sat down as every prince ought to sit. Then said the Princess, "Have you no servants with you? If you have, let me provide for them."

"I have come to your town," answered he, "unattended by any one."

Then she gave him sweetmeats and sherbet, paying him great attention, and when evening approached, three hundred and sixty maidens, all richly attired in coloured silks and adorned with necklets of flowers, entered the chamber and stood in a row before them. Then said the Princess to him, "You may be alone, and I may be alone; but when kings move about they are accompanied by troops and guards, and if no guards go with them, yet is the minister never forgotten. Tell me now, have you your minister with you or not? Because if you have, one of these maidens shall go and attend on him, so that he may not want for comfort in a strange land."

The Prince was so enchanted by all he saw that he forgot his promise, and, pointing to a beautiful damsel, he said, "Let this girl, then, be my minister's attendant."

Then the eyes of the Princess darted out sparks of anger, and crying, "You know the penalty—destruction to the suitor who lies to me!" she summoned some of her strongest women, who seized the Prince and cast him headlong out of the palace windows. Down and down he fell, but he escaped death by falling on the cotton, which was collected in abundance on the pavement beneath. Nevertheless, he was stunned, and all night long he continued to lie there in a profound sleep.

Next morning his minister discovered him, and roused him, saying, "Up, O Prince, why continue to lie here?" Then he went to the merchants, and to them he said, "Your cotton is not approved of, so take your goods and take also your money and go."

The two friends then sat disconsolately down just where they were, and began to consider their position.

"My counsel is that we return home," said the wazîr.

"Never!" answered the Prince; "with what face could I show myself at court without the Princess?"

"I warned you not to speak of me," said the wazîr's son, "but to say you had travelled alone, for I had a scheme to win her. Where was your memory?"

"Nevertheless," said the Prince, "you must manage affairs so well that I may visit the lady again."

"People who are in kings' houses," returned the wazîr, "speak but once. You will never be admitted again, and you will lose your life over her."

"As for me," said the Prince, "it matters little whether I go back alive or dead."

"O Prince," continued the wazîr, "you lack wisdom. With prudence you would have won her, but how are you to win her now? The only thing left for us is to turn fakîrs and don the yellow robe."

So the two friends disguised themselves as religious mendicants, and dressed themselves in the appropriate costume. "O King," said the wazîr's son, "the good fortune we had looked to find has slipped from our hands. Gone is all openness and all candour. Henceforth we deal only with deceit."

Now, in that town there was a certain vacant house, containing a courtyard and a double entrance, one to the front and the other in the back. This house, being suitable for their purpose, they hired, and while the attendant sat solemnly in a cell at the front door, his master occupied a secluded cell within the enclosure. The arrival of two strange fakîrs was soon hinted abroad, and many of the poor came to solicit their prayers. But the wazîr's son was wont ever to send them in to visit the Prince, saying, "I am only a servant, but the great saint, my master, dwells within." One by one he sent them in, nor would he allow more than one to enter at a time. And the Prince, in his character as a holy man, was for ever seen devoutly telling his beads and mumbling his prayers. And as he always kept under the corner of his robe a store of money which he distributed freely, his fame and his sanctity were soon the talk of the town. At last the Princess heard of him, and she said to her attendants, "I, too, must go and salaam those two holy men." So she set out with her three hundred and sixty damsels, half of whom walked before her and half of them behind her, and thus in grand procession they came to the gateway. But the wazîr's son said, "Only one at a time can be permitted to visit the holy fakîr, for that is the custom of his order." So the ladies filed in and out one by one, until at last the Princess rose and said, "Now I will enter also, but do you, my maidens, await my coming."

Now, in the courtyard there always stood, saddled and bridled and ready for the start, two swift coursers. When, therefore, the Princess entered the house, the wazîr's son instantly closed the door. At the same moment the Prince sprang to his saddle, and when the Princess had been thrown into his arms, he set spurs to his steed, and issuing from the opposite gate, he galloped away with his prize. Instantly also his friend mounted and followed, and they rode and rode until they arrived in all safety at their own palace, where the Prince and Princess were married in great state and ceremony, after which they spent many a happy hour together in mutual happiness and delight.

THE STORY OF THE PRINCE AND THE WAZÎR'S SON (*continued*)

Part III

Now, in course of time the King of that country waxed very old and resigned his kingdom to his son, who thus became King in his stead. There was a certain servant then living at court who possessed a flower of remarkable beauty, growing in an earthen jar, and every morning he used to come and gaze at it. This circumstance was reported to the young King, who, hearing that the flower was such as no one else in the world possessed, sent for his servant, and said to him, "Let me see the flower which you gaze at every morning." No sooner had he seen it and examined it, than he said, "I admire this flower of yours, therefore let me have it."

"I cannot part with my flower," answered the servant. "You may take my life and welcome, but not the flower."

"But why not?" returned the King. "I offer you a price for it, which will be useful to you, and what can you want with a flower which is fit only for a king's palace?"

"Yet my flower I cannot give," replied the man.

"But why cannot you give it?" asked the King. "You surely must have some secret reason for answering me thus."

"This flower," said the servant, "was given to me by my wife the night before I left her. 'Keep this flower by you,' said she: 'when it is blooming thus, know that I am true to you; if it droops, then you may be sure that I am false.'"

"But has it ever bloomed thus?" asked the King.

"It has," answered the guard.

"If you possess such a treasure," said the King, "why do you not return home?"

"I did a foolish thing," replied he, "on account of which I had to leave my home. But now I begin to think I must go back again."

"What foolish act was it?" said the King.

"What can I say?" answered the servant: "I am ashamed to speak of it. When I was in my father's house, and well off, my father was a merchant, and he used to trade. And when I grew up he chose a match for me, but I said I did not wish to marry."

"But what objection had you against marrying?" inquired the King.

"I will tell you," said he, "the whole story from the beginning. When I was a boy my father kept a servant who used always to be with me, and of whom I became very fond. One day it happened that the King of that country heard that a famous dancing girl had arrived in the town, and he said, 'Let her come and dance before me.' So she went as she was ordered, and my servant and I also went there to see her. Numbers of people were standing and looking, and we stood and looked too. When the dancing girl approached us, she glanced at my servant and at once fell to the ground. Then said the King, 'Why have you fallen?' and she answered, 'I have a pain in my chest.' And the King said, 'Had you ever this pain before?' Then the woman pointed her finger at my servant, and said, 'If you have that man killed my pain will go.'

"The King at once ordered his arrest, and he was seized by the guards, but my servant said, 'It is not the custom of kings to kill the innocent.' The King answered, 'Even now you know well you have committed something amiss. Owing to some fault of yours this dancing girl has fallen, and who knows but that she may die?' The servant replied, 'O King, tell this dancing girl to give up to me that which belongs to me, and then you may do with me even as you please.' The King turned to the girl, and said, 'This man is to die; nevertheless, get up and speak to him.' When she arose, she said to my servant, 'What do you want to say to me?'

"'Give me up,' answered he, 'what you have of mine.'

"'I have not anything of yours,' said she.

"'Very well,' replied my man, 'with words say to me, if you can, that you have restored to me that which you had of me.' And the woman said, 'Whatever I took from you I have given you back.' The moment she uttered these words she fell back dead. Then cried the King, 'I'll hang you, you villain! unless you tell me what that was which you gave to her, and which she has given you back again—the whole story.' Then my servant told the King, and I sat down by his side, and he said, 'Once we were all merchants well-to-do, and I was married to this woman, who has since become a dancing girl. We both loved each other dearly, and one day she said to me, "If I died, how much would you sorrow for me?" I replied, "If you died I should be wretched, but if I died what would your sorrow be for me?" "If you died," cried she, "I would make me a little cabin at your grave and never, never leave it." Then said I, "And I would do the same by you."

"'After a time it so happened that my wife died. When she was buried, I ran up a little hut by her grave, gave away all my goods to the poor, and lived by her grave. I, in short, turned fakîr, begging my bread, and spending my nights and days at her sepulchre.

"'One day a wandering fakîr chanced that way, and as he passed the hut he said, "Why have you come to live in the wilds among the graves?" I told him the whole story, and when the fakîr heard it, he said, "As you have done this thing out of pure love, I tell you that, if you consent to give up to her half the remaining years of your life, this woman will rise again, and the day of your death will also be the day of hers."

"'"Very well," I answered. "I give up to her one half my remaining life."

"'Then the fakîr by a miracle brought back my dead wife to life, and there she stood before me. To meet again like that I was glad, and so also was she; but as I had given away all my substance in charity, we set out for another town. After travelling for some days, we came to a certain river, and there on the bank, when I had taken some bread and water, I began to feel sleepy. As my head happened to be low, my wife sat up and laid my head in her lap, and I slept. I can just remember that action of hers before I dropped off, but afterwards she abandoned me, and when I awoke I looked for her in vain. Seeing no one there, I continued travelling, and at last I arrived at this city, and I obtained some employment from the father of this youth now sitting by my side. This morning the lad said to me, "Come along; a new dancing girl is to dance before the King: let us go there!" And so I came with him; but as soon as I came I recognized my lost wife; and when she looked at me, from disgrace and shame of mind she fell, and so she asked for my death, being afraid of me. You, O King, then gave the order for my death; but every one loves life, and therefore I asked her if she would give me back that which she had taken from me, and she answered, "I have taken nothing." So I said, "Only say with your mouth these words, *I have given you back what I took from you*, and I am satisfied." And she said it, and died once more.'

"When the King heard this story he was amazed, and gave my servant his life, and let him go. But as for me, having also heard these dismal things, I felt that it would be far better not to be married than to be married; and so, when my father wished me to marry, I refused. My father, however, was not to be gainsaid, and he said, 'If I do not have you marry, the world will reproach me, saying, "See that merchant, who is not able to find a wife for his son!" Tell me then,' continued he, 'what is the matter with you?' So I told my father I was well enough in both mind and body, but that I could only marry a woman who would allow me every morning to strike her five times with a shoe, and this I said in order that no one might consent to have anything to do with me. My father, however, undertook to find such a girl, but he did not succeed, because all his endeavours were rendered futile by my absurd condition.

"Time passed, and at last my father went to a certain merchant, and told him he was anxious to marry his son.

"'I have a daughter,' answered the merchant, 'who would suit your son; but she declares she must have a look at him first with her own eyes.'

"'But, my son,' said my father, 'will only marry the woman who will patiently allow him to smite her five times every morning with a shoe.'

"'I cannot assure myself of that,' replied the merchant; 'but I will speak to my daughter and let you know.'

"When he went home he described the proposed match to the girl, who at once said, 'Yes, I consent. Marry me to that merchant's son;' and so the message was sent that, after twenty days, I might come and marry his daughter. There was a grand wedding, with much spent, and on the day of the wedding my father gave me a separate house and servants, and in the morning I said to my wife, 'I must now be allowed my stipulation, namely, to beat you five times with a shoe.'

"But she begged off, saying, 'To-day do not beat me, and to-morrow you may strike me ten times instead.'

"The next day I said to her, 'You said I might give you ten blows, but let me have my will and give you five.'

"'Hush!' cried she, 'or the guests in the house will hear you. Let me off again to-day, and to-morrow you can give me fifteen.'

"The next day I spoke to her again, saying, 'To-day I must really give you the five blows.'

"My wife then turned on me, and said, 'When we were married, whose money was spent, yours or mine?'

"'No money of yours,' answered I, 'nor yet money of mine. Your father paid your expenses, and my father paid mine.'

"'And our expenses now,' said she, 'by whom are they paid?'

"'They certainly don't come from my earnings,' replied I, 'but from my father's. As for me, I have earned nothing as yet.'

"'If that be so,' cried she, 'what right have you to beat me at all, since you do not contribute a farthing to my maintenance? When you begin to earn wages to keep the house, then you may beat me, but you mustn't beat me before.'

"I got so angry that I left the house that minute, and set off to my father's and told him all.

"'Give me four thousand rupees,' said I, 'that I may go out and trade and make a living for myself!'

"So I hired servants, and loaded a ship with merchandise and sailed to a far country and steered up a river, and there I came to a wild desolate place, but still there was a garden in the midst of it, though no village or town could be seen. Then I ordered my men to moor the ship to the bank, but I myself sprang ashore and hastened to the garden to look at it. As soon as I entered I saw a tree covered with fine mangoes, one of which fell to the ground. It was so ripe and so tempting that I took it, and having eaten it, I threw the stone away. Then down came another mango, and as I was eating that the stone which I had thrown away took root and sprang up, a goodly tree, covered also with fruit, which ripened as I stood eating, and presently from this tree too fell down a beautiful mango. So I thought to myself, 'This mango I will not eat, but I will take it to the nearest city, and with this wonder I shall make money and grow rich.' So I went on, and coming to a large walled town, I entered the market-place and made a bet.

"'Look at this mango,' cried I; 'I will eat it and let the stone fall. If it grows and bears fruit at once, you will give me four thousand rupees, but if not, then I will pay four thousand rupees to you.'

"'Agreed!' cried they, gathering around me.

"So I sucked the mango clean, and threw down the stone before them, and at once it grew up and up into a big tree, but, alas! it bore no fruit at all, and I lost my bet and my money. To save myself from arrest, all my remaining servants and all my goods were sold by auction, and, like a beggar unable to move, I sojourned alone in that strange place. Poor and hungry, I grew sorrowful, stupid, sick, and even senseless, for I thought to myself, 'I do not know how to beg, and for work I am not fit. How am I to get my bread?' In this distress I went to a fakîr's place, and there I remained. After five or six days the fakîr spoke to me, and said—

"'It is time that you should do something for yourself.'

"Now, with that fakîr there was then living another wayfarer like myself, who every day used to bring in grass and sell it. This man, having pity on me, took me, and said—

"'Come out with me, and I will show you where grass is to be found, and how to cut it. As for me, I cut grass every day, and sell it in the bazaar, and cook my food here.'

"This, then, I did, and every day I brought in my bundle, and with my scanty earnings I bought flour and I lodged with the fakîr.

"Now, it happened that my wife, after waiting for some time, determined to seek me. So she dressed herself as a man, turned merchant, freighted a ship, and set sail. Coming up the same river, she at last arrived at the same garden. And having moored alongside, she entered and tarried there just as I did. And when a ripe mango fell at her feet, she took it up and sucked it and threw away the stone; and as she sucked another, up sprang the new mango and bore fruit, ripe and full, and even as she gazed it dropped one of its mangoes before her eyes. But she was wise where I was not, for she not only took with her the new mango, but also some of the garden earth, and returning to the ship, she at last arrived at the town in which I was living. But me she never saw, nor did she know I was there; but she made a bet with the same people for four thousand rupees, who, having won before, were eager to win again. Having, therefore, challenged them, she ate the fruit and threw the stone on to the earth, which she had first put down, and at once it shot forth a leaf, then grew into a mighty tree, and bore abundance of fruit, and the fruit began to fall. Thus my wife won the four thousand rupees. Then she came into the bazaar just as I arrived there with my bundle of grass on my head, and, looking at me, she said—

"'How much do you want for that bundle of grass?'

"'Two annas,' answered I.

"'Take three,' said she, 'and carry the grass to my camp at the river-side.'

"So I followed her to the river, and she paid me the three annas. As I was going away, she said—

"'If any one offered you work, would you take service?'

"'Yes,' answered I, 'why not? I do not like the drudgery of grass-cutting.'

"'If you will come to me,' said she, 'I will give you the management of my servants.'

"I accepted her offer, and she furnished me with all I needed, but she took from me my old clothes, my net and my sickle, and kept them by her.

"Then she issued her orders to all her attendants, 'Whatsoever this servant orders you will do. He is my steward, and manager of all my property. Absent or present, I am still represented by him.' Then came she to me, and said, 'You will remain here with the ship. As for me, I must make a short voyage to-morrow to see a friend, but only for a day, but, whether for a day or more, manage everything in my absence.'

"So she started, taking with her my old clothes, my net, and my sickle; but I saw her no more that day, nor yet the next.

"When ten days had passed and still she returned not, I said to myself, 'My master must be dead. He will come no more. I had better sail.'

"The next day, therefore, I hoisted sail and made down the river, and in due time arrived at my own city. There, in a certain house of mine, the servants stored all the goods, and I went home to my wife. When I saw her, I said, 'I am rich; I come laden with my own earnings; submit, therefore, to our bargain, and let me have my five blows.'

"'Certainly,' answered she, 'I will let you, but first sit down a bit.'

"'No, no,' replied I; 'I'll dismount from my horse only when you promise submission.'

"'Nay,' said she, 'get off and have some food, and then we can talk it over.'

"'You may talk for ever,' said I; 'your excuses will not avail. Submit, and I will dismount.'

"Then said she, 'Wait a little;' and going into the house, she brought out my old grass-cutter's clothes, my net, and my sickle, and held them up before me, and cried, 'Have your own way! The horse you are riding is mine; the clothes you are wearing are mine. Give up my horse and my clothes, and put on your own things, and take your sickle and your net in your hand, and then come, give me five blows with your shoe.'

"When I looked at everything, I was covered with confusion, nor did I remain a moment, but, getting down, I handed the bridle to a servant, and went at once to my father's house, where, in very shame and sorrow, I remained in the dumps for days. At last I considered, 'Why do I continue here? Let me go away!'

"One day, just as I was preparing to leave, my father surprised me, and, forbidding my departure, took me to my own house where my wife was, and there left me.

"'If you like to live here,' said she, 'do so—if not, go. But if you go, take this flower with you and keep it. When it is fresh and blooming, as it is now, know that I am true to you; but if it droop, then be sure that I have ceased to remember you.'

"So I took the flower and left my home once more, and came here and took service with the King your father. Therefore it is that I do not like to return, because I said I would have my own way. That is the disgrace which hinders me from going home to my wife."

When the King had heard the whole story, he was pleased, and doubled his servant's salary, and determined to retain him. Then he spoke to his ministers, and said, "You see that flower, how beautiful it is! The lady herself must be beautiful, too. So spare no pains to bring her here."

"Some women," answered the wazîr, "are wiser than men."

"True," said the King; "but old women, gossips and go-betweens, are equal to any enterprise;" and he ordered his ministers to collect some of these women and to bring them to the court to prove their skill in cunning, deceit and guile.

Numbers of women accordingly assembled, each anxious to surpass the others. Out of these the King chose four, and dividing them into two sets, two and two, he called the first and said, "Now what can you do?"

"We have such power," answered they, "that if we went into the sky we could bore holes through it."

Then to the other he said, "And what can you do?"

"So great is our craft," answered they, "that, if we went into the sky, we could not only bore holes through it, but so patch it up again that you would never know that a single hole had been in it at all."

Thus the two last were chosen, and the rest dismissed, and then the King and his ministers sent and brought those two old women before them, and said, "Go to a certain town. There you will find a merchant's wife living alone. Can you entice her and bring her here?"

"Is she not a woman?" answered they. "Women are so simple that they can be led to do anything. We could make even a dumb animal follow us."

"Bring her to me, and I will reward you," said the King. The old crones delighted him, and having given them money for their journey, he sent them away. So they disguised themselves as Mecca pilgrims, and put on rosaries; and coming to the town, they inquired for the house, which was pointed out to them, and they entered and found the lady sitting at her needle. Then they caught hold of her and embraced her, and began crying over her.

"My good women," said she, "who are you, and why are you crying?"

"Why, dear me!" answered they, "we knew you as a child. You do not remember us, but your mother was our own sister, and you are our niece. You were quite an infant when we two went to Mecca, and there we have been ever since; and now that we have at last come back, hearing that you were here, we have called to see you."

Then thought she to herself, "It is late, and I must get my aunts some food." So she told her slave-girl to go to the bazaar and buy a pound of flour, a pound of sugar, a pound of melted butter, and some *bhang*.[1] With these ingredients she made the women a nice dish, and they all partook of it, and began to tell the truth, until at last they sank into a deep stupor. With the same food she fed them day by day, and there they remained overcome with slumber and forgetfulness.

Meanwhile, the King was growing impatient, waiting in vain as the days passed and the women never returned. So he called his ministers, and said, "Those women have been detained in that country, send, therefore, some cunning rogues to look for them, and see if they are at the lady's house, or where they are."

Two great villains were accordingly sought for and found, and when they had approved themselves they were at once despatched. "Not only," said they, "shall we bring back the two women in a twinkling, but we shall bring back the lady as well!" So they set out, being disguised as respectable fakîrs; and finding the house, they went there and began praising, saying, "Ah, child, behold in us your uncles. We have not seen you for many years, because we have been travelling over many lands. And now at last we have come to see you."

"You did well," said she, "to come and see me."

So she made them welcome, and the same food which she gave the women she ordered her slave-girl to set before the men, until they also sank into the same condition; and thus they remained, for every four days she repeated the course, and so rendered them helpless and stupid. Not only that, but she shaved the heads of all the four impostors as well, and the beards and moustaches of the men, and covered their faces with lamp-black.

When many days had now passed away, the King called his minister, and said, "Even those villains have failed to serve us, therefore let us go ourselves." So to the town they came, and when they knocked at the door the lady sent her slave-girl to ask them who they were.

"I am a wazîr," said the minister, "and this is a king."

[1] Indian hemp—extremely stupefying.

And the girl told her mistress, who made ready a grand feast of seven courses, and waited on her guests herself, bidding the slave-girl to stand by. With each dish, as she brought it in, she appeared in a fresh suit, very rich and beautiful, and with different sets of jewellery to match. When the seventh course came in, the King whispered to his minister, "I heard there was only one merchant's wife, but it seems there are seven, and all alike."

Overhearing the remark, the lady said, "O King, what is this you are talking about?"

"What I have said," answered he, "it would not be proper for you to hear."

"Keep nothing secret from me," said she; "but speak out frankly, and let me know your thoughts."

"I said," replied the King, "there was but one woman here, yet now there are seven, and all alike."

"You said well," returned she. "There is but one."

"What!" cried the King, "I have seen seven, and you say there is only one!"

"Among the seven you have seen," said she, "you have not seen the merchant's wife at all—she never comes out."

"Then who are you," asked the King—"the merchant's wife or a slave-girl?"

"I am a slave-girl," said she.

"If you are her slave-girl," said the King, "and we give you a message for her, do you think she will attend to it?"

"I think she will," answered she.

Then the minister put into her hand a large bribe, and said to her, "Go and persuade your mistress to accompany us back to my palace, and your fortune's made."

"If you will agree to something which I propose," said she, "I think my mistress will go with you very easily. You must pass the night here; but first one of you must go to the bazaar and hire a strong doolie and eight stout bearers for the journey, and bring them here. If you will do this, early in the morning, when the merchant's wife rises, we can catch hold of her and force her into the doolie, and you can carry her off."

To this both King and minister agreed, and so the doolie and the bearers were brought and introduced into the house.

In the morning the merchant's wife got up, and when she had administered a double dose of *bhang* to the two men and the two women, and blackened their heads and their faces afresh, she dressed them up in women's garments, pulled their chuddas well over their faces, and put them all four, drowsy and stupid as they were, into the doolie. She then drew down the curtains, closed them up, and over all she spread a handsome cover, while she warned the bearers that if they uttered a word about the weight they would be well thrashed, but that if, on the contrary, they bore their burden without a murmur their reward would be fourfold.

Thus, then, it was arranged, and the King, mounting his horse, ordered the doolie to be carried away. After a day's march they arrived at his capital, where, by the King's direction, the doolie was carried to an empty wing of the palace and taken inside the enclosure, while a slave-girl was sent to attend to the King's new capture.

Now, as all four were dressed as women and their faces hidden, the slave-girl, when she lifted up the curtains, cried, "Not one queen has come, but four!" Dismissing the bearers, she went to the King and reported to him the arrival of four rânîs where only one was expected. So the King went himself to see, and found all four sitting in the position in which they had been left. Lifting the chuddas of two of them, he fell back in a fright, crying, "What evil things are these that have come to my house?" and without waiting to examine the others, he dropped their coverings and ran to his minister, to whom he said, "That merchant's wife has taken us all in dreadfully!"

"Why, what in the name of God," cried the minister, "has she done?"

"She has filled the doolie with four evil beasts," said the King. "Come and see!"

When the wazîr cast an eye on them, he was quite confounded, and, seizing one of them by the ear, he roared, "Who are you?"

Their stupor was then passing off, and their senses returning, and the creature replied, "I am that very woman who boasted of her skill."

Then the minister called for a mirror and showed the hag her own face, and said, "If you are that very woman, what do you call this?" And in like manner he showed up the whole of them, until one of the women mumbled, "Of course we are the two Princesses, and these men are the two thieves!"[1] upon which the King had them all soundly thrashed and sent about their business.

But the King was more in love than ever, and he now said, "What a wise woman she is! Not only my messengers, but myself and my wazîr as well, she outwitted!"

"You will try in vain to entrap her," said the minister. "Only one way remains: you must make her husband a councillor, and let him then understand that, if he continues to live apart from his wife, it will be most unbecoming, since the reproach will lie on the King himself."

So the merchant became a King's councillor, but when his wife was mentioned he demurred. "My pay is but small," said he, "and she is accustomed to luxury."

But his pay was raised, and when a handsome home had been prepared for him he went to his own city, and said to his wife, "If you will heed me, I have something to tell you. The wisdom of my father was never mine, and I cannot trade as he can. The King, my master, has given me a good appointment and a fine house, but he orders me to bring you home. So come with me."

"I am your wife," answered she. "You are my master. Whenever you wish me to go I am ready."

So she went back with her husband, and he and she lodged at the same house. Leaving her there, he went to the King, who was overjoyed. "You are now one of my ministers," said he. But to his wazîr he said, "Contrive something. So manage this affair that my man may be despatched on some distant expedition."

"But even then," replied the wazîr, "he will still be alive, and able at any time to return. Let him be despatched, therefore, to procure something which has no existence, and ordered not to return until he has found it."

As they were thinking this over, both the King and the wazîr began to laugh. At first they were whispering, but when the King laughed and the wazîr laughed, the new minister began to laugh too.

"Why are you laughing?" asked the King of him. "What have you seen or heard that you should laugh?"

"I have seen nothing," answered he, "and I have heard nothing, and I laughed."

Said the old wazîr, "Laugh at nothing? Since the day

[1] Referring to a popular tale.

I was born I have never seen what nothing is. Be good enough to show me what nothing is."

"How can I show you nothing?" asked the man. "Neither have I, since the day of my birth, seen nothing."

"Nevertheless, nothing you must set out for and find, since the King commands it," said the wazîr.

Evening now came on, and they all went home. And when the wazîr saw the King again, he said to him, "This new minister will never discover nothing—he has entrapped himself, so let us send him to seek it."

But when he reached his home his wife noticed his downcast looks, and asked the reason. So he told her the story, and said, "They have ordered me to go forth into the wilds and bring them nothing, and to show it to them."

"Never mind," answered his wife. "Leave the affair in my hands, and I will manage it." And her husband grew cheerful. "Now," said she, "give immediate orders that all those who go out shooting game shall bring to me the feathers of all the birds they kill, and promise that you will reward them with the weight in money." Then she directed her husband to send for two masons, who, when they came, constructed two vats in the floors of adjoining chambers. One of these vats she filled with liquid glue, and the other with the quantities of feathers which the hunters and sportsmen had brought in to her.

Meanwhile the husband was attending the court, but his wife had warned him, "If the King should ask you if you have found nothing, say, 'I am not yet sure. I shall learn more about it when I go home.'" Scarcely had he entered the presence when both King and minister at once spoke to him, and he answered, "To-day I have not found it, but I shall make a further report to-morrow."

"That woman," said the King aside to his wazîr, "is sure to outwit us with some cunning answer."

So in the evening he again went home, and his wife counselled him, so that when morning came, and he was once more before the King and was asked for nothing, he answered, "Give me a year's leave, and I'll go and bring you nothing, but if I return within a month with nothing, let me still have my year's leave and also my full pay."

"If in eight days," said the King, "you bring me

nothing, you shall still have your year's leave." But the wazîr whispered, "Give him all the leave he may wish, for never will he be able to find nothing."

So the merchant, promising that he would set out the next day, once more turned his steps towards his home. "Now," said his wife, "have made at once a pair of large brass tongs, with a ring at the end of them, and two sets of bells for the ankles, and in the morning go to the King, and say, 'Now I am going;' but go not far, only at midnight be sure to come back to the house, and knock at the door."

These things, therefore, he did, and at night the King considered within himself, "Hitherto I have followed the advice of my wazîr. Now I shall act for myself. By this time the lady is alone. I will go and visit her." When he came to the house he found the door bolted, so he knocked, and the lady within cried—

"Who are you?"

"I am the King," answered he. "Open the door."

So she opened it, and the King entered, and she closed the door once more. As they were sitting together on the couch, the husband came, and loudly knocked, and she cried—

"Who's there?"

"Your husband," answered he.

"You went to look for nothing," said she. "How have you returned so soon?"

"I forgot my arms, and I have come back to fetch them," replied he.

Then the King was in a fright, and he said—

"Hide me somewhere, or he will kill me. Not a soul knows I am here."

"There is no hiding-place for you," protested she.

"For the love of God," pleaded he, "put me anywhere, and save my life;" and he began to beseech her.

"There is a closet here," said she, "with a vat in it, but it is full of size."

The King rushed to the closet; and as he was in haste, he fell at once into the vat, and the glue was in such a state that he was unable, with all his struggles, to get out again.

"For mercy's sake, pull me out!" cried he.

"But where can I put you?" said she.

"I will never forget your goodness," groaned he, "if you will but take me out of this mess."

So she had pity on him, and took him out, and hid him in the room full of feathers, and, as he entered, down he fell, and all the feathers stuck to him like pegs in a caldron. Then she opened the door to her husband, and told him—

"Come along," said she, "I have found nothing for you; it is even now in the house. See here! It is neither bird nor man. It is nothing. Tie the bells to its ankles, and put a rope round its neck, and take a torch and the tongs and lead it to the palace of the King, and as you go, give it a good crack with the tongs occasionally, and so take it to the King's very footstool."

All this the husband did, never suspecting that the object before him was the King himself. So he led him to the court, and when he arrived there he cried, "Wazîr, wazîr, summon the King; I have brought him nothing!"

The wazîr looked out from a balcony, and said—

"Such a thing as this I have never seen since the day I was born! What is it?"

"And do you not remember," answered the merchant, "how you said that from the day you were born you had never seen nothing? Look at it now, then. This thing is nothing."

"I am afraid of this nothing which you have brought," said the wazîr. "In the morning, when the King attends court, bring it again, and then we shall look at it."

"Nay, you are the wazîr," answered he, "and must take charge of it now, as I have had so much trouble in capturing it, and, besides, it must not escape. If you do not consent, it will be my duty to report the matter to the King."

So the old wazîr called a servant, and had a tent-peg driven into the ground, to which he tied the King by the rope.

After this the merchant returned home, and his wife said to him—

"Did you see the King?"

"The King was not there," answered he; "but I gave the thing to the minister."

"You have obeyed orders," said she, "and now keep quiet."

When the King was left alone with his wazîr, he called to him, and said, "Come near to me, and hear what I have to say." But in a fright the wazîr edged further away. "I am the King," continued the unhappy being. "That woman has turned me into nothing." The wazîr would hear no more, but, taking up two stones, he cast them at the evil thing, and went to his house. Seated in his chamber, he began to reflect, "What thing is this? It speaks like a human being, but has feathers like a bird. It may escape, and do me a mischief." So he bolted his doors, and went to bed.

The next morning he repaired to the court to report to the King the adventures of the night. But no King could be found, nor could his officers give the slightest tidings of him. Then went the wazîr to the place where the King was tied to the peg, and the King cried, "For God's sake, wazîr, help me, and restore me to my condition! Even you have forsaken me."

"But I am afraid of you," said the wazîr, "for to me you seem to be some evil spirit. In the name of Heaven, how came you into such a misfortune?"

Then the King disclosed the whole story, and the wazîr said, "This must indeed be the King, and no one else, because the King was always keen to go to that woman's house, and she is deep, and will not permit liberties." So he went to some attendants, and said, "Prepare a hot bath, then take this thing and cleanse it." At first they were afraid, but, nevertheless, they obeyed. The glue was of such a nature that the King lost both his hair and his beard. However, when he was cleaned, the wazîr had him dressed in his robes and brought to a mirror, and the King was filled with shame at the sight of his beardless face and bald head. But his wazîr advised him to put on his turban and to wear a false beard, and so, when he had eaten food and rested, the King appeared once more in his court.

Meanwhile, the woman said to her husband, "Go now to your duty, and find out whether the King has seen nothing or not." So he went, and when he saw the King's false beard he said, "Why, O King, have you put that beard on your face? Last night I brought you nothing, even as you commanded me. Have you seen it?"

Then thought the King to himself, "This fellow must be an owl. He put bells on my ankles, and a halter round my neck, and now he wants to know why I have a false beard; and sometimes he gave me a crack with his tongs, and made me dance and set the bells jingling, and cried out, 'See how pretty she is; see how pretty she is!' And after all this he wants to know if I have seen nothing!"

Then the man said to the wazîr, "Did you show the King that nothing I brought in last night?"

"Yes," answered the wazîr; "the King has seen it, and I have seen it."

So the man claimed his discharge, which the King gave him, and he and his wife went to their own place.

"And will you, O King," said the old wazîr, "visit that lady again?"

"God forbid!" answered he, holding his ear. "Never shall I approach her house again. Whoever made that woman, never in the world made any woman like her."

But, as for the merchant and his wife, those two lived in peace for the rest of their days.

Told by the bard Sharaf at Torbela, December 1880.

LIX

OF THE FAMINE AND THE WEAVER

A GREAT famine was once raging in the land, and the villagers died in hundreds. A certain weaver was riding along, and he, seeing the numbers of unburied corpses, and hearing the cries of the survivors, who besought him for a morsel of bread, addressed himself to Heaven, and exclaimed, "O God, if you have not food enough to give your children, why are you so simple as to bring so many of them into the world?"

LX

OF THE TWO WEAVERS AND THE GRASSHOPPERS

Two weavers took guns, and went out for a day's sport. As they passed through the fields, one of them espied an immense grasshopper sitting on a madâr plant, which, as they approached, flew on to the shoulder of his companion. "See, see, there he is!" cried he, and, levelling his piece, he shot his friend through the heart.

LXI

OF PATHÂN GREEDINESS

THERE is a certain small black plum grown in the Hazâra district called the amlôk, which, when dried, looks like a species of black beetle. One day a Pathân stopped in a bazaar and bought some of them, laying them in a corner of his lûnghî (turban). As he went along he took out a handful, in which there chanced to be one of these beetles alive, and the little creature, feeling the pressure of the man's hand, began buzzing and squealing. But the Pathân, determined to be deprived of no portion of his money's worth, said, "Friend, you may buzz, or, friend, you may squeal, but in the measure you came, and in the measure you'll go."

Saying which, he clapped the whole handful, plums and beetle together, into his mouth and devoured them.

LXII

STORY OF SHÎSHAT KHÂN OF LAHORE

In the time of the Great Moguls of Delhi, whose Indian Empire included so many vast possessions, there lived a governor at the city of Lahore whose name was Shîshat Khân. His reputation was by no means good, for he oppressed the poor people under his rule, and exacted from all classes heavy taxes, while his private life of luxury and pride was a notorious disgrace to his name and to his high office.

Now in Lahore there also lived at that time a certain couple who though poor were respectable. They earned a scanty living by the sale of glass bangles which they hawked about to the houses of the rich. One day they found themselves below the palace of the governor. "Bangles for sale! Bangles for sale! Who'll buy glass bangles?" cried they. These words were heard by a lady who was sitting at a closed lattice belonging to the apartments of the zenana, and she sent her slave-girl to bid the woman come up and exhibit her wares. The poor woman, who was both young and beautiful, followed the messenger, and presently she was ushered into the presence of the lady herself. But it happened that Shîshat Khân at that very time was sitting there with his three wives, of whom the lady at the lattice was one. He, when the bangle woman had salaamed and sat down on the ground to unfold her bangles, having looked on her beauty with admiring eyes, said to her, "Is there any one else with you, or are you alone?"

"My husband is with me," answered she. "He is standing in the street below."

"Call him hither!" said the governor.

"God forbid," exclaimed the poor woman, putting up her hands, "that my husband should set foot in the King's zenana!"

"Call the man up!" then said the governor in a voice of authority to the slave-girl, who instantly left the room for the purpose of obeying his orders.

Descending to the gates, the girl summoned the husband

to the presence of the governor, and led him through many apartments richly and luxuriously furnished, until at last they came to the door of the principal apartment of all. There the man hesitated.

"So far I have come," said he, "but farther I dare not intrude."

The slave-girl, finding persuasions in vain, passed through the door, and made her report.

"Come in!" cried the governor to the man. "Come in instantly!"

The poor bangle man then entered into the presence of the governor and of the five assembled women.

"What relation is this woman to you?" asked the governor.

"My lord, she is my wife," said he.

"Look you," said Shîshat Khân; "here are my three wives. Choose one of them—which you please—and hand over your wife to me." This, however, he said, not that he really meant it, but to find an excuse if possible for doing away with the husband of the poor woman on whom he had fixed his fancy. But the bangle seller, putting up his hands together, said, "O my lord, my wife is poor, and has to work hard for her living, but these three are great ladies!" Then the governor pretended to fly into a great rage, and, hunting the man out of the palace, took possession of his wife, who, as she loved her husband dearly, was in not less distress than himself.

So the poor man went away bemoaning his fate, but still quite determined to leave no stone unturned to recover his lost wife. He betook himself to the camp outside the city, and told his story to certain of the soldiers. "This governor," said he, "has seized my wife by force and wrong. Can you not rescue her?"

"We cannot help you at present," said one of the soldiers, "but go you to the King of Delhi and tell your story to him, or if you are afraid to do that, go to Râwâl Pindi, to the house of the great saint Shâh Chamchirrâg, and see what he can do for you."

The bangle seller listened to this advice, but considering that Delhi was too distant, and that he might never be permitted to approach the person of the King, he said, "I will go to Râwâl Pindi," and that evening he started on the journey. It was not many days before he arrived, and going straight to the squalid hut of the saint, he found him sitting over a little fire, for the weather was cold. The bangle seller put up his hands and began his petition, telling the whole of his story, how that he was a poor man, and that the wicked governor of Lahore had seized his wife, and kept her in his palace. When he had ended, the old man answered roughly, "Do you think I have troops at my command to march against a governor? You should have taken your petition to the King of Delhi," and he turned his back and went into his hut.

The bangle man, repelled and disappointed, was turning away, and, indeed, had gone some paces, when the fakîr suddenly cried, "Wait, wait! Don't go away just yet!" Then the fakîr took out a scrap of paper, and upon it he wrote the following words—

Letter written by Shâh Chamchirrâg to Shîshat Khân.

Let us eat and let us drink,
Yet of God let us think,
The swing in the end must sever!
What is it though we rise
At a bound to the skies?
We cannot swing on for ever!
Do we glory in our pride?
It must all be laid aside,
The Guest of the Grave enjoys it never.

"Take this letter," said the saint, "to the governor of Lahore, and your wife will be restored to you."

Joyfully the poor man received it, and his haste was such that he would scarcely stop for food. When he reached Lahore he heard that the governor had gone out for a day's hawking, but he went to the palace, and giving the letter into the hands of one of the chief officers, he ran as quickly as he could to his own house, fearing lest he should be seized and instantly thrown into prison.

When the governor returned home in the evening, he retired as usual to his zenana to enjoy the company of his wives. As the moon was shining and the night was fair he was sitting with them on the roof of his house listening to the strains of one hundred hidden musicians, and the wife of the bangle seller, who had never ceased to pine for her husband, was sitting disconsolate at his feet. Just then one of the palace slave-girls entered, and said, "Here is a letter for your Highness, brought from Râwâl Pindi by Karîm the bangle seller."

"Read it aloud!" said the governor. So the woman (who was very accomplished, as people of her class usually are) read out the letter of Shâh Chamchirrâg. When the governor heard it, and as soon as he understood that he was listening to the words of Shâh Chamchirrâg, the great prophet of his time, a sudden trembling came upon him, his face changed, his eyes started, and, before any help could reach him, he fell backwards from the terrace into the courtyard below and broke his neck.

So died Shîshat Khân, by the judgment of God, and in the confusion which instantly followed, the bangle woman made her escape from the palace, and, joining her husband, she and he both set out that night for another town, where they dwelt for the rest of their lives safe and happy.

LXIII

OF THE PHILOSOPHIC BANERWÂL

A BANERWÂL said to his wife one night, "Man is but a bird, without wings!"

"How is that?" asked the woman.

"Do you not see?" answered he. "Yesterday you were squatting on this side of the oven, and I was crouching on the other. And this is the state of man: one day perched here, another day perched there, always on the hop, never abiding in the one place. Truly, man is only a bird without wings."

LXIV

OF GOD AND THE NOBLEMAN

A CERTAIN poor weaver, naked and hungry, was sitting shivering by the roadside, when a great man passed by, followed by a large retinue of servants, who were well mounted, well clothed, and well fed.

"O God!" exclaimed the beggar, "if you would know how to treat your servants properly, you should come here and learn it from this noble gentleman!"

LXV

STORY OF THE NINE-KILLING KHÂN

IN a certain village there once lived a poor weaver, who one day said to his wife, "I work long and hard, and you feed me with dry bread. Why do you not bake my bread sometimes with a little butter?"

His wife, thus reminded, set to work, and baked her husband some cakes with abundance of melted butter and sugar, and the weaver rested for an hour to enjoy the feast with her.

When he had satisfied his appetite, he wiped his greasy hands on his bare arms and resumed his work; but the sun being warm, and his hands and arms covered with butter, swarms of flies began to gather about him. Irritated by their attacks, he suddenly ran his right hand along his left arm, and killed nine of them at a stroke. "See," said he to his wife, "what havoc I have made at a stroke! From this day forward you must call me Nomâr Khân" (*i. e.* the nine-killing prince).

"What is the good," answered his wife, "of my calling you Nomâr Khân here? Here you are only the village-weaver, and every one knows it. Nay, let us set out for some other country, where you will not be known at all, and then I will call you Nomâr Khân."

So the two put together a few trifles for their journey, and left their native village to seek their fortune. After travelling many a league, they at last came to a strange town, where the husband said to the people, "I have come here to look for employment."

"And what are you called?" asked they.

"My name," answered he, "is Nomâr Khân, the nine-killing prince."

The news of the arrival of so redoubtable a warrior was at once carried to the King, who was beyond measure glad, saying to his ministers, "Bring this man before me. It will be an excellent thing to have such a hero in our service. He will command our armies, and he will slay the man-eating tiger, which is ravaging the country."

So the weaver was brought into the royal presence, and the King showed him honour and kindness. But the ministers, who were jealous of favour lavished on a stranger, said, "Your Majesty pays this man so much respect that his bravery and worth must indeed be great. Send him, therefore, to attack the band of robbers whom no man has yet captured."

This advice pleased the King, who at once ordered the weaver to set out on the adventure.

Then the weaver, by no means perplexed, returned to his wife, and said to her, "I have a grand name, but what will that avail me against those ferocious robbers, who are seven in number? Make me, therefore, some poisoned cakes, and let me capture them by guile."

The poisoned cakes, seven in all, were accordingly made, and the weaver took them and started for the mountains; but he took with him no arms of any description.

As he was going along the road the thieves met him in a body, and they said to each other, "This fellow has only a bundle. Let us set on him and see what is in it."

When the bundle was opened, it was found to contain exactly seven cakes, which tallied with their own number, so each of them took one, and sitting down among the rocks, they began to eat them. Having eaten, they drank of some water, which was flowing close by, and then they all lay down and died.

After a bit the weaver got down from the mountain-path on which he had been seized, and came to see what the fellows were about. Finding them dead, he stripped them of their arms and accoutrements and took them into the city and laid them at the feet of the King.

His master, when he saw the valiant weaver laden with the spoils of war, was astonished, and said, "But where are your own arms?"

"I heard," answered the weaver, "that there were only seven of these rascals. I had, therefore, no necessity to arm at all. If they had numbered ten or twelve, I might possibly have girded on my sword, or, perhaps, have provided myself with a stout stick; but for seven—never!"

The King now showed greater kindness than ever to his new ally, and made him commander-in-chief of all his forces, which angered his ministers greatly.

After a time tidings were brought in that the king of another country was advancing with a vast army to besiege and capture the city. Troops were at once levied to resist the invader, and the weaver was ordered to lead them forth to battle. Unfortunately he was no rider, having never bestridden a horse in his life. But he was quite equal to the occasion, for, having arrived in front of the enemy, he said to his attendants, "When I mount my charger, tie my legs down with a stout rope."

"But, sir," said the soldiers, "this is a thing which is never done either in peace or in war. We never tie the legs of our riders."

"Oh, but I am the Nine-killing Khân!" cried he. "Whenever I see the enemy, I am perfectly mad to rend them—yea, to devour them; and no horse in the world can charge fast enough for me! Therefore, tie down my legs."

So his legs were bound under his horse's girths, and when the troops charged, he galloped furiously with loose rein towards the ranks of the enemy. Coming to a tree, he laid hold of one of its branches, but so great was his impetus that the whole tree came up by the roots, and the enemy, perceiving it aloft over his head, imagined that he was a giant, or some being of supernatural power; and being seized with a panic, they all threw away their arms and fled dismayed from the field.

The brave Nomâr Khân now returned, and when he had ordered his legs to be untied, he dismounted in the midst of the acclamations of the army. The King was enchanted, and, sending for an elephant, he had him carried back to the city in state; but the jealousy of the ministers increased ever more and more.

News was now brought in that the man-eating tiger had visited a neighbouring village and carried off some of the inhabitants, and the ministers advised that Nomâr Khân should be sent forth to bring in the animal's head.

"Nomâr," said the King, "go forth now and capture the tiger!"

The weaver, nothing daunted, first returned to his own house to consult his wife, but as he entered his door he saw the tiger lurking outside.

"Wife!" bellowed he with a loud voice, "I am now going to kill the tiger!"

"Nay," said she; "stay at home. The night is cold and wet."

"What do I care for the cold or the wet?" cried he. "I don't care for the wet, and I don't care for the tiger, but I do care for the drip, drip, dripping of the rain from the roof of my house. Tigers? Fiddlesticks!"

The tiger's spirit was so cowed by the valiant words of this famous hero that he stood stock-still with fright, and then slunk away with his tail between his legs and hid himself in an outhouse. Instantly the valiant weaver, who was on the watch, pulled the door to, put up the chain, and secured it with a padlock, after which his wife and himself went to bed and slept profoundly.

Next day he waited on the King his master, and made his report.

"What arms had you?" inquired the King.

"No arms needed, your Highness," answered Nomâr Khân. "I merely laid hold of the savage beast by the two ears, threw him over my shoulder, and clapped him into one of my sheds. Therefore let your troops now go down and capture him alive."

So the King sent his ministers and a regiment of soldiers all armed to the teeth, who fought the tiger, having burned him out, and thus at last the beast was taken, paraded and caged.

The fortunate weaver, invested with more honours than ever, now became the King's favourite companion, and lived in happiness, prosperity and renown all his days.

LXVI

OF THE SILVERSMITH AND HIS MOTHER'S BANGLE

(SILVERSMITHS as a class bear a bad reputation for mixing up an undue quantity of alloy in the silver of their customers.) There was once a silversmith who, in a moment of disinterestedness, promised his mother that he would give her a bangle which should contain nothing but pure silver.

"You are my mother," said he, "and I, as your son, who owe you so much, cannot do less."

So he cast a bangle for his mother out of unmixed silver, and when it was finished he stored it up for her and went to bed. But he was quite unable to get a wink of sleep. He turned from side to side, and moaned and fretted in torment, frequently exclaiming, "Ah, that wretched bangle! What a simpleton was I to make a bangle without alloy!"

At last he could stand it no longer, so he got up, lighted his lamp, and did not rest until, having melted down the silver once more, he had recast it with a considerable admixture of base metal. Then, with a conscience purged of offence, he returned to his deserted couch, and in an instant he was asleep, while a fat smile of pleasure and contentment betokened the satisfaction of his mind.

LXVII

HOW A WOMAN COULD NOT KEEP A SECRET

ONCE upon a time there was a certain weaver who became so indigent and poor that he went to a grain-seller and borrowed forty rupees. "If I do not return within a year," said he, "take my house and all it contains—they are yours."

So the weaver wandered off over the hills, and in a lonely place he saw a light, and going to it, he found there a man sitting on the ground. He sat by his side, but the man spoke never a word. At last the weaver said, "Why, man, can't you speak? Say something, at least. Do you not see I am a stranger?"

"My fee," answered the man, "is twenty rupees. Hand me twenty rupees, and I will speak."

The weaver counted out twenty rupees and gave them to him, eagerly waiting to see the result. But all the man said was, "Friend, when four men give you advice, take it."

Said the weaver to himself, "I have only twenty rupees left, and if I venture on another question I shall lose that, too!" But a weaver's curiosity is very great, so he counted out his balance, handed it to the man, and said, "Speak again."

Then the man spoke a second time, and what he said was this, "Whatever happens to you—even if you rob, steal, or murder—never breathe a word of it to your wife."

Soon after the weaver took up his wallet and trudged along until he came to another desolate place, and there he saw four men sitting on the ground round a corpse.

"Whither away?" said they.

"I am going to that village across the river," answered he.

"Do an act of charity," said they. "We were carrying this body to the river. Take it up, as you are going that way, and throw it in for us."

Immediately they laid the corpse on his bare back and started him off. But as he went along he felt the most horrid pricking across his loins. "In the name of God," he cried, "what is this corpse doing? Are these knives or needles?" He could not stop to lay the corpse down, because it was a fat corpse, and he would never have been able to get it up again. So he went on groaning to the river, dropped it on the bank, and began to examine it. What was his surprise to find fastened round the waist of the corpse numbers of little bags filled with diamonds! He at once pounced on them, threw the corpse into the river, and started for home. Arriving in all safety, he paid off the grain-seller, presenting him as well with five gold mohurs, bought a handsome mare and a nice saddle, hired servants and took to fine clothes, and lived on roast fowl and rice-pudding every day.

In the same village the lambardâr was a man well-to-do in the world, and he, noticing the style in which his humble friend lived, sent his wife to gossip with the weaver's wife.

"Not long ago," she began, "I used to give you cotton to spin for me, and now what a lady you are! However, I am now your friend. Your husband, I see, has bought a mare and a handsome saddle, and he has a servant to follow him. Where did he get all the money? You might tell *me*."

"Indeed I don't know," answered the woman.

That night the wretched weaver had no rest. "Tell me," said his wife again and again, "where you went to, and how you got all that money."

"No, no," answered he, "I can't tell you. The best thing you can do is not to tease me, as, once you know the secret, it will be told everywhere, for women are like sieves."

The next morning he went out half dead with worry, and when he returned for his food, he found his wife still asleep, and nothing ready. "Get up, wife," cried he; "get up, I want my breakfast."

"Why should I get up?" said she. "What kind of husband are you, and what kind of wife do you take me for? You treat me like a child, and tell me nothing."

"Best for you not to know," replied he.

"Yes, but tell me," said she. "Not a word shall pass my lips."

"Well," said he, "I was told on my travels that if I drank half-a-pint of mustard-oil in the morning, when I got up, I should see treasure everywhere."

In the course of the day in came her friend, and the woman laughs and says, "Oh, I have found out everything, I have found out everything!"

"What is it?—quick, tell me!" said the lambardâr's wife.

"My husband says," answered she, "that when he drinks half-a-pint of mustard-oil he sees all the treasures buried by the old kings, so I advise you to give your husband and your six children half-a-pint each, and drink some yourself, and you will see treasure, too."

The woman at once ran home, bought some mustard-oil, and at night persuades her whole family to drink it, though she took none herself. In the morning she rushes into their rooms and cries, "Get up, get up, and look for treasure!" but, alack! she finds them all lying dead and stiff.

Now, when the King heard of this, he called for her, and all she could say was, "The weaver's wife deceived me, and told me to do it." But the weaver's wife denied it, saying, "I never told her. I expect she is carrying on with some low fellow, and, not to be interfered with, she got rid of her husband and children." So the lambardâr's wife was hanged, and so ends the story, all the trouble having been caused by a woman who could not keep a secret.

LXVIII

THE STORY OF ALI THE MERCHANT AND THE BRAHMIN

THERE was once a Brahmin who had two sons. But the Brahmin was very old, and his sons were unlettered and ignorant. So the old man began to think, "My sons are so ignorant that they cannot even recite the creeds and the prayers on which we beggars depend for our daily food. How will they live? Who will give them a morsel of food when I am taken away?" The thought of this preyed on his mind, and gradually rendered him silent and desponding.

One day he was sitting at a shop in the bazaar, brooding over his troubles, when a fakîr came up, and, seeing him so sad and wobegone, he began to ask him the reason.

"Why are you so deep in thought?" said he.

"For no reason," said the Brahmin; "there is nothing the matter."

"Nay, but there is," replied the fakîr.

"But even if I were to tell you," said the Brahmin, "you could not divide my sorrows with me."

"You are mistaken," returned the fakîr. "I am a fakîr. Therefore tell me your trouble."

"Well," said the Brahmin, "my only trouble is this: I am old and not likely to live. My sons are untaught and ignorant. They cannot say even a creed, and when I die they must both starve."

"Nay," said the fakîr, "not so bad as that, not so bad as that. Listen to me, and I will make you an offer. You say you have two sons who want training. Hand them over to me for a year and I will be their tutor, if only at the end of the year you will agree to give me one of the boys, keeping the other for yourself."

This proposal seemed so reasonable to the Brahmin that he joyfully accepted it, and, rising up, he led the way to his home. There he introduced the boys to their future master, and the fakîr took them away to his own village. But both the Brahmin and the fakîr had quite omitted to specify which of the sons was to be the property of the fakîr at the end of the year.

It was the habit of the fakîr to sit at the door of his miserable hut, where he had two hookahs for all passers who chose to stop and smoke hubble-bubble. Very few thought of passing without giving him alms, and by this means he was able to provide food for himself and the two boys, and he had ample time as well for teaching them their letters. Very soon it became apparent to him that of his two pupils the younger developed far greater intelligence than his elder brother, so to him the fakîr determined to communicate all the secrets and the arts of fakîrs, such as witchcraft, magic, and soothsaying, while he taught the elder only such ordinary knowledge as was suitable to poor Brahmins.

When the year was up the fakîr said to the boys, "Now come along with me. Let us go and visit your father." So they set out together, and came and put up in the town where the children's father and mother were living. The next morning the younger boy asked the fakîr's permission to go and see his parents, to which the fakîr agreed, and both brothers took their way to their old home. When the younger son had greeted his father, who was overjoyed to see them both, he whispered to him, "Remember, father, when you choose between us, you are to choose me."

In a few minutes the fakîr himself arrived, and said, "Brahmin, you see I have fulfilled my side of the bargain. Now let me choose which of the two I shall have."

"Nay," said the Brahmin, "I will choose for you. Take the elder; the younger is mine."

But the fakîr would not have this on any account. "Nay, master," said he, "the younger boy I love; let me have him." So there arose a dispute between the two men, the father and the teacher, until at last, after much argument, they agreed to call in arbitrators to settle their differences.

When the arbitrators had entered the room, the Brahmin addressed them, explained to them all the circumstances of the case, and concluded by saying, "I have decided to retain my younger son for myself, but do you judge between us."

Upon this the neighbours turned to the fakîr and said, "It is evident that both the boys are the sons of the Brahmin; therefore, do you take the elder and be satisfied." But the fakîr flew into a rage, and cried, "The younger is mine; I will have him or none! I will have him or none!" Saying this, he instantly left the Brahmin's house, muttering a dreadful revenge.

After a day or two, said the father to his younger son, "You advised me to choose you, and you I have chosen. But know we are poor and destitute, and you must help us to live."

"Father," answered the lad, "I know something of magic. If you will trust to me, we shall have no lack of money. This very night I will enter the empty house on the opposite side of the street. You shall see me enter, but you must not follow me till the morning, and then you will find there a bullock tied. Him you must lead out, and sell him for not less than a hundred rupees; but remember, you are not to part with the headstall, and, above all, beware of the fakîr."

In the evening the boy entered the empty hut, as he had said, and the next morning it was found that a fine bullock had been brought into the world by his magic.

When the Brahmin had examined him, he untied him and led him by the rope into the market-place for sale.

"What is the price of your bullock?" cried half-a-dozen voices at once.

"One hundred rupees without the headstall," answered the Brahmin.

After some discussion a farmer counted out one hundred rupees, and bought the bullock. "But you must give up the headstall as well," said the people. The Brahmin, however, refused to part with it, and the purchaser then agreed to buy another.

Then the Brahmin, taking off the headstall, laid it on his shoulder, and turned himself homewards. After a time he missed the headstall from his shoulder. He supposed it to have fallen, but as it was useless to search for it then, he continued his way. Arriving at his house, he said, "Son, I have sold the bullock, and, see, here are the hundred rupees. But, alas! by some misadventure I have lost the headstall."

"Don't be distressed, father," answered the son; "I was myself the headstall, and you see I have found my way back all right."

The Brahmin, who had been wretchedly poor, was now rich enough to pay off his debts, and to live in less discomfort. But as the money was not inexhaustible it was soon spent, and then he had to apply to his son once more.

"Always depend on my power," said the boy, "and you will never need."

In a few days he took his father aside, and revealed to him another scheme. "To-night I shall again go into the empty hut and shut the door. In the morning you will find there a handsome horse. Take him and sell him for not less than one hundred rupees, but remember you are not to part with the bridle, and, above all, beware of the fakîr, who is still lurking somewhere in the village. He is the master of magic, but I am only the pupil."

Early before sunrise the Brahmin opened the door of the house, and saw before him a beautiful riding-horse bridled. Leading him forth, he mounted on his back, and rode him into the market-place to sell him.

"How much?" cried the people.

"One hundred rupees without the bridle," said he.

Now, the fakîr himself happened to be one of the crowd assembled about the horse. Laying aside his bag, and retaining his staff, he began to walk round the animal as if to observe its points; and as soon as he saw that the Brahmin was absorbed in making terms with the dealers, he suddenly lifted his staff and struck the horse a violent blow on the back. The horse sprang several feet into the air, unhorsed the Brahmin, and instantly galloped away, while the fakîr ran after him at the top of his speed. As he ran in pursuit, he kept crying out, "My young fellow, I was the making of you. You know it. It seldom happens that the moustaches grow longer than the beard. How far do you intend to make me run—two miles, three miles? Because in the end you simply *cannot* escape me. I am the master."

Hearing these words, the lad in the shape of the bridle began to consider that escape was impossible under these conditions, and compelled the horse to stop short. Then, by the power of his magic art, the horse suddenly vanished, and the boy himself became a dove.

"Ho! ho!" said the fakîr. "You turned yourself into a bridle, and you are now a pigeon. But do you not know that I can become a hawk?" And the fakîr, in the form of a hawk, gave instant chase. The poor dove wheeled, and turned now here, now there—sometimes in the open, sometimes in the tangled wood, until at last he found that it was all of no avail. He would have been struck down by his pursuer if he had not happened to arrive at a lake, when, changing the form of a dove, he became a fish and dropped into the water.

"Ha! ha!" laughed the fakîr. "A horse, a pigeon, and now a fish! But what is the use? I shall now become an alligator, and you cannot possibly escape, for I will devour every fish in the lake."

So the fakîr then changed himself from a hawk into an alligator, and in that shape he raged through the waters of the placid lake, eating voraciously every fish he could find. At last he came to the dark creek where his pupil was hiding, and peering in he made a hideous dart at him. But in extremity of despair his intended victim made one final effort, and succeeded in leaping on to the bank, whence, perceiving that the corpse of a man was hanging from the branch of a tree, he transformed himself into a mosquito, and hid himself in the dead man's nostrils. Out now came the alligator, having observed the whole proceeding, and resuming his original form of a man, he took up a small piece of soft clay, and with it he stopped up the nostrils of the corpse, being determined that this time there should be no escape. He then slid down from the tree, and squatted on the ground beneath to consider how he should next proceed. Just then there passed by a respectable countryman riding on a horse, to whom the fakîr cried out, "O beloved of God, give me, I pray you, a little cloth."

"I can give you but little," answered the traveller. "Why do you not go into the town, where Ali the merchant lives? He is rich, and gives away freely of everything."

"So I shall," said the fakîr; "but, meanwhile, I am begging from you." The man, thus appealed to, handed to the fakîr a piece of linen, and continued his journey. This linen the fakîr tore into three slips, and climbing the tree once more, he tied up the corpse's head, binding it round over the nostrils with the linen slips, so that the mosquito could not possibly force his way out. Having done this he came down. "Now I shall visit Ali," said he. And without more delay to Ali's house he went, and took up a position with other beggars outside the door. By-and-by Ali the merchant came out and sat down to his prayers. As soon as he appeared the fakîr approached him and put up his joined hands, as beggars always do. "O Ali," said he, "your name and your liberality are spoken of everywhere. From a distant land I have travelled to see you, but just now I want your help, for God's sake, in a matter of importance."

When Ali had looked at him, and perceived that he was a fakîr, he answered, "My goods are your goods. If you want a horse, speak; I will give it you, or money or clothes."

"I want neither horse, nor money, nor yet clothes," replied the fakîr. "I only want you to do me a small favour. For God's sake, promise me that you will do it."

"Of course," said Ali, "I will oblige you, and it is not necessary for you to invoke the name of God so much. Why do you do it, when you see I do not refuse?"

"Never mind," said the fakîr, "come aside and hear my story."

So the fakîr took simple Ali the merchant apart and said, "For God's sake, my friend, perform this favour for me. You are a Hindoo, I am a Mussalman. In a certain spot there is a body hanging from a tree. Go yourself, cut it down, and bring it here to me."

"O what a difficult task you have set me!" cried the merchant. "I certainly cannot do this thing in the day-time; what would the people say? Still, for your sake, and as I have passed my word, and because you are a fakîr, I will go at night and bring the body in to you."

When darkness had set in, Ali mounted his horse and rode out of the town, and when he had arrived at the spot indicated he dismounted and began, in spite of his unwieldy bulk, to climb up the tree. When he got within reach he cut the rope with a knife which he had been holding between his teeth, and down fell the corpse with a thud. He then descended, thinking to take up the body in order to set it on his horse, and so to carry it back to the town. But, lo! when he got to the ground he was astounded to perceive that the corpse was once more hanging from the same branch. Believing that he had made some mistake, he again swarmed up the tree, and again cut down the body. But precisely the same thing was repeated, for as soon as he had reached the ground the corpse was seen to be still dangling from the bough. A third time he essayed his difficult task, and the third time this extraordinary corpse resumed his position in the tree. Ali now began to feel seriously alarmed. "There is something wrong here!" cried he. And getting on his horse, he rode swiftly back to the town.

When the fakîr, who had been looking out for him, saw that he had not brought in the body, he began to reproach him.

"What!" said he, "you could not do for a poor fakîr such a trifling service as that?"

"The blame is not mine," said the merchant. "The corpse is bewitched. Every time I cut it down it jumped up again into the tree, and there it is hanging now!"

"Ali!" replied the fakîr, "if this had been so easy a thing, I should have brought in the corpse myself. But, as you say, there is magic in it! O Ali! to me you are a king, though only a merchant; and a king you shall really be if you will only bring in that body! And now remember my directions. First, do not dismount from your horse, and next, for God's sake, contrive so to manage as that the corpse shall fall on the horse and not on the ground."

With these instructions, Ali set out again; and coming to the tree, he called upon God, and cut the string. He had so stationed himself that the corpse fell in front of him on the horse's withers. So he settled it evenly, with his stirrup-leathers, and then, uttering a sigh of relief, he started once more for the town.

As he went along, Ali cast his eye over this singular corpse, and began to address it with playful humour: "Now, here you are," said he, "a dead body, though how long dead I don't know. Pretty tricks, indeed! I wonder how you managed to get up into that tree again and again!"

Hardly had he spoken the words, when the dead body began to quiver and shake and wriggle as if it had ague. Seeing this, Ali seized it, and held on to it with all his strength. But he held on in vain, for the body easily shook itself off the horse, and in another second it was suspended once more from the branch of the tree.

"The devil!" muttered Ali. But he was in no mood to turn back that night, for the sky was dark and murky, and his mind misgave him. So he made the best of his way back to his home.

When the fakîr saw that he had returned a second time without the body, he began to reproach him once more.

"O Ali!" said he, "what, no body yet? How is this? For God's sake, tell me!"

"Why are you perpetually calling on the name of God?" said Ali peevishly. "Listen, and judge if I am to blame."

Then Ali related to the fakîr the whole of his adventure.

"I see how it is," said the fakîr; "the body is certainly bewitched. I knew that before; but, Ali, the next time you are not to open your mouth to speak a single word to it on any account whatever."

The night following Ali again saddled his horse, and rode out to the fatal tree. He acted precisely as on the last occasion, and, with the body balanced in front of him, he began his journey to the town. As he rode along, the body began to mutter and to appeal to soft-hearted Ali's feelings.

"O Ali!" moaned he, "we all know you to be a great

man, wise and prudent, and of excellent judgment. For God's sake, then, halt a moment until I ask you a question!"

So Ali pulled up his horse in the moonlight, for the night was fair, and then the corpse resumed his speech—

"Listen," said the corpse; "I'll tell you a story of a frightful tyranny, a piece of consummate cruelty, which has been witnessed in this very country. There is a certain Brahmin. The Brahmin's family consists of four persons: himself, his wife, his son, and his daughter. What the mother orders, the daughter does not obey, and what the father orders, the son does not obey. In the midst of all this domestic disunion, the daughter grows up and becomes marriageable. Without consulting with his wife, the father goes out to the house of a neighbour, betroths his daughter to a certain youth, and receives for her a hundred rupees. The marriage is fixed for the fifteenth day after the betrothal. Having done this, he returns home; but he keeps the business secret from every member of his family.

"About the same time the mother also goes out, and betroths her daughter to some one else, and she also receives one hundred rupees for her. Then she comes home; but she also keeps her deed a secret from the rest of her family.

"After a day or two, the son thinks to himself, 'It is time now for my sister to be married. I had better go and get her betrothed somewhere.' So he goes to the house of one of his friends, and betroths her to an acquaintance, receiving a hundred rupees for her, and fixing the same day for the wedding as his father and mother had chosen. Then he, too, comes home; but he takes care not to breathe a word of the matter to any one.

"On the morning of the wedding-day the father gets up, and, going to the bazaar, he buys five rupees' worth of rice and curry-stuffs, which he brings back with him to the house. When his wife sees him entering with such a quantity of food, she asks, 'What is all this rice for?'

"'This is our daughter's wedding-day,' answers the Brahmin. 'The guests will all assemble here this evening, and this rice is for their entertainment.'

"'Alas!' exclaims the wife; 'something dreadful has happened. I also have betrothed our daughter, and this is the day fixed for the wedding. My friends will also be here this evening.'

"She has no sooner spoken these words than the son enters the door, and says, 'Why, father, why are all these preparations?'

"'It is your sister's wedding-day,' answers his father. 'I have betrothed her, and the guests will be here to-night.'

"'Sir,' replies the son, 'I also fixed this day as the day of my sister's wedding, and the guests whom I have invited will also be here immediately.'

"After hearing these heavy tidings they all sit down in silence and await the issue of events. By-and-by the three grooms and the whole of the three parties of invited guests arrive at the house, and begin to ask for explanations.

"Now, the poor young girl herself knows nothing of these arrangements. She is playing innocently with some of her companions in the court, when one of them who has overheard the angry expostulations of the guests runs to her and says, 'Your father and your mother and your brother have engaged you to three different persons: to-day is your wedding-day, and all those people are the guests.'

"The daughter now thinks to herself, 'Can this be so? But if I go with the man of my father's choice, my mother and brother will be angry. Neither can I consent to marry any of the others. Let me go and see whether this can be true.'

"So she goes to her mother, and learns what fatal mistakes have been made. Beginning to weep, the poor girl says to herself, 'What's to be done now? Better die than survive this disgrace. If I leap from the house-top it will be all over, and my troubles will end.' And she mounts the outer steps and throws herself down, but life is extinct before her body reaches the ground. Her playmates, seeing this catastrophe, cry out, 'Alas, alas! help! your daughter has killed herself!' And the whole assembly comes rushing to the spot. But it is too late. The child lies upon the ground with her eyes open, but her spirit has gone for ever. Such is the mournful end of an innocent girl!

"This," continued the corpse, "is the tyranny to which

I referred as going on in this country. And now, O merchant, answer, what have you to say to it?"

As Ali had been adjured in the name of God, he felt bound to answer. Besides, in his indignation, he had utterly forgotten all about the fakîr.

"My opinion is this," said he. "The unhappy girl saved her whole family from well-merited disgrace. That is my reply."

As soon as the merchant had finished speaking, the corpse began to shake as before, and in another minute it fell, glided rapidly over the earth, and once more it hung itself up in the tree.

By this time it was close upon dawn, and the astonished Ali, not willing to be seen near so unlucky a spot in the light of day, hastened away home. As soon as he appeared, the fakîr again began to upbraid him. "Such a trifle it is, O Ali," said he, "which I ask of you, and all in the name of God! Have you not accomplished it yet?"

"O fakîr, do not be hard on me," answered Ali. "Have I not passed my word? If it cost me my head, that wretched corpse I am determined to bring to you."

At the close of day, Ali the merchant once more rode forth to try his luck on the bewitched corpse. He arrived at the tree, cut down the body, settled it on the horse, and set off for the town once more. He had not gone half-a-mile when the corpse began to wheedle and coax him again. "O merchant," said the body, "you are a great man—who can deny it? Listen to me, for I have something more to tell you of what is going on in this country.

"In the morning her friends bathe the poor girl's dead body, and, laying it on a stretcher, carry it away to the place of burning. The three wedding parties now separate and betake themselves to their homes. Not so the three young men. 'Let us all perish with her,' cries one, and sadly they join in the funeral procession. When the mourners arrive at the pile, the same youth, he to whom the brother had betrothed her, exclaims, 'For me life is over. I will ascend too.'

"'Nay,' answer the people, 'do not be foolish. A woman might indeed make this sacrifice for a man, but a man should know better.'

"Yet when the body is laid on the top of the pile he springs up, and sits him down beside it, wringing his hands. Then the faggots are lighted, and in an hour this devoted couple are burnt to ashes.

"When this is all over, the youth to whom the girl had been betrothed by the mother collects all the charred bones together and buries them on the spot. Then he turns fakîr, and, taking up his station there, watches by the bones day after day, and never leaves them, excepting on those rare occasions when he goes into the village to beg for his food.

"When the third youth, he to whom the father betrothed the child, witnesses all these things, he goes up to the one who is sitting over the bones, and he says to him, 'Friend, we all loved the girl; we all had a share in her, for each gave his hundred rupees. The bones of one of us are mingling with her own. You are now the guardian of her dear remains. As for me, I shall also turn fakîr, and for the sake of that bright one I will travel over the whole world.'

"So he dons the garb of a fakîr, and with a wallet on his back and a staff in his hand, he starts on his travels. After travelling many a weary mile, at last, one day towards evening, he arrives at a village, and sees a woman spinning at the door of a house. To her he goes forward, and says, 'O mother, I have here a little flour, bake me some bread!'

"The woman merely answers, 'O yes,' and goes on with her spinning.

"The fakîr, being tired, sits down and waits patiently. At last he speaks again. 'Mother,' says he, 'the sun is now setting. By this time I could have walked on some three or four miles. Bake me, I pray you, a little bread.'

"The woman, who was a witch, answered, 'Don't be in a hurry. Your bread shall be baked, and you shall have it immediately.'

"Saying this, she rises from her spindle, takes a handful of dry grass, puts it in the stove, and on it she drops a little fire. Then she catches up her little girl, who was sleeping on a couch hard by, and puts the child's feet into the fire, and they begin to burn and burn like dry wood, nor does the child once awake, though the whole of her feet, almost to the knees, consume slowly away. The fakîr looks on with speechless horror, watching the woman baking his bread over that horrible fire.

"When the bread is quite ready, the woman enters the house and brings out a little vase. Pouring some coloured liquid from it into a large vessel, she fills it up with water, and, lifting her child, she puts both her legs into the mixture. Then, snatching her up once more, she lays her as before in the bed, and covers her over with a sheet.

"'O fakîr,' she cries, 'come and eat. Your bread is ready.'

"'Nay, woman,' answered he; 'I eat not, I am a fakîr. As for you, you are worse than a cannibal. Such tyranny as this is outrageous!'

"'Your eyes beguile you,' says she; 'this is true bread, fit for fakîrs. Come and eat it.'

"As they are arguing and disputing, the husband with his two sons approaches the spot, and cries in angry tones, 'Woman, will you never be quiet? Whenever I come home I find you quarrelling with fakîrs. You must be worse than human. You are a devil, and no woman at all!'

"He then turns to the fakîr and says, 'Eat the bread; eat the bread!'

"'No, no!' replies the fakîr. 'Never shall I eat bread which has been baked with the feet of a poor child.'

"'What nonsense, man!' exclaims the husband. 'Was it ever heard of that a child's feet could be burnt like that? It is quite impossible.'

"'But what if I saw it with my own eyes?' says the fakîr. 'And what would you say if I prove it to you?'

"With this the fakîr steps forward to the couch and lifts up the sheet which covers the sleeping child. But he starts back astonished still more than before, for the child's feet are whole and well, and there is not a sign of fire upon them.

"Meanwhile the mother comes and rouses the child, who wakes up crying.

"'Come and eat bread, child,' says the mother; 'come and eat bread.'

"'Don't give me any bread, mother,' says she; 'O, no, I don't want bread, mother. Give me some *dâl*.'[1]

"But the fakîr, sitting apart upon the ground, loses himself in reflection, thinking of the wonderful power of the witch. 'If I only knew her secret,' says he to himself,

[1] Dâl is a vetch largely used for food in India.

'I might throw some enchanted water on the bones of my betrothed, and we might marry and be happy still.'

"So the fakîr feigns a complaisance which he does not feel, and eats a little bread. He then says, 'O mother, have you any old bedstead you can lend me? If so, let me have it, as I am tired and would like to sleep.'

"Early in the morning the fakîr rises, takes up his wallet and goes out to beg. On his return in the evening, he hands over all his alms to the woman. In short, he takes up his abode with her, and each day he walks as many as ten or fifteen miles to all the villages round, but he never fails on his return to give the woman everything he collects. At last she says to him, 'O fakîr, once you scorned to touch my very bread. But now there is nothing which you do not give to me. What is it you really want of me?'

"'All I want,' answers he, 'is some of your skill in the art of magic. Teach me a little of your knowledge.'

"So the woman imparts to him all the knowledge she possesses herself, and he soon acquires it, after which he leaves that country and hastens back to visit his own.

"Four days is the length of the journey from the one country to the other, but his eagerness to visit the grave of his betrothed is such that he accomplishes it in a single day. It happens that when he arrives at the spot the other fakîr is in the village begging. So he digs up the whole of the bones and lays them reverently on the ground, after which he throws over them a sheet, and, sitting down, he keeps reading his magic words, and sprinkling the remains with his enchanted water. Presently he removes the sheet, and sees lying under it the living forms of his betrothed and of the other youth who was burnt with her on the funeral pile. At this moment comes back also the other fakîr. And so it happens that they all find themselves sitting side by side at the tomb, the three suitors and the young girl, all four living and breathing face to face, as they lived on the earth before.

"And now, O merchant," concludes the corpse, "this is the question which in God's name I implore you to answer. Of all these three, whom is the girl to marry?"

In spite of his promise the forgetful merchant hastened to give his opinion.

"My judgment is this," said he. "The two who were burnt together, the youth and the maiden, having been the same dust, must be regarded as brother and sister now that they are restored to life. Therefore they cannot marry. The suitor who raised the pair from the dead must be viewed as their father, since he was the author of their second birth. Therefore the maiden cannot be married to him. But the third suitor, who merely watched by the bones, must be considered differently. He bears no relationship whatever to these children of resurrection, and to him therefore the girl belongs, and him she must marry."

Having so delivered himself, Ali the merchant looked for the corpse, but it had slipped down from the horse, and was moving with surprising swiftness over the fields towards the tree, from which in a few minutes it was once more swinging in the wind.

Again the merchant rode on to encounter the disappointed greeting of the fakîr, who met him at the city gates, and cried, "O Ali, Ali, lacs and crores of rupees in charity you squander abroad, yet for poor me you will not do this trifling favour."

"I was beguiled again into speaking," pleaded Ali. "Let me try my hand once more."

"For the love of God," urged the fakîr, "speak not a word to the body on any account."

That night away rode Ali again, and acted precisely as on former occasions, cutting down the corpse and bringing it away on the neck of his horse. And as on former occasions so now, the corpse endeavoured to impose on Ali's simplicity. "For God's sake," he implores, "hear me but this once; listen to the rest of my story, and I promise to go whithersoever you please. All the former part of the adventure I have reported exactly, and you cannot accuse me of perverting the truth. Yet once more will I speak. Only, as the night is warm, undo these bandages, and take from my nostrils the clay which closes them up."

Ali felt glad when he heard the promise of the corpse, and he had no hesitation in complying with his request. He first untied the bands of linen, and then removed the clay. In a moment the mosquito escaped with a buzz, and, flying to the earth, turned at once into the son of the Brahmin, who walked rapidly away in the direction of the town, to the intense amazement of the bewildered Ali.

"Hullo!" cried he, "who are you? Hi! stop and say who you are and whence you have come."

But the boy answered him never a word.

Meanwhile the corpse had fallen heavily to the ground, where it lay perfectly still. Then the merchant dismounted, and having replaced it once more, he continued his journey, and arrived with it safely at the town.

The fakîr was overjoyed. He advanced to meet the merchant, and helped him to lift down the corpse; but when he missed the bandages and the clay with which he had secured the mosquito, he turned away and set up a howl. "Ah, miserable Ali!" cried he. "What have you done? You have let my enemy escape me!"

He was not a man, however, to lose time in useless repinings, so he made his way at once to the house of the Brahmin, and, peeping in through a hole in the door, he saw, as he expected, his runaway pupil. He therefore decided to remain in that town a little while longer. When a day or two had elapsed, he sent a request to the boy to come and see him. The boy knew well that all this time he had been withstanding his master, and, as the old influence was still upon him, he said to his father, "I have been called by my master; do you also come along with me." He went, therefore, to the house at which the fakîr was lodging and made his salaams to him. "Bravo!" cried the fakîr, "you have done your old master credit. The world used to say that moustaches never grew longer than the beard, but you have proved the old saw to be false. Come, sit down."

The boy, with a smile of triumph, sat down by his master, who then said, "All this time you have outwitted me by mere tricks. If you trick me this time, I promise you something which will be the death of you outright."

"O master," answered the boy, "let me give you a friendly challenge, and so let us decide who is the better man, you or I. I propose that you turn yourself into a tiger, while I shall turn myself into a goat. If the goat eat the tiger, then the world will see that the pupil has surpassed his master. But if the tiger devour the goat, it will acknowledge the master to be still paramount."

The fakîr at once agreed to this proposal, but in the boy's mind there existed treachery unsuspected by his master. It was arranged between them that the boy in the form of a goat should be tied outside the town, and that at a certain hour in the evening the tiger should approach the spot and endeavour to carry him off.

Leaving the house of the fakîr, the boy and his father, the Brahmin, went round to a certain number of the inhabitants and revealed to them that the next evening a large tiger would be prowling about outside a certain part of the town, and that, in order to capture it effectually, it would be necessary for marksmen to be stationed in ambush behind the neighbouring walls. So every one was on the alert, armed, some with guns, and some with bows and arrows. Then the boy turned himself, as agreed upon, into a goat, and was tied by the Brahmin to a stake near one of the entrances of the town. Presently a large, full-grown tiger was seen issuing from the jungle and creeping cautiously up the slope in the direction of his prey. Just then one of the concealed marksmen fired, but missed his aim, and the next moment the tiger had leaped upon the goat and had seized it by the neck. An indiscriminate volley was now poured in from all sides, and tiger and goat, both pierced in a score of places, rolled over and over dead upon the ground. And so ends the Story of Ali the Merchant and the Brahmin, or, as it might be named with greater exactness, the Story of the Fakîr and the Brahmin's Son.

LXIX

OF THE TWO MISERS

Once upon a time, two misers hobnobbed together to eat their food. One of them had a small vessel of ghee, into which he sparingly and grudgingly dipped his morsels of bread. The other miser, observing this, protested vehemently against such wasteful extravagance. "Why waste so much ghee?" said he; "and why do you risk the waste of so much more, seeing that your bread might slip from your fingers, and become totally immersed? Think better of it, and imitate me. I take my vessel of ghee, and hang it just out of reach to a nail in the wall. Then I point at the ghee my scraps of bread, one by one, as I eat, and I assure you I not only enjoy my ghee just as well, but I make no waste."[1]

LXX

OF THE KING AND THE ROBBERS

In former days it was the delight of kings and princes to disguise themselves and to visit the streets of their cities, both to seek adventures and to learn the habits and opinions of their subjects. One night the famous Sultan Mâhmûd of Ghaznî dressed himself up, and, assuming the character of a thief, went into the streets. He there fell in with a gang of notorious robbers, and, joining himself to their company, he gave himself out as a desperate villain, saying—

"If you are thieves, I am a thief too; so let us go and try our good fortune together."

They all agreed. "Be it so," said they; "but before we set out let us compare notes, and see who possesses the strongest point for the business in hand, and let him be our captain."

[1] This anecdote is an instance of the truth of the saying of Solomon: "There is no new thing under the sun." Many readers will be reminded of the Irish dish, "Potatoes and point," consisting of a large supply of potatoes and of a very limited supply of meat, bacon, or even fish. The potatoes are eaten, but the more solid food is merely pointed at. The following passage from Carlyle's "Count Cagliostro" refers to this singular custom: "And so the catastrophe ends by bathing our poor half-dead Recipiendary first in blood, then after some genuflexions in water; and 'serving him a repast composed of roots,'—we grieve to say, mere *potatoes and point!*"

"My strongest point," said one, "is my hearing. I can distinguish and understand the speech of dogs and of wolves."

"Mine," said the next, "is my hands, with which I am so practised that I can jerk a rope to the tops of the highest houses."

"And mine," said another, "is my strength of arm. I can force my way through any wall, however stoutly built."

"My chief point," said the fourth, "is my sense of smell. Show me a house, and I will reveal to you whether it is rich or poor, whether it is full or empty."

"And mine," said the fifth robber, "is my keenness of eyesight. If I meet a man on the darkest night I can detect him and point him out in the daytime."

The King now spoke and said, "My strong point is my beard. I have only to wag my beard, and a man sentenced to be hanged is released immediately."

"Then you shall be our captain!" cried all the robbers at once, "since hanging is the only thing of which we are afraid."

So the King was unanimously chosen as leader, and away the six confederates started. The house which they agreed to rob that night was the King's palace. When they arrived under the walls a dog suddenly sprang out and began to bark.

"What is he saying?" asked one.

"The dog is saying," said the robber with the fine ear, "that the King himself is one of our company."

"Then the dog lies," answered the other, "for that cannot be."

The robber who was so dexterous with his hands now threw up a rope-ladder, which attached itself to a lofty balcony, and enabled the party to mount to the top of one of the houses.

"Do you smell any money here?" said one to the robber whose scent was his principal boast.

The man went smelling about all over the roof, and at last said, "This must be some poor widow's quarters, for there is neither gold nor silver in the place. Let us go on."

The robbers now crept cautiously along the flat tops of the houses until they came to a towering wall, richly carved and painted, and the robber of the keen scent began smelling again. "Ah!" exclaimed he, "here we are! This is the King's treasure-house. Ho, Strong-arm, do you break open a way through!"

The robber of the strong arm now proceeded to dislodge the woodwork and the stones, until at last he had pierced the wall, and effected an entrance into the house. The rest of the gang speedily followed, and their search was rewarded by the coffers full of gold which they found there, and which they passed out through the aperture, and carried away. Well laden, they all by common consent hastened to one of their favourite haunts, where the spoil was divided, the King also receiving his share with the rest, while at the same time he informed himself of the robbers' names and learnt their places of abode. After this, as the night was far advanced, they separated, and the King returned alone to his palace.

The next morning the robbery was discovered and the city cried by the officers of justice. But the King, without a word, went into his audience-chamber, where he took his seat as usual. He then addressed his minister, and told him to send and arrest the robbers. "Go to such and such a street," said he, "in the lower quarter of the city, and there you will find the house. Here are the names of the criminals. Let them be taken before the judge and sentenced, and then produce them here."

The minister at once left the presence, and taking with him some attendants, he proceeded with all despatch to the street in question, found and arrested the robbers, and took them before the judge. As the evidence of their guilt was conclusive, they made a full confession and implored mercy, but the judge condemned them all to be hanged, and sent them before the King. As soon as they appeared the King looked sternly at them, and demanded what they had to allege in extenuation that their sentence should not be carried out. Then they all began to make excuses, excepting the one whose special gift it was to recognize in the day those whom he had met at night. He, looking fixedly at the King, cried out, to the surprise of his comrades, "The moment has arrived for the wagging of the beard."

The King, hearing his words, gravely wagged his beard as a signal that the executioners should retire, and having enjoyed a hearty laugh with his chance acquaintances of the preceding night, he feasted them well, gave them some good advice, and restored them to their liberty.

"The moral of this story," continued the story-teller, "is this: The whole world is in darkness. At the last day no faculty, however strong, will avail a man but that which will enable him to discern the face of God Himself."

LXXI

OF THE PAINTED JACKAL

A PROWLING jackal once fell into a large vessel full of dye. When he returned home all his astonished friends said, "What has befallen you?" He answered, with a curl of his tail, "Was there ever anything in the world so fine as I am? Look at me! Let no one ever presume to call me 'jackal' again."

"What, then, are you to be called?" asked they.

"'Peacock,' you will henceforth call me 'Peacock,'" replied the jackal, strutting up and down in all the glory of sky-blue.

"But," said his friends, "a peacock can spread his tail magnificently. Can you spread your tail?"

"Well, no, I cannot quite do that," replied the jackal.

"And a peacock," continued they, "can make a fine melodious cry. Can you make a fine melodious cry?"

"It must be admitted," said the pretender, "that I cannot do that either."

"Then," retorted they, "it is quite evident that if you are not a jackal, neither are you a peacock." And they drove him out of their company.

LXXII

OF THE JACKAL AND THE EWE-SHEEP

ONCE upon a time a certain jackal made a dash at a ewe-sheep, hoping to catch her. The sheep rushed into a half-dry tank, where she stuck in the mud. The jackal, attempting to follow her, stuck in the mud too. Then said the jackal, "O aunt, this is a bad business!"

"O nephew," answered she, "it is by no means so bad as it will be soon, when my master appears. On his shoulder he will carry a *sângal* (forked stick), and behind him will follow his two dogs, Dabbû and Bholû.[1] One blow with his stick will hit you in two places, and his dogs will drag you out by the haunches. Then, dear nephew, you will know this business is not so bad now as it will be then."

LXXIII

A STORY OF GHOLÂM BÂDSHÂH AND HIS SON MALIK

"THIS STORY IS OF AN EARTHLY KING: THE TRUE KING IS GOD."

GHOLÂM BÂDSHÂH had four principal ministers, of whom three were Hindus and one a Muhammadan. But his son Malik loved only the son of the Muhammadan minister, whose name was Mîrzâ, whom he made his young wazîr, and with whom he was constantly seen. The three Hindus, noticing the friendship existing between Prince Malik and the boy Mîrzâ, became envious and plotted their separation. So they went one day to the King and said, "O King, your son is always consorting with Mîrzâ Khân, the son of your Muhammadan minister, an un-

[1] "Spot" and "Speak."

principled young ruffian, and if you should die what would become of your kingdom? Before more mischief ensues let Mîrzâ be banished." Hearing this, the King sent for his Muhammadan minister, and ordered him under penalty of death to send his son into banishment.

Arriving at his house, the Muhammadan minister began to ponder, "How shall I do this thing?" and his sadness was such that his son, perceiving it, went to him and with uplifted hands inquired the reason of his grief.

"O son," said the father, "I cannot disclose the reason. If I tell you, I am disgraced before you; and if I do not the King's anger will fall on me."

"I would not wish," said Mîrzâ, "that you should be distressed for me. Tell me, therefore, what it is."

So the father told his son of the enmity of the Hindu ministers, of the King's anger, and of the King's decree.

"O father," said Mîrzâ, "this surely is no such great matter! Let me go and serve some other king."

So the son, taking costly gifts and servants, left his home. He passed through two kingdoms without stopping, and coming to a third, he rested in a certain town, where he was met by a man who asked him, "Who are you?" It was one of the officers of the King's bodyguard who thus accosted him, and Mîrzâ told him the story of his misfortunes, ending with the words, "Give me service with the King." The officer went at once to the King and made his report, upon which Mîrzâ was summoned to the presence, and going there he took a handsome present and paid his respects. When the King saw his beauty and his stature, he said, "I have already three viziers, and this handsome youth shall be the fourth." So Mîrzâ was advanced to great honour, and the King trusted him in everything.

Meanwhile, Prince Malik dreamed a dream. In his sleep he saw a lovely garden, and in the garden walked graceful as a guinea-fowl a beautiful princess in the midst of flowers only less lovely than herself. When he awoke he thought of Mîrzâ, and said, "Now I have no longer a friend to confide in." He became melancholy, and from over-thinking and from longing for the lady of the garden of flowers, he went out of his mind. His father sent everywhere for the best physicians, who physicked him to no purpose. What good was medicine, when all the time he was sick of love and of pining for his friend? The more the doctors wagged their heads over him the worse the patient became. At last he rent his clothes and wandered away into the wilds, where, in a foreign country, he turned fakîr, begging for a morsel of bread, and suffering so much misery that his very appearance became changed.

Four or five years went by, and Mîrzâ, the absent son of the Muhammadan minister, bethought him of his parents, and sent them a letter in which he said, "What news have you about my friend, Prince Malik? Does he sometimes think of me?" The letter was duly received, but the father hesitated to disclose to his son the sad story of the Prince. On second thoughts, however, he wrote and told him all that had happened. Mîrzâ, on reading the doleful news, cried, "Alas! with him I was brought up. He is my foster-brother. I must set out and look for him." So he went to the King and made his petition, and the King gave him leave for three months; "but," said he, "promise to return to me, lest Gholâm Bâdshâh take you again into favour, and you never come back to me more."

After taking leave Mîrzâ reflected that he must go in disguise, fearing that his former master should discover him and visit him with punishment. So, leaving his attendants to follow with bales of goods and to figure accordingly, he disguised himself as a merchant, mounted a horse, and rode to his own home. Meeting his father and mother, he cautioned them to secrecy, and then inquired for the whereabouts of the Prince. His mother was about to tell him, but his father stopped her, told her to keep quiet, and said, "The King's son is well." After two or three days, however, Mîrzâ becoming impatient, his mother let out the secret, and he began to take on, saying, "This is dreadful! From a child I was reared with him. If I am indeed faithful I must go forth and find him." Then he spoke to his parents, saying, "My servants are coming on behind. I have told them that I am a merchant; but they are strangers to this country. Take, therefore, my likeness and seal, and when they come give them as tokens to my overseer and receive the goods, after which send him and my retinue back." Saying this, he got on his horse, and with a few articles and some money he started off to seek his friend.

As he passed out of the city he met a countryman, who asked, "O horseman, where are you going?"

"The King's son," answered he, "was a great friend of mine. He is out of his mind, and I go to look for him. Who knows where I may have to go, and where not?"

"You are going," said the countryman; "but do you know what manner of man he is?"

"Yes," replied Mîrzâ. "He may have changed, but once I look on his face and figure I shall know him among a thousand."

Leaving the countryman, and travelling on, he came to a village, and meeting a villager, he questioned him. "The man for a time was here," answered he, "wandering about, and sleeping in the fields, but he has gone, nor has any one found him or seen him since."

Mîrzâ searched the place in vain, and he thought to himself, "Now, where shall I look?" So he went on and on, seeking high and low, until he came to a second village, but no one there knew anything about the matter. Soon after he passed a Hindu fakîr, seated in front of his tiny shrine. "Some fakîrs," said he to himself, "are hard-hearted and some are soft-hearted." The fakîr, noticing Mîrzâ's anxious looks, wondered, and asked the reason. "I am looking for a friend," answered he, "who has gone distraught."

"O," answered the fakîr, "he stayed with me ten days. Go on to the next town and inquire."

On he went and inquired at the next town, but he was directed to go still further. So he followed, and came nigh to a large city, and there at the meeting of two roads his friend was lying on the ground. At first he rode by, but turning to ask for tidings, he dismounted. Gazing on his face, he at once recognized him as the son of Gholâm Bâdshâh. Then the sleeping man awoke, leaped up and embraced him.

The vizier's son now put up his hands, and asked the reason of his grief, and Prince Malik told him his dream. "In my dream," said he, "I saw a beautiful Princess, and I awoke; but I had no friend to speak to, and I went mad."

"Oh," answered Mîrzâ, "I know the Princess. I know where she is."

But he lied to the Prince, in order to comfort his mind

and render him happy. He then got him a bath and procured him suitable clothing, and set him on his own horse, he himself walking on foot before him. So they entered the city, and there they rented a fine house, and bought a second horse. Every morning the two friends rode out into the country, examining everything, and every evening they came back to the house. After some days they took a longer journey than usual, Mîrzâ growing more and more anxious on account of his deceit. After a ride of eighty miles they arrived at another city, where again they rented a handsome house, and there also they made daily expeditions into the country. But Prince Malik was perpetually urging him to go to the Princess, while Mîrzâ perpetually excused himself, holding out false hopes. Having journeyed again, they at last came to the capital city of that kingdom, and there, as before, they hired a house.

The next morning the two friends rode out as usual, and by chance they came to a royal garden, in which at that very moment the Princess was walking with sixty attendant maidens. "This," cried the Prince, "is the place of my dream, this is the garden of flowers!" By the time they arrived at the door the Princess had left, and as they were about to enter they were met by the gardener's wife, who threatened them with a club, saying, "No man has ever dared to enter this garden, and how dare you?" But Mîrzâ gave her twenty-five rupees and calmed her down, and she admitted them. "Only," said she, "sit not in the Princess's seat, nor touch the Princess's favourite flowers. Sit on this side, and you may pluck the flowers which grow there."

After sitting still for some time, Mîrzâ began to ask the gardener's wife all particulars concerning the Princess, her times of visiting and departing, her age, her looks, her disposition.

"O she is sweet," cried she; "but for some years she has been in trouble. She frets and sighs, and speaks of a king's son named Malik, whom she saw in a dream, and so she does not give me her accustomed presents, nor think of me at all."

The Prince and his friend were delighted, and said to her, "We shall tarry some time in this city. Let us remain here, and we will pay you well."

"Outside the walls," answered the woman, "there is a pavilion, of which we reserve only a small part. Take your servants and horses and stay there."

So they gave up their house in the city and lived in the garden pavilion, and to the gardener and his wife they gave from their table day by day.

One morning the woman brought a number of flowers and began to make garlands of them.

"What are you doing?" asked Mîrzâ.

"I take them to the Princess, whose heart is broken," answered she, "and she takes comfort from their sweetness."

"This is your doing," said Mîrzâ to the Prince. Then to the woman, "Bring me a needle and thread, and let me make a necklet, which you can also give to the Princess."

So next day she brought flowers and needles and thread, and put them before him, and from the flowers he made a lady's dress most curiously.

"Does your Princess," said Mîrzâ, "choose for herself the top flowers of the basket, or those which are beneath?"

"Her maidens," answered she, "first take the upper flowers and then the Princess keeps those which are beneath."

Then Mîrzâ wrote a letter on scented gold paper, in which he recounted Prince Malik's misfortunes, and when he had finished it he concealed it in the dress of white roses, and, handing it to the woman, bade her go and deliver her basket to her mistress. This then she did, and, as usual, the maidens took the upper necklets for themselves; but when the Princess Hasan Bâno lifted the dress she was delighted, and said to the gardener's wife, "O what work is this! What a dainty hand! Who made it?"

The gardener's wife began to feel embarrassed, and so she answered, "My niece, who is in the service of another queen, came yesterday to see me, and it was she who made this coat of roses."

Now, as the Princess was examining the dress, the letter fell on the floor. Instantly snatching it up, she hid it in her bosom, and going into another room, she read it. All her pain vanished, and she became radiant with delight. Then returning, she rubbed her finger on the dark colour of the wall and marked the gardener's wife's face with it.

The woman, who expected money, was angry, and said, "What a reward for all this trouble!"

"Keep quiet," said the Princess, "and tell me—did your niece bring horses and baggage with her?"

"Yes," answered she, "baggage plenty, and two horses."

"Bring me the basket," said the Princess.

And when the basket was laid before her, she went and half filled it with gold mohurs, which she covered over with grain, and giving it to the woman, she said, "Go; this is for your niece, who made my coat of roses." So the gardener's wife put the basket on her head and went away, muttering to herself, "No present for me—only a smutched face!"

Arriving at the pavilion, she began to complain, "Reward I have had none, and the Princess is angry. All she gave me was this wretched grain. Here, take it and feed your horses with it." Then she put down her load and began to fume with anger. But Mîrzâ took off the grain, and finding the gold, he gave the old thing a handful which mollified her. As he handed her the money he noticed the black mark on the woman's face. "In this," thought he, "the Princess has sent us a riddle to guess, and the meaning is this, 'At present the nights are moonlight; I cannot meet you until the nights become dark.'"

The same evening a slave-girl came in to say, "When the nights are dark, expect to see me in my place in the garden. Then come and make merry." Several days passed, and when the moon had waned the same messenger came to say, "Expect me to-night!" True to her word, the Princess came to the garden, and Prince Malik met her, and the two lovers plotted an escape. Everything was entrusted to Mîrzâ. "So contrive," said she to him, "that I may go with the Prince, and that yet no disgrace shall attach to my name. Anything rather than that people should say I have gone away with a strange man unwed."

The next day the same slave-girl came again with the message, "I have confided in my maidens, and they are eager to see the King's son. So send the Prince to the palace and forget not a disguise." Therefore, Mîrzâ clothed the Prince as became his rank, and over all he put a red sheet that he might pass as a woman. When all was ready he advised him thus, "Attend," said he, "and follow my counsel in all things, that you be not arrested and hanged. Enjoy yourself with the Princess Hasan Bâno, but do not drink all the wine she offers. One drop of this liquid will secure her to you for ever. Pledge each other, therefore, changing cups, and when she has succumbed to insensibility take off all her jewels and with your nail make three deep scratches behind her right ear—remember, her right ear—and so come away."

The Prince started, and at the door he was met by the trusty slave-girl bearing a purdah, or disguise, but when she saw him already disguised she did not use it. So the Prince entered the zenana, and all the girls came about him clapping their hands with joy, and they began to dance and be merry. After a time Prince Malik rose to go, but the girls said to their mistress, "Keep him still with you, the night is long; and as for us, we will retire and rest a little."

Then the Prince asked the Princess to pledge him, and she sent for wine, and when the goblets were filled he said, "Give me a cup with your own hands and accept a cup from me." But he only sipped, remembering his friend's caution, while she, overjoyed, drank deeply, until at last she sank into insensibility, overcome by the drowsy liquid. As she lay on her cushions the Prince took off the whole of her jewels and hid them in his clothing, and then he scratched her to bleeding in three places behind her right ear. This done, he summoned the slave-girl, and said, "Lead forth!" And having been guided in safety past all the guards, he arrived at the garden-house, where Mîrzâ inquired, "Is all done correctly?" and he answered, "All."

Then said his friend, "So far, so well; now for more. To-night we must dress in saffron robes and turn fakîrs. You are my pupil; I am your priest and master. Let us take tongs in our hands and go and sit in the place where the Hindus are accustomed to burn their dead, and in the morning I will place in your hand one of the Princess's jewels, which you will take to the bazaar and offer in sale." So to the burning-place they went, and in the morning Mîrzâ gave Prince Malik the jewel and sent him off, saying, "Go, sell it in the bazaar. And remember in the King's palace there will be a great outcry, for it will be said a thief has entered and robbed the Princess. You with this jewel will of course be arrested and arraigned before the King, but say, 'I know nothing whatever. My master-priest sits in the place where the bodies burn. Send and inquire from him.'"

Thus the Prince did. When he reached the bazaar the sun was risen and he heard a great commotion. Men were beating tom-toms, and criers proclaiming the theft everywhere. The Prince, disguised as a fakîr, took the jewel to the very jeweller who had himself supplied it. The moment he saw it, knowing his own work, he seized the supposed thief and conducted him to the King, and the King questioned him. "Ho, you fakîr," said he, "where did you find this jewel?"

"I know nothing," answered Prince Malik; "my *gûrû* gave it to me this morning. He sits in the place where Hindus burn their dead. Send, O King, to him and inquire."

Now kings fear fakîrs, so this King turned to his ministers and said, "Kings have their ways, and fakîrs have theirs. Instead of sending to him, I will go myself."

So the King, followed by his nobles, started to see the priest. When he arrived at the spot the pretended fakîr, standing in the midst of fakîrs, with hands clasped and with a staff under his chin to keep up his head, was gazing fixedly at the sun. The King salaamed him, but the fakîr did not deign to notice him even with a wink of his eye. The King remained standing there for an hour, but still the fakîr gazed as if no King existed.

Now, Prince Malik had sat down near the priest, and by-and-by, when the hour had elapsed, he took down the support from the chin of his master, who then, gazing round, said to the King, "And who are you?"

"I am the King," answered he.

"Nay," said the fakîr, pointing to the heavens, "the King is up there. Then what King are you?"

"I am an earthly King," replied he.

"Ah," said Mîrzâ, "say not, as you said at first, 'I am the King,' but say rather, 'I am an earthly King.'"

Then said the King, "O fakîr-master, that jewel of my daughter's, where did you get it?"

"Listen, O misguided one," answered he. "Last evening, before dark, I came and sat here. My pupil sat with me and slept, but I rose to pray. While praying, I perceived fifty or sixty evil spirits in the forms of beautiful young women who assembled together and began to devour the bones of the dead. Enraged, I picked up my three-pronged fork and ran after them. They fled. One of them caught her foot in the folds of her dress and fell, and I struck her with my trident behind the right ear and rendered her insensible. Then I took off her jewels. You have one. Behold the rest!"

Then was the King confused, horrified, and astounded. Instantly he sends his vizier to the palace to see, and the vizier goes, examines, comes back, and reports to the King, "Your daughter is lying insensible, and behind her ear are the three bloody marks of the trident."

Then, turning to the fakîr, the King salaamed and said, "I came not here to disgrace you, but merely to discover the truth. Now I send my guards to take my daughter away to a desert place and to disperse her guilty maidens."

So the order was given and carried out. But the two pretended fakîrs hastened home, assumed their proper dress, mounted their horses, and rode with loose rein after the Princess. She, poor thing, had been abandoned in the midst of the wilderness, and when she awoke from her stupor she looked up and cried, "Where in the world am I now among all this jungle?" The first persons she saw were Prince Malik and Mîrzâ, for as to her sixty attendants, they had all run away for their lives excepting two. So the Prince dismounted and set the Princess on his own horse, while he sat behind Mîrzâ and the two slave-girls walked. At last they reached a town, and there they bought doolies for the Princess and her maidens, and started once more for the kingdom of Gholâm Bâdshâh.

But the Princess said to Mîrzâ, "I am as your sister. We are now only a few. Let us enter my husband's country with full retinue. In your hands I leave it." Thus admonished, Mîrzâ promised to manage, and some marches further on he sold the jewels, and with the money hired an escort of horsemen to accompany them.

When within two marches of the kingdom Prince Malik wrote a letter to his father, saying, "The cause of all my madness I have now with me, and in two days I shall arrive home safe and well." This letter changed sorrow into joy, and the King mounted at the head of a guard of honour and set out to meet his son. But Mîrzâ became troubled. " Your father," said he to Prince Malik, " now approaches. It is my duty to pay my homage to him; but if I do, and his anger revive at sight of me, what then?"

" If my father," answered the Prince, " so much as frown on you I will give my head for you."

At last the King arrived, and the Prince dismounted to kiss his hand. But the King dismounted also, and they fell on each other's necks. But the King did not recognize Mîrzâ, nor did he notice him until the camp had been pitched under his direction, and he was sitting exchanging confidences with his son. Then it was that Prince Malik told him the story of his friend's devotion, which affected the King to tears, so that he sent for him and embraced him as a son, saying, " My anger exists no more. You are now as dear to me as my own."

Next day they arrived at the capital, and all the troops and the people turned out to welcome them, and when everything was settled the King called for Mîrzâ and seated him by his side. Then he sent for the three false Hindus who had plotted against him, and said, " What now shall be done with these men?"

" Spare my life," besought Mîrzâ, " and I will tell you."

" Speak on," said the King.

" We have been always taught," answered Mîrzâ, " that when a man has wronged us we should try to do him good."

" But," said the King, " what if he do wrong again?"

" Try to do him good," replied Mîrzâ.

" But he might do wrong a third time," protested the King.

" Still try to do him good," again replied Mîrzâ. " By that time, if he persist, God Himself will punish him."

After some time Mîrzâ took leave of absence and journeyed to the court of the King who had befriended him in his exile. On his way he met a messenger coming to inquire the reason of his long absence, and with him he continued his march, while his servants brought up the rear with handsome gifts. Arriving at the end of his journey, he waited on the King, who said, " Why have you been so long away?"

"Kings," answered Mîrzâ, "have troubles too. My King sent me into exile, and I came to you. But now my King is kind once more, and I have come all this way back to show that I am grateful to you and to ask for leave for ever."

So he returned to his old King, Gholâm, and having recounted his adventures, he said, "O King, you banished me. But I was innocent, as you now see. For the future do not go by hearsay. See for yourself. Use your ears, but not your ears only; use your eyes also."

LXXIV

STORY OF THE QUEEN AND THE GOLDSMITH

WHEN the kings of the Sassanian line ruled over the East, many hundreds of years ago, there lived a Queen who was in love with her goldsmith. It happened one day when the goldsmith was in the Queen's apartments that the attendant who was on the watch at the casement cried out, "Alas! here comes the King!" This news threw the Queen into the greatest possible confusion, as it was then too late for her lover to escape unobserved. "What's to be done?" cried she; "there is not a single outlet for this man to escape, and he will be detected and slain." Her slave-girl, who was clever and judicious, thought of a trick which promised success. Taking one of the long handsome mats with which the floor was covered, she rolled up the terrified goldsmith in it, and set it up in a corner of the chamber against the wall. She had scarcely completed her task and resumed her place at the window, when the King entered and began to converse with his consort. But the goldsmith was in such a fright that he could not restrain his trembling, and as he trembled the mat trembled too. Then the slave-girl, to give him confidence and to obviate any dire mishap, sang out aloud—

> "O happy bee, inhaling love's sweet breath,
> Within the flower,
> Love's own enchanted bower,
> O why art thou afraid of death?"

The King, startled both by the words and by the unexpected manner in which they were sung, turned and said, "What does the girl mean?"

Then answered the slave-girl, "O King, a little time ago I went into the garden, and I saw a bee enter a flower; but the flower closed upon it and imprisoned it in its sweet embrace. I see from this casement that the bee is still there, and that its foolish fluttering causes the blossom to tremble on its stem, so I sing—

> "O foolish bee, bewitched with love's sweet breath,
> Within the flower,
> Love's own delightful bower,
> Ah, why art thou afraid of death?"

The King, marvelling at the girl's ingenuity, resumed his conversation with the Queen. But at that very moment the wife of the wretched goldsmith was seen by the slave-girl to be approaching the palace. She had heard of the unexpected return of the King, and being in great alarm for her husband's safety, she had come to inquire concerning his fate. As soon as the girl saw her beneath the window, foreseeing a new danger, she sang once more—

> "O bee, no need to mourn thy partner's fate!
> When shadows fall
> He'll burst his amorous thrall,
> And join again his lawful mate!"

Once more the King, being surprised, turned round and said, "And what now is the meaning of this?" And the slave-girl, ever ready, answered him, "O King, the bee flutters in alarm within the closed doors of the flower. Round and round flies the female bee, but she does not know that when the dews begin to fall the petals will relax, and that her loved one will escape. And so, to allay her anxiety and to send her comforted away, I sang, as I sing again—

"O murmuring bee, why quake with vain alarms?
At sunset hour
Thy spouse shall quit the bower,
And seek once more thy faithful arms!"

"This wisdom," said the King, "is wonderful. Where did you learn it?"

"My wisdom," replied the girl, "was got by constant intercourse with people of all classes. But you, O King, spend your whole life between your palace and your court of justice. You meet your ministers for a brief moment day by day, and then you return to your zenana. How can your Highness expect to learn wisdom, or to understand the ways of men, still less the minds of women?"

When the King had reflected on these words of the slave-girl, he found that she had spoken only too truly. So, determined to pursue a different policy, he sought counsel with his ministers, to whom he told all that had occurred in the apartments of the Queen, and whose advice he required. One of his ministers perceived the true explanation of the case, and said, "O King, there comes a thief to your house."

"I cannot believe in so dire a calamity," answered the bewildered monarch. "But, at least, I am determined not to return to my palace until the mystery has been solved."

Then answered the chief vizier, who was by no means anxious that the King should take any more active part in public affairs, "O King, the slave-girl's statement was probably true, and there is no mystery in the matter. But even if it be otherwise, need the heart of the King be troubled? Have not women from the time of Adam played similar tricks? And has there ever lived a man who could fathom the depths of their cunning? Therefore, O King, be comforted, and live happily and unconcernedly as before."

To this advice the King assented, deeming it the best, and knowing his vizier to be the most sagacious man in his kingdom.

Meanwhile, as the goldsmith was being unrolled from his narrow enclosure, the Queen said to the slave-girl, "The King my husband is certainly a mere bullock."[1]

[1] As we apply the term "donkey" to a stupid man, so the Panjâbis name him a "bullock."

"If he were a bullock," answered the girl, "he would have horns."

"And do you not know," returned her mistress, "that there are bullocks without horns?"

And with these words she dismissed the goldsmith in safety to his home, laughing herself at the strangeness of the adventure.

LXXV

OF THE WILD DOG OF PÎHÛR

A TRUE STORY

ON Mount Pîhûr, on the banks of the Indus, there lived a wild dog. This dog, whenever he heard the sound of funeral drums, used to say to himself, "Ha! there's a funeral, and to-night there will be feasting!" Nor did he ever fail to attend, and he always carried off some spoil. At last the people on either side of the river determined to compass his destruction. So at a given signal one party stationed themselves on the eastern bank, and another party on the western bank, just as night was closing in. Then those who were on the eastern bank struck up their drums, and the wild dog, leaving his lair, made his way to the water and began swimming across. When he was nearly over the drums ceased, and as he was hesitating in doubt, the drums from the other side began to beat and he turned back. But scarcely had he reached mid-stream again when he sank exhausted and was carried away.

LXXVI

STORY OF THE WEAVER AND THE PRIEST[1]

ONCE upon a time the friends of a young weaver betrothed him to a girl of a distant village. After a few days his mother said to him, "It is time to pay your future father-in-law a visit, but do not go alone, take your best man with you, and, above all things, remember, you are not to grab at the food like some hungry farmer's son, but eat delicately, choosing the smaller bits, and then your new friends will say, 'What a well-bred lad you are!'"

Accordingly the youth set out with his friend, and paid his call, but the food with which he was entertained was not bread, but vermicelli. Bearing in mind his mother's advice, he picked up the vermicelli bit by bit, but as fast as he did so the morsels slipped from his fingers again, and he ended the meal as hungry as a tiger, while his friend, deterred by no such scruples, fed himself by handfuls, and fared well.

It was a summer's night, and the sleeping-place reserved for the two guests was the housetop, while the members of the family slept, in accordance with their custom, in the court-yard. After they had all retired to rest, the weaver said to his friend, "I am starving with hunger."

"It is night now," answered his friend. "What are we to do? I think if you could get down into the house by this chimney-hole you might find something below."

Now, the hole was very narrow, and they were compelled to enlarge it a bit. Then the best man tied a rope to both his friend's legs, and lowered him like a bucket, head first, down the chimney-hole, nor did he release him when he felt that he had reached the bottom, but held stoutly on. The weaver, with his feet elevated in mid-air, and his elbows on the floor, now began groping about in the dark, and at last he found a large earthen jar containing flour, into which he thrust his head, and he began to eat. When, however, he desired to withdraw his head, he found himself unable with all his struggles to do so, owing to the narrowness of the neck. So, half suffocated, he was compelled

[1] For a variant of this story see "The Four Weavers."

to cry out to his friend with might and main, "Chick, chick!" (Pull, pull!)

His friend, hearing his sepulchral cries, began to tug at the rope, but found the weight so increased that he pulled in vain. "One man only I let down," said he, "but now there must be two or three;" and he sat down in amazement.

Meanwhile the repeated cries of "Chick, chick!" roused the whole household without, and all the members of the family began to say to each other, "Certainly some devil must have entered our house, and his name is Chick." In the greatest alarm the women cried to the master, "Go at once to the village and call for help!"

In a short time several of their neighbours came running to the spot, but not a man had the courage to enter the house, while the cries of "Chick, chick!" with increasing violence continued to assail their ears. At last some one said, "Send for the priest," and straightway the priest was summoned.

When the good man heard the mysterious cries of "Chick, chick!" he turned to the people, and said, "What have you in there?"

"The house is haunted," answered they, "by some evil demon named Chick, and we want you to drive him out."

"Very well," answered the priest. "I will enter the house, but do you arm yourselves with sticks, and stand by the door. If the evil spirit escape me, and if he make for the door, set on him with your sticks and knock him down."

All this time the best man was still pulling away at the rope, but he had only succeeded in raising his friend a few feet from the floor, while the poor man's cries grew more and more desperate, as he embraced the vessel with his arms to prevent its weight from breaking his neck.

The priest, going into the room, and perceiving some dark object moving up and down, struck at it with a club with which he had armed himself, and his blow, lighting on the jar, smashed it into numerous pieces, which fell to the ground with a horrible clatter, while the clouds of rising flour covered him all over and filled the whole apartment. Then, while the weaver flew up the chimney, the bewildered man cried, "Alas, what devil's dust is this, which threatens to choke me?" and in a fright he made a rush for the door. The people, who were on the alert, perceiving a strange figure, its head, face, and hands of a ghastly white, in the act of escaping, laid on it with their sticks and knocked it over.

"Hold, hold!" cried the unfortunate man. "I am the priest! I am the priest!"

"No, no," said the neighbours. "None of your palaver with us. You are a devil, and you know it. Our priest went in one colour, but you come out another;" and they trounced him more heartily than ever, until they had bruised him all over, nor would he have escaped with his life if some of his own friends had not appeared on the spot and rescued him.

"It is the priest indeed," said they; "and as for the white colour, it is merely flour. You have half killed him, and you must suffer the consequence."

The people, who were unfeignedly sorry for their mistake, now explained that they had only followed the orders of the priest himself, and peace being restored, the poor victim of their misapplied zeal was carried off to his house and put to bed.

Meanwhile the weaver and his companion, in fits of suppressed laughter, settled their clothing about them, and without a word to their friends below composed themselves to sleep.

LXXVII

OF THE JACKAL AND THE FLEAS

THERE was once a jackal so infested with fleas that life was a burden to him. Determined to be rid of them, he sought for a pool of water, and snatching up a small piece of dry wood in his mouth, he began to enter the water with "measured steps and slow." Gradually, as he advanced, the astonished fleas rushed up his legs and took refuge on his back. The rising water again drove them in multitudes from his back to his head, and from his head to his nose, whence they escaped on to the piece of wood, which became perfectly black with them. When the sly jackal perceived the situation of his foes, he suddenly bobbed his head into the water, relinquished the wood, and with a chuckle swam back to the shore, leaving the fleas to their fate.

LXXVIII

OF A SILLY JACKASS

A JUNGLE TALE

A CERTAIN man possessed a donkey which, as it was in extremely bad condition, he sent into the jungle to graze. It happened that close to the spot to which the donkey strayed there was a tiger whose leg had been broken by an elephant, and in attendance on the tiger there was a jackal. "I am helpless and unable to move," remarked the tiger to his friend; "go out and forage, and bring me home some meat."

Then the jackal went to the donkey, and, addressing him as an old acquaintance, said, "The grass here is poor and scanty. Follow me, and I will show you good pasturage."

Now, when the tiger saw the donkey following close on the heels of the jackal, he forgot all about his maimed leg, and attempted a spring, but he fell short, and the donkey galloped away to his old grazing ground.

After a day or two the tiger again said to the jackal, "Here am I dying of hunger; go forth again, and forage for food."

"It is entirely your own fault," retorted the jackal. "I brought you a donkey, and you foolishly scared him away." And the two friends came to hard words.

At last the tiger said, "Well, try once more!"

So the jackal went again to the donkey, but the latter abused and reviled him.

"You cheat," said he, "you wretched impostor; like all your tribe, you are cunning and deceitful."

"Nay, nay," protested the jackal, with an innocent air, "you entirely mistake me. What you saw was not really a tiger at all, but merely the appearance of one—a mere shadow. Look at me, how fat I am! If it was really a tiger, why has he not eaten me? However, if you will not come to the good grass, never mind; it is no business of mine, and certainly I don't care; so farewell!"

Then the jackal went off. But he had not gone many yards before the foolish donkey began to follow, and this time he was seized by the hungry tiger and killed.

After eating a part of the carcase, the tiger, oppressed with thirst, drew himself along the ground, and went to a spring to drink water. In his absence the jackal pulled out the donkey's heart, and ate it up. The first thing the tiger did on his return was to search for the heart, but he searched for it in vain. Scowling at the jackal, he cried, "How dared you eat the heart, which I wanted myself?"

"This donkey," coolly answered the jackal, "never had any heart."

"And how will you prove that?" asked the tiger.

"The proof is this," said the jackal. "The donkey escaped you once, and yet he came within reach of you again. How could a simpleton like that have had any heart to think at all? He who has once escaped death and risks his life again deserves his fate, and why? Because he has no heart."[1]

[1] The heart among the Panjâbis being the seat of reason.

LXXIX

OF THE FRIENDLY RAT

A RAT met a camel in the forest, and said to him, "O camel, you ought to make a friend of some one. Make a friend of me, and it will go well with you."

"Pooh, pooh!" answered the camel. "What possible use can you be to one like me?" And he raised his head aloft, and began eating the leaves of a thorny plum-tree.

When he desired to pass on, he found that his nose-string had caught in a branch, and that no effort of his could detach it. Seeing this, the rat exclaimed to him, "O camel, you should have listened to good advice and accepted my offer. Behold the proof!" And running nimbly up the tree, he nibbled the string asunder, and relieved the camel from his difficulty. "And now," said the rat, "remember, I am your friend. If you are ever in trouble, appeal to me."

Some time after this the King with his army was passing through those parts, and the camel was seized by some of his attendants.

"Whose camel are you?" said they.

"I belong to a rat," answered he.

"Nonsense!" said they; "rats don't own camels;" and they led him away. Then the rat went to the King and complained, but the King laughed at him and bade him begone. Upon this the whole of the rats of the jungle assembled together, and, having visited the camp of the King by night, they gnawed to pieces the saddle-girths of all his horses and cattle, so that on the morrow when he met his enemies in battle he sustained a severe defeat and was taken prisoner, while the camel, making his escape in the confusion, returned with his old friend to the jungle.

LXXX

ON THE STUBBORN NATURE OF THE AFGHANS

A PATHÂN was one day sitting in a ferry boat which was moored to the bank of the Indus. His tulwâr, or sword, lay by his side. Presently down came a countryman driving a donkey, and requesting to be ferried across the river. The donkey, however, having come to the boat, refused to enter, utterly regardless of entreaties, threats, and blows. Suddenly the Pathân sprang from his seat, seized his tulwâr, and at a blow smote off the donkey's head. "To a Pathân," cried he, "this stubborn pride is permissible; but to a jackass—never!"

LXXXI

A STORY OF A BARBER

ONCE upon a time a barber and a farmer found themselves in company, travelling together to visit a common acquaintance who lived at a distant village. The barber was moon-blind; his sight during the day was perfect, but at night he was quite unable to see anything. It happened that his companion, the farmer, suffered from exactly the same defect of vision, but neither of them knew of the other's infirmity. They were both welcomed by their friend, who, after the custom of the country, brought out a low bed for them to sit upon in the enclosed space in front of his house. "Rest here," said he, "I will go in and bake some bread, and call you when it is ready."

As they were waiting darkness came on, and the farmer, lifting a hookah from the ground, began to say to himself, "I should like to have a smoke, but I am moon-blind, and cannot find my way to a light. If the barber now were to ask me to bring fire, and I refused, he would think me a funny, churlish sort of fellow. I had better ask him to go."

So he filled the bowl, and, handing it to the barber, said, "Here, take the hookah, and fetch a little fire in it."

Now, the barber was also ashamed to confess that he was moon-blind too. He therefore took the hookah, and rose to look for some fire. It happened that, instead of going in the direction of his friend's house, he passed through a doorway into an adjoining yard, and, not seeing where he was going, he fell over a bullock which was lying on the ground quietly chewing the cud. The owner at once cried out, "Hi, sir! what are you rolling over my bullock for? Are you blind?"

"No," answered the ready barber, "I am not blind, but I have been having an argument with a friend of mine as to the age of your bullock, and as we could not agree, I said I would go and find out the bullock's age by a touch."

"What opinion did you give?" inquired the owner.

"I," replied the barber, "said your bullock was young, but he said no, your bullock was old."

"You are right," said the owner; "the bullock is young."

The barber now ventured to ask for a little fire, which the man brought out for him, and placed in the bowl of his hookah. His next difficulty, however, was how to find his way back, as he had no idea on which side of him the doorway lay. Not to be outdone, he cried out to the farmer, "Well, friend, is the bullock young or old?" The farmer, who on the other side of the wall had been a puzzled listener to the conversation, answered in as loud a tone, "The bullock is young. As you are a barber, you, of course, were right." And so the barber, guided by the direction of the voice, made his way successfully to the doorway, and passed back without further mishap.

Meanwhile, however, the farmer had been considering, "Surely the barber must be moon-blind too, to have gone headlong over a bullock!" So, as the barber was handing him the lighted hookah, he remarked, "I suffer from the moon-blindness. Do you too? If so, why did you not say so, and we might have sent some one else for the fire?" But before the barber could answer, their friend came and called them to their food, and having all three eaten their supper, they went to sleep.

The next morning a certain woman, hearing that the barber had arrived, brought to him her sick child and said, "My child has boils."

"I will bleed him for you," answered the barber. But he used his lancet so clumsily that he pierced the child's body, and the child died. Seeing this, the mother began to cry, and the people seized the barber and charged him before the King with murder. "This is unfortunate," thought the barber. "I must see if I cannot get off." Meanwhile he was ushered into the King's presence.

"How came you to kill this child?" asked the King.

"Spare my life," answered he, "and I will tell you."

"Be it so," replied the King.

The barber then said, "It was the fault of the woman herself for having borne a thin-skinned child. If she had borne a child with a proper skin the knife would never have pierced it and the child would never have died."

Hearing this, the King laughed and let the man off, and so he returned in safety to his own home.

LXXXII

THE ADVENTURES OF RÛP AND BUSSANT, THE TWO SONS OF RÂJÂ BANS

ONCE upon a time two swallows built their nest in the rafters of a veranda in one of the palaces of Râjâ Bans. This veranda was a cool and pleasant place, with an agreeable prospect of plain and river, and Râjâ Bans came often there to rest. One day he noticed two swallows which flew into the veranda several times, bringing food for their young ones. Being curious to learn their habits, he continued to watch them day after day. One evening he noticed that though both birds had flown forth for food, only the male bird returned. The next day he looked again, hoping to see both the birds, but the young ones were again fed by the male bird only. Surprised at this, he issued an order, "If any one in the city has caught a swallow he is to let it go immediately." In a short time a falconer came and reported that he had caught a hen-swallow. "Then let it go," said the King.

"But, sir," answered the falconer, "I gave the bird to my hawk."

"Ah, cruel one!" said the King, "you have killed the mother of a brood of poor young birds."

The falconer excused himself, saying, "I was not aware she had young," and the King sent him away.

For several days after this the King was pleased to notice that the male bird, though deprived of his mate, was unremitting in his care of his offspring, and he hoped that all would yet be well with them. On a certain morning, however, when the swallow flew back with food as usual, he came accompanied by another mate, which seemed so strange a thing that it set the King thinking. "Is this the real mother," thought he, "or is it another? Perhaps it is the very one herself." Then the King's heart felt glad, and he continued to watch. The next morning the two birds came in together again, but instead of coming and going many times, as before,

[1] The accent in "Bussant" is on the second syllable (pronounce Bussŭnt).

they visited the nest only once during the whole day. Another day passed, and the King found that the hen-bird came alone, but that the cock-bird never appeared at all. "Can anything have happened to the cock-bird?" then said he to himself. "Has he been caught too?" So he issued a second order, "Whosoever has caught a swallow, be it male or female, he is to let it escape." But his vizier brought answer back, "No one has caught any swallow whatever." Then King Bans returned to his palace veranda and began to consider this, "Both birds brought in food yesterday, and to-day the hen-bird only appeared. How is this? Where could the cock-bird have been?" Looking up towards the nest, he was surprised to notice an unusual silence. "Can the young ones be sleeping?" said he to himself. So he called for a ladder, and mounting, he put his hand into the nest, and found that all the four young birds were dead. "Ah," said the King, "some snake must have come and drawn their breath away!" But when he began to examine them he found a little thorn sticking in the throat of every one of them, which had deprived them of life. He now concluded that the second hen-bird was a stepmother, and that she had purposely given the young ones thorns instead of worms in order to destroy them.

Now, Râja Bans had two sons named Rûp and Bussant, and as he considered the fate of the poor fledglings he thought to himself, "If my Queen were to die and I were to marry again, my new wife would treat my sons cruelly too. If a silly bird can be so wicked, what might not be expected from a designing woman?"

As fate would have it, it happened after some time that the Queen, the mother of the two boys, died and was buried. The King mourned for her, and the whole of his court mourned for her too, both because she was young and beautiful and on account of all her endearing qualities. Many months elapsed, and as the affairs of the kingdom were suffering neglect owing to the King's continued sorrow, his ministers all assembled together and advised him to marry again.

"No," answered the King. "I have learnt a lesson from the birds of the air; I have seen what atrocities even the stepmothers of swallows can commit."

Again and again his vizier and his other ministers

begged him to marry again, and their words prevailed, so that at last, as it is easier to gratify men than to please God, he gave his consent. So proposals of marriage were made to the daughter of a neighbouring king, and in due course of time the bride was brought home, and lodged in a splendid palace of her own.

Time passed, and the two boys went to school together, and learnt their lessons day by day in the classes of learned pundits, where many others used to come too, to win wisdom and knowledge out of ancient books. This was the golden period of their lives, and they were happy in the innocence of their boyhood and in the full measure of their father's love.

The Queen, however, entertained for these two young princes sentiments of a far different description. She was their stepmother, and she possessed all a stepmother's feelings towards the children of her predecessor. One day, when the two brothers had returned from school as usual, they were amusing themselves with some tumbler-pigeons in the court of the palace. The younger brother threw his pigeon high into the air, and it alighted on the terrace of the Queen's apartments, on which she was then pacing backwards and forwards. Seizing the bird, she at once put it under a basket and hid it, and sat and looked as if nothing had happened. The boy, who was strong and active, climbed up the terrace, and seeing his step-mother, he said, "Mother, have you seen my pigeon?" The Queen answered, "No." The boy looked doubtfully at her, and just then an old nurse, who had tended both the Princes in their infancy, and who was a favourite of the former Queen, made signs to him that the pigeon was hidden under the basket. He reached the basket at a bound and rescued the pigeon, which he took away with him, while the discomfited Queen retired in anger to her chamber. Coming down again to the court, he told his brother, "My pigeon flew on to the terrace, and the Queen hid it, and but for the nurse I should never have recovered it."

A few days passed, and the same accident occurred again. The pigeon lighted on the terrace and was hidden by the Queen. Then said the younger brother to the elder, "It is your turn now. Do you go up and bring the pigeon back."

Up climbed the elder brother as quickly as possible, and when he arrived at the top he looked all round for the pigeon, but it was nowhere to be seen. Feeling certain that the Queen, who was sitting by her chamber-door, had hidden it, he went towards the basket, but as he approached the Queen caught hold of him, saying, "You are not to go there." As his strength far surpassed hers, he released himself from her hold, and rescued his pigeon. But the Queen set up a cry of distress, and began to weep loudly and bitterly. All her maidens came running about her, wondering what had occurred, and then came the King himself, to whom the Queen said, "Either your sons must quit the kingdom, or I must."

"What have the Princes done?" inquired the King. "And how have they annoyed you?"

"Yesterday," answered she, "the younger, Prince Bussant, and to-day Prince Rûp, the elder, scaled the palace-wall, and having insulted me, they would have treated me with violence, but I cried out and they escaped."

Then was the King filled with sorrow. "Ah!" thought he, "that which I feared has befallen me at last." Going to his vizier, he said, "Do you not see? From the first I foresaw this trouble, my mind misgave me, and as I expected, so has it come to pass, and now either the Queen or the Princes must leave the palace. I can no longer keep both wife and sons. What am I to do?"

Some of his ministers counselled the King to have pity on the youth of the two Princes, and to forgive their offence, but the King, swayed by his wicked wife, was so convinced of their guilt, that no arguments were strong enough to induce him to regard them again with a favourable eye. Then said his vizier, "O King, if you banish your children the scandal will not be so great. But if you dismiss your wife evil tongues will remark it, and a bad report will spread abroad in the kingdom."

Led, therefore, by the advice of his vizier, the King determined on the banishment of Rûp and his brother Bussant. Now, in those days, it was the custom with kings, whenever one of the royal household was to be disgraced and banished, either to place a pair of wooden shoes turned upside down at the door of him who was sentenced to exile, or to order his rooms to be swept out backwards instead of being cleaned in the usual way.

The next day the two boys came home from school, and the elder was chasing the younger, and they were racing towards the court. On reaching the palace, Bussant, the younger, caught sight of the upturned shoes at the door of their rooms, and he said to his brother, "See, brother, the King's signal! It is our sentence of banishment, and we must leave the country."

They were brave boys, both of them, and when they entered the house they sat down and conferred together and made their plans. "Yes," said the elder, "let us go to the stables and choose out a couple of swift horses, and let us see the treasurer and provide ourselves with money, and let us be gone, otherwise the Queen will compass our death."

As they agreed, so they acted, and having provided themselves with everything necessary for a long journey, and having armed themselves with their good swords, they set out from the palace without bidding farewell to any one. On and on they rode over mountain and plain; day succeeded day, and they found themselves astray in a gloomy forest. "God is in heaven," said the elder; "but where are we?" Just then they met a wayfarer, and inquired of him, "Is there any town or village hereabouts?"

"Yes," answered the man; "there is a village close at hand."

So they continued their journey, but instead of arriving at human abodes they appeared to plunge deeper and deeper into the forest, and evening coming on, they sat down to rest under a great *tâlî* tree, both wide-spreading and high.

"Either we were misled," said Bussant, "or we have mistaken the traveller's directions."

"Here let us rest," answered the elder brother, "for there is abundance of grass and water. Let us tie up our horses, and watch through the night by turns."

"True," said the younger, "this spot is cool and delicious, and though our food is exhausted, and we are hungry, we can at least lie down and sleep by turns. Let the first watch be mine."

"Nay," said the elder, "you are more fatigued than I am. Brother, you shall rest first."

"Not so," returned Bussant.. "You are the elder, and to rest before me is your right. Therefore, if you really love me, suffer me to mount guard for the first few hours. O let me watch while you sleep and dream of happier days to come!"

Then the two boys picketed their horses, and having washed, they commended themselves to the protection of God in the usual prayers, and while Rûp, the elder brother, lay down and slept, the younger watched.

The place was lonely and wild, and the silence of night was broken at times by the cries of wild animals on the quest for prey. To scare them away, Bussant collected some dry leaves and sticks, and having struck out a spark from his sword-blade, he lighted a fire, and having blown up the glowing embers into a bright blaze, and heaped on more wood, he sat down and began to warm himself, because the air, though still, was cold. He had been thinking over all their misfortunes, longing for his home, and guessing at the uncertain future, when he suddenly heard a strange fluttering of wings in the *tâlî* tree. Looking up, he could dimly discern two pearl-eating flamingoes[1] struggling together among the branches.

"What!" said one of them to the other. "You, a female, presuming to contend with me! Let me tell you that, if any one were this moment to kill me and eat me, to-morrow morning he would be a crowned King."

"And hear what I have to say, also," answered the other. "If you are great, I am great also, for if any one were to kill and eat me he would become a king's counsellor."

When Bussant heard what the birds had to say he wondered greatly, and he thought to himself, "If now I could so manage as to kill both these birds, I would give the male bird to my brother, and the female I would eat myself."

He then thought of his God, and, putting two arrows to his bow, he drew it with a steady aim and shot them both. Down fell the two flamingoes at his feet, and picking them up, he plucked them and laid them on the red ashes. Then he turned to his brother and roused him, saying, "Brother, wake up, God has sent us some food."

When Rûp saw the two birds roasting on the embers, he said, "One of these fowls is smaller than the other.

[1] In Panjâbi—*Hâns*.

Let me have the smaller one, since I can bear hunger better than you."

"No, no," answered Bussant. "You are my big brother, and yours is the larger bird. The smaller one is mine." And, to prevent mistakes, he took the smaller bird and began to eat it.

When the two Princes had finished their supper, the elder said, "It is your turn now to lie down. Brother, it is midnight; rest, and I will keep watch."

In the morning they were about betimes, and, having again washed in the stream, they saddled their horses, mounted, and rode on their way.

After going some little distance, the younger brother said, "Ah, brother, how unfortunate I am! I have forgotten my whip under the *tâlî* tree, and I shall have now to ride back to fetch it."

Then said the elder, "If you will return, I will go on slowly. Make haste, and overtake me." And the brothers separated, but little did they suspect how long a separation their parting was to prove.

Let us first see what happened to the elder brother.

He rode on, and presently he fell into a reverie, and quite forgot all about Bussant. Before he was aware of it he found himself approaching the gates of a large well-walled city, where he was surrounded by crowds of eager people all vociferating loudly, and hailing him as their King. "What means this greeting?" asked Prince Rûp of one standing by his bridle, who by his appearance seemed to be a person of consequence.

"Our King," answered the vizier, for that was his rank, "died last night, and it is an unalterable law of this realm that when the reigning sovereign dies his successor shall be the first strange horseman who comes riding into the town."

So Rûp was escorted by guards of honour to the public place, and thence to a palace of exceeding beauty, where, in the midst of applauding multitudes, he was throned a crowned King. But, as if some strange spell had fallen upon his mind, he never once remembered his younger brother, but forgot him as completely as if he had never existed.

But where was Prince Bussant?

After parting from Rûp, he rode back to the spot where

they had spent the night; but as he approached the tree he observed that a deadly snake was lying across his whip, which still remained on the ground where he had left it. "If I spur my horse into a gallop," said Bussant, "I shall be able to stoop down and pick up the whip as I ride by." So Prince Bussant urged his horse forward at a gallop, but it so happened that the snake was on the alert, and just as the lad stooped over to grasp his whip the venomous reptile drew away his breath and he fell from his horse in a swoon, while his horse also, arrested by the poisonous influence, stood still by his master's side. Then the snake glided rapidly away, and disappeared in the depths of the forest.

For several days Prince Bussant remained lying unconscious under the *tâlî* tree. To all appearance he was dead, for he neither breathed nor moved. At last an old beggar-man and his wife happened to pass that way in their journeyings from one country to another. And when they came to the place and saw a handsome boy lying, as they imagined, cold and stiff upon the ground, they began to feel alarmed, and the old man said to his wife, "Come away, come away, we shall both be hanged; his death will be fastened on us!"

"Stay for one moment," answered the woman; "let us see what is the matter."

"Nay, nay," said he, "we shall get into trouble; let us go."

The woman, however, had her own way, and, having carefully felt and examined the boy, she said, "No one has shot him, and no one has cut him down, nor is he really dead, but his breath has been drawn out of his body by a snake. If you will not come here and try to restore the lad to life, you and I must now separate. You are a fakîr and a snake-charmer, and all the snakes know you and fear you. Come nigh, therefore, and let us not abandon this beautiful youth to perish in the wilderness."

Thus entreated, the old beggar-man approached, saying, "I will do my best. If it is the will of God that he shall live, doubtless he will live."

Then the old man drew upon the ground his magic lines, and, kneeling down, he began to recite and to pray with intense energy. As he proceeded with his incantations, all the snakes of the forest began to crowd around him, some of them centuries old, others small and young, until he was surrounded by them on all sides. But the snake which had wrought the mischief came not. Then the old beggar-man took four cowrie shells, and, having repeated certain words over them, he sent them flying to the four winds, to the north, to the south, to the east, and to the west, to search for and to bring back the missing snake. Three of the shells failed in their quest, but the fourth succeeded, and, finding the snake, it compelled him to return. And when the snake appeared, he was seen riding as a king on the back of another snake; but he was proud and disdainful, and when all the other snakes bent their heads to the earth and touched the magic lines, he alone refused to do so.

When the beggar-man saw this, he prayed and prayed and prayed again, until he had subdued the power of the snake, and then he spoke roughly to him and said, "What tyranny of yours is this? By what right have you stolen the breath of this beautiful boy, and left him to be devoured in the forest?"

"No tyrant am I," answered the snake; "but this boy is himself the tyrant, for with his bow and arrows he shot my two flamingoes."

Then the beggar-man added entreaties to his spells, and prevailed on the snake to relent and to restore the boy to life. And when the snake had breathed into his mouth, Prince Bussant opened his eyes, and, looking round, he said, "O what a beautiful sleep I have had! Why have you wakened me?" But the fakîr answered, "O boy, the sleep which you have had, may God in His mercy never grant you again!" By degrees the Prince remembered all the circumstances which he had forgotten, and the beggar-man explained to him how he had been restored to life. Very grateful he felt when he understood how truly he had been served, and he said, "O fakîr, my brother is now lost; let me therefore go with you." But the old man answered, "It cannot be; you are a king's son, and we are only poor folk. We should be taken up and hanged on account of you. Therefore, wherever you go, we shall not go. We'll have nothing more to do with you." And the old couple salaamed the Prince and went off.

Left to himself, Bussant determined to mount his horse

and to ride on through the forest in the hope that fortune might lead him to his brother, or at least to some village or town. One evening, after the sun had set, he found himself before the walls of the very city in which his brother Rûp reigned as king. But the gates were closed and fast barred, and the watchman on the battlements refused to open them. In vain Bussant pleaded hunger and fatigue.

"Too late," said the watchman; "a man-eating tiger infests this neighbourhood, and the King's order is that the gates shall not be opened after sundown. No one can enter now before the morrow."

Finding entreaties unavailing, Bussant retired to some ruined huts close by, and, dismounting from his horse, he tied him to a tree, and determined there to spend the night. Scarcely had he closed his weary eyes when he heard the growl of the tiger, and looking out, he saw the beast, close to the door, about to make a spring upon his horse. Said Bussant to himself, "You may roar, my friend, but with luck I hope to have your head."

He had his good sword drawn in his hand, and as the tiger, in the act of springing, flew past the doorway, he smote him with might and main and nearly cut him in two.

This tiger had been the terror of the town for many a year, and one of the decrees made by the late King proclaimed that whoever should bring in his head should marry his daughter and be made governor of the fourth part of the kingdom. It might seem that Bussant's troubles were now about to end, and that a life of happiness in the enjoyment of his former rank was about to open to him. But this was far from being the case, because it so happened that the watchman, from his tower, had observed the whole of his proceedings and noted the death of the famous man-eating tiger. "Ah," exclaimed this villain to himself, "to-night my star is in the ascendant, and if I can only get rid of this stranger, and secure the tiger's head, my fortune is made."

For an hour he remained at his post, but when he felt assured that the Prince was fast asleep he stole down from the tower, and cautiously approaching the hut, he entered, sword in hand, and hewed at the unfortunate boy without mercy. Having thus, as he supposed, killed him outright, he took up the unconscious body and, carrying it to a lonely place, threw it among some reeds by the river's side. Then, returning, he hid the horse, and cut off the tiger's head, which he took back with him to his watch-tower, and in the morning, presenting himself at the palace, he displayed his prize and claimed the promised reward. Every one belauded the courage of the watchman, who suddenly became famous and was regarded by the whole city as a hero. Nor were his supposed merits unrequited, for he was raised to the position of a councillor of state, he was made governor of a province, and the hand of a lovely princess was bestowed on him in marriage.

Early on the next day a poor washerman loaded his donkey with the clothes of his customers, and, driving him before him through the city gate, went to his usual washing-ground by the river's side. There he heard a most lamentable groaning.

"What can this be?" said he. "Perhaps the tiger has mauled some wayfarer." Having searched among the reeds, he found the wounded Bussant, whose face seemed to him so beautiful that he exclaimed, "This boy looks like a rose. But O," continued he, "how he has been cut to pieces!"

Finding that life still breathed in him, he raised him gently and placed him on his donkey, and so led him back to the city and took him to his own home.

When his wife saw her husband returning so soon with a strange youth on the donkey's back, she assailed him with five hundred curses. "I sent you out to wash the clothes," said she, "and here you are back again already."

"Hush!" answered he. "Keep still, keep still! God has sent us good fortune."

And as soon as she saw the state of affairs, and looked at the boy's handsome face and deadly wounds, she also pitied him, and she received him kindly, and took him in, and laid him down, and dressed his wounds, and she tended him so carefully that in a short time he recovered and became quite well again.

But these good people were very poor, and they could not afford to keep a young man in the house idle, nor had he any hope of ever meeting his brother again, for he knew not what had become of him. But as he felt grateful to the worthy couple for all that they had done for him, he offered to serve them in any way they pleased. So the woman taught him sewing and embroidery, and he became so expert with his needle that the King and all the nobles heard of his fame and sent him orders for their robes of state. Little did he think when he was busy toiling as a tailor on some royal garment that he was working at the clothing of his own brother.

So time went on, until at last, as his evil genius would have it, his old enemy, the city watchman, now a governor, came that way and recognized him as he sat over his needle in the washerman's doorway.

"Ah," said the villain, "can this be true? I thought I had despatched him, but it seems I was mistaken. I am undone if I do not find means of destroying him. I had better have him stolen and killed without delay."

Now, it happened at that season that a merchant vessel, which had arrived at the harbour, had become stranded, and though every device was tried to float her again, she still remained embedded in the sand. Despairing of success, the sailors consulted a certain sorcerer, who said, "The vessel will never move until you offer in sacrifice an only son, who must be slain, and whose blood must be caught and sprinkled on the deck."

Having received this answer, the sailors went to the King and stated the whole case, at the same time begging that an only son should be surrendered to them for slaughter. As it was the custom of that country to perform these hideous rites on occasions of emergency, an order was made out for them, and it was entrusted for execution to the wretch who had been promoted from obscurity to honour.

Overjoyed at his good fortune, he hastened to the house of the washerman, and with his own hands dragged forth the unfortunate Bussant and led him away to the ship, saying, "This is my day of revenge." In vain followed the washerman and his wife, weeping and lamenting. The youth was handed over to the sorcerer, and the merchants prepared to sacrifice him to the sea.

"What are you going to do with me?" asked the boy.

"We are going," answered they, "to sprinkle your life-blood on the deck of the ship, and then she will float and we shall be able to sail. So prepare, for in two minutes off comes your head."

Now, Prince Bussant had himself learnt something of magic and charms from his wicked stepmother, and at the same time he was also wise and intelligent. So, addressing the merchants, he said to them, "Sirs, what is it you really desire? Do you wish to take off my head, or only to float your ship?"

They all answered, "What we really want is to set sail as soon as possible."

Then Bussant took out his knife, and, opening a vein in his arm, he sprinkled the deck with his blood. At the same time the sailors and the people all pushed with a will, and in a moment the ship slid from the bank into deep water, where, having quickly righted herself, she was soon riding at anchor.

The merchants and the sailors were all delighted, nor did they desire anything more, but the villainous watchman conspired with their chief, and said, "By the King's gift this boy is yours. Your ship may ground somewhere else; therefore, be prudent and take your prisoner with you." So Bussant was immediately seized and carried on board.

No time was wasted in weighing the anchor and in unfurling and raising the sails, and in less than an hour the disconsolate washerman and his wife saw the vessel ploughing the river to the neighbouring sea before a favourable wind.

Long was the voyage, but Bussant commended himself to all by his gentle manners and willing obedience, and the principal merchant, to whom the ship belonged, began to regard him with favour.

At last they reached their destination, and the ship was moored to one of the wharfs of a great seaport. Then the merchants and the sailors carried their bales and boxes of merchandise on shore, and betook them to the bazaars, leaving Bussant to keep guard on the deck.

Now, it happened that quite close to the wharf at which the vessel was moored rose the walls and turrets of the King's palace. This King had a most lovely daughter, who often came and sat at a lattice overlooking the sea, and as she was young and romantic, she loved to lean her cheek upon her hand and gaze over the moonlit waters.

Once when she was thus engaged she heard the sound of weeping rising from the deck of the strange ship, but it was so dark that she could not see who it was that thus bemoaned his fate. In the morning, however, she looked out again and saw Prince Bussant sitting in the stern with a book in his hand, from which he was reading aloud. As she gazed at his face, she thought to herself, "Surely never was any one so handsome!" and as she listened to his voice she thought, "Was ever voice more beautiful than his?" That night she watched and heard him weeping again, and soon she discovered that thus he spent most of his time, reading aloud while the daylight lasted and crying over his troubles in the dark hours of the night.

Resolved to become acquainted with this mysterious visitor to her father's kingdom, she told her slave-girl to go down and find out who he was. So the slave-girl went as she was ordered, and, entering the ship, she approached the spot where at that time Bussant was lying asleep in the moonlight. Looking closely at him, she came away again, and returned quickly to her young mistress, to whom she said, "I have just seen a youth more beautiful than the moon."

Then said the Princess, "Come along with me. I must go and see him too." And, disguising herself, she descended to the wharf, ran across it, and went on to the deck, where she felt as she gazed that her whole soul was ravished with love. And so she returned weeping and sighing to her chamber.

While she was sitting sadly at her window the Prince awoke and said, "Have I been dreaming, or did some beautiful lady really visit me in my sleep?" He then looked up, and in the full moonlight he saw the lady of his dreams gazing at him from the lattice, and as his eyes met hers his soul escaped from his body, and he fell hopelessly in love with her. Then the Princess called the slave-girl and bade her go down quickly to the ship and tell Bussant how much she loved him, and that if so he pleased she was ready to marry him, since her father's affection for his daughter was such that he had given her liberty to choose her own mate and to marry the man of her heart.

A happy time they had together, these two young people, day after day and night after night exchanging signs and tokens of mutual love. For the sake of the Princess the King accepted Bussant as a son-in-law, and believing him to be the son of the principal merchant of the ship, he loaded him with favours and bestowed on him ample wealth. Nor were the merchants themselves less kind and friendly on account of his fortune, though in secret they were always plotting how they might ruin him and enrich themselves at his expense.

In due time the wedding was celebrated and the Prince lodged in the palace, but the next day the merchants came and said, "The ship is laden, the breeze is fair, and we must set sail. Come, boy, it is time to be off." The Prince at once went and informed the King. "Our vessel," said he, "sails to-day. What am I to do?"

"Take ample gold," answered the King, "and take your wife on board with you, and when you have both travelled all the world over come back and see me again."

So they went on board the vessel, the Prince, the Princess, and the company of merchants, and to pass away the idle time the Prince began from that very day to tell his wife the story of his life.

When she had heard the whole of his adventures she was grieved, and cried, "O why did you not tell me of this before? Both my father and I believed you to be the son of the merchant. But you are a Prince, and none of his, and his past treatment of you augurs ill for the future. We are now in this man's hands, and Heaven knows what he may do to us!"

From that day she watched and guarded her husband with the most assiduous care, expecting she knew not what, but fearing the worst. Nor was her dread destitute of foundation, for the merchants had conspired together, saying, "Let us wait our opportunity, and throw the lad overboard, and then we can divide his money amongst us, while, as for the Princess, we can take her to the King's palace and sell her at a fabulous price as a slave."

With all their malice, however, they found no opportunity of carrying their schemes into practice, until they had fairly entered the river and had arrived within a few miles of the city which was governed by Prince Rûp. Then, as the weary Princess rested apart, they approached Bussant, who was sleeping on a carpet on the deck, and, tying the four corners of the carpet hastily together, they lifted him up and threw him overboard into the river, which was running fast astern.

But the ship continued her course, and when they arrived at the city the merchants took the weeping girl to the palace and sold her for an immense sum in gold. Prince Rûp as soon as he saw her thought she surpassed in beauty every other lady whom he had ever beheld. And he had a mind to marry her at once; but the Princess said to him, "I am married already."

"That can hardly be," answered he. "Are you not a slave?"

"I am married," repeated she. "Grant me, therefore, just three years to mourn and to inquire for my husband. If in that time he does not come for me, you are free to marry me; but if you attempt to wed me by violence, know that I am a Princess, and that I will kill both you and myself."

The King heard these words without anger, assigned to her a separate palace, and gave her a bevy of maidens to attend upon her.

Meanwhile Fortune had not altogether abandoned the younger Prince. Finding himself in the rushing water, he struggled with all his might, and, having freed himself from the carpet, he struck out manfully for the neighbouring banks. But the current was set in strong towards the sea, and it was with the utmost difficulty that he made the shore before it was too late.

[In that ardent region of the earth's surface, where the rays of the sun are very powerful, in order to secure the fruits of their fields farmers have to depend on artificial irrigation. On the alluvial lands which stretch along the borders of the rivers they are accustomed to sink down shafts in the perpendicular banks to the flowing water. These shafts are open all the way down on the river-side, being semi-cylindrical, and the water is drawn up by means of Persian wheels turned by bullocks.]

Into one of these singular wells Prince Bussant was driven by the force of the current, and, seizing the suspended ropes to which the numerous pitchers were attached, he held firmly on.

It happened that the gardener who owned the land above was just then watering his fields, and perceiving that some accident had stopped the wheels from working, he went to the well and looked down, when to his surprise he saw Bussant, half drowned, clinging to the ropes. Calling for help, he succeeded in rescuing the lad from his woeful plight, and in restoring him once more to solid ground.

Prince Bussant was so exhausted that he fainted away, and the gardener and his wife had to carry him home. There he was seized with a violent fever, which lasted for weeks, and which left him so feeble that he was unable to walk for several weeks more. All hope of ever recovering his lost Princess had now vanished from his mind, for he knew well that if she had not been shut up in the house of the merchant she had been sold into slavery. When therefore he was well enough, he offered his services to his benefactors, who gladly accepted them, and the King's son became a gardener.

Now, this old man and his wife were accustomed to make a little money by selling their vegetables; and so one day they said to Bussant, "You are now strong and well enough to earn something for yourself. Fill up a basket with cucumbers, and carry them into the market for sale."

"If," answered Bussant, "you would have me go in and out of the town without fear of violence, give me the clothing of a girl, because in that place lives a certain man who has twice attempted my life."

So the Prince was dressed up as a girl, and in that disguise he accompanied the gardener's wife day by day, whenever she went to the town to sell her vegetables and to buy food.

One day, as they were passing through the bazaar, they met the town-crier beating a drum and crying aloud, "Ho people, by order of the King, if any one was ever shipwrecked or lost at sea let him come with me to the court and tell the story, and his reward shall be great!"

"Mother," said Bussant, "my chance has come to reward you as you have befriended me. Let me go to the palace and tell the story of my adventures."

"But who will believe you?" said the gardener's wife. "You are no longer a boy, but a girl."

"Still, give me leave," pleaded he, "and let us trust to chance."

So the woman went to the crier and said, "Here is this daughter of mine who knows a story of the sea."

And the crier took Bussant disguised as he was, and he was brought to the palace, and seated before the Princess, who bade him tell his adventures at sea. Bussant, therefore, sat down and began the story of his life from the very beginning, about his father and his stepmother and his exile from home; but when he came to tell of himself and his brother sleeping at night under the *tâlî* tree, he there stopped short, and said, "Of that story I can remember no more to-day."

Then the Princess turned to a slave-girl and said, "This is the very person I want. She will remember perhaps to-morrow. Give her money, therefore, and tell her to come again." And to the watchman or crier she sent word that he should watch for the girl's return, and that when she came again to the town with her basket of vegetables he should bring her before her.

The next day the old woman and Bussant, laden with vegetables, again came to the town, and again they heard the crier beating his drum and proclaiming the will of the Princess, and again the Prince said, "Mother, if you will allow me, I will go and tell the rest of the story to-day."

And the old woman answered as before, "Go, son, go." So to the Princess he went, and he continued the story of his life from the point at which he left off the day before. But when he came to the account of the manner in which he had been tied up in his sleeping-carpet on the deck of the ship, he again stopped and said, "The rest I do not know, I cannot tell, but I will come again some other time and finish the story." So the Princess ordered him splendid presents and dismissed him. All this money he faithfully took to the gardener and his wife, who were both overjoyed.

The next day came the old woman and Bussant to the town as usual, and again the town-crier was seen beating his drum and delivering his message. The woman went up to him and said, "Take my daughter to the palace only once more, and she will finish her story of the sea."

So Prince Bussant again sat before the Princess and took up his story, but when he got to the tale of the well, and how he had escaped, and how the gardener and his wife had nursed him back to life, the Princess rose from her seat and ran to him and embraced him, crying, "My husband, my husband!"

"Nay," said he, "I am only a poor gardener's daughter."

Then she wept over him and kissed him, and he revealed himself to her, and when he had bathed and dressed in princely robes he returned to the chamber again. So the Princess sat down and wrote to the King, saying, "My lost husband is found again, but if you do not believe, come yourself and see him."

As soon as they met, the younger brother at once recognized the elder, but the elder did not recognize the younger, and he said to him, "What is your history, that you come here to claim the Princess?" Then Bussant began to tell his direful story again. The King sat down and listened with interest growing deeper and deeper, and when the story was ended he hailed his younger brother with joy, there was full recognition, and the palace resounded with the welcome news.

The next day the King took his brother and his wife and gave them quarters in his own palace. And the younger said, "Is that wicked watchman here still?"

"He is," answered Rûp, the elder. "The order of the late King was that whoever killed the man-eating tiger should be advanced to honour, and the watchman is now the governor of a province. But I have sent to have him seized and produced before me."

"Alas!" answered Bussant, "it was my fate, and one's fate who can avoid? Therefore spare the man's life and let him live for my sake."

Nor did he forget the old gardener and his wife, who received promotion and lived in comfort all their days.

So Bussant became his elder brother's chief counsellor, and at his brother's court he lived for many months. But the time came when he longed to return to his father's house to see if the old man was yet alive. So, taking his wife, he set out and journeyed towards his own country, and when he arrived within the borders of the kingdom he sent forward a message to report his approach. But his father was now old and blind, and every one had long given him up for dead, and his story was not believed. So he called for a cunning artist to paint his picture, and this picture he sent to the court by the hand of a friend. And when the vizier saw the picture he at once knew it to be the likeness of the lost Prince Bussant, and he sent out a guard of honour to conduct him to the capital, where he was received with joy.

The old King was so glad to meet his son once more that he placed his crown upon his head, and said, "Now you shall be King in my stead;" and having done this he turned fakîr, and soon after died happy and content.

Meanwhile the Prince had taken his wife to see his step-mother. But she hated the Prince more than ever, especially now that he was King; but she dissembled her hatred, and said to him, "I am now your friend, and I wish also to be considered your brother's friend as well. Give me, therefore, an escort, and let me go and visit him."

The Prince gladly agreed, and she started for the kingdom of Prince Rûp; but evil thoughts were burning in her heart as in an oven, and she had determined to set the brothers one against the other.

Arriving at the elder brother's court, she began her wicked schemes. "Your younger brother," said she, "is a tyrant. He deposed his blind father and cast him into a dungeon, where he perished miserably. Me also he would have served in like manner, but I escaped, and he has seized your inheritance and rules the land."

Unfortunately, the elder brother believed this cruel woman, and he gathered his armies and prepared to make war. In vain Bussant sent messenger after messenger to explain the true story. He was compelled to arm and advance too, and when the two armies met there was a great battle, in which the elder brother, Prince Rûp, was defeated and slain. Then for her life fled the wicked Queen, and never halted until she had put herself far beyond the reach of pursuit. As for Prince Bussant, he mourned for his brother all his days; sorrow like a shadow dogged his steps, and never was he seen to make merry again.

Told at Ghâzî by a villager, May 1880.

LXXXIII

OF THE BANÉYRWAL AND HIS MOTHER

A Banéyrwal went out coursing on the hills, and he took his mother with him to assist him in the sport. The woman had charge of the hound, but instead of simply holding the leash in her hand, she tied it in a fast knot round her wrist. When the game was put up, the dog made a sudden bound, by reason of which the unfortunate woman was jerked forward, and, as she came into violent contact with a sharp rock some distance in advance of the hound, she was unluckily killed. The dutiful son, with mingled feelings of admiration and sorrow, carried his mother home and buried her, and never afterwards did he cease to honour her, saying to his friends, "My poor mother was such an excellent courser that she outstripped the very dogs and left them far behind her."

LXXXIV

STORY OF FAZL NÛR AND THE DEMON

Once upon a time there were two men, Waîs by caste, named Muhammad Bax and Amîr Khân, who by chance became friends. Muhammad Bax used to visit Amîr Khân pretty regularly, and Amîr Khân and his wife always received him with respect. One day Amîr Khân thought that he also would go to his friend's house, and so he did. But Muhammad Bax's wife was a decided termagant; and the poor man, when he saw his guest approaching, got into a terrible way. So he went to his wife and spoke softly to her. "Dear wife," said he, "Amîr Khân is coming. You are the daughter of a noble family, and I hope you will treat him kindly. Whenever I went to his house, his wife came and washed my feet with warm water, and has always treated me very civilly; so I wish you to do the same."

"All right," said she; "don't worry yourself. I shall not put you to disgrace before your company. But if you are wise, you will also be careful not to vex me, but to remain quiet at table and keep a civil tongue in your head."

The meal was prepared accordingly, and the table spread in a room adorned with all kinds of nice furniture. The lady of the house, Fazl Nûr by name, served up delicious food, but, as there were four at table, the host and his friend and his two grown sons, there was by no means enough for all. When therefore they began to eat, the food fell short; seeing which, Muhammad Bax became anxious, but at the same time he was in mortal fear of his wife. At last he ordered his servant to go and ask her for something more. So the servant went and brought in a fresh mess, but neither was that enough for four hungry men, and Muhammad Bax, trembling with fright, sent her out again. But this time, no sooner had the servant gone into the room and given her message, than Fazl Nûr flew into a rage, seized the earthen pot, and, coming into the guest-room herself, she smashed the pot on her husband's head, and while the pieces were scattered on the floor, the rim of the pot remained round his neck intact like a horse-collar. On seeing this, Amîr Khân was transfixed with astonishment, but he tried to satisfy his host by saying, "Dear friend, every woman suffers from temper, and these things often happen in my house also. Let us go out for a little walk."

So the two friends went out, and Muhammad Bax appealed to his companion and begged him to get rid of his wife for him. "As to myself," answered Amîr Khân, "I do not like to do such things, but I will see my son and we'll do our best for you."

Amîr Khân then left for his own home, and, arriving there, he called his son, Akbâr Khân, and said to him, "Son, go to Muhammad Bax's, and entice his wife to come here with you under pretence of coming to a marriage-feast; but on the way, when you get to a lonely place, do away with her, that my friend may be rid of her."

So the son went to the house of Muhammad Bax, and stayed the night there. In the morning he said to Fazl Nûr, "Dear aunt, will you accompany me to my father's? We have a marriage-feast going on, and your attendance is most urgently required." At first she refused, because she had a lively recollection of the reception she had given the young man's father the day before. But afterwards, when her husband also urged her, she got ready, and, having dressed in her best and put on all her ornaments, she set out with her husband and Akbâr Khân. For many miles they took her through a wild forest, when, towards noon, they came to a well. There they halted, and in their usual manner told her to go to the well and fetch water. No sooner had she got to the edge of the well than Akbâr Khân with the greatest violence pushed her in. Fortunately for her the well was dry, but she fell on to the back of a demon who had his abode in that place, and there, not a bit the worse, she sat. The demon trembled excessively, not knowing what gruesome thing it was that had come and sat on his back. "Who are you," cried he, "that so fearlessly have come on to my back?"

"As for you," answered she, "you are merely a wretched demon, while I am own sister to the devil. Still, I saw you once and fell in love with you, and I have been looking for you everywhere—oh, ever so long! To-day some people told me you lived here; so I came, and in this well sure enough I have found you."

"Will you then be my wife?" asked the demon, fairly taken in.

"With all my heart," answered she, "but only on one condition."

"What is the condition?" inquired he. "Quick, let me know it soon!"

"It is not a hard one," replied she. "It is merely that I administer every morning a hundred strokes on your head with a slipper."

At first the demon was surprised to hear this. But afterwards, when he considered her beauty, he gave in. So he married her, and for a long time he continued to live with her, but by and by he began to get tired of his perpetual beatings, because there was a great wound in his head;

and one day, when he went outside, some flies settled on it and laid their eggs there, and he was tormented with pain. Moreover, whenever he went to see his relations, they despised him and railed at him as a poor demon, a miserable demon, on account of his sores. So he began to droop. He got very mournful, and he longed to get rid of his bargain. With this object in view, he made off, transformed himself into a man, and hid himself from her in a mosque, where women never come and mustn't come.

Now, it so happened that Muhammad Bax, the woman's former husband, had turned fakîr, or dervish, and was then living with some other dervishes in the same mosque. The demon, never suspecting who he really was, met him, and taking him aside, said, "My brother, all the work which you do shall be done in future by me. I will fetch the water for ablutions, and I will sweep the mosque and keep it in good order, but in return you and your friends shall go to the villages, collect bread, and give me also a share."

So Muhammad Bax and the other dervishes took out their begging bowls day by day, and in the evening returned with bread. But, at supper-time, the moment they squatted down, the demon invariably clutched all the food with both hands, swallowed it up, and left nothing for them. At last one morning Muhammad Bax went to the demon privately, and said, "Brother, I think you are not a man at all. You look very stout, and you eat like some evil spirit. Tell me the truth—what are you?"

"Tut, tut!" answered the demon, "I am a man, of course!"

"You are not," said Muhammad Bax; "I don't believe you. I can guess from your mode of eating that you are not a man."

"My friend," then said the demon, "you are right. I am really a demon, but be kind enough not to betray me. I have escaped to this place, fleeing from my wife." And then the demon went on to tell him the whole story: how he was living in a dry well, and how a certain woman, own sister to the devil, calling herself Fazl Nûr, had come there and married him, and what a terrible life he had led with her. All this reminded Muhammad Bax of his own wife, and he guessed that she was the same person. "My friend," said he to the demon, "I also have been ruined by Fazl Nûr; but now that you have betrayed yourself, perhaps she will be coming round here to look for you."

"O friend," cried the demon, "for God's sake keep my secret. Do not betray me for the world. Let her not cross my path again. Promise me this, and in return I will marry you to the daughter of the King."

So at once the demon disappeared, made his way to the palace, and entered into the body of the Princess. Upon this, the most beautiful damsel in the whole world became mad, and the King sent for all the wisest men in his kingdom to cure her, but none of them could. The demon caused her to put every doctor and physician who came near her to the greatest disgrace. She tore off their turbans and threw them down; she tweaked their noses, and pulled their beards; and sometimes she threw dust in their faces: so that all the most learned pundits, astrologers, doctors, and magicians became wearied out and indeed quite sick of her.

All this soon came to the ears of Muhammad Bax, who then, as previously agreed upon with the demon, went to the King, and said, "I will drive out the evil spirit from your daughter; but first promise that, if I do, you will give her to me in marriage." The King gladly consented, and the pretended dervish went into the sick-chamber. As soon as he appeared the raving Princess rose up from the floor, and fell at his feet, to the great astonishment of all her attendants. The King also was much moved, seeing the respect which she paid to so common a man, but he thought to himself, "Perhaps he is some saint." Then Muhammad Bax raised the Princess, and said, "Demon, within, I know you well; even your relations I know. Set this innocent Princess free and go away, otherwise I shall clap you into prison." But the demon, having acquired such comfortable quarters, was no longer minded to stand to his bargain. Therefore Muhammad Bax bent nearer, and whispered in the lady's ear, "Brother, that old virago, Fazl Nûr, your wife, has come!" Scarcely had he spoken the words, when the Princess began to tremble and the scared demon left her at once. The King kept his word, gave Muhammad Bax his daughter in marriage, and conferred upon him one half of his kingdom.

But the demon still hovered near the city, and one day he came to Muhammad Bax, saying, "Friend, I have given you a kingdom, but now be careful and attend. I am in love with the daughter of the King's vizier, and I am going to her. I shall enter into her, and stay there; but if this time you come and interfere with me, I will tear you limb from limb and crush you into pieces." So the demon went to the house of the vizier, and entered into the body of his favourite daughter, and there he lodged and the girl went frantic. To see his daughter thus afflicted, the vizier was overwhelmed with sorrow, and he sent for all the physicians and learned men to cure her, but they tried in vain. Then he besought the King to send him his son-in-law; "I shall go mad myself," said he, "if you do not send him." And the King ordered him to go. But the young man refused, saying, "My lord, I am quite powerless in this matter. It was by the favour of God that I cured your daughter." But the King insisted, and afterwards said, "Look here, sir, if you obey my order, you will gain respect and honour more and more every day; but if you do not, you will come to grief."

So Muhammad Bax consented and went to the house of the vizier. As soon as the demon saw him, he raged with fury and began to cry out. But his friend said, "Demon, I have not come here to interfere or to drive you out—I shall keep my promise to the last—but I have come to inform you of something which concerns you deeply. Let me, therefore, have just one word in your ear."

The demon consented, and Muhammad Bax came near and spoke in the girl's ear thus, "My dear friend, that day at the palace I was merely joking when I told you Fazl Nûr had come. But to-day I tell you seriously that she is now at the door of this house waiting for you, and no doubt she will find you out. Hark! I hear her coming up the stairs!"

The demon fell into such a state of fright that he cried, "For God's sake, friend, get the vizier to send her away, and I promise never to come back any more."

So Muhammad Bax spoke a few words to the vizier, and the demon, when he thought the coast was clear and the woman driven off, said, "Now I am going," and off he went.

Then the girl fell a-trembling and was straightway cured, while the demon fled away into the wilds, and was never heard of again.

Told at Ghâzî by bard Sharaf, July 1880

LXXXV

CONCERNING THE SEVEN WISE MEN OF BUNEYR

SEVEN men of Buneyr once left their native wilds for the purpose of seeking their fortunes. When evening came they all sat down under a tree to rest, when one of them said, "Let us count to see if we are all here." So he counted, "One, two, three, four, five, six," but, quite omitting to reckon himself, he exclaimed, "There's one of us missing—we are only six!"

"Nonsense!" cried the others, and the whole company of seven began counting with uplifted forefingers, but they all forgot to count themselves.

Fearing some evil, they now rose up, and at once set out in search after their missing comrade. Presently they met a shepherd, who greeted them civilly and said, "Friends, why are you in such low spirits?"

"We have lost one of our party," answered they; "we started this morning seven in number, and now we are only six. Have you seen any one of us hereabouts?"

"But," said the shepherd, "seven you are, for I have found your lost companion; behold—one, two, three, four, five, six, *seven!*"

"Ah," answered the wise men of Buneyr, "you have indeed found our missing brother. We owe you a debt of gratitude. Because you have done us this service, we insist on doing a month's free labour for you."

So the shepherd, overjoyed with his good fortune, took the men home with him.

Now, the shepherd's mother was a very old woman, in

her dotage, utterly feeble and unable to help herself. When the morning came he placed her under the care of one of the Buneyris, saying to him, "You will stay here and take care of my old mother."

To another Buneyri he said, "You take out my goats, graze them on the hills by day, and watch over them by night."

To the other five he said, "As for you, I shall have work for you to-morrow."

The man who was left in charge of the old crippled mother found that his time was fully occupied in the constant endeavour to drive off the innumerable flies which in that hot season kept her in a state of continual excitement and irritation. When, however, he saw that all his efforts were fruitless, and that he flapped the wretches away in vain, he became desperate, and, lifting up a large stone, he aimed it deliberately at a certain fly which had settled on the woman's face. Hurling it with all his might, he of course missed the fly, but, alas! he knocked the woman prone on her back. When the shepherd saw this he wrang his hands in despair. "Ah," cried he, "what has your stupidity done for me? The fly has escaped, but as for my poor old mother, you have killed her dead."

Meanwhile, the second Buneyri led his flock of goats up and down among the hills, and when mid-day came he rested to eat his bread, while many of the assembled goats lay down beside him. As he was eating he began to observe how the goats were chewing the cud and occasionally looking at him. So he foolishly imagined that they were mocking him, and waxed wroth. "So," cried he, "because I am taking my food, you must needs crowd round and make game of me, must you?" And, seizing his hatchet, he made a sudden rush at the poor animals, and he had already struck off the heads of several of them, when the shepherd came running to the spot, bemoaning his bad luck and crying to the fellow to desist from slaughter.

That night was a sorrowful one for the trustful shepherd, and bitterly he repented his rashness. In the morning the remaining five wise men of Buneyr came to him, and said, "It is now our turn. Give us some work to do, too!"

"No, no, my friends," answered he; "you have amply repaid me for the trifling favour I did for you in finding your missing companion; and now, for God's sake, go your way and let me see you no more."

Hearing these words, the wise men of Buneyr resumed their journey.

Told, with the five following, at Ghâzî, February 1878.

LXXXVI

OF THE FOOLISH QUACK

ONE evening, as the sun was setting, some travellers stayed to rest under a clump of trees, and, loosing their camels, set them to graze. It happened that one of the animals entered a melon-field, and that a melon stuck in its throat. The owner, seeing this and fearing to lose the beast, tied a blanket round its throat, and then struck the place with the greatest violence. Instantly the melon broke in the throat of the camel, and it was then easily swallowed.

A certain man who had just come up, looking on and observing this proceeding, shouldered his bundle, and, going to the next village, pretended that he was a doctor.

"But what can you cure?" asked the villagers.

"I can cure the goître," answered the quack.

An old woman, whose throat was swollen to a frightful size, exclaimed, "O my son, if you would only cure my goître, I would bless you for evermore!"

"Certainly," answered the man; "here, bring me a blanket and a good-sized mallet."

As soon as they were brought, he tied up the woman's throat, and struck the swollen part with so much force that the poor old creature instantly expired.

"Ah," cried the people, "this fellow is a villain!"

So they seized him, being minded to carry him before the King. One of them, however, said, "She was a very old woman, who must have died shortly in any case. Let us therefore compel the wretch to dig her grave, and then we can beat him and let him go." So they took him and set him to work, but the ground was so stiff and hard that he made but slow progress.

"If you do not dig it," said they, "before the King you shall go, and then you will be hanged."

Thus exhorted, the unfortunate man, in the greatest fear, laboured away with all his might; and at last, when the villagers saw that he had finished his task and buried the victim of his mistaken treatment, they beat him well and let him go.

Uninfluenced by the severity of his punishment, the man mounted his camel and went on to the next village, and again gave himself out as a great doctor.

"And what can you cure?" said some.

"I can cure goître," answered he.

This time it was an old man who offered himself for treatment. But the pretended doctor said, "Look here, good people. I shall do my best to cure this case; but remember, if I am so unfortunate as to kill him, I am not to be compelled to dig the man's grave."

"A pretty sort of doctor you must be!" cried they. "Before you begin your treatment, you are talking of digging the patient's grave! Away with you; we shall have nothing to do with you."

Hearing this, the pretended doctor began to say to himself, "What an extraordinary thing this is! My best plan surely is to return to the camel-men, and tell them they have not shown me the right way to cure this disease. Perhaps they will advise me."

When he had overtaken them, he cried, "What foolish men you must be! I met an old woman who suffered from goître just like your camel; and I tied a blanket round her neck and struck her with a mallet, but, instead of recovering like your camel, she died, and instead of getting a fee I was compelled to dig her grave!"

"It is not we who are stupid," answered the camel-men, "but you. We are not stupid at all. These animals are camels of prodigious size and strength. How was a feeble old woman to stand the blow of a mallet? No; it is you, and you only, who are stupid."

One of the men now stepped forward, saying to his friends, "You remain quiet, and leave this fellow to me."

Then, addressing himself to the newcomer, he cried, "Hear you, sir, these men do not understand the matter at all. I can set it all right for you in a minute." Saying this, he lifted a heavy stick, bound with iron rings, and struck a camel which was feeding off the leaves of a wild plum tree. The stolid creature, scarcely feeling the blow, merely moved a step or two forward. "You observe," said the man, "the effect of this treatment on the camel. Now observe its effect on a human being!" He then struck the man himself a similar blow, which felled him to the earth like a log. When consciousness returned, his bewildered victim inquired, "Why, sir, this cruel usage?"

"Do you not perceive?" answered the camel-man. "I wished to show you that what is good for camels is not therefore good for poor old men and women."

"Ah," said the wretched man, "I now begin to see my error. Never, never again shall I set myself up for a doctor!"

LXXXVII

OF THE CAMEL AND THE RAT

A CERTAIN camel, having strayed from his owner, was walking in unfrequented ways with his nose-string trailing upon the ground. As he went slowly along, a rat picked up the end of the string in his mouth, and trotted on in front of the huge animal, thinking all the time to himself, "What strength I must have to be leading a camel!" After a little time they came to a bank of a river which crossed the path, and there the rat stopped short.

Said the camel, "Pray, sir, go on."

"Nay," answered his companion, "the water is too deep for me."

"Not at all," said the camel; "let me try the depth for you."

Halting in the middle of the stream, the camel looked

round and cried, "You see, I was right—the water is only knee-deep, so come along!"

"Ah!" said the rat, "but there is a trifling difference between your knees and mine, don't you see! Pray carry me over."

"Confess your fault," replied the camel; "consent to acknowledge your pride, and promise to be humble-minded for the future, and I will carry you over in safety."

To this request the rat gladly agreed, and so the two passed over.

LXXXVIII

OF THE CROW AND ITS YOUNG

An old mother-crow was once engaged in giving sound advice to her newly-fledged young ones.

"Remember," said she, "your principal enemy will be man. Whenever you detect a man in the act of even stooping towards the ground as if for a stone, at once take wing and fly."

"Very good," answered one of her precocious youngsters, "but what if the man happens to have a stone already in his hand? Can you advise us as to how we shall proceed then?"

LXXXIX

OF THE TWO SIMPLE BANERWÂLS

ONE Banerwâl asked another, "If the Indus were set on fire where would the fishes go?"

"They would get on the trees," said the other.

Then said the first, "Are fishes like buffaloes, then, to climb up trees?"

XC

OF THE BANÉYR MAN AND THE BOAT

A COUNTRYMAN who had spent the whole of his life in the fastnesses of Banéyr, and had never seen the Indus, determined to perform a journey. Descending to the Yusafzai plains, he made his way to Attock, and, when he saw one of the large six-oared ferry-boats crossing with the flood to the opposite bank of the river, he cried, "What long legs that great creature has!"

XCI

THE STORY OF GHOLÂM BÂDSHÂH AND HIS SON GHÛL

THERE was once a King by name Gholâm who had an only son named Ghûl. From his early years this young Prince was passionately devoted to the pleasures of the field, and though now grown to manhood, his whole time was spent in hunting. The King, his father, could not behold such a condition of things as this without concern, and one day he called his ministers together and said to them, "It is time for my son to marry. Choose out a wife for him and let him settle."

The ministers, however, chose in vain. The Prince continued to hunt, and though the King remonstrated with him every evening on his return from the chase, his remonstrances were all disregarded. "If you do not marry," said the King, "every one will say it is because no one will have you, and you will suffer in reputation accordingly."

"But I do not want to marry," the Prince would answer, and so the matter would remain until the next day.

One evening in the hot weather the young Prince, weary with hunting, was returning home, when he stopped to rest by a well. "Let me drink from your vessel," said he to one of the damsels who were drawing water.

"O," answered saucily the young girl, "you are the Prince whom no one will marry!"

Prince Ghûl was so angry when he heard this speech that he refused to accept the water which was offered to him, and, rising, he walked away. "When I get home," said he to himself, "I shall announce my intention to marry, but my wife shall be the girl who taunted me."

Meeting an old woman, he asked of her, "Whose daughter is that?"

"She is the daughter of Alîm the blacksmith," answered the woman.

"Whether a blacksmith's daughter or a king's," thought he, "it is she whom I shall marry."

That evening his father again addressed him on the subject of marriage, and joyfully learnt that his son was willing to abide by his counsel and to marry. So he summoned his ministers once more, and bade them arrange for the marriage and to choose out some suitable lady. The ministers answered, "Name the King with whose house you desire an alliance, and we will set out for his court forthwith, and the Prince shall bring the bride home."

But the Prince answered, "Nay, there is no need for

you to look abroad. I have made my choice. I will marry Alîm the blacksmith's daughter."

Then was the old King filled with anger. "What," cried he, "is my nobility to be mated with people of low degree?"

But the ministers craftily answered him, "What harm will it do? This is merely a young man's fancy. Let him have the girl, and meanwhile we will look out for another lady worthy of his rank."

The King now consented to the match, and ordered his ministers to procure the blacksmith's daughter in marriage for Prince Ghûl. When they went to the house the poor man held up his hands in dismay and said, "Why does the King ask where he can command? But, indeed, as he asks for her, I am by no means willing to part with her."

This answer was reported to the King, who would brook no denial in the matter, and ordered that the blacksmith should surrender his daughter within two months. But the daughter herself, who felt that she was not fitted for such a destiny, implored her father to petition the King to grant her relief for the space of one year. The petition was granted, and the King finally agreed that the girl should enjoy her freedom for one year more.

"Alas," said she, "I am only a poor blacksmith's daughter! What shall I do in order that people may feel respect for me when I am the wife of the Prince? Let me see if I cannot test the wisdom of the King's counsellors themselves." Addressing her father, she said, "The water-melons in our little garden are as yet small. I shall make some large unburnt jars, and these I shall paint and enamel, and I will lay a water-melon in each, and when the fruit is full-grown I will challenge the King's ministers to take out the fruit without breaking the jars. And then we shall see whether kings and their ministers are better or wiser than poor folk."

So the girl did as she proposed, and having made the earthen jars of unburnt clay, she painted them, and in each she laid a growing melon. When the melons were full-grown so as to fill the empty space, she sent two of the jars containing the melons to the King, and wrote a letter requesting that the ministers should be ordered to free the melons without breaking the vessels. This letter the King read to his ministers, and commanded that they should display their wisdom accordingly. But the ministers tried in vain. For two or three days they felt the melons through the narrow necks of the vessels, and examined them carefully, but they had not the sense to perceive that the jars were formed of unbaked clay, which they could easily have discovered by sounding them. At last the King sent back the jars to the daughter of the blacksmith, saying, "There are no such wise people in the whole of my kingdom."

The girl was delighted beyond measure when she received this news, and when she had taken the jars into her hands she said, "I now begin to understand what kings' courtiers are, and what kings are also." Sending to the palace, she requested permission to attend, and when she entered the presence of the King, she took a wet cloth and wrapped it round the jars until the clay was quite soft. She then stretched the necks and drew forth the melons, after which she restored the jars to their former shape. Handing them to the abashed ministers, she said, "A man is known by his words, and a vessel is known by its sound. As by sounding a vessel of clay you find out its true nature, so I have sounded you, and I find you wanting in sense, and now, when the year is over, the King's commands shall be obeyed."

When the term of probation was nearly over, the blacksmith wrote to the King a petition praying that, as his means were small, the guests to be entertained in his house should be few. The King answered, "Four hundred will attend from the court, and for these only I will myself be chargeable," and he sent him a sum of money.

At last the day arrived and the guests assembled, but the blacksmith, finding the sum insufficient, said, "There is a great number of people here;" and he went to a certain nobleman and stated his difficulty. The nobleman advised him to keep the money as dower for his daughter, and to send it back with her to the King, and meanwhile he spoke to the court party, who all promised their assistance in entertaining the rest of the guests, and the feast passed off very well.

When all was over, and the Prince and the girl were united in wedlock, the King's party returned to the palace, and the bride and her dower were taken home and she was lodged in the apartments reserved for her.

When two or three days had passed by, Prince Ghûl rose up early one morning, and, taking a whip, he lashed his new wife unmercifully. "This is what I owe you," said he, "for your taunt to me at the well." The girl bore the beating in silence. Every two or three days the same scene was enacted, the Prince with his own hands baring the shoulders of his unhappy wife and ill-using her.

One morning, when he got up as usual to beat her, she said to him, "What glory do you gain by beating a poor working man's child? If you are a man, you will go and marry a king's daughter. Win her if you can, and beat her if you dare: but I am only the daughter of a blacksmith."

On hearing this taunt, the Prince was so incensed that he dropped the whip and vowed never to enter the house again until he had married the daughter of a king.

Now, there was a certain Princess, the daughter of a neighbouring King, whose beauty was justly celebrated, though she was said to be dumb, and she it was whom the Prince determined to marry. So he chose out a trusty slave and his best horse, and, having loaded several mules with jewels and presents of inestimable value, he set out one morning for the court of the King her father. March by march he travelled along, until at last he reached the kingdom, but in answer to his inquiries all he could learn from the inhabitants was that the Princess could not speak, and that every prince who came before her as a suitor had to consent to play chess with her, and that the penalties which she inflicted on his presumption when he lost the game were of the severest description. Nevertheless, Prince Ghûl had so much vain confidence in his own powers that, nothing daunted, he sent forward his slave to announce his arrival to the Princess, and to request the honour of her hand in marriage.

"It is necessary," answered the Princess, "that your master should understand the conditions. He must try his skill with me in three games of chess. If he lose the first, he forfeits his horse; if the second, his head is to be at my mercy; and if he loses the third, it shall be my right, if I choose, to make him a groom in my stables."

The Prince at once accepted these proposals, and the event was made known in the city by the sounding of a great drum. "Ah," said the people, when they heard the familiar sound, "another prince endowed with 'blind wisdom' has come to play with the Princess, and he will lose, as all others have lost before him!"

When the Prince arrived at the palace, he was admitted, and there he found the Princess seated on a rich carpet, while the chess-board lay on the carpet in front of her. The first game he lost, and the second, and the third. "Begone, presumptuous pretender," cried she, "and take your place with your predecessors; you are only fitted to groom my horses!" So the unfortunate claimant for her hand was led away and set to mind one of her horses.

Some time had elapsed, when the blacksmith's daughter began to wonder at the continued absence of her lord, and she determined to follow him in order to learn his fate. So she disguised herself as a young nobleman, and very handsome she looked in her new attire when riding her beautiful steed. After a journey of many miles, she came to a river broad and deep, and, as she stood on the bank waiting for the ferry-boat, she observed a rat being carried down by the stream. "For God's sake," cried the drowning rat, "save me! Help me, and I will help you!"

The blacksmith's daughter said to herself, "No rat can possibly help me, yet I will certainly save you;" and she lowered the point of her lance to the water, and the rat, seizing it, climbed up to her and was saved. Taking the dripping creature in her hand, she placed it in safety on her saddle-bow.

"Where are you going?" asked the rat.

"I am going to the kingdom of the dumb Princess," answered she.

"What is the use of your going there?" said the rat. "What will you gain? The Princess possesses a magic cat, and on the head of the magic cat there stands a magic light which renders her invisible, and enables her to mix up all the chessmen unperceived, so that the Princess's suitors invariably lose the game and are ruined."

Hearing this, the blacksmith's daughter began to fondle and pet the rat, and to say to it, "Assist me, for I also would try my fortune with the Princess," while at the same time she felt that her husband had tried his fortune and had lost.

Then the rat looked at her, and said, "Your hands and your feet are those of a woman, though your dress is that of a man. First, tell me truly, are you really a man, or am I lacking in wisdom?"

Then she began to tell the creature all her history from beginning to end, and how she had set out in search of her husband, Prince Ghûl. "And now," said she, "I want your assistance to recover my husband's liberty and to restore him to his rank and position."

This was a rat which never forgot a kindness, but, on the contrary, always endeavoured to repay a benefactor tenfold. "You must take me with you," said he, "hidden in your clothing, and if you will follow my advice you will beat the Princess and you will attain your utmost desires." The rat then instructed her in the means of achieving a victory, and so at last in conversation of a pleasing description they approached the capital and there rested.

The next day, when the blacksmith's daughter was admitted to the Princess's reception-room, she began by requesting that she might change places with her at the chess-board; and, as her request was granted, she secured the side on which the magic cat invariably entered the room. Then the game began; but soon she perceived that the board was becoming confused, and that she was gradually losing ground. Seeing this, she produced the rat, holding it the while firmly in her hand. Immediately she felt a sudden rush as of some animal, which, in fact, was the cat herself, which had that moment entered, and which in her eagerness to pounce on the rat had forgotten all about the game and her mistress's interests. The blacksmith's daughter, though she could not see the cat, still struck at her with her hand, and the magic light fell to the floor. Poor pussy was now rendered perfectly visible, and, having been scared by the unexpected blow, she ran with hair erect out of the room.

When the Princess perceived these untoward occurrences, she trembled and lost heart, so that she was easily beaten, not only in the first game, but in the succeeding ones as well.

At that moment the sound of the great drum was heard

reverberating through the city, and the inhabitants knew by that signal the result of the game.

Now, there was one more condition attached to the wooing of this Princess, which she had the privilege of insisting upon before she could be compelled to surrender her hand. It was that her suitor should prevail upon her to speak three times before sunrise; and it was ordained by a decree that each time she spoke the great drum should be sounded by an attendant slave, for the information of all the King's subjects.

"You see," said the rat to the blacksmith's daughter, "the assistance I have rendered you has not been in vain. And now let us see if we cannot make this obstinate Princess speak. Your sleeping places will not be divided even by a curtain. Keep me with you, and when you are both in bed, set me loose, and I will get on the Princess's bed, while you must coax her to speak."

When they had retired and had lain down each on her own side of the apartment, the blacksmith's daughter in her feigned voice began, "Charming Princess, light and glory of my eyes, will you not speak to me?"

The Princess vouchsafed not a word. But the rat, which was sitting by one of the legs of her bed, imitating the Princess's voice, exclaimed with the utmost tenderness, "Dear Prince, sweet Prince, at your request I could speak on for ever!"

When the Princess heard these dreadful words, she thought to herself, "This Prince is such a master of magic that he makes the very leg of my bed imitate my voice and answer for me." Then, shaking with rage, she cried to the inanimate wood, "To-morrow morning you shall be hacked off and burnt in the fire for disgracing your mistress."

The instant these words were uttered by her, the attendant slave ran to the tower and sounded the drum, and all the people heard and wondered. At the same time the blacksmith's daughter cried joyfully, "Salaam Alaikim, to the leg of my charmer's bed!" to which the concealed rat replied, "To you also, my King, Alaikim salaam!"

After a minute or two the blacksmith's daughter, again addressing the angry Princess, said in coaxing tones, "As I have to lodge under your roof to-night, O sweet Princess, pray tell me a story to send me to sleep!" The rat, having moved away to another leg of the bed, immediately answered, "Shall I tell you what I have witnessed with my own eyes, or merely something which has happened to me?"

"The best story," replied the blacksmith's daughter, "would comprise both what you have seen and what has happened to you."

"Very well," said the rat, "I will tell you what I have seen, heard, and encountered myself: In a certain city there lived a robber who used to rob on a large scale. Once upon a time, in order to carry on his tricks, he left his own country and went into another country, leaving his wife behind him. During his absence the woman was visited by a thief: now listen to me well, and do not fall asleep. This thief came and practised such deceit on her that she took him for her husband and admitted him to her house, her true husband having been a very long time away. At last the robber returned, and, finding the thief established in his home, he was astonished, saying to himself, 'Has any kinsman of my wife's come to see her?' However, he salaamed and entered the door, when the thief exclaimed to him roughly, 'Sir, who are you?'

"'This house is mine,' answered the robber; 'my wife lives here.'

"'Nay,' said the thief, 'the woman is not your wife, but mine. You must be some bad character, and I shall send at once for the police and have you well thrashed.'

"The robber was astounded. 'Wife,' said he, 'do you not know me? I am your husband!'

"'Nonsense, man,' replied the woman, 'this is my husband—I never saw you before.'

"'This is a pretty thing!' cried the robber, and he was fain to sleep elsewhere.

"In the morning all the neighbours assembled and welcomed the robber as an old friend; and to the wife they said, 'You have made a slight mistake; this is your real husband, the other fellow is not.' A regular fight ensued between the rival claimants, and they were carried off to the judge, when the woman settled the difficulty by saying, 'I am the wife of him who brings me home the most money.'

"Then said the thief to the robber, 'Who and what are you?'

"'I am a robber,' answered he; 'who are you?'

"'I am a thief,' said the other.

"The thief, who would by no means relinquish the woman, now said, 'Listen to me. Let us make trial of our skill. First, show me what you can do, or, if you please, I will begin. I am a thief and a cheat. If you can do more in robbery than I can perform in deceit, the woman is yours; but if otherwise, she is mine.'

"The thief then hired some fine clothing, got into a palanquin, and, going to a city, gave himself out to be a rich merchant. As he passed through the streets, he stopped at the door of a jeweller, who considered himself so honoured by a visit from one whose great fame had preceded him, that he rose up and made him a humble obeisance.

"The pretended merchant, with a lordly air, now asked, 'Have you any pearls for sale?'

"'Yes,' answered the jeweller.

"'Let me see the best you have,' said the thief.

"The jeweller immediately produced a beautiful casket, which the thief opened, and found therein several strings of pearls, which he proceeded to examine. After a pause he gave back the casket, saying, 'These are not what I require. I want pearls of a better quality than these. Have you no more?'

"The jeweller then brought out three or four other caskets, one of which the thief opened, and, while pretending to examine the worth of the contents, he adroitly cut off two strings of pearls, and, unseen by the owner, hid them in his sleeve. He then said, 'How many boxes of pearls do you possess of this description?'

"'Altogether I have seven,' answered the jeweller.

"'You shall hear from me again,' replied the thief, and, getting up, he went at once to the King, who was sitting in court, and paid his respects.

"'Well, merchant,' said the King, 'how has it fared with you since coming to my capital?'

"'O King,' answered the thief, 'I have been robbed of seven boxes of pearls of the greatest value, and, according to information which I have received, they are in the hands of a certain jeweller.'

"Immediately the King gave the thief a guard, and

ordered that the jeweller's shop should be at once closed and the unfortunate man arrested.

"On their arrival at the shop, the thief pointed out the box out of which he himself had stolen the pearls, and said to the guard, 'All my caskets were like that one.' The soldiers hereupon took the box and the jeweller back to the King, to whom the thief said, 'O King, this casket is mine.' But the jeweller protested, 'Nay, your Highness, this casket is not his property, but mine.'

"'If it is yours,' replied the thief, 'tell the King how many strings of pearls it contains.'

"'It contains one hundred,' at once said the jeweller.

"'No, no,' said the thief, 'not one hundred, but ninety-eight.'

"'Let the strings be counted,' commanded the King.

"This order was accordingly obeyed, when it was found, to the satisfaction of the court, that the thief had spoken truly. 'The whole of my pearl-caskets,' said the thief, 'have been stolen from me, and are now unlawfully held by this jeweller. If this casket had not been mine, how could I have known the number of strings contained in it?'

"'True,' said the King, 'the casket is evidently yours.' And he ordered the other caskets also to be delivered to him, but the jeweller was beaten with rods and cast into a prison.

"The robber, who had witnessed the whole of this knavery on the part of the thief, was amazed, and how to overreach such matchless impudence he was puzzled to say. However, he now joined him, and both the rogues went together to the woman's house and related the story.

"Now," cried the rat, "you must understand that the father of wisdom, who handed over these pearls to a common swindler and cheat, is also the father of this adorable Princess. That is what I saw and what I heard, and so I have told you."

The Princess was so enraged at hearing these concluding words that, being quite unable to restrain herself, she cried out to the leg of the bed, "When the morning comes you shall be cut off too, and thrown into the fire with your lying brother!"

Hardly had she spoken when the great drum was heard to resound for the second time, and all the people remarked it. "Salaam Alaikim!" cried the blacksmith's daughter, laughing. "Alaikim salaam!" answered the rat.

Some little time now passed by, when the blacksmith's daughter again broke silence.

"Delightful creature and most charming Princess," said she, "you have regaled me with an excellent story. But the night is long and tedious. Pray tell me another."

The rat, who had moved his position to the third leg of the bed, answered, "Good, I will tell you what I saw with my eyes and heard with my ears. My former story was all about the thief. You shall now hear the adventure of the robber.

"It was the next day that the robber said to the thief, 'It is now my turn. It is necessary, however, that you promise not to open your mouth to say a single word, since I kept strict silence with you. Otherwise you lose the prize.'

"To this condition the thief agreed, and both started once more and travelled to the same town. For some time the robber cudgelled his brains to no purpose for some device by which to surpass the thief. 'I must contrive some scheme,' thought he, 'to have the thief imprisoned and his gains transferred to myself.' On inquiry he learnt that the King was in the habit of sleeping on the roof of his palace, which was built in a pleasant place by the river-side. Said he to the thief, 'You must of course attend me as I attended you, and be a silent witness of my work.'

"Taking some iron pegs with him, the robber went to the palace, and, by fixing the pegs in the joints of the masonry one by one, he managed to climb to the roof. When he got to the top he perceived that the King was asleep, and that he was attended by a single guard who was pacing up and down. Watching his opportunity, he cut down the guard and threw his body into the river. Then taking up the musket, he assumed the sentry's functions, and begun pacing backwards and forwards, while the thief sat down at a distance and looked on.

"After a short time the King stirred, and cried, 'Sentry!'

"'Here I am, sir,' answered the robber.

"'Come near to me,' said the King, 'and sit down, and tell me a story, that my soul may rejoice.'

"So the robber approached the monarch, and, sitting down as he was directed, he told him the story of the jeweller, the thief, and the pearls. As the story progressed the thief began to tremble with fright, and made repeated signs to the robber to change the subject, or at least not to divulge his name or to betray him; but the robber pretended not to notice him, and went on with his tale. Then suddenly breaking off, he began to tell the King his own story, and how by means of iron pegs he had scaled the palace roof and killed his sentry.

"'Good heavens!' cried the King, looking round in consternation. 'Who are you? Tell me this instant!'

"'Sire,' answered the robber, 'be not alarmed—I am the robber.'

"'And where is my sentry?' asked the perplexed monarch.

"'I have just thrown his lifeless body into the river,' said the robber.

"The King was greatly alarmed. 'And yet,' thought he, 'this scoundrel might also have cut me down and disposed of me in the same way, and he didn't! He must be a good sort of fellow.' This consideration relieved the King's mind. 'Come near to me,' then said he aloud.

"'But,' replied the robber, 'I was telling your majesty the story of a thief. This person, you must know, now standing behind you, is the very thief in question, and the jeweller is innocent of any crime.' Saying these words, he led the thief forward by the ear.

"Morning now dawning, some attendants appeared, the thief was seized, and in due time the jeweller was released out of prison. Then the King, sitting on his judgment seat, gave orders that the pearls should be divided equally between the robber and the jeweller, and that the thief should be blown away from a gun. After this the robber joyfully returned home to his wife and took possession of his house.

"And now," continued the rat, "all I have to add is that the father of wisdom who rewards robbers with the property of other people is also the father of this charming lady."

Hearing these words, the Princess became more angry than ever, and cried, "O lying spirit, when morning comes I will burn you too!"

Then sounded the drum for the third and last time, and

the people of the city heard it, and, turning in their beds, said to their children, "To-morrow the Princess will be married."

"Salaam Alaikim!" said the blacksmith's daughter.

"Alaikim salaam!" answered the rat, after which the two friends parted, the rat going his own way, while his benefactress closed her eyes and slept.

The next morning the whole city was astir, eager for news of the Princess's wedding, and by common consent there was universal holiday. The blacksmith's daughter rose betimes, and, dressing herself with the utmost care, she went out to the stables, and there she saw her husband, Prince Ghûl, in the costume of a groom, rubbing down a horse with curry-comb and brush. She gazed at him very tenderly for a moment, while a tear came into her eye, but she hastily recovered herself, and returned to the palace. The whole day was devoted to feastings, games, and rejoicings; and by-and-by the priest came, and in the midst of the assembled dignitaries of the court the blacksmith's daughter and the Princess were united in marriage according to the forms in vogue among Muhammadans. When the ceremony was over the sham bridegroom addressed her bride and said, "I have fairly won you in spite of every difficulty, and now it is my will that for six months you are not to enter my chamber."

The wisdom of the pretended Prince was so great that her father-in-law paid her the greatest possible respect and consulted her in all affairs of state, and her manners and speech were so charming that she won all hearts. One of her earliest acts of grace was to petition the King to release all the unfortunate Princes who were engaged in menial attendance on her wife's horses, and to permit them to return to their homes. Her request was granted; but as she herself bore the order, she was careful while dismissing all the rest to except her own husband, and on him she laid her commands to bring to her his horse every morning saddled and bridled, and to attend her on her expeditions. Prince Ghûl, noticing all his companions restored to their liberty, could scarcely on these occasions forbear crying with vexation and disappointment as he said to himself, "I alone am left in slavery!"

After many days the blacksmith's daughter went to the King, and said, "O King, a favour! Give me leave to visit my own country and my own kindred." Her prayer was granted, and she was provided with an escort of horsemen, and with every comfort for the journey both for herself and for the Princess. Then she ordered Prince Ghûl never to leave her horse's side, and over him she set guards lest he should attempt to escape.

After several marches had been accomplished the Prince said to himself, "I perceive that we are going to my own country. Alas! what would the blacksmith's daughter say if she saw me in such a plight as this?"

When the cavalcade came within two or three marches of the capital, and had halted for the night, the blacksmith's daughter sent for her husband, and said to him, "I have now urgent business on hand, the nature of which I cannot communicate. It is enough that I require a disguise. Do you give me your groom's clothing, and, accepting some of mine in its place, represent me in my absence. Halt here for a month. In a short time I shall see you again."

The Prince, wondering at her request, obeyed, and assumed the dress of his supposed master. But she, having received his groom's clothing from a trusty attendant, together with his curry-comb and brush, locked them all up in a box, and, taking them with her, stole off in the darkness to her father's house.

A day or two having elapsed, and the blacksmith's daughter not returning, Prince Ghûl said, "This Prince bade me to remain here for a month with the Princess and her retinue. My father is a powerful King, and his capital is near. Why should I not carry off the Princess to my own home and swear that I won her?" So that night he gave order accordingly, and on the third day he arrived at his father's palace. He entered in triumph, and proclamation was made everywhere that Prince Ghûl had returned, and that he had won the famous dumb Princess; and when the people saw him riding through the street by the side of his father, who had gone forth with troops to escort him in, every house resounded with acclamations.

The next day Prince Ghûl sent a message to the house of the blacksmith, and ordered him to send his daughter to the palace. As soon as she appeared, he said to her, "Oh, you taunted me about this Princess, did you? Now what have you to say? Have I not won her?"

"Did you win her," quietly answered she, "or did I?"

"I did," protested he.

"Nay, I did," replied the girl.

She then stamped her little foot, and a servant brought in a box. When the company had been ordered to retire she unlocked the box, and took from it the old curry-comb, the brush, and the old suit of groom's clothes. Holding them up before the Prince, she asked, "Whose are these—yours or mine?"

The Prince was confounded, and for a moment he could not speak. He then stammered, "They are mine!"

"Did you, then, win the Princess," demanded she, "or did I?"

"You did," answered he.

"Ah," said the blacksmith's daughter, "if you with your father's ministers were not able even to tell the secret of the earthen jars, how could you possibly have won the dumb Princess? But now take her, and marry her, and let us all be happy at last."

Told at Hâji Shah, November 1879.

XCII

THE STORY OF LÂL BÂDSHÂH AND THE TWO LITTLE PRINCESSES

THERE was once a king, not Lâl Bâdshâh, but another, whose wife died, leaving him with two beautiful little daughters.

After a time, as he had no son to be his heir, his vizier said to him, "O King, it is right that you should marry again, so that your people may not be left without a Prince to rule over them hereafter." With this advice the King complied, and he brought to his palace a second wife. But she was of a morose and cruel disposition. She hated the two little Princesses, and starved them, and, in short, she acted the stepmother to the life.

These little girls, in their unhappiness, used to go out

hand-in-hand, and sit and pray by their dead mother's grave; and to their simple minds it did not seem at all strange that, when they had said their prayers, they should find by the grave a dish of food, which they always partook of. Day by day at their mother's grave they found a meal, and they said that God had sent it to them.

But the stepmother had a cat, and this cat took it into her head to follow the Princesses whenever they went to the grave, and the Princesses took notice of her and fed her with scraps.

One day the Queen was eyeing the children, and thinking to herself, "I give them only bran bread, and very little of that; how is it they are so fat?" Then the cat, who divined her thoughts, said, "The Princesses visit their mother's grave every day, and their mother feeds them. That is the reason they look so plump."

When the Queen heard this, she turned so sick with spite and vexation that in a day or two she had to take to her bed. But she pretended to be worse than she was, and at last she persuaded the King that she was at the point of death.

The King was greatly concerned, and said to her, "Can nothing be done for you?" This was just what the wicked woman wanted; so she answered, "I shall never recover until you have dug up the bones of your former wife and scattered them over the earth."

The King was very sorry, but to save her life he consented to do it, and his first wife's bones were taken up and scattered, and the stepmother then became quite well again all at once.

The two little girls now conferred together as to what they should do next. "What now?" asked the little one of the elder. Her sister answered, "We must trust in God. What is to be is to be, and our destiny must be fulfilled."

Now, though their mother's bones had been taken away, these two children continued their visits to the grave as before. Soon they observed a beautiful tree growing out of it, which bore delicious fruit; and, as they constantly ate of it, they were never hungry. One day, however, the cat followed them again, and when they saw her coming, the elder said, "Hide your fruit!"

"Nay," said the younger; "let me give her one plum."

"If you do," said the other, "she will know, and will tell the Queen."

So they hid their fruit, but one plum fell to the ground by accident; and when the cat saw it, she pounced upon it, and, putting it in her ear, took it away to show it to the Queen.

Then this wretched Queen fell sick again, and, going through the same pretence as before, she said to the foolish King, "I shall never be well until you cut down the tree which grows out of your first wife's grave and throw it into the fire."

The King therefore gave his orders, and the tree was removed root and branch, and they made a fire and burnt it up.

The Queen, however, was not satisfied even then. Her hatred of the Princesses increased, and she could no longer bear the sight of them: so, with first one reason and then another, she persuaded her husband to take them far away into the desert or into the forest, and to abandon them to their fate.

Early in the morning the King set out with his two little girls, and when he came to a lonely spot, he said to them, "Children, gather the pretty flowers and play and amuse yourselves, while I go down to that brook and wash my turban." Even kings were not above doing for themselves in those days, but this time the King only spoke to deceive.

Going to the brook, he set up an empty jar on the top of a long stick, and put a cloth over it, and the blowing of the wind made the side of the jar knock and knock against the stick, so that the children, when at intervals they heard the sound of the jar, believed it was their father who was washing his turban on the stones, after the manner of the country. At last, however, the day wore away, and it began to get late. Then they sought the brook to rejoin their father, but he, alas, was nowhere to be seen, and they called and called his name in vain.

The little girls were so distressed to find themselves forsaken and alone in the middle of the wilderness that they sat down and cried for a good hour. "O what now shall we do?" cried the younger one. Looking up, they saw a lofty rock towering over the trees, and they climbed to the top of it, and gazed all round. Then they saw some smoke rising up far in the distance, and, descending, they set out in the twilight to seek for it.

Before very long they arrived in front of a gloomy castle, where they found an old woman of great stature sitting before the door and blinking at the stars. She was an ogress, but she had the heart of a human being; and when she saw the children, she, being a woman, felt pity for them, and said, "Poor things! my son is a man-eater, and when he comes home he will eat you both up!"

"O hide us somewhere!" cried they.

Then the ogress took them up and turned them both into flies, and, when she had stuck pins into them, she fastened them to the wall.

Hardly had she done so, when, with a great roar, the ogre returned from the jungle. "O, O," cried he—

"'I smell man's flesh,
I smell man's blood!'"

"My son," said his mother, "there is no man here. There is no one but you and me only."

Then he sat down to his hog's flesh and his wine, and fell fast asleep.

In the morning early, after the ogre had gone out as usual, the old ogress pulled out the pins, and turned the children into their proper shapes. "Get away," said she, "as fast as you can; you will be getting me into trouble, too."

Right glad were the children to escape from that dreadful place, and they hastened away as fast as they could run. At last they came, towards evening, to a most pleasant spot, where there was an immense tree full of shade. In this tree they both passed the night, feeling thankful that they were safe from wild beasts and ogres.

The next day the elder sister remained in the tree sewing with silk, but the younger got down and went into the forest and collected some deer, which willingly followed her everywhere. So the two sisters lived on deer's milk and berries, and, as each had her own occupation, they passed a pleasant time.

One day the elder gave the younger sister a flower, and said to her, "Sister, you go out every day, and while you are away something might happen. When this flower fades you will know that I am in trouble, and when I drop my needle I shall know that you are in trouble."

Some time after this it happened that a King, named Lâl Bâdshâh, with all his retinue, came out hunting in that very forest, but after a long day's chase he succeeded in shooting only a single partridge. As he was hungry, he said to his minister, "Vizier, go—see, there is smoke!—cook this partridge for me, and bring it back."

So the vizier took the partridge and began to cook it over the fire, to which he was easily guided by the smoke. But it was the fire of the two Princesses, the younger of whom was still in the forest. As the vizier was cooking the partridge he happened to look up, and he saw the elder sister in the tree. The sight of her so astonished him that, instead of attending to his duty, he kept staring at her, wondering who and what she could be, and so the partridge got burnt.

When the vizier perceived that the bird was spoilt, he began to mutter in great distress, being quite in despair, fearing the King's anger. Then the Princess said to him, "Why are you crying?"

"Because," answered he, "I have burnt the King's partridge."

"If you will make a solemn promise of secrecy," said she, "I will help you."

The vizier faithfully promised, and the Princess, descending, made up a delicious dish of partridge and deer's milk, and sent it to the King.

The King was quite delighted, and he said to his minister, "Vizier, who cooked this partridge?"

"I cooked it," answered he.

"Who cooked this partridge?" repeated the King.

"I cooked it," repeated the vizier.

"Who cooked this partridge?" once more cried the King.

"I cooked it," once more replied the vizier.

"Bury him alive!" screamed the King.

Some of the guard came forward, and, digging a great hole, they thrust in the unlucky vizier, and began to throw the earth over him. When he was buried as high as the neck, the King asked him once more, "Who cooked this partridge?" and still the vizier answered, "I cooked it."

"This is a very obstinate fellow," said the King. "In with the earth!"

When he was buried to the mouth, the King for the last time asked him, "Who cooked this partridge?"

"Take me out, take me out," cried the vizier, "and I will confess."

So he was released from his grave, and then he told the King the whole story.

Lâl Bâdshâh was astonished beyond measure when he heard that a beautiful young Princess was living in a tree. Nor was it long before he visited her, when he was so struck with her great beauty and refined manners that he married her there and then, and carried her off on his horse.

The poor girl would have been better pleased if she had been allowed to remain in the tree, and, as she thought of her absent sister, she became very sorrowful. Fortunately, she had a bag of mustard-seed, which she took with her, and as she rode along she dropped the seed on the ground to mark the way.

The younger sister was some distance off, when she suddenly observed that her flower began to fade. So she hastened back as fast as she could; but she was too late: her sister had gone. "Alas!" cried she, "what new misfortune is this? Where can my sister be?" She then noticed the mustard-seed, and perceived that it was a track leading into the forest. Instantly she decided to follow it, and, with her deer gambolling about her, she at once set out.

The track led her to a fine city, where she heard that her sister was now the most favoured Queen in the King's palace. Resolving to remain in that place, in the hope that she might some day be able to communicate with her, the younger sister made herself a little wicker cabin on an ancient mound, past which flowed a brook, just outside of the city gates. Here she dwelt, by day taking out her deer to graze, and by night sleeping with them in the cabin.

The elder sister, however, though she was so beloved by the King, was hated by all her rivals. They were jealous of her power and of her superior beauty. And when, in the course of time, the poor Queen had a baby, they stole it and threw it out of the city, close to the old mound, and instead of it they placed by her bed a basket of charcoal.

Having done this, they went to the King, and said, "This new Queen of yours has been brought to bed. But, instead of a baby, she has given birth to a basket of charcoal." Naturally, the King was very angry, and he ordered his young wife to be cast into a dungeon.

It so happened that the poor little outcast infant was rescued by its aunt, the younger sister, and as the story of the Queen's disgrace was soon bruited abroad, she easily recognized the child as the King's. So she took to it, showering on it the greatest affection, and nursing it with deer's milk.

Some time elapsed, and the child had grown into a handsome little lad of four or five years, when the aunt observed that the King frequently rode out past the mound, and that he sometimes stopped to water his horse at the brook. So she made for the little Prince a wooden horse as a plaything, and she told him to look out for the King. "Whenever," said she, "the King stops to water his horse, do you water your horse, too, and say, 'Drink, O horse!'"

The child was quite charmed with his new toy, and already imagined himself a gallant knight charging his enemies. When the King came to the brook, as usual he stopped to give his horse some water, and the Prince, seeing him, pranced down to the brook, too, and cried, "Drink, O horse!"

"Silly boy," said the King to him, "can a wooden horse drink?"

In the evening the child reported all this to his aunt—how the King had come, and what he had said. "Tomorrow," said she, "you must do exactly the same thing, and to the King's question you are to answer, 'But, O King, did a woman ever give birth to a basket of charcoal?'"

The next day Lâl Bâdshâh was again watering his horse at the brook, and by his side the little Prince was watering his, saying, "Drink, O horse!"

"Foolish boy," said the King, "how can a wooden horse drink water?"

"And, O King," answered the child, "how can a woman bring forth a basket of charcoal?"

This answer quite startled the King. "Now, what can be the meaning of this?" he said; and, noticing that the little boy entered the wicker cabin, he approached it, and, dismounting, went behind it to listen. He then heard the aunt saying, "Did you repeat to the King what I told you?" And the boy answered, "Yes," and related all that had happened. Then said the aunt, "Lâl Bâdshâh can by no means be a wise King, or else from your answer he would have guessed the truth."

On hearing these words, the King approached the door, and the aunt at once rose up to pay him respect. "This boy of yours," said he, "has just given me a most mysterious answer. What does it mean?"

So the aunt told him the whole history of her life and of her sister's life, and revealed to him the secret of the boy's birth. Never was the King so pleased in the whole course of his life. He acknowledged his son as heir to his empire, he restored his injured Queen to her position and rank, and he amply provided for her younger sister. And so, after many misfortunes, the two sisters, who loved each other so truly, were united once more, and lived happily ever after.

Told at Torbela, July 1880.

XCIII

STORY OF PRINCE BAIRÂM AND THE FAIRY BRIDE

ONCE upon a time the king of the giants from the mountains of Kôh Kâf came to visit the kingdoms of men. His name was Safeyd. As he was wandering over the earth he entered a forest, and there he saw a merry company of huntsmen chasing the deer. Their leader was a young prince named Bairâm, and the beauty of this youth was so striking and so unusual that the giant Safeyd felt that he loved him, and that he would never again know happiness or contentment unless he became possessed of him. So he turned himself into a fine horse, with a skin like snow and a neigh like thunder, and in that form repeatedly crossed the path of the Prince to attract his attention.

The Prince was enchanted when he saw so noble a steed, and gave orders that he should be caught. Safeyd was only too glad to permit himself to be saddled and bridled, and to suffer the Prince of whom he was enamoured to vault on to his back. No sooner did he feel him safely seated, however, than he galloped away, and never stopped until he had arrived at his own palace in the mountains which girdle the earth. There he heaped on him every favour, loaded him with gold and precious stones, gave him splendid steeds and hundreds of attendants, clothed him in the richest apparel, and lodged him in a magnificent palace.

After eight days the giant Safeyd came to Bairâm and said, "I shall now leave you for eight days. I must go to my brother's wedding. You, however, will remain here; but take this key, which will admit you into an inner garden, which hitherto no one has entered but myself. When you go, go alone, and remember to lock the door again when you return." So the giant gave the Prince the key, and at once set off for the kingdom of his brother.

That very evening Bairâm went to the garden, which surpassed all he had ever imagined. There stood within it a wonderful pavilion of jasper, set with precious stones: fountains played on all sides, and the trees, instead of fruit, were laden with rubies, emeralds and sapphires. Sitting down, he watched the fountains throwing up golden spray, and the reflections mirrored in the beautiful pools. Just then four milk-white doves flew on to a tree, and then settled in the shape of four fairies by the edge of a tank of clear crystal water. Their beauty seemed to dazzle his eyes. Having unrobed, they entered the water and began to bathe; and as they were bathing one of them said to the others, "I have had a dream, and by my dream I can tell that one of us shall be parted from the rest." They then stepped one by one out of the water and began to dress; but the most beautiful fairy of all could not find her clothes. Meanwhile, the others, having finished dressing, turned once more into milk-white doves and flew away, the fourth fairy, whose name was Ghulâb Bâno, exclaiming as she bade them farewell, "It is my kismet. Some different destiny awaits me here, and we shall never meet again." She then looked towards the steps and saw the Prince. At once her heart escaped from her body, and she fell in love with him. Now, it was the Prince himself who had stolen the fairy's clothes and hidden them, and, as he knew that if she recovered them she would change into a milk-white dove again, he now brought out another suit, and she clothed herself, and the two lovers remained in the garden.

When eight days had passed the giant Safeyd returned once more to his house. And when Bairâm saw the huge chains which encircled his waist he began to tremble with fear; but the giant reassured him, saying, "Fear not; are you not master of all I possess?" and he ordered music to play and dancing girls to assemble in numbers to beguile and cheer his spirits, but they were all invisible.

"Do you see them?" asked the giant.

"No," answered the Prince; "I see nothing, but I hear the music and the tinkling of anklets."

"I will give you some of King Solomon's antimony," said the giant. "Touch your eyes with it."

And when Prince Bairâm had touched his eyes with King Solomon's antimony he saw the whole place filled with troops of exquisite damsels, dancing to the music of viol and drum.

Now, the beautiful fairy whom the Prince had captured in the garden was one of the wives of the giant, and the giant knew all that had passed. But his love for Bairâm was so great that he said to him, "Take not only Ghulâb Bâno, but all I possess you can take as well."

One day the fairy grew sad and said, "Give me leave to visit my father and mother and to return." So the Prince brought out her fairy clothes, and she changed into a milk-white dove and away she flew. But her parents, when they heard the news, were angry that she had married a mortal, and they imprisoned her in a gloomy subterranean city. Therefore she did not return; and as time went on and still she came not, Prince Bairâm began to pine and droop from sorrow, and for his sake, too, the giant grew sad and melancholy. At last the Prince cried, "I must follow her, and never come back till I find her."

"Are you quite resolved to go?" asked the giant.

"I can no longer live," said he, "without her."

Then the giant gave him three things; his invisible cap, some of King Solomon's antimony, and one of his own hairs. So the Prince set out, and after many days he came to the subterranean city. But because it was all in darkness, and he could not see his way, he rubbed his eyes with the antimony, which made everything plain and clear before him. Then he inquired, and found that the fairy Ghulâb Bâno was imprisoned in a lofty tower of one hundred iron doors. And when he found himself before the tower he put on his magic cap, which rendered him invisible, and which also compelled all the doors to fly wide open. He then entered, and when he saw the fairy Princess he took off his cap and rushed into her arms, and with her he remained for many days.

A woman can never keep a secret.[1] It was not long before Ghulâb Bâno began to whisper to some of her favourite maids, and to tell her intimate friends the good fortune which had smiled on her in the midst of her banishment. Then the news spread until it reached the ears of her father. He collected his giants together, and, going to the tower, they found the Prince with the Princess. They were horrified, and cried, "Come, let us kill him!" Immediately the Prince awoke, and, seeing his peril, he put on his magic cap, which made him invisible. Then he took the giant Safeyd's hair, and held it in the flame of the lamp; and as the smoke rose a thousand squadrons of giants at once assembled. There was a great battle, the enemy was routed, and the enraged father compelled to surrender his daughter to Prince Bairâm. After this Safeyd and the Prince and the fairy returned in triumph to their beautiful home.

By-and-by, when some years had now elapsed, the Prince began to long for his own kingdom, and his longing grew so great that at last he determined to go. The giant became very sad, but on account of his love for him he allowed him leave. Then Ghulâb Bâno changed herself into an enormous bird, and the Prince mounted between her wings, and in a moment they alighted close to the capital. There the Prince disguised himself as a poor fakîr, while his wife became a milk-white dove. Then he entered the city and called on his old nurse, who at once recognized him, and told him that his vizier had seized the kingdom and was reigning in his stead.

[1] This sentence is literally translated, and reflects the views of the Panjâbîs.

"And where are my wives?" asked Bairâm.

"Three of your wives," answered she, "he took to be his wives; but the fourth defied him, and because of her fidelity he imprisoned her in a pit. There a son was born, and there the mother and the babe still remain, and he feeds them with the leavings of his hounds."

For a time the Prince lodged with his nurse, the fairy having resumed her own shape, but one day when he was out news was taken to the false King that a woman surpassing in beauty all the women of the earth had been seen at the house of the old woman. So the false King rushed to the spot, seized Ghulâb Bâno by the arm, and cried, "Come along with me!"

"O King," answered she, "let me first go in and change my clothes."

So she left him waiting at the door, but having entered her chamber, she put on her fairy suit, and, at once changing into a milk-white dove, flew out of the window, and sped far away, but the false King went back to the palace vexed and defeated.

When Bairâm returned, the first thing he said was, "Where is my wife?"

"She has gone to the vizier's," said the woman. "He came and carried her off."

So the Prince took out the giant's hair and held it again in the flame, when instantly there rushed to his help thousands of giants with clubs and swords, and the city was taken, the vizier and the three false wives were slaughtered, while the faithful wife was delivered from the pit and restored to the palace as queen once more. With her Prince Bairâm lived for some time, being always kind and good to her; but he sighed for the fairy Princess, who had flown back to her father's house and had never returned. By degrees his melancholy increased more and more, until, becoming mad, he wandered about the city and the palace and the forest, seeking in vain for his lost love.

Meanwhile the giant Safeyd grew melancholy also, and at last he could bear his grief no longer. So he set out for the kingdom of his friend Bairâm, and, having found him, he carried him away and restored him again to his fairy queen. With her he recovered his health, and his whole after-life was spent in happiness and delight, sometimes with Ghulâb Bâno among the mountains of Kôh Kâf, and sometimes with his faithful wife in the capital of his own kingdom. But at last he left his wife for good and never returned again.

XCIV

OF THE SILLY WEAVER-GIRL

A CERTAIN quarter of a village was inhabited only by weavers. One day a fine young weaver-girl was sweeping out the house, and as she swept she said to herself, "My father and mother, and all my relations, belong to this village. It would be a good thing if I married in this village, and settled here too, so that we should always be together. But," continued she, "if I did marry here, and had a son, and if my son were to sicken and die, oh, how my aunts, my sisters, and my friends would come, and how they would all bewail him!" Thinking of this, she laid her broom against the wall, and began to cry. In came her aunts and her friends, and, seeing her in such distress, they all began to cry too. Then came her father and her uncles and her brothers, and they also began to cry most bitterly; but not one of them had the wit to say, "What is the matter?—for whom is this wailing?" At last, when the noise and the weeping had continued for some time, a neighbour said—

"What bad news have you had? Who is dead here?"

"I don't know," answered one of the howling uncles. "These women know; ask one of them."

At this point the head-man arrived at the spot, and cried, "Stop, stop this hubbub, good people, and let us find out what is the matter." Addressing himself to an old woman, he said—

"What is all this disturbance in the village for?"

"How can I tell?" blubbered she. "When I came here, I found this weaver-girl crying about something."

Then the weaver-girl, on being questioned, said, "I was weeping because I could not help thinking how, if I married in this village, and had a son, and if my poor son were to sicken and die, all my aunts, my sisters, and my friends would come round me, and how we should all bewail him. The very thought of it made me cry."

On hearing her answer, the head-man and his followers began to laugh, and the crowd dispersed.

XCV

OF THE TIGER AND THE CAT

TIGERS at first were ignorant, until the king of the tigers once came to the cat and begged him for lessons. The cat, consenting, taught the tiger to watch, to crouch, to spring, and all the other accomplishments so familiar to the race. At last, when he thought he had learnt everything the cat had to impart, the tiger made a spring at his teacher, intending to tear him and eat him. Instantly the cat ran nimbly up a tree, whither the tiger was unable to follow.

"Come down!" cried the tiger, "come down instantly!"

"No, no!" replied the cat. "How fortunate for me that I did not teach you more! Otherwise you would have been able to pursue me even here."

XCVI

THE STORY OF THE PRINCESS AND THE OGRES

"MY STORY IS ABOUT EARTHLY KINGS, BUT THE TRUE KING IS GOD."

ONCE upon a time a certain king went out hunting in the forest. After chasing his game the whole day, he found a wild, fierce woman sitting alone, who, as soon as he came near, sprang to her feet and caught hold of his bridle.

"Who are you?" cried the startled King. "Are you a woman or a demon? Let my horse go!"

"My name is What-will-be-will-be," replied the woman, "and one day I shall make you feel my power."

The King asked her, "But when will this thing be?"

"Choose, O King," answered she, "whether I shall bring it upon you now or at some distant period!"

"Let me not answer you now," said the King; "let me first go and consult my Queen, and I will return and tell you."

"Go," said the fierce old hag; "I shall await you here."

So the King rode home, and as he entered his palace his looks were distressed. Said the Queen to him, "Your looks betoken trouble; what is the matter?"

"Oh, do not ask me what is the matter!" answered he. "I met in the forest an old witch named What-will-be-will-be, and she has bidden me choose whether adversity shall fall upon us now or hereafter. What shall I tell her?"

"You and I," replied the Queen, "are both of us young and strong. Choose, then, that the trouble may visit us soon, while we are well able to meet and to bear it."

Then the King returned to the forest, and to the old woman, whom he found in the same spot, he said, "Whatever is to befall us, let it come now, and not hereafter."

"Be it so," answered the woman. "You have your wish."

Scarcely had the King arrived at his capital when a mounted messenger met him and informed him that the king of another country was at hand with a vast army to make war upon him. In the battle which ensued this unfortunate monarch was totally routed, and his kingdom fell into the hands of his enemy. But he himself, with his Queen and two Princes his sons, and his sons' two wives, having all armed themselves, and having mounted upon swift horses, fled away from the city and escaped.

On and on they went, as strangers in strange lands, until at last the whole of their money was expended, and poverty and want began to stare them in the face. Then the King said to himself, "If we could only leave my sons' wives somewhere, and steal away from them unperceived, our troubles would diminish, for we should have fewer mouths to provide for."

Having formed this cruel design, he soon carried it into practice, and one night, when the two young Princesses were wrapt in slumber, the rest of the party, leaving the unfortunate girls a couple of horses and some arms, abandoned them in the wilderness.

When the two Princesses awoke, they looked about them, and found themselves alone; and having cried for their friends in vain, they began to say to each other, "What shall we do now?"

"If we both travel in these wild places as women," said the elder and wiser sister, "we shall be robbed and cruelly treated."

So she set to work, and in a short time she had altered her feminine robes into a man's attire, and having assumed her arms, she mounted her horse, and she then looked a noble young prince, both valiant and strong, while her beautiful sister, in her own raiment, rode beside her.

The two Princesses now set out again to search for their friends, but they rode and searched in vain. No signs of them were to be discovered or seen, neither could they hear any tidings of them.

One day they came to a certain city where there was a king, and in this city the elder sister determined to tarry. So she took a small house for herself and her sister, and every day in her masculine disguise, mounted, and armed with sword and lance, she attended the court of the King, until at last the King observed her, and said to his vizier, "Who is that stranger who comes every day to court?"

Then the minister approached the Princess, and asked

her, "Who are you? Are you a king's son or a merchant's son? What are you, and whence came you?"

"I am in need of nothing," answered the Princess. "I am merely looking for a lost brother."

Then the King called for her, and said to her, "If honourable service were offered to you, would you accept it?"

"Yes," answered the girl, "but only to become one of your own body-guard."

The King, who had taken a fancy to this handsome youth, as he supposed the Princess to be, immediately made out an order for her, and she was enrolled as a member of his body-guard.

Her duties were light and her payment liberal. She was most assiduous to please, watching the King with careful fidelity whenever she was on guard, ever active and alert, but never forgetting that her chief concern was to scan the faces of all new-comers, if by any chance her own friends should be among them.

Now, it was a custom in that country that if a criminal were sentenced to death he should be conducted by the executioners to a wild place and hanged on a tree or a gallows, and there at once abandoned, either to escape if he could, or to be the prey of the vultures. One evening, when the Princess was on sentry over the King, a notorious robber was thus taken out and hanged. In the middle of the night the Princess heard a dismal howling and wailing, and fearing that some danger was approaching, she boldly entered the forest to find out the cause of the disturbance. In a few minutes she came to the gallows-tree, on which the dead robber was swaying in the wind, and under the tree she noticed what appeared to be a miserable gaunt woman, who from time to time set up the dismal howling which had so greatly alarmed her. In reality, however, the creature was not a woman, but a female ghoul—that is, a demon in human form, who, like the vampire, wanders about at night and feeds upon corpses.

"Who are you?" demanded the Princess.

"This man who has been hanged is my son," answered the monster. "He hangs too high for me to reach him, for I am old and feeble. If you would lift me up, O strong young sir, I might perhaps kiss him once more, as I shall never see his face again."

The Princess, who did not suspect her true character, raised her up to the body; but the ghoul, instead of kissing it, seized it by the neck with her teeth, and began to suck the blood. Perceiving this horror, the Princess instantly dropped her, and, drawing her sword, she struck at her; but the ghoul evaded the stroke and fled. Nevertheless, the Princess had severed a piece of her clothing, which she picked up, and, examining it, she found it was composed of the very richest material, worked in strange and fantastic figures, with threads of gold.

Returning at once to the palace, the Princess found the King sitting up awake. "You are posted here," said he, "to guard me from intrusion. Where have you been?"

Then the Princess related to the King the whole story, telling him of the dismal wailings and of the female ghoul who had sucked the blood of the robber. The King was incredulous, and said to her, "Have you any proof of the truth of this extraordinary adventure?"

Then she showed him the piece of cloth, which the King inspected with astonishment and admiration. "This cloth," said he, "is of the rarest quality and most precious."

He was so pleased that he gave the Princess a bag of gold, and sent the cloth as a present to the Queen his wife, who, as soon as she had seen and examined it, longed for more of it, and so she sent word to the King, "Such beautiful cloth has never before been seen in the kingdom. I would have a whole suit of it."

The King now said to the Princess, "Wherever it was you obtained this wonderful cloth, you must depart instantly and fetch me more of the same pattern."

The Princess was amazed at such an order, and answered, "Who knows whence the ghoul came or whither she has gone? Where am I to look for her?"

This objection the King merely waved aside. "If you bring the cloth it will be well with you," said he, "but if not, your head shall answer for it!"

"Be it so," said the Princess, with confidence. "But, O King, grant me time."

To this request the King assented, and, giving her both time and abundance of money, ordered her to set out forthwith.

The next morning she bade her sister farewell, and started on her quest of the ghoul's coat. Many a day she journeyed, until at last she found herself in the territories of another king. In the midst of this kingdom she arrived at a half-abandoned city, where grass was growing in the streets, and where the few inhabitants wore a melancholy and woe-begone aspect. Here she perceived an old woman surrounded by one or two others, all of whom were kneading huge quantities of dough. As she gazed in wonder, she noticed that the old woman was crying and lamenting.

"O mother," said the Princess, "you are both baking bread and crying! What is the matter?"

"Every eighth day a ghoul comes here," answered she —"a monster from the mountains; and the tribute he receives by the King's order is a human being, a buck goat, and two hundred pounds of bread. The reason I am crying is that to-day it is my turn, and that I have to give the ghoul my only son."

Then said the Princess to the old woman, "Mother, do not cry. When you have the bread ready, let it be taken with the goat to the usual place, and thither I also will go instead of your son."

"But who in the world," said the woman, "would give his life for another?"

Now, the King of that country had made an order that whosoever should kill or drive away the ghoul should be rewarded with riches and honoured with the hand of one of his daughters. And the Princess, having heard of this order, turned to the old woman, and said, "But is no one able to kill the ghoul?"

"No one whatever," answered she.

"Well," said the Princess, "at least come and show me the place where he is accustomed to feed."

When the bread was all ready, the old woman and her son, and the buck goat, proceeded with the Princess to the spot. In that dismal place, which lay without the city-walls, there stood an old hut, and there the whole tribute used to be put for the ghoul, who always came at night and devoured it all before the morning. Going into the hut, the Princess first dug a great hole. Then she placed the goat and the heap of bread on one side, and on the other she set up a log of wood dressed up to look in the darkness like a boy. Having completed these arrangements, she dismissed the old woman and her friends, and descended herself into the pit, where, with her sword ready drawn in her hand, she crouched down and hid herself. In the middle of the night she heard a roar, and the ghoul, in the form of a gigantic man, rushed into the hut and began to devour. When he had eaten the bread and the buck goat, he went to the log and seized it ravenously. At that moment the Princess rose from her pit, and smote and cut off one of his legs, which so startled the brute that he instantly fled from the hut on his other leg, and made his escape to the hills with the utmost despatch.

In the morning the Princess returned to the city, and said to the old woman, "I had an encounter with the ghoul last night, and he has been punished so handsomely that he will never trouble you or your neighbours again."

Every one was astonished, and some cried "Nonsense!" but the most hopeless were convinced when the Princess displayed to them the monster's horrid leg. Then the old woman gave away both money and food in charity for the sake of their glorious deliverer, and because of herself and her son, whom he had delivered from destruction.

When the King, who dwelt in the citadel, heard the news of this exploit he also was surprised beyond measure, and he sent for the Princess and treated her with the utmost honour.

"How did you manage to accomplish this great achievement?" asked he.

Then the Princess told him the history of her adventure without adding to or diminishing aught from the simple truth. The King listened with gratified interest, and rewarded the heroine by saying to her, "It is a decree of mine that whoso shall kill the ghoul or drive him out of my dominions shall receive the hand of my daughter in marriage. The lady is ready, and, therefore, if you are willing to marry her, pray do so."

The Princess was more than grateful for this proof of the King's generosity and goodwill, yet she answered him, "O King, I have still another enterprise on hand, but when that is safely accomplished I shall again return to your court."

The King then suffered her to depart, and so, mounting her horse, she travelled on and on again for weeks and months. At last, in the midst of craggy mountains and gloomy defiles belonging to a third kingdom, she came to a lonely fortress with frowning walls and forbidding appearance. Entering the open gateway, she found herself in a courtyard, and there she saw a gentle maiden sitting spinning, but no one else was visible anywhere. When the girl saw the Princess, she first laughed, and then she cried. The Princess was amazed, and, going up to her, she said, "Why do you both laugh and cry?"

"Never since the day of my birth," answered the girl, "have I seen a man, and when I saw you, therefore, I laughed. But I cried because the ghouls who live in this castle will certainly eat you up."

"How many ghouls are there?" asked the Princess.

"There are two of them," answered the girl, "and one of them is the husband of the other."

"But is there no way of escape for me?" inquired the Princess.

"For this one night," said the girl, "I may be able to save you from them, but not for more."

She then rose, and with looks of love conducted the Princess to a lonely chamber, and having left some food and some water with her, she fastened the door and came away.

As the shadows began to fall, the two ghouls returned to their gloomy castle, bringing with them some buck goats and the remains of a human being. Having made their horrid evening meal, they poured out quantities of wine into golden goblets and began to quaff and to make merry. Then, looking at the girl, one of them said to the other, "About this girl of ours, whom we stole as a baby: it is time that we should find a husband for her. If now we could capture a brave man, we might marry them together."

"I could recognize the man who cut off the skirt of my coat," answered the female ghoul. "If we could find him, we might marry her to him, for a braver man never lived."

"Ah," replied the male ghoul, "but he was a braver man a great deal who cut off my leg."

The two ghouls now began to dispute and to fall out as to which of the two men was the braver, the male ghoul asserting that the girl should be married to the man who cut off his leg, and the female protesting that she should be the wife of the man who cut off the end of her embroidered coat. And so they fell asleep.

In the morning the two ghouls went away as usual to hunt for man's flesh, and the girl, going to the secret chamber, released the Princess from her lonely tower, and brought her forth, telling her as she did so all that had passed between the two ghouls the night before.

"But," continued she, "I would rather marry you, dear Prince, if the ghouls would allow me."

Then the Princess inquired further into their history, and the girl told her the story of the ghouls' misfortunes: how one lost part of her garment, and the other his leg.

"But," said the Princess, "it was I who deprived them of both; I cut off the leg of the one, and I cut off some of the cloak of the other. Would they, then, give you to me?"

"They would be most willing to do so," replied the girl, astonished and pleased.

That day passed in visiting the rooms of the castle and in wondering at its vast treasures and stores of all manner of rarities, and in the evening the Princess was again hidden in the secret chamber.

When the ghouls returned, they feasted and caroused as before, and when warmed with wine they again began to dispute as to who should marry the girl, each, without knowing it, extolling the bravery of the same hero. Then said the girl, "But perhaps it was the one man who achieved both those wonderful exploits. If so, would you allow him to marry me?"

"Marry you?" cried they. "Of course he should marry you, and take you wherever he pleased."

"Then," said the girl, "give me your most solemn assurance that, if he can be found, you will not kill him."

"We make the promise, of course," said they.

Then, going to the secret chamber, the girl brought forth the Princess, and took her in before them, and both the savages, at once recognizing her, gazed at her with wonder, admiration, and astonishment.

"How did you contrive so well to cut off my leg?" asked the male ghoul.

"I dug a hole in the floor of the hut," answered the undaunted Princess, "and in that I hid myself, and the goat and the bread I put on one side, and a dressed-up log on the other; and when you passed by me to seize the log, I raised my sword and at a blow off came your leg."

"Wonderful!" cried the male ghoul, in tones of awe.

"And how did you cut off the skirt of my coat?" asked the female ghoul.

"When I saw what a monster you were," answered the Princess, "and when I heard you sucking the blood of the dead robber, I dropped you on the ground, and, drawing my sword, I made a stroke at you, and thus it was that I cut off the skirt of your coat."

"O most wonderful Prince!" cried the female ghoul, equally amazed.

Then said they, "Now take away this girl with you. You have won her; she is yours. Take her to your own country, and marry her."

When the Princess and her bride were all ready for the journey, the ghouls loaded them with heaps of money and presents.

"One thing only I care for," said the Princess, "and that is the coat of embroidered gold of which I have already a piece."

Her wish was no sooner expressed than it was gratified, and for the sake of the girl the ghouls presented her with much more of the same material as well. After this they accompanied the pair to the borders of their own territory, and there they left them.

Journeying on, the Princess and her young bride arrived at the city which had formerly suffered so greatly from the exactions of the male ghoul. The King was enchanted to welcome her back, and gave her his daughter in marriage in accordance with his promise, together with riches in abundance, after which she continued her journey to the country of her own King; and having arrived at the capital she committed her two wives to the custody of her younger sister, and at once rode on to the palace. There she presented the whole of the wonderful cloth which she had brought from the castle of the ghouls; and the King was so delighted that he instantly said to her, "Now you shall be my prime minister, and you shall live in a palace of your own."

"Very well," answered the Princess, and at once the

order was made out, the decree published, and she was promoted to the head of affairs.

The Princess was now both powerful and wealthy, but she never for a moment forgot the one object of her life, which was to find her lost friends. With this thought ever present in her mind, she one day said to the King, "If you will allow me, I would make a large garden to contain trees and plants of every kind."

The King approved of her plan, and gave her an immense tract of land for the purpose. Her design was that her garden should be the wonder of the whole world, and so there was not a country to which she did not send her messengers to make known that whosoever would bring her a plant for her garden should receive two gold mohurs. But all the time she was thinking of her dear friends, and hoping that in their poverty and obscurity, wherever they were, they might hear tidings of her wonderful garden, and be induced to bring her some plants for the sake of the reward.

For months this good Princess was doomed to disappointment, for, though thousands came with plants of the rarest varieties, her own relations came not. At last the King, her first father-in-law, in his distant exile, heard the proclamation, and, as he was very poor, he and the Queen his wife, and their two sons, searched for the rarest plants, and carried them to the famous garden. There, notwithstanding their altered condition, their ragged clothing, and their attenuated frames, they were immediately recognized by the Princess. But she refrained herself, and ordered them to be confined in a certain house, over which she placed a guard, while at the same time she herself occupied a room in which she could overhear all they spoke about.

The first thing the King said was, "Strange! all others receive rewards and are allowed to depart, but we only are placed here under restraint."

"I suppose," said the Queen, "we are being punished by God for having so cruelly abandoned those two poor girls in the desert."

No longer able to restrain herself, the Princess left the house and at once ordered her friends to be conducted into sumptuous chambers, and to be supplied with baths and rich clothing, and with food and wine of the best. Then she had them all brought into her own palace, and, in her character and disguise of prime minister of the kingdom, she received them as if for the purpose of a mere audience, nor had any of them any suspicion of her real identity. Having seated them on chairs, she gazed on them, and said, "What is your history?"

"We were once a royal family," answered the aged King, "but misfortune befell us, and we were driven from our kingdom. Then, in our need and distress, we abandoned the young wives of my two sons in a lonely place, and ever since we have lived poor, unblest and unknown."

"Yes," said the Princess, "I suppose you left the Princesses because of your necessity. Notwithstanding, every child of man has to eat his own kismet."

Then she left the room, and for the first time for years she assumed her own proper habit, and taking her sister by the hand, she led her into the apartment, and looking at the young Princes, their husbands, she said, "You left behind in the desert your two wives, but now God has restored them to you once more."

Then she turned to the King and Queen, and there followed many a fond embrace, with tears and words of surprise and of love, and they were all reunited in a lasting reconciliation.

The next morning the Princess went to the King, and said to him, "The time has come when I must reveal to you the secret of my life. No longer a man, I now assume my proper character, for I am really the wife of a prince of ancient lineage, and my husband is here."

Then she related the story of her life, and said, "And now assist us with a suitable army, that we may take the field and recover our own lost inheritance. But if not, then permit me to remain here, and give my friends positions near your own person."

"Choose," said the King, "which you will have."

"Let us, then, have the troops," answered she, "and the treasure to wage a campaign."

To this proposal the King joyfully agreed, and the Princess, with all her friends, set out at the head of an invincible army, and having routed the usurper in a signal battle, they recovered their lost dominion, and the old King ascended his throne and reigned once more. Then, having provided splendid matches for the two beautiful girls whom the Princess had married in her expedition against the ghouls, the whole united family settled down in peace and prosperity, and lived happily ever afterwards.

Told by a villager of Ghâzî, November 1881.

XCVII

OF THE PRIEST WHO FEIGNED TO BE DEAD

THERE was a certain priest who was constantly preaching, "Give of your goods in charity, give of your goods to the mosque! Whosoever will give to the mosque, whether bread, or milk, or fowls, the same shall have houris in heaven."

One day his wife accidentally overheard his exhortations, and instantly going home, she prepared quantities of most delicious food, which she sent by a safe messenger to the mosque, in the devout belief that houris of the opposite sex would await her also in Paradise. The priest, not knowing whose food it was, took it in with the utmost pleasure, crying aloud, "Hear, you people, to-day some one has sent to the mosque a proper offering! Some excellent person gives good things! May God show mercy on him! He shall be blessed with houris!"

So saying, the priest sat down to the mess, part of which he ate himself, while some he gave to the people. Then, when his duty was over, he went home never so jovial to his wife, who greeted him with smiles, saying, "Come, sit down and eat bread!"

"I think I could manage a little," said the priest, "but I have already eaten most heartily."

"But you don't know," answered his wife, "that all that nice food was sent to the mosque by me!"

"What!" cried the priest; "you sent those dishes?"

"Yes, certainly!" answered his wife.

On hearing the news the priest nearly fainted away.

"I overheard you preaching," said the woman, "and I made a vow, and my vow I shall keep!"

Then said the priest, "Now let me die! What is life to me if you are going to play the fool with my goods like that?"

"Nay, don't die," said his wife; "don't die, there's a good soul! Surely we have plenty, and the more we give, the more we shall get. It was yourself who said so!"

"Yes," said the priest; "but my sermons are for the people, not for you to go and destroy my house and bring ruin on your husband!"

Then he stretched himself out on his cot, saying, "Now will I die!"

"Whether you die or whether you live," said his wife, "I have made a vow, and my vow I shall keep."

As they were both determined, he to die, and she to give of his goods, all the people of the village came about her and said, "What is the matter?"

"Alas!" answered she, "my good man, the priest, is dead!"

So they began to lay him out; but as they were doing so his wife whispered in his ear, "What's the use of all this tomfoolery? Even if you die, your goods will still go in funeral expenses all the same!"

"Spend no money on me," answered he; "only get ready my shroud and lay it over me. But if you promise not to waste any more of my goods, I will then get up and live."

"No, no!" answered she; "I have made the vow, and the vow must be kept."

So the shroud was got ready and put over him. Then said she to the people, "Stand aside a bit." And going near, she spoke quickly to him, saying, "Don't be so absurd! They are now going to carry you to your grave."

"Even now," murmured the priest, "I will consent to live, if you will only promise to obey."

But again she answered, "I have made the vow, and the vow must be kept."

Then came the people and carried him forth, and laid him down by the edge of his grave, and some one began the prayers, and the burial service went on. The wife, however, had also followed behind, and the people, when they saw her, said, "Go away, go away; what do you want out here?" But others said, "Never mind, leave the poor creature alone."

"I only want," answered the woman, "to have one last look at him."

So she entered the (shallow) grave in which he had been laid, and stooping low, she whispered, "In another minute *maunds* and *maunds* of earth will be thrown over you!"

"Will you promise, then?" said he.

"The vow has been made, and the vow must be kept," answered she.

"Then," said he, "let them cover me up, and the sooner the better."

So she stepped out of the grave again and said to the people, "You can now shovel in the earth."

As soon as a spadeful or two had been thrown in, the wife cried aloud and said, "O brothers, hear me! now that the priest is dead, the whole of his house and all his goods I give to the poor!"

Hearing these words, the priest got a shock, and he said to himself, "Before it was only a little she vowed in charity, but now my whole house is not too much for the hussy to squander away!" Instantly he sprang to his feet, and, leaping from the grave, he dropped the shroud from about him; and, eager to forestall possession, tore back to his house as fast as his legs would carry him. But, as he fled naked away, the people were astonished, holding up their hands and saying, "Ah, this priest of ours must be a great saint, a very great saint indeed! He died, and, lo, God has raised him from the dead again!"

Thus that rogue of a priest became more famous than ever. Nor was his wife called upon any more to break her vow; she was able to give, since offerings of nice food and other good things flowed in upon them both more abundantly than ever.

Told at Abbottabad by a bard, December 1882.

L'ENVOY

Sadâ nâ bâgịn bûlbûl bole,
  Sadâ nâ bâg bâhârâṇ;
Sadâ nâ râj khûshi de honde,
  Sadâ nâ majlis yârâṇ! [1]

Freely rendered thus—

For evermore, within the bower's recesses,
  No bulbul sits and sings melodious lore;
No verdant April leaf the garden blesses
  For evermore!

A monarch, robed in might and wrapt in splendour,
  Reigns not for aye from sounding shore to shore;
And friends companionship must fain surrender
  For evermore!

[1] There is scarcely a Pànjâbî who has not this stanza by heart. It expresses the resigned philosophy which suits him best, the philosophy of the Preacher—Vanity of Vanities!!—

The bulbul is not always singing in the garden,
The garden is not always in bloom,
Kings are not always reigning in happiness,
Friends are not always together.